AF559625

THE COBRA'S GAZE

Also by Stephen Alter

NON-FICTION

Wild Himalaya: A Natural History of the Greatest Mountain Range on Earth

Becoming a Mountain: Himalayan Journeys in Search of the Sacred and the Sublime

All the Way to Heaven: An American Boyhood in the Himalayas

Amritsar to Lahore: Crossing the Border Between India and Pakistan

Sacred Waters: A Pilgrimage to the Many Sources of the Ganga

Elephas Maximus: A Portrait of the Indian Elephant

Going for Take: The Making of Omkara and Other Encounters in Bollywood

FICTION

Death in Shambles: A Hill Station Mystery

Birdwatching: A Novel

Feral Dreams: Mowgli and His Mothers

In the Jungles of the Night: A Novel About Jim Corbett

Guldaar

The Rataban Betrayal

Renuka

Aranyani

Aripan and Other Stories

The Godchild

Silk and Steel

Neglected Lives

FICTION FOR YOUNGER READERS

The Phantom Isles

Ghost Letters

The Cloudfarers

The Secret Sanctuary

THE COBRA'S GAZE

Exploring India's Wild Heritage

STEPHEN ALTER

ALEPH

ALEPH BOOK COMPANY
An independent publishing firm
promoted by ***Rupa Publications India***

First published in India in 2024
by Aleph Book Company
7/16 Ansari Road, Daryaganj
New Delhi 110 002

Copyright © Stephen Alter 2024

The author has asserted his moral rights.

All rights reserved.

The views and opinions expressed in this book are those of the author and the facts are as reported by him, which have been verified to the extent possible, and the publisher is not in any way liable for the same.

The publisher has used its best endeavours to ensure that URLs for external websites referred to in this book are correct and active at the time of going to press. However, the publisher has no responsibility for the websites and can make no guarantee that a site will remain live or that the content is or will remain appropriate.

No part of this publication may be reproduced, transmitted, or stored in a retrieval system, in any form or by any means, without permission in writing from Aleph Book Company.

For sale in the Indian subcontinent only.

ISBN: 978-81-19635-35-1

1 3 5 7 9 10 8 6 4 2

Printed in India

This book is sold subject to the condition that it shall not, by way of trade or otherwise, be lent, resold, hired out, or otherwise circulated without the publisher's prior consent in any form of binding or cover other than that in which it is published.

Dedicated to the many individuals and institutions,
including the forest departments of each state,
that have worked together to conserve India's
wildlife and wild spaces.

Ramapithecus and I

The young swamp he came to
Six million years ago,
His unfazed mother beside him,
His father recently dead,

Is the wall-map's mixed forest
A dotted power line along its edge
And the window's low, clouded hills,
Dolomite and fossil rich.

Making his home
Where his implements took him,
He waited for the rains to break.
Cutting my finger, it's his blood I taste.

—Arvind Krishna Mehrotra

CONTENTS

PART III
ON HIGHER GROUND
Hills–Mountains–Uplands

AUTHOR'S NOTE

Being neither a wildlife scientist nor an authority on conservation, I need to make it clear that the observations and opinions expressed in this book are those of an amateur naturalist who has simply had the privilege of visiting wild places across the length and breadth of India. In my travels and research, I have relied heavily on the knowledge and perspectives of friends, guides, and experts of all kinds, as well as the published works of experienced ecologists and dedicated conservationists. While writing about various species and landscapes, I have discovered, more than anything else, how little I know of the natural world and how it works. The only reassurance I have gained in this process is the realization that all of us begin studying birds, plants, reptiles, or mammals—whatever living things intrigue us—from a position of ignorance, which is, after all, the foundation of knowledge. In this, I keep reminding myself of the words of E. H. Aitken, one of the founding members of the Bombay Natural History Society, who was an outstanding naturalist and writer. Faced with the prospect of discovering new creatures, facts, and ideas, Aitken exclaimed with effusive delight: 'How abysmally ignorant we are!'

For the most part, I have used common names for species, primarily in English but also from Hindi and the regional languages. At the end of the book is a list of species mentioned herein, with common, local, and Latin names.

PREFACE

BHIMBETKA

An irregular line of eroded sandstone crags surmounts the crest of a broad ridge. This low escarpment, fringed by jungle, rises only a hundred metres above the plain. From a distance, the rocks appear to be the ruined battlements of an abandoned fortress though their uneven profiles reveal the architecture of geology rather than the hand of man. Here, amongst these natural formations, in the foothills of the Vindhya Range, our ancestors sought refuge for many thousands of years.

In 1957, Dr Vishnu Shridhar Wakankar, sometimes referred to as the pitamaha or grandfather of Indian rock art studies, discovered Bhimbetka, while travelling by train from Bhopal to Itarsi Junction. Through the window of his railway carriage, he spotted the unusual outcroppings along the western horizon and his sixth sense told him that something significant lay nearby. Getting down at the next station, he made his way back to the ridge, which lies only a couple of kilometres from the railway tracks. Other than a few scattered villages, the area was mostly forest and he had to approach on foot, following game trails through the underbrush and up the boulder-strewn slopes. What Wakankar came upon is one of the most extensive archaeological sites in the world, as important as the cave complex in Lascaux, France, which contains similar prehistoric rock art. Bhimbetka became Wakankar's greatest find and he spent much of his career studying and documenting the paintings on the walls, as well as unearthing ancient dwellings and tombs.

In her book, *India through Archaeology: Excavating History*, Devika Cariapa writes that Bhimbetka provides a window into the world of stone age hunter-gatherers and their descendants:

> Tools, bones and artefacts found at an excavation give us a lot of information about our ancestors. We know about their diet, their clothes, their houses, their lifestyle, even the size of their brains. But it is only with

> their art that we can finally see them as living, breathing people with hopes, fears, dreams and feelings, as well as a sense of humour. We finally get to see prehistoric people *from their point of view.*

The majority of images at Bhimbetka are of wild animals that lived in this region long before science assigned them names. Being hunter-gatherers, the early inhabitants acquired first-hand knowledge of the creatures they pursued. Though they had no written language, the visual record they left behind conveys a closely observed taxonomy by which they classified and differentiated the biology and behaviour of various mammals. Altogether, Cariapa notes that twenty-nine different species can be found on the walls at Bhimbetka, ranging from squirrels and porcupines to leopards and tigers. In some instances, the inner organs and bones of the animals are depicted, showing the anatomy of a species. In a few cases, a foetus appears within a pregnant mother. After they killed an animal, the hunters would have cut it open with stone knives, removed the skin, and butchered the meat, dividing it amongst their tribe. More than likely they also performed prayers and rituals to propitiate the spirit of their prey, as well as the life-giving forces of nature upon which their survival depended.

Some of these creatures, like Asian elephants, one-horned rhinoceroses, and wild buffaloes, are no longer found in this part of Central India because of the pressures of habitat loss and indiscriminate hunting. But others, including sloth bears, nilgai, wild pigs, and sambar still live in the forests of the Ratapani Wildlife Sanctuary where Bhimbetka is located. Their living presence underscores the significance of the paintings both as a record of the past as well as a point of comparison with wildlife distribution today. Naturalists, as much as archaeologists, can learn a great deal from the artworks, which are, in essence, the first field guides to Indian mammals.

The rock shelters show evidence of continuous habitation reaching back to the Palaeolithic Age, approximately 100,000 years ago, which makes them one of the oldest and most enduring settlements on earth. The caves lie empty now and the forest has closed in around them, reclaiming the landscape. The trees are typical of the dry deciduous forests of Central India—mostly sagun or teak, as well as tendu, saaj, khair, and ghiriya (bhirra). Each of these species would have served a purpose for the early inhabitants, providing firewood, tools, resins, and medicinal extracts. Many of the huge boulders are held in the clutches of gadasi trees, a tenacious lithophyte of the ficus family that germinates in the crevices of rocks and sends out serpentine roots to reach soil and moisture beneath. Its pale grey bark resembles the colour and texture of an elephant's trunk and looks as if it has the same pliable strength.

In 2003, Bhimbetka was declared a UNESCO World Heritage Site. Unlike

Wakankar, visitors can now drive to the top of the ridge, where the rock shelters are preserved and labelled with informative signage. Of the 700 shelters that have been identified, roughly 250 contain paintings but only fifteen of these are open to visitors.

Entering the complex, it feels as if the shelters were only recently abandoned and it is easy to imagine ancient communities living within the shallow cavities beneath these massive rocks. Some of the dwellings are narrow ledges tucked below an overhang, while others are deeper chambers, though none of them are completely enclosed. Open to the air, the living spaces offer protection from sun and rain but admit both wind and daylight. Trees grow in amongst the shelters and the paths between them are littered with leaves. Looking out over the plain below, from the terrace of one cave, I can picture men returning from a successful hunt, carrying the carcass of a boar while a gaggle of excited children scurry out to greet them.

Though the rock shelters are natural formations, the clustered settlement resembles a village, with narrow intersecting lanes and separate dwellings that would have been occupied by family groups. On some of the walls, I can see scenes of domestic activity, people holding utensils or carrying what look like baskets. Hides of animals are stretched and dried. At places, handprints decorate the walls. In the earliest paintings, human figures appear to be naked, while later on they are dressed in simple garments. Rituals of celebration are also evident, lines of dancers with their arms linked, moving to the rhythm of a drummer. Though the sounds and voices of these people have been silent for centuries they seem to echo amidst the stillness of the rocks, between the distant whistle of a passing train and birdcalls in the trees.

The largest shelter, which Wakankar dubbed 'The Auditorium', has high ceilings and is open on both sides, more of a tunnel than a cave. Several beehives are suspended from an arched cornice 15 metres above the entrance. Further on, an image of honey gatherers harvesting the combs appears in one of the other shelters. Tribal people in Madhya Pradesh still collect wild honey that is sold primarily for medicinal purposes. In many ways, their lives remain remarkably similar to the foraging existence of the figures in the paintings. Indigenous communities of forest dwellers like Gonds, Bhils, and Korkus have taken up agriculture and animal husbandry but still retain a close connection to wild landscapes and wild creatures. Their religious ceremonies and rituals reflect an animistic tradition that has its roots in prehistory. Most significantly, the decorative murals on the walls of their homes are similar to the rock art—stylized paintings of peacocks, deer, and tigers. Scenes of drumming and dancing that adorn the shelters could easily be images from tribal festivals today.

One cave, with a broad, sloping ceiling, is known as the 'Zoo Rock' because sixteen different species of animals are pictured here. A large herd of deer, gazelle, wild cattle, and other ungulates stampedes across the surface of the rock. Simple stick figures of hunters with bows and arrows or spears, roam in their midst. Most of the paintings are done in mineral hues—rusty browns, umbers, and ochres produced from the soil and mixed with animal fat or other natural fixatives, possibly the sap from saaj trees. These pigments stand out against the tawny sandstone slabs. Some of the images are painted in white lime and a few are outlined in sooty greys and blacks. Though many of the paintings have faded and become indistinct, others are remarkably well preserved considering their age, each brushstroke visible and precise. In a number of shelters, more recent paintings are superimposed upon older images from different periods of history, a complex palimpsest representing the layered strata of collective memory. Instead of displaying a linear progression of images that follows an orderly chronology, different timelines converge and flow across the textured surface of the rocks. Each of these open-air galleries lead from one to the next with a freedom of movement that reflects the transient, migratory lives of early hominids and the mammals they pursued.

Wandering through Bhimbetka, I am conscious of the spiritual resonance of nature, the invisible threads that tie us to other forms of life through memory, dreams, and desires. A three-striped palm squirrel scampers up and over a rock, then down the other side, chittering and raising its bushy tail in alarm. While running away it tempts me to follow it into the jungle beyond. A baronet butterfly alights on a stone, its orange wings like petals of fire blooming in the bright sunlight. The colour ignites my imagination as if through spontaneous combustion. Corrugated, cork-like bark on a ghiriya tree has been rubbed off by the antlers of a chital stag that must have come here after dark, unafraid of the primal hunters silhouetted on the walls and unaware of its own likeness sketched upon the rocks. The deer's cloven hooves have left prints in the dust by my feet, as if it were spoor from hundreds of centuries past.

More than just decorative motifs, the rock art is imbued with layers of meaning, though we can only speculate about the original purpose of these images. They appear to be a catalogue of animals found in the surrounding jungle as well as a record of hunting techniques that included stalking game or driving creatures towards hidden archers who waited with arrows drawn. These paintings also convey a sense of curiosity and wonder at the abundance and diversity of nature. The scenes are full of life and could be an attempt to invoke the presence of these animals and ensure success in the chase. For those ancient people whose survival depended on plentiful prey, these were reassuring tableaus. Though it is unlikely the painters had any idea that their art would be preserved for millennia, the images were certainly executed with an eye to posterity, even if only a few years hence.

It is tempting to imagine that the paintings have some religious significance. Though the shelters are not temples, each dwelling probably contained a small shrine. At places, circular depressions have been carved into the rocks. Archaeologists believe these 'cupules' were receptacles for flowers and other votive offerings. In their book *Madhya Pradesh Rock Art and Tribal Art*, Meenakshi Dubey-Pathak and Jean Clottes include interviews with individuals from contemporary tribal communities regarding their understanding of rock art. Without exception, the descendants of those ancient artists emphasize the spiritual significance of the images. Some believe they were painted by supernatural beings, while others imply that they might be a form of ancestor worship. Animals and human figures embody the ageless mysteries of life and cycles of existence that nature sustains. A few abstract symbols have been drawn on the walls at Bhimbetka, with floral or geometric designs, but no written inscriptions can be found.

The most recent paintings from the historical period (3000 BCE onwards) include images of men on horseback wielding swords. Pathak and Clottes suggest these are 'spirit riders' that memorialized individuals who had passed away. Equestrian figures are a common motif in Bhil, Gond, and Korku iconography, though tribal people seldom used horses, which are not indigenous to India and were brought here by pastoralists and invaders. By elevating their ancestors to the status of warriors on horseback, the hunter-gatherers venerate their dead while acknowledging the changing face of human society and the arrival of outsiders who conquered their lands.

Memorial tablets, placed at the foot of sacred mango and mahua trees in Central India, often depict a rider on horseback. The implication is that a deceased person's soul is conveyed into the afterlife astride a mythical horse. In sacred groves throughout India, guardian deities are often depicted as heroic figures riding a horse and wielding a sword. This represents the paradoxical connection between arboreal myths and historic legends, where ecology and conquest meet. Throughout recorded history, horses have served as powerful symbols in Indian culture. On one level, of course, these images portray a relationship in which man's dominance over nature and the land is symbolized by his superior position on the animal's back, holding a sword in one hand, whereas the earlier hunting scenes depict a less developed society before the age of iron blades, when human beings with crude, stone-tipped weapons pursued other species on foot.

More than anything, the images that artists painted with brushes made from twigs and the bristles of wild creatures they killed are part of a story that comes to us from the advent of time, an epic without beginning or end. Long ago, before history was measured, these nomadic hunter-gatherers felt a need to narrate their adventures through pictorial art that still speaks to us with wisdom, eloquence, and wit. They recount the pursuit of prey, acts of bravery and cowardice, as well as victory and celebration. Like all good hunting tales, the rock art contains elements of exaggeration and embellishment. In one of the shelters a giant, seemingly mythical boar appears, with horns as well as tushes, chasing a terrified hunter. This monster, four times the size of a man, is both frightening and comical at once. Studying the image under the shadow of an overhanging rock, I can almost hear a tribal bard telling this story as he traces the creature's outline with his forefinger.

Bhimbetka is a place of myths and legends projected onto the walls of sedimentary rock. It takes its present name from Bhim, one of the five Pandava brothers in the Mahabharata. A powerful giant and champion warrior capable of lifting and moving huge boulders like these, Bhim rested here after his exertions. The name Bhimbetka, which means a place where Bhim sat, was probably assigned to this site long after the rock artists departed, when the caves were occasionally used in more recent times by mendicants and mystics who retreated into the forest.

Prehistoric paintings occur in many parts of India, some of them similar and others unique. In Ladakh, a thousand kilometres to the north, high in the Himalaya, petroglyphs were etched on rocks by nomadic hunters along the Indus and its tributaries. The mountain mammals they depicted—snow leopards, ibex, yak, and bharal—are entirely different from animals that appear in the rock art of Central India but what links them is an appreciation for the diversity of life, the wild, agile, dynamic forms rendered by anonymous artists who committed their stories to stone.

∽

Some of the earliest recorded observations of India's natural history underscore the spiritual significance of species other than our own. These primal images and symbols suggest a mystical connection between humankind and the rest of nature. Ancient rituals of hunting, blessed by tribal shamans, sanctified both predator and prey. In oral epics, ballads, and folklore, the medicinal and hallucinogenic properties of wild plants were often linked to supernatural or magical powers. For thousands of years, nature's fecundity has been revered and worshipped in India, assuming the iconic forms of mother goddesses, sacred trees, serpent spirits, and other divine animals.

Tigers and elephants, being dominant creatures of the Indian jungle, were often chosen to represent attributes of strength and authority, linking them to omnipotent deities or rulers. Clay seals from the Indus Valley civilization, during the third millennium BCE, depict what may be a god seated astride a tiger. The Mahabharata contains a passage that is probably the earliest call for tiger conservation: 'The forest has tigers and it should never be cut nor should the tigers be chased away from the forest. Not living in the forest is death to the tiger and in the absence of the tiger, the forest is annihilated. The tiger protects the forest and the forest nurtures the tiger.'

But more than these so-called 'apex species', a bestiary of lesser creatures captured our ancestral imagination. In an ocean of stories, turtles and fish were identified as avatars of benevolent water gods protecting the world from demonic destruction. On land, spiders were seen as emblems of creation, spinning an intricate web of existence that connected all forms of life. Geckos were interpreted as symbols of good luck while bats were seen as harbingers of death, though in some parts of India they were believed to bear wealth and prosperity on their wings. Birds of all kinds have been classified according to reverential taxonomies that assign celestial virtues to vultures, parakeets, and cranes, as well as dozens of other genera.

Spectacled cobras are considered one of the most sacred animals in India, invoking awe and terror. They are an essential part of the iconography of deities like Shiva and Vishnu. Carved images of cobras adorn Hindu temples but also appear on simple stone tablets tucked into the roots of peepul and banyan trees. An abundance of botanical lore is found in Buddhist and Hindu literature. Tulsi (holy basil) is an aromatic herb venerated in many Indian households. Verses from the Vedas celebrate a mythical plant called soma that produces the 'nectar of the Gods', causing divine intoxication. Today a variety of common species from marijuana to the flowering mahua tree elicit the same mind-bending response. Ayurvedic medicine synthesizes indigenous knowledge of plant-based therapies that are used to treat everything from gallstones to depression. Tribal communities in different parts of India maintain unique systems of classification for forest resources like wild grasses, tubers, seeds, bark, leaves, and flowers that are gathered for nourishment and healing. Fragrant herbs and resins produce incense and perfumes used in rituals of devotion.

This book chronicles a quest to uncover multiple layers of meaning associated with the wild flora and fauna of India's woodlands, mountains, rivers, deserts, and coastline. It includes first-hand observations of rare and unusual forms of life as well as jungle lore. In the same way that biological specimens were gathered and catalogued by early naturalists, the stories of each species can be collected and compiled. Scientific research and discourse is a form of storytelling that provides an intriguing counterpoint to myths and legends. Though the scope of this book spans the entire subcontinent of India, focusing on life forms as diverse as scorpions, mangroves, pheasants, fungi, and wild cattle, this is not an encyclopaedic project. Instead, it is an effort to weave together a coherent and compelling litany of proverbs, parables, and prayers that draw inspiration from the wild. At the core of these braided metaphors lies the moral imperative of conservation, voicing an urgent call to preserve the diversity of nature as well as the poetry, folk tales, and hymns that commemorate threatened biomes.

Wild creatures and wild places are part of our natural heritage, providing a link to the past but also an ecological perspective for the future. Through observation, reflection, and enquiry, we can learn to appreciate the life stories of other beings. As a species, *Homo sapiens* are inextricably connected to the larger, multifaceted narratives of evolutionary history—an ongoing epic of survival, coexistence, and change. Curiosity and wonder, as well as the recognition of biological kinship, compel us to share the earth equitably with other life forms, whether they are dangerous or docile, fearful or indifferent to our presence. As we look at them, we must also know that they are looking at us. By meeting their gaze, we can begin to comprehend the conflicts and commonalities that bind us, so that we can fulfil our responsibility to preserve what little is left of the natural world.

PROLOGUE

A NATURALIST'S TRANCE

On a clear September morning several years ago, I went for a walk by myself to Jabarkhet Nature Reserve, about a kilometre north-east of my home in Landour. I have been visiting this forest for more than fifty years. When I was a boy, it was a place where I collected butterflies, beetles, and snakes. As a teenager, I also hunted here for kalij pheasant, kakar (barking deer), and goral, a goat-antelope that is common in this part of the lower Himalaya. At the age of twenty-two, I gave up hunting, though I continued to explore the forests with binoculars and a camera instead of a gun. Jabarkhet Nature Reserve was established in 2015—a 40 hectare (100 acre) private wildlife sanctuary adjacent to several thousand hectares of government forest. The highest point in the reserve is a rounded summit known as Flag Hill because of Tibetan prayer flags tied to trees at the top. Further along this ridge is another summit called Bear Hill, where Himalayan black bears sometimes come to eat acorns from the banj oaks.

My walk that morning had a purpose, though it was also an excuse to get out in the woods after weeks of near-constant monsoon rain had kept me indoors much of the time. I was looking for a specific plant, *Drosera peltata*, commonly known as sundew. The only insectivorous plant in this part of the Himalaya, it blooms in late August and early September. Having written about it in one of my books, I wanted to see if I could find it again and take a photograph.

When I reached the intervening ridge that connects Flag Hill and Bear Hill, I knew there was a good chance that the plant might be growing in one of the clearings. The uneven spine of the ridge is about a hundred metres long. Because of the monsoon, the grass and herbaceous plants were lush and thick. Head lowered, I kept a sharp lookout for the sundew's tiny white flowers and sinuous stems. My attention was fixed on the ground near my feet. Moving slowly, one step at a time, I traversed the ridge but after covering three quarters of the distance, I suddenly felt that I was no longer alone.

Raising my head, I looked up through the forked trunk of an oak about 2 metres away. At that same instant, on the opposite side of the tree, a goral raised its head and stared directly at me. We were less than 4 metres apart, but the animal hadn't sensed my approach because its attention was focused on the grass it was eating, while I was moving slowly and the breeze was in my face. Both of us were so surprised that we froze and locked eyes for what must have been thirty seconds. The goral had short, tapered horns that curved back sharply between its large ears. A young male, his coat was a ruddy grey, with a prominent white patch on the throat. His eyes were an amber green.

I had seen many goral before, but never this close. Both of us were alone and it was one of those moments when people like to say, 'time stops', which is a clumsy cliche. Instead, it was as if nothing before or after this encounter mattered as much as it did right then and there. I must have taken a breath or two and my heart was still pumping but it seemed as if everything within me had paused, except for the signals passing from my eyes to my brain, registering this wild creature in front of me. At the same time, I was acutely aware that the goral was watching me with the same stillness and intensity. Though I would never claim to comprehend what the goral was thinking, the two of us were transfixed by each other's presence.

After my initial surprise, I began to raise my camera very slowly until the goral appeared in the viewfinder. He was standing so near I didn't need to use the zoom. Pressing the shutter button, I focused on his face, framed between the forked trunks of the tree. And then, as soon as the camera clicked, the spell was broken. The goral let out a sneeze of alarm and plunged down the other side of the ridge, disappearing into a steep ravine full of larger oaks and underbrush.

Unable and unwilling to move for several minutes, I remained where I was. The encounter left me with an overpowering feeling of awe and elation. Looking into the goral's eyes had aroused in me a startling sense of shared consciousness, as if our separate perceptions of where we stood in this wild place had merged for the briefest fraction of time—a revelation so sudden it was immeasurable, yet infinitely profound.

'The hunter's trance' is a phrase that I first came upon in a book by naturalist and physician, Carl Von Essen. The concept has intrigued me ever since. Essentially, it describes the moment when an archer draws a bowstring taut and takes aim, focusing intently on his or her target, just before an arrow is released. It also suggests an ephemeral moment of transcendence when the hunter and prey become one.

E. O. Wilson, the eminent ecologist, picked up on this phrase in his book *Biophilia* which explores the relationship between human beings and other species. He describes experiencing what he calls 'the naturalist's trance' while searching for rare ants in a coastal forest in Surinam:

> In a twist my mind came free and I was aware of the hard workings of the natural world beyond the periphery of ordinary attentions, where passions lose their meaning and history is another dimension.... The effect was strangely calming. Breathing and heartbeat diminished, concentration intensified. It seemed to me that something extraordinary in the forest was very close to where I stood, moving to the surface and discovery.

The hunter with his bow is one of our most ancient archetypes that can be traced back to prehistoric cave paintings in places like Bhimbetka. This primal figure, embedded in human consciousness, is an integral part of mythology, folklore, literature, and art, as well as other cultural practices and discourse. Yoga, for example, teaches an asana called akarna dhanurasana—the archer's pose. An individual performing this asana requires considerable flexibility and discipline. In a seated position, one leg is extended straight out in front of the body while the other is drawn back until the toes are aligned with the ear. One hand holds this foot like a bowstring while the other arm stretches forward, like an arrow. Classical dance forms in India also include gestures and postures that represent an archer poised at the moment of releasing an arrow.

Aside from being illegal in India, hunting is no longer a necessary or ethical pursuit. With the depletion of wildlife and wild habitats, there can be no argument to justify it, especially for sport. Nevertheless, naturalists use many of the same skills and knowledge that even the earliest hunters employed—an awareness of climate and terrain, the direction of air currents, seasonality, and the times of day or night when birds and animals move about. They also interpret the calls of wildlife and other behaviour, as well as hoofprints, pugmarks, and various spoor. Perhaps the most important insight that naturalists have inherited from our hunter-ancestors is a basic understanding that the vast majority of wild animals still perceive us as predators, no matter whether we are conservationists or not.

The impulsive connection or empathy that we feel while observing wild animals, particularly when they look back into our eyes, often leads us to anthropomorphize these creatures. Consciously or unconsciously, we impose human emotions, gestures, and cognition on species other than our own. Robert Macfarlane, in his book *The Wild Places*, cautions against this self-centred human response:

> Wild animals, like wild places, are invaluable to us precisely because they are not us. They are uncompromisingly different. The paths they follow, the impulses that guide them, are of other orders. The seal's holding gaze, before it flukes to push another tunnel through the sea, the hare's run, the hawk's high gyres: such things are wild. Seeing them, you are made briefly aware of a world at work around and beside our own, a world operating in patterns and purposes that you do not share. These are creatures, you realise, that live by voices inaudible to you.

While we can certainly feel an affinity towards other fauna and perhaps even flora, it is essential to recognize the dissimilarities in nature and our fundamental ignorance of the various ways in which other species respond to the world around them, including us. Moreover, we must accept that wild animals are not likely to reciprocate our feelings or fascination for them. The young goral that stared at me briefly, with surprise and alarm in his eyes, registered in his own way that I was looking at him, but it is highly unlikely that he experienced anything similar to my response. Those feelings were exclusively mine, not his.

In his recent book *An Immense World*, the American nature writer Ed Yong explores how each species perceives the world through a unique perspective, distinctly different from that of other species. Yong uses the German word 'umwelt' (and its plural, 'umwelten'), which was coined by a zoologist, Jakob von Uexküll, in 1909. Essentially, each of us has our own umwelt or 'sensory bubble' through which we experience and perceive our immediate environment, including other species. Yong gives the example of a bat that uses high frequency sonar to locate its prey and navigate in the dark, or a rattlesnake that senses heat through the pits on its face.

> Even when animals share the same senses with us, their Umwelten can be very different. There are animals that can hear sounds in what seems to us like perfect silence, see colors in what looks to us like total darkness, and sense vibrations in what feels to us like complete stillness. There are animals with eyes on their genitals, ears on their knees, noses on their limbs, and tongues all over their skin. Starfish see with the tips of their arms, and sea urchins with their entire bodies.

The goral and I each possess separate umwelten which may coincide on some levels but diverge in other ways. Not only is the goral's sense of smell and hearing more acute than mine but our consciousness is attuned to different things. Our appreciation of the grass and trees, the air around us, is determined by the stimuli that we respond to and the many ways in which our brains filter and focus the information we gather.

As Yong explains, a person's umwelt can vary from one individual to another. Some people are colour-blind, for example, while our human sense of taste is highly subjective. In addition to this, our perceptions change over time, particularly as we grow older. A child absorbs and processes vast amounts of information, from new experiences or sensations. Therefore, his or her umwelt is naturally going to be quite different from that of an adult, who is more familiar with the same environment. Children are constantly discovering things they do not recognize or understand, which can result in a more diffuse, and sometimes easily distracted consciousness, but it can also lead to an intensely sensitive and focused awareness of the world around them.

∽

My interest in wildlife began at an early age. One of my first memories, from when I was four years old, is of a blackbuck antelope that we kept as a pet. My parents had bought it from tribal hunters who brought it to our bungalow on the mission compound in Fatehgarh, where we lived at the time. I was too young to have any memory of the hunters, though I heard the story often enough from my parents to form an image in my mind. Two barefoot men, armed with bows and spears, carried the baby blackbuck in a wicker basket. I do not know how the baby had been captured, though it is likely the hunters had killed its mother. The men were accompanied by a pack of three or four lean dogs. Later, I would occasionally see other hunter-gatherers like them walking past our compound gate or camped along the roadside when we were driving somewhere. Growing up in western Uttar Pradesh, I was always fascinated by their nomadic presence.

My parents raised the blackbuck in our aangan, a walled courtyard connected to the bungalow. I have clear memories of the antelope once it had grown into an adult. A male, with long, spiral horns, he had a dark brown coat, almost black, and white eye patches that made him look perpetually startled. The blackbuck's underbelly and the insides of his legs were also white. His slender, supple limbs were built for speed, though confined to the aangan, he could only pace about in circles, leaving heart-shaped prints in the dust. A custard apple tree grew in the courtyard and the antelope would nibble on its leaves.

We called him Hira, which means diamond, though his name came from 'hiran', the Hindi word for blackbuck. He was tame enough to eat biscuits from my hand, but I was never left alone with him because his sharp horns could have easily skewered me. I remember petting Hira's soft, flexible ears and looking into his dark, almond-shaped eyes that were moist and alert. When full grown, he must have stood about 75 centimetres at the shoulder and weighed roughly 45 kilograms. Hira lived with us in Fatehgarh until 1961, when our family went on furlough to America for a year.

Upon our departure, he was adopted by Dr Lois Visscher, a colleague of my parents, who worked at the mission hospital in Fatehgarh. She was fond of Hira and had an Alsatian dog with which he got along and played. A tall, imposing woman, Dr Visscher spent most of her life working as a medical missionary in Uttar Pradesh. I remember Aunt Lois, as I called her, grabbing both of Hira's horns. To give him some exercise, she would wrestle with him, just as he might have sparred with his rivals had he lived in the wild.

Fatehgarh is a military cantonment that is part of the larger town of Farrukkabad, which lies on the southern bank of the Ganga, about 150 kilometres from Kanpur. The surrounding landscape is mostly dry and flat, covered by sparse, thorny jungles and open grasslands, the ideal habitat for blackbuck. This region is known as the Doab, the area between two rivers—Ganga and Yamuna. Much of the land came under cultivation after the construction of irrigation canals in the nineteenth century. Among the many memories I have of our home in Fatehgarh is the presence of a large banyan tree that grew in front of our house, where I would play with my friends, trying to climb into its spreading branches and swinging on its aerial roots.

While driving along the highway, we would occasionally see herds of blackbuck on the plains, usually far off in the distance, like a shimmering mirage. My father told my brothers and me that their numbers had dropped dramatically from when he was a boy in the 1930s. He described riding in trains while herds of blackbuck raced alongside the railway tracks, with graceful, leaping bounds, like dolphins keeping pace with a ship at sea. Blackbuck are one of the fastest animals on earth, and they used to be chased down for sport using trained cheetahs, until those swift predators became extinct in India in 1947. Illegal hunting and the destruction of open grassland habitat has led to the depletion of blackbuck in most parts of the country.

While we were in America, a letter arrived from Lois Visscher telling us that Hira had died. I can't recall the cause, except that he had been sick for a while. I was five years old, attending kindergarten in Ithaca, New York—about as far away from Fatehgarh as we could get—and I remember weeping at the news. However, what I recall most clearly, after my tears had dried, was asking my father if Hira's head and horns would be mounted on the wall like a hunting trophy. Both my parents were horrified by this suggestion and anxiously explained that nobody would do that with a pet.

My father and other men on the mission compound hunted, mostly for ducks that migrated in winter to shallow wetlands, known as jheels. They also shot nilgai, a large antelope, which provided enough meat for the entire compound community. Years later when I was a teenager, I joined a hunt in another part of the Doab, when a female blackbuck was flushed from a sugar cane field where she had taken cover. Unlike males, the doe had no horns and was a light fawn colour. One of the hunters fired at her with a shotgun, and she was wounded, falling to the ground and then struggling to rise on trembling legs. Her eyes were wide with fear and anguish. Just before she died, the doe let out a moaning sound, so full of pain that I can still remember it today, fifty years later. It was an awful, tragic cry that seemed almost human, though it was a sound only a wild creature could make, full of desperation and despair beyond my understanding. This cruel incident was one of several experiences that ultimately turned me against hunting.

A few years afterwards, when I was in college, I read a book about Persian and Urdu poetry in which the author—I cannot remember who—mentioned that the ghazal, a form of poetry that expresses the pain of separation and loss, takes its name from the cry of a wounded antelope. The word 'ghazal' from Arabic and Farsi, is also the root of the English word gazelle, an animal closely related to the blackbuck. Suddenly, the etymology of this literary term brought back for me the desperate moan of that injured antelope and a sense of my own guilt at having witnessed her brutal death.

Anwar Farrukhabadi (1928–2011) was a Sufi poet whose pen name identifies his birthplace, the town where I spent part of my early childhood. Also called 'Fana', which translates as 'Annihilation', he was well known for his ghazals, many of which were used as lyrics for Hindi film songs in the 1960s and 1970s. Farrukhabadi's poems have been sung by celebrated vocalists like Pankaj Udhas and Nusrat Fateh Ali Khan. One of Fana's best known ghazals begins with the lines: 'Jab se dekha unki aankhon ko/ Halka halka sa suroor rehta hai/ ... Yeh teri nazar ka kasoor hai.... From when I first looked into her eyes/ A mild intoxication overcame me/ ...Your gaze is to blame.'

Nazar is the Urdu word for gaze and it can imply many things, from a romantic glance to casting an evil eye upon someone. In poetry, it often means to observe an object or a person with intense desire. Essentially, nazar suggests an unabashedly subjective perspective—the opposite of dispassionate, scientific observation. And yet, when we look at wild creatures and they look back at us, an element of poetic fascination occurs, a kind of nazar that is both intimate and possessive but also invokes a rational quest for knowledge. Of course, irony does not exist in nature. Wild things are what they are, distinct from any human emotions or language.

~

After we returned from furlough in America, our family moved to Etah, another small town in Uttar Pradesh, about 70 kilometres west of Fatehgarh. Once again, our home was a brick bungalow on a mission compound at the outskirts of town. Next to us lay the Slater Poultry Farm, which had been established by an American Presbyterian missionary named A. E. Slater, who had preceded my parents. The compound was home to about twenty Christian families, some of whom worked on the poultry farm as well as at an Agricultural College across the road. Our family lived simply and frugally, though our position in the community was certainly privileged and we were far better off than our neighbours. My friends and playmates lived in homes much smaller than ours, some in single-roomed quarters. Despite having spent the past year in upstate New York, experiencing snow and ice for the first time, as well as television and other American distractions, I was delighted to be back home in India again. What I enjoyed most was the freedom of being outdoors, both within the compound and beyond.

As I think back on those early years of my life, it strikes me that my companions and I were constantly playing out the role of hunter-gatherers. A good part of our day was spent foraging for things to eat or to satisfy our curiosity. For some of my friends it was a necessity, since they came from the poorest families on the compound and they sought anything that might add variety to a daily diet of dal and roti. Even rice was a luxury for some. My brothers and I, of course, did not need to worry about putting food on the table, though we did get caught up in the challenge of hunting for whatever we could find to eat.

From almost the moment I woke up in the morning until I went to bed, I carried a catapult in one hand. We learned how to make these crude weapons using a Y cut from the branch of a shisham tree, a sturdy hardwood that acquired a smooth lustre when polished by callused fingers and palms. The black rubber thongs were cut from old bicycle inner tubes, which had so many punctures and patches they were finally discarded by the cycle repairman who had a shack outside the compound wall. From the same rubber we cut thin bindings to fasten the thongs to the Y and attached a leather pouch, fashioned from the tongue of an old shoe that was also beyond repair.

My first catapult was made for me by older boys, Saroj or Eddu, who also taught me how to use it. In Hindustani, which I spoke with my friends, it was called a gullail. Pulling the rubber thongs with all my strength, I would aim between the two tines at whatever target presented itself. We hunted mostly for collared doves that perched on trees and electric wires. When they flew overhead their wings made a whistling sound. We also hunted black-naped hares that lived along the edges of the compound. Our ammunition consisted of a pocketful of kunkar, rough limestone pebbles that littered the ground and were used for paving roads. On most of these expeditions we were accompanied by a straggling pack of compound dogs that didn't seem to belong to anyone in particular.

Instead of a bow and arrow, my earliest awareness of wild species and my focused pursuit of animals and plants is inextricably linked to catapults. It was through that Y of shisham wood and the parallel lines of those taut rubber bands that I began to observe the many birds and animals that flocked about the mission compound in Etah. In a poem titled 'Catapult', Reshma Aquil, a poet from Allahabad, echoes my memories of observing the world around me through the forked tines of a gullail.

> Between the space of wood and leather,
> Imagining, holding the forest and its beast;
>
> Within my palm and pull of pebble,
> Time and attention peaked....

In defence of that young boy and those formative experiences of hunting wild things, I can only say that my aim was so poor I never actually hit or killed the small game we pursued. Most of our expeditions ended on a vegetarian note. After stalking hares and doves in the open scrubland to the north of the compound, roaming as far as the distant railway tracks and returning empty-handed, my friends and I would raid the fields of the Agricultural College and make off with fistfuls of green channa (chickpeas), which we roasted over an open fire and ate hungrily, peeling the blackened husks between our fingers and popping the charred green kernels into our mouths.

Our gullails were also effective at shooting down the knuckled brown pods from the high branches of a tamarind tree that grew in one corner of the compound. The raw imli was so sour it made my teeth and gums itch, though I ate it with relish. Another popular target were mulberries that grew on trees in the poultry farm, their limbs stretching over the chicken-wire fences. We would aim at the bunches of drupelets, firing into the air, and then race to collect the fallen shahtoot that were dusted off and eaten with salt and red chilli powder, another memorable flavour that remains with me from childhood.

Most of the boys were better marksmen than I and they would occasionally bring down a dove that came within range of their catapults. A few other birds were considered good eating: pigeons that roosted on the roof of our bungalow, francolins and quail, as well as the grey hornbills that nested in the hollows of a giant gulmohur at the edge of our yard. Through the process of hunting, I learned to recognize each of these species and differentiate them from mynahs, crows, egrets, and parakeets, which my companions avoided shooting because they were considered inedible. Before I knew what these species were called in English, I learned the Hindi names—phaakta, kabootar, titar, bater, kavua, bagla, tota, lamdor. I also learned to recognize a hornbill's flight, flapping its wings several times and then gliding with a syncopated rhythm. One day, there was great excitement when Saroj killed a grey hornbill with his gullail. We plucked it and carried the dead bird home to his mother, who cooked it up with onions and spices. The hornbill produced just enough meat for each of us to have a mouthful of the dark, gamey flesh.

My early knowledge of birds and animals was supplemented by books my parents owned—Hugh Whistler's *Popular Handbook of Indian Birds* and Salim Ali's *The Book of Indian Birds*, as well as S. H. Prater's *The Book of Indian Animals*, all of which were kept in a bookcase in the living room. I studied the coloured plates and recognized many of the species we found in our garden, including baya weaver birds that constructed long nests of dry grass that hung from the trees like stockings with their toes blown out or coppersmith barbets that hid out of sight and marked time with their monotonous cries.

A variety of mammals lived in and around the compound in Etah, everything from bandicoots that tunnelled underground to jackals that cried out hysterically at night and prowled the perimeter of the poultry farm, hoping to find a way into the cages. Behind our bungalow was a large yard, encircled by flower beds. At the far edge of this cultivated expanse lay a strip of jungle that blocked off the motor road beyond. It was about 15 metres deep and very dense with a tangled growth of wild shrubs and vines, forming an understorey beneath taller date palms, babool, ber, bistendu, and eucalyptus. Though my brothers and I played games of gulli danda and kabbadi in the yard with our friends, it was that ragged hemline of wild scrub that attracted us most. It was a place in which we could hide and pretend we were somewhere far away from home in an untamed and unexplored wilderness where creatures known and unknown lurked in the perpetual green twilight beneath a sheltering mosaic of shadowy leaves.

Though we were told there were cobras and kraits in the overgrown margins of the compound, I never saw any as a boy. But I do remember a grey mongoose with fiery red eyes that used to appear now and again. My mother had read the story of Rikki-Tikki-Tavi to me many times and I wondered if there was any chance of adopting this creature as a pet. Kipling's story was set in a bungalow like ours and I could imagine the mongoose standing guard over a young boy as the cobra spread his hood. From time to time, snake charmers stopped by the compound and men with performing animals, mostly sloth bears that danced to the beat of a dumru, or rhesus macaques that turned somersaults and begged for coins.

Living in the company of wild creatures, I grew to appreciate the ways in which we cohabited with other species. Palm squirrels raced back and forth in the branches of neem trees, ducking for cover when raptors appeared. Frogs lived in the wells that supplied water to the houses and the poultry farm. Indoors, common house geckos clung to the walls and made clicking sounds at night. These chipkalis would often perch on the overhead commode in the bathroom and dart away whenever I pulled the chain to flush the toilet. We slept under mosquito nets, and I could hear insects whining in the dark when the electricity stopped, and the ceiling fans went still. Centipedes and spiders crawled about on the brick floors and bats often entered through the roshandans, or skylights, and flew about frantically overhead. One night, I remember stepping out onto the veranda with my father who shone a torch across the yard where the eyes of a jungle cat lit up, bright yellow discs that flashed for a moment before its tawny, long-legged form disappeared into the hedge that bordered the driveway.

The Kali Naddi flowed about a furlong west of the compound, a narrow, sluggish stream that attracted sarus cranes and other waterbirds, especially in winter. We fished in its weedy green waters, catching mostly minnows and occasionally a kind of catfish called lanchi. Striped hyenas lived in the ravines that drained into the river, as well as ratels, a honey badger that was rumoured to dig up graves and feed on corpses. Saroj and Eddu's father, Charaunji Lal, told us stories about the ill-tempered lakarbagga and bejoo, which only came out of their dens at night. Each of these nocturnal species haunted my dreams and whenever I walked past the Christian cemetery, on the far side of the motor road, I would nervously glance through the gate to see if any of the graves had been dug up.

~

When I was a boy, one of my favourite books was Ylla's *Animals in India,* a volume of wildlife photographs, both in colour and black and white. I was fascinated by the pictures of tigers, leopards, and other wildlife, which were part of the stories my parents had read to me but for which I had no clear image in my mind. I still have this book, the pages dog-eared and coming apart at the binding.

Born Camilla Koffler in Vienna, in 1911, Ylla was the daughter of a Croatian mother and Hungarian father. She began her career as an apprentice to the famous Parisian photographer, Ergy Landau, but soon set up her own studio, specializing in portraits of pets. After Germany invaded France in 1940, Ylla moved to America, where she reopened her studio in Manhattan. Aside from producing posed photographs of dachshunds and Siamese cats, she also trained her lens on zoo animals. In 1952, Ylla travelled to Kenya and Uganda and published *Animals in Africa*. Her photographs also illustrated storybooks for children, including bestsellers like *The Sleepy Little Lion*.

Ylla's visit to India in 1954–55 was funded, in part, by a commission from *Sports Illustrated* magazine to cover a tiger hunt in Cooch Behar, organized for the Hollywood director, John Huston. Though she fulfilled this commitment, tiger hunting didn't impress her and she wrote, 'I do not understand that need in man to affirm himself heroically by killing. It seems to me that only creative effort can give one a true sense of fulfilment. Photography fills me with a satisfaction no dead animal could possibly give.'

Mysore seems to have appealed to Ylla more than other part of India, largely because of the generous hospitality of 'HH', Jayachamaraja Wodeyar, the erstwhile maharaja. She took pictures of royal tuskers decorated for the Dussehra festival as well as wild elephants along the Kabini River. Though independent India had abolished the princely states in 1950, the maharaja still owned vast tracts of land and asserted his authority through political office. He hosted a procession of visitors at his palace, including Dennis Conan Doyle (son of the British author Arthur Conan Doyle) who was in Mysore at the same time as Ylla. She notes, with amusement, his belief that a hidden sanctuary of dinosaurs and other prehistoric beasts still existed in Africa, as described in his father's novel, *The Lost World*. Intent on leading an expedition to find these extinct creatures, Conan Doyle invited Ylla to join him and promised her exclusive photographic rights.

After her visit to Mysore, Ylla travelled to Bharatpur to photograph migratory birds in the famous wetlands that later became Keoladeo National Park. It was here that she died on 30 March 1955, in a fatal accident, falling off the hood of a moving jeep while photographing a bullock cart race. *Animals in India* was published posthumously in 1958 and includes extracts from Ylla's journals. She writes about meeting Prime Minister Nehru and Indira Gandhi in New Delhi, where they kept a pair of red pandas in an enclosure on the grounds of Teen Murti Bhawan, sending them up to Nainital in summer. Ylla also met the tea planter and naturalist E. P. Gee, author of *The Wild Life of India*.

Animals in India was enshrined in my parents' bookcase from as long ago as I can remember. Ylla's photographs entranced me at an early age and looking at the book now, the pictures still elicit a sense of curiosity and wonder, though they are very different from most wildlife photography published today. Many of the images are obviously of animals in enclosures, though the walls and cages are not visible. In some cases, the pictures have the quality of pet portraits, as in a shot of a nilgai that stares balefully at the camera, or a mouse deer photographed at such close range it would have been impossible to take this picture in an open forest. The book also features photos of performing animals and their handlers including a sloth bear, leopard, and two brahminy kites, as well as several rhesus macaques dressed up to dance like living marionettes. Among the most arresting images is a simple shot of a cow and a peacock passing each other on a city street in Mathura.

The book also contains images of cobras. One of these is of worshippers during the Naga Panchami festival, offering prayers to a snake with its hood extended. Another shot is of a spectacled cobra emerging from a snake charmer's basket. Two photographs depict a fight between a grey mongoose and a cobra, which was clearly staged. The mongoose is a blur of fangs and fur, while the cobra rises up like a hooded question mark.

Despite the limitations of her equipment and the pictures of zoo animals, many of Ylla's photographs have a raw immediacy that evokes a sense of the wild. A young tusker in a bamboo jungle raises his trunk and faces the tame elephant from whose back she took the photograph. Another picture, of a dead tiger and hunters on elephant back, presents a grim tableau of blood sport. Accompanying this is a shot of white-rumped vultures feeding on the skinned carcass of the tigress John Huston shot. The hunched, long-necked birds pick the flesh from its bloodied ribcage and the only recognizable part of the animal is its feline skull with giant canines.

Wildlife photographers today follow a different code of professional ethics and have the advantage of the latest optical and digital technology. While some of Ylla's photographs may seem contrived and naïve in comparison to images published today, she captures the fierce intensity in a leopard's eyes as it stares down at her from a shadowy branch or the wide-open jaws of a lion-tailed macaque, glaring at the bursting flashbulb.

Though I didn't know it at the time, Ylla was the inspiration for a character in one of my favourite films from childhood—Howard Hawk's *Hatari* in which John Wayne plays the part of a big game trapper, collecting animals for zoos. Riding on the hood of a Land Rover, he lassoes giraffes, ostriches, zebras, and, finally, a rhino. The female lead, Anna-Maria D'Allesandro, nicknamed Dallas, and played by Elsa Martinelli, was based on Ylla, who had gone to Africa in 1952. The prejudices and fantasies of that period, including a woman's place in the jungle, were firmly entrenched though Ylla challenged those limitations. John Huston, who emulated Ernest Hemingway's brand of masculinity and was famous for directing Hollywood classics like *The Maltese Falcon* and *The African Queen*, must have found Ylla something of a puzzle, as would the son of Sherlock Holmes's creator, dreaming of a lost Eden full of dinosaurs. Ylla took far greater risks than either of these men and, ultimately, paid with her life.

As a young boy, poring over the pages of *Animals in India*, I had no understanding or appreciation for these nuances and complexities. Instead, the intimate yet expansive vision of Ylla's camera inspired me to learn the names of birds and animals, hoping that someday, I might actually be able to encounter them 'in the wild'.

Of course, by this time, I had seen some of these animals in circuses and zoos. Whenever our family drove across from Etah to Delhi, visiting my aunt and uncle who lived there in the early 1960s, we would visit the Delhi Zoo with my cousins. It was always an exciting experience and I have strong memories of seeing tigers, lions, and leopards in their enclosures, as well as the white tigers that were one of the prime attractions. The other animal that fascinated me were hoolock gibbons that swung about their cage like long-limbed acrobats, hooting wildly. In addition to these, there were more familiar animals like nilgai and blackbuck. The zoo was always the first place we went to in Delhi. Situated between Purana Qila, the old fort, and Humayun's Tomb, there was a sense of surrounding history to the place, though it had only opened a few years earlier in 1959. Like every child, I suppose, I was fascinated by the animals but also felt a strange sense of sadness seeing them confined and I wished they could be set free.

The other book that made an indelible impression on me at an early age is *Chendru: The Boy and the Tiger* by Astrid Bergman Sucksdorff, a copy of which was given to me on my eighth birthday. A children's picture book, illustrated with photographs, it is based on a Swedish documentary film, *En Djungel Saga,* made by Sucksdorff's husband, Arne. Released in 1957, the film's English title is *The Flute and the Arrow.*

Chendru is a young boy from the Muria tribe in the Bastar region of Chhattisgarh. His family are hunter-gatherers though they also have paddy fields and a flock of goats. One day, after returning from a hunt, Chendru's father and grandfather arrive in their village with a tiger cub. Chendru adopts it and the two of them become inseparable companions, wandering through the forest together. Carrying a bow and arrows, Chendru lives a simple, idyllic life within the Muria community. The tiger is named Tambu and he grows up quickly during the course of the book, which ends on an ambiguous note, suggesting that the relationship between the boy and the tiger cannot last forever.

The photography is beautiful and presents glossy images of tribal life. How much of the story is true to the actual events in Chendru's life, it is hard to say, but the narrative was obviously scripted from the filmmaker and author's point of view. In 1955, the Sucksdorffs had travelled to India after hearing of the story of a tribal boy who had adopted a tiger cub. From this they constructed a happy fable of life in the Indian jungle.

Being about Chendru's age in the book, I was intrigued by the unlikely 'friendship' between him and Tambu. I also readily accepted the writer's premise that Chendru was 'a young Indian boy of the primitive Muria tribe...a laughing, singing people from the jungle', as the cover text explains. Looking at this book today, I can see the obvious distortions and concocted scenarios, as well as a patronizing European perspective, full of prejudices and stereotypes. But for me as a child, the story resonated with my naive imagination of the Indian jungle and the people and animals that lived there.

For a brief period, Chendru became a star—the 'Tiger Boy' from Bastar. According to an article in the *Times of India,* published soon after his death in 2013, Chendru met Jawaharlal Nehru and travelled with the Sucksdorffs to Sweden, where he lived in their home for several months, but eventually his celebrity waned, and he returned to his village. After that, his life settled into a tragic yet predictable struggle for survival, unlike the joyful scenes of Muria society depicted in the book. Ultimately, Chendru worked as a labourer, earning daily wages from the forest department. Following a stroke, he died destitute and all but forgotten. Tambu's fate is unrecorded, but another source suggests that the tiger shown in the book and film wasn't a wild foundling from the forest, but a captive animal brought to Bastar from West Bengal. He was probably procured from either a circus or a private menagerie of tame wildlife rented out to moviemakers. Once the film shooting was completed, he went back to his cage.

Our relationship with wild animals, particularly our fellow mammals, is often a story of exploitation and wilful destruction. The evolutionary success of our species has led to an arrogance that subjects other life forms to selfish human whims and fantasies, as well as false claims of our dominion over the earth and all its creatures. This sense of superiority, often reinforced by religious scripture, has given licence to many of our most pernicious activities and an indifference to the fate of other living things.

The assumption that our umwelten—those inner lenses, mirrors, and prisms through which we perceive our environment—take precedence over the umwelten of other species, is a fundamental misconception. Yet, we have been taught to believe that human beings know nature better than nature knows itself. That is the flawed logic behind so much of our interaction with wildlife. A goral or blackbuck understands its habitat more intimately than we do and knows how to survive, so long as we don't interfere.

Instead of trying to assert human perspectives and priorities, we need to maintain an open-minded awareness of the unique and complex diversity of the natural world. In this process we must be guided by a sense of humility and compassion. That doesn't mean a sentimental or patronizing approach to conservation but instead a recognition that human beings cannot always dictate, regulate, or engineer solutions to ecological crises. Instead, more often than not, we must allow nature to take its own course by limiting our intrusive, wasteful, and ruinous activities while recognizing that we are, undeniably, the root cause of the problem. As the twentieth century British philosopher, R. G. Collingwood, once wrote, 'Whatever nature depends on, it does not depend on the human mind.'

I

LIVING LANDSCAPES

Forests–Jungles–Grasslands

1

AT AGUMBE

The monsoon has stalled off the Malabar Coast, but a light rain falls for most of our drive along the highway between Goa and Karnataka. Low, dark clouds obscure the forested crestline of the Sahyadri Range, except where an occasional blue ridge protrudes above layers of mist. Whenever the ocean comes into view, its frothing waves are the same colour as the milky coffee served with my breakfast at a roadside canteen. Crossing one of many bridges over broad estuaries, I can see a fleet of fishing vessels safely docked and lashed together to protect them from impending storms. Palm trees sway like toddy drinkers in the gusty, moisture-laden air.

As soon as we turn inland, the two-lane road begins to wind its way through a narrow belt of rolling foothills. Within a few kilometres, the Sahyadri, also known as the Western Ghats, rise abruptly 664 metres above the sea. This extensive chain of mountains stretches for 1,600 kilometres along the western coast of India. In Kerala, Anamudi peak stands 2,695 metres above sea level, India's highest summit outside the Himalaya.

A looping skein of hairpin bends leads us up through shadowy arcades of foliage as we ascend the near-vertical slope. At one or two places, the trees and clouds part just enough to provide glimpses of the rugged landscape beyond, but most of the drive is through dense rainforest, curtained with dripping leaves and verdant coils of clambering lianas. When we stop at a lookout point to take a photograph, my glasses and camera lens steam up as soon as I step outside the air-conditioned vehicle. Super-saturated air closes in around me like a clammy embrace.

At the top of the climb, where the twisting road levels off and takes a last turn, we come upon a pair of weathered stone survey markers, erected in 1839. The inscription reads: 'Head of the Ghaut', and gives the distance from Shimoga as 55 miles, 1 furlong, and 122 yards. We have arrived at Agumbe.

This village of scattered farmhouses and fields, serves as a wayside halt for buses travelling between Shivamogga, the current name for Shimoga, and the town of Udupi on the coast. A couple of hotels and restaurants have come up at a crossroads but other than that it is a quiet, unassuming dot on the map, surrounded by Someshwar Wildlife Sanctuary and Kudremukh National Park. Agumbe is one of the wettest places in India, with almost as much rainfall as Mawsynram and Cherrapunji in Meghalaya. It is also well known for a prevalence of snakes including both spectacled and king cobras. My destination is the Agumbe Rainforest Research Station (ARRS), India's premier field research centre for reptiles. Founded by Romulus Whitaker, it is managed and operated by the Madras Crocodile Bank Trust.

The natural heritage of Agumbe extends far back in time, long before India became a peninsula. Pranay Lal, in his bestselling book *Indica: A Deep Natural History of the Indian Subcontinent*, emphasizes that the Malabar Coast was originally connected to Madagascar, 135 million years ago, well after the protocontinent of Pangea began to break apart. Though these two landmasses—both of which are biodiversity hotspots today—ultimately ended up on opposite sides of the Indian Ocean, they contain many similar species and share corresponding geographical features. Lal points out that, '...the eastern coastline of Madagascar fits snugly with India's western coast like pieces of a jigsaw puzzle.' He goes on to describe how the separation occurred, as tectonic forces ripped the Western Ghats and the highlands of Madagascar apart, 'like a zipper along the range of mountains which tore down the middle....'

This ancient cataclysm is known as the Marion volcanic event, a prolonged series of violent eruptions that began 88 million years ago, reshaping the earth's crust and setting the subcontinent of India on a collision course with Eurasia. Ultimately, the ocean that formed in its wake became the source of the southwest monsoon, which brings vast reservoirs of airborne moisture to the Malabar Coast before moving further north towards the Himalaya. Though the volcanic activity in this region ceased long ago, these dramatic weather patterns continue. An average of 7 metres of rain falls on Agumbe every year, most of it during the monsoon, and the record is more than 11 metres. The rainforests of the Sahyadri are home to millions of life forms, many of which are endemic species such as lion-tailed macaques and Kottigehara dancing frogs, as well as unique birds, reptiles, insects, arachnids, land molluscs, plants, and fungi. The monsoon supports this diverse array of life that clings to the broken rim of India, reminding us how climate and ecology can be a consequence of continental drift.

∽

'Four Malabar pit vipers are in the tree in front of you. Can you see them?'

Ajay Giri, field director of ARRS, challenges me with this question as he shines his torch into the tangled mass of creepers that have engulfed the trunk and lower limbs of the tree. A steady drizzle sifts through the pale beam of light and a chorus of frogs are calling from the surrounding darkness. For several minutes I search the illuminated circle of wet foliage without success until I am finally able to recognize the reticulated markings of a Malabar pit viper stretched out along a branch above me. Though it blends into the patterns on the bark, the regularity of its checkered markings gives the snake away. About three quarters of a metre long and thinner than my index finger, the viper resembles an arrow, with its triangular head that tapers to a point.

After another minute, I spot a second snake, only an arm's length away and level with my chin, its body wrapped around a twisted vine. The head and neck are cocked in a hunting position, waiting to ambush its next meal. Pit vipers hunt in the dark using a pair of sensors between their eyes and nostrils that can locate and identify heat radiating from their prey. The third snake, which lurks at the edge of the torch beam's aura, is a distinctly different colour from the first two, with a greenish tinge to its scales, while the others are mottled shades of brown and bronze. Ajay explains that Malabar pit vipers, which are endemic to the Western Ghats, morph into different hues from a bluish grey to varying shades of green, brown, orange, and even yellow. Neither of us can see the fourth snake.

'It was here five minutes ago,' Ajay insists as he casts about with the light, searching through the lower branches of the tree. We are standing ankle deep in weeds and ferns, near an open well, a few metres away from the main building at ARRS, but in the darkness we could just as easily be in the middle of the jungle. A trickle of rain seeps under the collar of my shirt and my glasses are beaded with moisture.

'There it is!' Ajay exclaims.

Crouching, I spot the fourth pit viper, hanging upside down from a slender tree limb, its body stretched like a bungee cord. The snake's jaws are clamped onto the hind leg of a bright green frog, which is motionless in the glare of torchlight. The frog's throat pulses slowly and it is clutching a twig with one foreleg. Bulging round eyes stare into the light, though it makes no attempt to escape. Whatever initial struggle took place allowed the pit viper's venom to circulate through the frog's body and it now appears to be paralysed. We watch for another quarter of an hour but neither the nocturnal hunter nor the frog moves, suspended from the arched branch above, which is drawn taut like a bow. The other three pit vipers remain where they are—a quiver of poisoned arrows.

The victim is a Malabar gliding frog, about 8 centimetres long. These arboreal amphibians can leap as far as 10 to 12 metres between trees, spreading their webbed feet and flattening their bodies like parachutes to help them sail through the air. Earlier, at dusk I heard several calling, a loud, grating sound, as if someone were repeatedly playing with the handbrake on a car. I also saw a mating pair, the male being smaller, hunched on the female's back as if hitching a ride. Gliding frogs have unique breeding behaviour. After mounting the female, the male uses his hind legs to kick up a froth of excretions that looks like a lather of soap bubbles. The frogs then deposit their eggs and sperm in this foam nest, where fertilization occurs. Later, when the tadpoles hatch, they drop from the nest into pools of water below, where they grow to adulthood and continue this curious cycle of life.

Rhacophorus is a large family of tree frogs, consisting of more than 300 species, distributed mostly in South and Southeast Asia. A subfamily, Mantellidae, are found in Madagascar and may have shared the same ancestor as the Malabar gliding frog, before the island separated from India. While Madagascar has many snakes—upwards of eighty different species—no vipers are found there; neither are cobras or pythons. These predatory reptiles probably entered India only after the subcontinent collided with Eurasia. Both the pit viper and gliding frog that we observe in Agumbe are endemic to the Western Ghats but their origins lie hemispheres apart. In this way geological and biological history converge even if they follow very different timelines.

∽

Dawn in a rainforest is the noisiest hour of the day and I wake up to a rousing chorus. Some of the frogs and insects I heard the night before are still carrying on a syncopated medley of clicks, chirps, and chuckling. But most of the vocalization comes from birds, beginning with the Malabar whistling thrush, which has a plaintive, flute-like song that sounds as if someone is trying to whistle a half-remembered tune. The notes are clear and musical but don't follow a predictable pattern, rising and falling in pitch with improvised virtuosity. As I step out of my cottage, a fine mist lies on the grass while grey clouds hover just above the treetops, filtering the pre-dawn light. The hammering of a woodpecker on a hollow tree trunk sets the tempo for a raucous jam session of hoots, warbling, trills, and shrieks. Most of these calls are unknown to me though I recognize barbets, leafbirds, and possibly an oriole. One bird I can't identify sounds like a clarinet, and another reminds me of the high-pitched honk from an old-fashioned claxon.

Because of the density of the foliage, it is impossible to see most of the birds, even those that are calling nearby. A large woodpecker flies across from one line of trees to the next, probably a greater goldenback, though in the half light it is hard to tell. Several greater racket-tailed drongos, mischievous mimics of the Indian jungle, are flitting about in search of flying insects, trailing extravagant plumes. Aside from their own chiming cries, they are probably the source of some of the other calls too. Manoj Nair, a senior IFS officer and expert birder, has described how these drongos can replicate the sound of temple bells as well as the alarm cry of a giant squirrel. He also recounts '...an apocryphal anecdote of a rather famous racket-tailed drongo at Thekkady, an adept mimic of the local range officer's motorbike and, more amusingly, his alarm clock, having woken up the poor fellow many a time, often at unearthly hours.'

This morning I am hesitant to wander too far from my cottage because Ajay warned me last night that a lone tusker is in the vicinity. This elephant, who makes a habit of visiting Agumbe at least once a year, has charged Ajay and other staff members on more than one occasion. Forest guards in the Someshwar Wildlife Sanctuary recently spotted the tusker. Though he doesn't do much damage other than ripping apart palm trees to get at their succulent hearts and sometimes raiding fields and village homes, *Elephas maximus* can be one of most dangerous animals in the forests of India.

'Though elephants are a threat, the most common cause of human–animal conflict is snakes,' Ajay explains, over breakfast. The 'big four' are the Russell's viper, the common krait, the Indian or spectacled cobra, and the saw-scaled viper, which are responsible for most of the venomous snakebites in India.

A combined (polyvalent) antivenom has been developed by injecting small amounts of venom from each of these four species into a horse. The animal's immune system generates antibodies to fight the effects of snake toxins. Blood is then drawn from the horse to produce a serum that can be injected into a person who has been bitten by a snake. If given soon enough, ideally within half an hour, this treatment is effective and significantly reduces the risk of death. Nevertheless, more than 50,000 people in India die of snakebite every year, usually because they are unable to receive antivenom. In many cases they are unaware of the treatment or can't get to a hospital in time. A large number of snakebite victims are taken to local healers, whose nostrums and other treatments are useless.

ARRS keeps a supply of antivenom for emergencies, but Ajay says that whenever someone is bitten in the surrounding area, they advise them to go to the nearest hospital where the serum can be given intravenously under medical supervision. Of course, the most effective antidote is taking precautions to avoid being bitten. All visitors at ARRS are required to wear shoes when they step out of their rooms and to use a torch at night. Common sense and being alert to the presence of snakes is the best protection.

'I've been here thirteen years,' Ajay tells me. 'And Kumar, the manager, has been here fourteen. Neither of us has ever been bitten.'

Both Ajay and Kumar are trained and experienced in rescuing and releasing snakes that have entered homes and other buildings. They are often called by villagers nearby to remove cobras and king cobras that pose a threat to humans and livestock.

'King cobras seldom bite people,' Ajay says. 'But there is no antivenom for them.'

The Indian cobra (*Naja naja*) is a separate species from the much larger king cobra (*Ophiophagus hannah*) and their venom is not the same. The only place that produces a serum using king cobra venom is Thailand, where these huge snakes are also found. Though ARRS has a couple of Thai vials in stock, researchers have shown that the king cobra's venom from India is quite different from samples collected elsewhere and the serum is unlikely to be effective. Even king cobras from different parts of India have significant variations in the neurotoxins that flow from their fangs. All of this means that if Ajay, Kumar, or anyone else is bitten by a king cobra, it could easily be fatal.

Much of the research in Agumbe occurs when king cobras and cobras are rescued, and a detailed record is kept of their distribution and behaviour as well as the conditions under which the conflict with human beings occurs. At the same time, Ajay and his teammates have been conducting telemetry studies on king cobras since 2008. Because these snakes shed their skin four or five times a year, attaching radio collars is impossible. Instead, a small transmitter, about the size of an AAA battery, is surgically implanted in the king cobra's coelomic cavity under its skin. Transmitters last for two to three years. Ajay explains how the snakes are captured and anaesthetized. A veterinarian performs the simple surgery, and it takes only a few hours for the king cobra to recover and be released back into the wild.

'The operations are performed right here,' Ajay says, pointing to the communal dining table where meals are served at ARRS. King cobras can grow up to 5 metres long, 'stretching from here to there'. He gestures to indicate three quarters of the length of the table, which can seat more than thirty people. The largest king cobra Ajay has handled was an estimated 4.5 metres and weighed 16 kilograms.

Telemetry studies allow the researchers to track a snake's movements and map the territory it occupies as well as study its behaviour, particularly during the breeding season. Using handheld antennae, they follow the king cobras through the forest on foot.

'It's very hard work,' Ajay tells me. 'Especially during the monsoon. You have to go wherever the snake leads you. There are a lot of leeches and ticks and it rains all the time.'

In addition to telemetry, the forest department has given ARRS permission to implant microchips in a few king cobras, which allows them to identify individual snakes.

'Recently I rescued a king cobra and when I scanned it,' Ajay says. 'I found it was one that I had tagged four years ago.'

When I ask him how he got interested in snakes, Ajay tells me that he has always been fascinated by reptiles, ever since he was a boy of seven or eight, growing up in a small town in Maharashtra.

'Nobody else in my family would touch a snake,' he admits with a smile, but he wasn't afraid and handling them came naturally to him. As he grew older, people began to call him to remove snakes from their homes.

Ajay speaks of his work in a quiet, understated manner, without bravado, though he is obviously passionate about protecting cobras. At the age of thirty-five, he seems to have found his mission in life and is apparently content living in a rainforest far from home. A lean, easy-going young man, with a trimmed beard and a casual manner, he talks of snakes the way others speak of cricket or films. When he moved to Agumbe from Maharashtra thirteen years ago, Ajay did not speak Kannada and he was clearly an outsider, but over time he has learned the language fluently and become part of the community.

'I have developed a trust with the local people,' he says. 'They will call me whenever a cobra is found and everyone knows that ARRS does not charge them anything. We also don't harm the snakes.'

There are plenty of professional snake catchers who will remove cobras for a price, as well as those who make a show of handling venomous serpents, as if they were circus performers. Many of them post photographs and videos on social media.

'When people come to watch me rescue a snake,' Ajay explains, 'they are usually disappointed because I do it quickly, without any drama.'

He tells me about a journalist who complained and argued with him when he refused to pose for photographs with one of the cobras he'd caught. But a few days later, there was an incident in which a professional snake wrangler died after he was bitten several times by a cobra that he had draped around his neck. When this story came out in the press, the journalist apologized to Ajay and wrote an appreciative piece about ARRS and its approach to conservation.

A number of wildlife documentaries have been shot in Agumbe, and Ajay has featured in several of them. He laughs when he tells me how most filmmakers arrive with specific scenes already planned out and they expect king cobras to perform like actors. But nature doesn't follow a script and often the snakes don't even show up.

'One director came here with his camera crew for a week, a few years back. He had plans to film king cobras but after the third day, when he hadn't seen even one, he told me that an ordinary cobra would be okay,' Ajay jokes. 'By the fourth day, he was willing to make a film about rat snakes.'

When audiences watch wildlife documentaries on television they often don't realize how many hours of patient waiting are required to record a few dramatic sequences, while clever editing, narration, and music are used to fill in the gaps. Many wildlife films present deceptively intimate, suspenseful, and action-packed storylines that compress months of preparation and shooting into a few minutes of fast-paced footage.

Through telemetry research, Ajay and his team have learned that king cobras spend most of their lives within a relatively limited territory of a few square kilometres, though several males had a home range of 15 to 30 square kilometres. If one of these snakes is released far away from its home, it may not survive. But for a villager who discovers a king cobra in his or her house, it is difficult to accept that the snake will be released only a few hundred metres from where it was found. Ajay and others at ARRS educate people to become more accepting of the king cobra's presence.

When people understand that king cobras eat other venomous snakes like vipers, spectacled cobras, and kraits, they are more willing to have them around. Ajay relates a story about a king cobra that built her nest near a rural settlement. At first the people were alarmed but as they watched the female gathering leaves in her coils, they gained a new appreciation for this creature. They even suggested that maybe they should offer her some water because she must be thirsty. An elderly woman said, 'She has such a difficult life. We should gather some leaves to help her.' Nevertheless, the core message that ARRS conveys is that human beings must allow nature to take its own course. Instead of conflict and interference, peaceful coexistence with snakes is possible, so long as boundaries are maintained. ARRS conducts workshops for forest department staff and other groups to help them understand the behaviour of snakes and how to work around them.

While we are talking, Ajay's mobile phone rings. He answers and speaks in Kannada for a few minutes, asking questions. When the conversation ends, he tells me that the caller has found a cobra in his house. We quickly gather up our gear and climb into the ARRS jeep but by the time we reach the main road, the phone rings again and the man reports that the snake has left on its own. Rather than returning to the research station, Ajay decides to carry on to the nearby town of Tirthahalli to buy some supplies.

As we drive along, he tells me another story about a group of tourists that stopped by the side of the road for a picnic. A few minutes later, they saw a king cobra emerge from the forest and disappear under their car. In a panic, they immediately called for help, but before Ajay arrived the tourists decided that the snake must have gone away, so they got in their car and drove on to Agumbe. When Ajay met them there, he made them get out of the car and jacked up one side of the vehicle so he could look underneath. The king cobra was still coiled up in the car's chassis. After removing and bagging the snake, Ajay was able to take it back to the picnic spot and release it into the forest.

'If I hadn't stopped them and checked, they would have taken the king cobra all the way back to Bangalore with them,' he says.

The mobile phone rings again and Ajay pulls over. There is a short discussion in Kannada, which I'm unable to follow, but it is clear that another snake has been found. Making a quick U-turn, Ajay explains that a spectacled cobra has entered a farmhouse, about 5 kilometres away.

Technology has changed dramatically since ARRS was founded in 2005. Many more people have access to mobile phones now and Ajay can respond to a situation almost immediately, whereas earlier it would have taken hours to receive an alert. Within ten minutes we reach an unpaved side road, where a farmer hails the jeep and directs us to his house. He is a tall, lanky man wearing a hat made from the pithy frond of an areca nut palm, the traditional headgear of this region.

The farmer's home is about 400 metres off the main road. Ajay parks the jeep in a fallow field and exchanges his flip flops for a pair of boots, then takes his snake hook and a green canvas bag from the back of the jeep. Descending a flight of steps, we come to the outer courtyard of the house. The cobra is in a cowshed at the back where the farmer has rigged up a chicken box at shoulder height. He explains that a brood hen was sitting on a nest full of eight eggs when the cobra arrived less than an hour ago. Realizing that something was wrong when the hen suddenly ran outside squawking with alarm, the farmer investigated and found the cobra inside the box, swallowing the eggs.

Ajay switches on his headlamp and cautiously enters the cowshed, while we wait outside. It is a dark, cramped space and the floor is covered in dung and leaf mulch. The roof consists of sheets of corrugated plastic, and the sides are slatted bamboo. In one corner, under the sloping roof is the chicken box made of plywood and wire mesh, with straw inside. It is open at the front. After a few minutes, Ajay comes out and suggests that we enter the shed from the opposite side. He tells me that the cobra is probably a female and gestures for me to follow. As we step over a low barricade of bamboo poles at the rear of the cowshed, I can see the cobra moving about inside the box, her body coiled up within the confined space. She is a couple metres from where I am standing.

The snake's scales glisten in the yellow beam of Ajay's headlamp as he goes closer. After taking a GPS reading to mark the spot, he photographs the snake using his mobile phone. Watching over his shoulder, I can see only a section of the cobra's body and tail but a few seconds later she raises her head and stares at us. In the electric glare, the broad ventral scales on her throat and belly are a creamy white. She has flared the skin on either side of her neck but it is not fully extended as a hood. The smaller scales on her head and back are an olive brown.

Her small, black eyes appear alert, with dark streaks beneath that look like smudged mascara. The snake seems to be watching me with wary alarm, though her eyes are probably blinded by the light and do not register much more than blurred shadows and silhouettes. Herpetologists used to think that cobras were colour-blind, seeing only black and white or shades of grey, but recent studies have shown that their retinas contain cone cells that are sensitive to pigments.

The cobra's forked tongue provides more information than her eyes, and she extends it every five or ten seconds. A snake uses its tongue to collect pheromones and other chemicals in the air that are conveyed to a vomeronasal organ on the roof of its mouth, also known as the Jacobson's Organ. This sensory information is then passed on to the reptile's brain. Human beings also have a vomeronasal organ but it is not nearly as sensitive as a snake's. Though I am looking into the cobra's eyes, her perception of me is more subtle and complex. She studies us with her tongue, possibly sensing the odour of my sweat as well as other chemicals I release into the air, some of which may signal my anxiety. The tongue flicks nervously as the cobra tries to gauge what threat we pose.

Aristotle believed that a snake's forked tongue provided 'a twofold pleasure from savours, their gustatory sensation being as it were doubled', but this cobra has swallowed the chicken's eggs whole and probably tasted very little. As Ajay manoeuvres into position and raises his hook, I take a step back and watch him draw the cobra out of the box. With expert ease, he gently grasps her tail and supports the rest of her body with the hook, holding her out in front of him as he makes his way to the door of the cowshed.

Earlier when we first arrived, Ajay had positioned a canvas bag next to one wall of the farmhouse, with a short PVC pipe protruding from its mouth. As he and the snake emerge into the sunlight, I can see the distinct shapes of the eight eggs inside her body like beans in a pod. The cobra is about a metre and a half long and her head stretches out, attempting to escape. She keeps flicking her tongue to help her understand what is going on. Guiding the cobra towards the pipe and the bag, Ajay lets her slither inside. The dark hole of the pipe looks like a burrow or a drain and the snake enters it instinctively. All of this takes less than a minute and the cobra is soon safely confined to the bag, which Ajay closes and tightly knots after removing the pipe.

The farmer and his family have watched the entire process with apprehension, but their faces now register a sense of relief. Sitting in the courtyard, Ajay fills in a form that provides details of the rescue. Data from the GPS reading has already been saved but he notes down the farmer's name and address, as well as the date and time. A daughter, about thirteen years old, gives Ajay the number of her family's mobile phone and he hands over his card with the ARRS contact information.

After this, the bag containing the cobra is placed in the back of the jeep and Ajay stows his gear before we drive off. Less than a kilometre down the road, he turns onto a secluded track with dense shrubs on either side and no houses nearby. As he lifts the bag, I can see that one side of the canvas is wet. The cobra has regurgitated some of the eggs and the shells have broken. Stepping across to an overgrown ditch at the side of the road, Ajay unknots the bag and releases the cobra while I watch from the jeep. Moments later, I can see the snake gliding through the weeds on the far side of the ditch before she vanishes into the undergrowth.

Ajay explains that nobody in Agumbe would kill a cobra because it is considered sacred. Fear and revulsion for the snakes is combined with awe and reverence.

'Sometimes religious and cultural traditions can be used for conservation,' he says. 'Even if a cobra gets run over by a vehicle on the road, people will leave money at the spot to pay for a priest to perform the final rites and cremate the dead snake. There are many temples here dedicated to cobras and one for king cobras too.'

On our way back to ARRS, we take a detour to the banks of the Bhadra River. A large peepul tree stands in the yard of a temple, facing the flowing water. More than fifty stone carvings of cobras have been placed at its roots, stacked together like tiles. Many of these images are of two cobras entwined and all of them are depicted with their hoods open. Someone must have worshipped at the shrine earlier this morning because fresh hibiscus flowers have been placed in front of the tree and the stone images are covered with a dusting of yellow turmeric powder. Though snake idols are common throughout India, I have never seen so many together in one place. Peepul and banyan trees are often associated with cobras and this riverside shrine celebrates a spiritual connection between *Ficus religiosa* and *Naja naja*, both of which are considered holy species.

Walking over to the Bhadra's edge, I can see that the water is flowing high because of recent rain. The broad, slow-moving current separates into several channels where it spills over a shelf of grey rock, polished by centuries of floods. Sahyadari rainforests are the source of many rivers, large and small, most of which flow eastward across the plateau.

Nobody else is around and the temple complex is deserted. A peaceful sense of sanctity and solitude infuses this place—the constant movement of the water, a breeze rustling the peepul leaves, and a lone cormorant opening its wings to dry in the sun. I try to imagine what it must have been like before the temple was built, long ago when there was no motor road or fields and villages nearby. The natural beauty of this setting, the calm yet powerful momentum of the river, and perhaps a cobra basking on the rocks must have inspired someone to venerate this spot in recognition of nature's fecundity.

As we return to the research station, drops of rain spatter against the windshield and it soon begins to pour, a heavy monsoon deluge that continues for most of the afternoon. Finally, at about four o'clock, the rain eases and I am able to emerge from my cottage. The trees are still dripping and pools of water flood the ground. Keeping a lookout for the lone tusker, I walk along the jeep track for several hundred metres to a place where a muddy footpath enters the trees. Not more than 30 metres inside the jungle, I come to the entrance of a sacred grove, marked by a string of dry mango leaves suspended overhead between two bamboo poles. This morning, as we were leaving, Ajay had pointed out this forest shrine which is hidden in the foliage.

A light rain begins to fall again as I step into a shadowy clearing next to a spring that feeds a shallow pond fringed with ferns. Three masonry altars have been built at this spot, all of them green with moss and algae. Atop each altar is a dark, uncarved stone about 30 centimetres in height. A couple of clay oil lamps that burnt out long ago are now full of rainwater. Withered garlands have been draped around the stones as a gesture of devotion. Faint colours are visible too, where yellow and magenta powder was daubed on the altar, though the rain has washed most of it away. Leaves have fallen from the trees above, mingling with the mouldering petals of floral offerings. The only recognizable religious symbol is a small iron trident propped against one altar, rotting lemons impaled on its tines. Earlier, Ajay had told me that the previous owner of the property, who sold his land to ARRS and moved into a house in the village, comes here occasionally to propitiate the forest gods. Sometimes he sacrifices a chicken, spilling blood on the stones and sharing its meat with the researchers.

I have no idea what deities are represented by these stelae or what prayers are offered here but in the dank twilight of the rainforest, I can sense ancient, arboreal myths—not of gods and goddesses or even formless spirits—but of wild, unpredictable forces sheltered by these trees. The stones retain geological evidence and mineral memories of fiery volcanoes and primordial continents ripped apart millions of years ago. Their irregular shapes reflect the rough contours of the mountains from which they come.

For once, the jungle is silent, no calls of insects, frogs, or birds. The only sound within this natural sanctuary is of falling rain, lisping from leaf to leaf, the persistent murmur of the monsoon.

Agumbe Rainforest Research Station is a 2-hectare (5 acres) nature preserve, which has been rewilded over the past eighteen years. Surrounded by the forests of Someshwar Wildlife Sanctuary, it attracts sambar and other wild mammals like common palm civets, wild pigs, and Indian crested porcupines, as well as leopards, including one melanistic or black panther. What used to be paddy fields are now a marsh, where great egrets and woolly-necked storks hunt for worms and snails. An abandoned areca nut plantation is still standing but it has not been sprayed or harvested and the jungle has reclaimed most areas of cultivation. Jackfruits as large as misshapen basketballs with spiked green hides grow from the trunks and branches of several trees within the complex. The buildings are all low, single-storey structures, providing accommodation for staff, volunteers, and guests, though the majority of the inhabitants are wild creatures that flourish in the lush surroundings outdoors.

Under the eaves of my cottage lives a bat that feeds on rudraksha fruit during the night, dropping the hard, wrinkled pits on the veranda along with its dung. Beside the path to the dining area, a long-horned spiny orb weaver crouches beneath a leaf, waiting for miniscule insects to get entangled in its web. About the size of a melon seed, it is a living gem, with bright blue horns and an orange-yellow body decorated with black dots. The colours are so bright they seem almost artificial.

Behind the kitchen, ARRS's manager, Kumar, points out a green vine snake draped on a plant. The colour of fresh grass, it looks like the coiled tendril of a creeper that has wrapped itself around the plant's stem. About a metre long and thin as a bootlace, it is sometimes called a whipsnake and has a narrow, diamond-shaped head with a tapered snout. Its large eyes are a yellowish green with horizontal black pupils like chevrons, which give it a sinister demeanour. Its genus name, *Ahaetulla,* comes from a Sinhala word meaning 'eye pecker'. Vine snakes have binocular vision thanks to grooves on either side of their heads, which makes their eyesight much sharper than other snakes like vipers. It hunts for small frogs, lizards, skinks, and other snakes. *Ahaetulla nasuta*'s bite is mildly venomous, though it has little effect on humans. A rarer species of brown vine snake is also found in Agumbe and while driving around, we come upon two of them crushed on the road.

Another interesting reptile is the southern flying lizard, which is relatively common in this part of the Western Ghats. Though these miniature dragons are masters of camouflage, Kumar helps me spot one clinging to the trunk of an areca nut palm, blending in perfectly with the mottled bark. Males have a bright yellow dewlap under their chins, which they flash to attract their mates, but most of the time *Draco dussumieri* remain hidden. A thin membrane on either side of their bodies, between their front and hind legs, allows them to soar from tree to tree, sometimes covering a distance of more than 30 metres. Flying lizards feed on ants and other insects and are most active when the sun comes out and warms their cold-blooded bodies.

Next to the steps of a storehouse, Ajay shows me a hump-nosed pit viper a few metres away from the well where we saw the four Malabar pit vipers last night. This one has the same distinctive shape of head but its colouring is different, a pale, rusty brown with black dashes along its back and sides. It blends into the dull, red soil, partly hidden beneath a layer of ferns. Though hunting in daylight, it has the same pits on either side of its face that contain heat sensors to help detect its prey. The hump-nosed pit viper's venom is much more toxic than the Malabar pit viper's, causing kidney damage. Fatalities have been recorded in Sri Lanka.

On my last afternoon in Agumbe, Ajay insists that we go and look for Kottigehara dancing frogs. Classified as a critically endangered amphibian on the International Union for the Conservation of Nature's (IUCN) Red List, it is relatively easy to find along streams in this part of Karnataka. Driving west through the village, we turn off on a forest road that takes us to Jogigundi, one of many waterfalls in the area. A popular tourist destination, it is located inside Someshwar Wildlife Sanctuary but when we come to the entrance, the gate is locked. Nobody is in sight, so we park the jeep and duck under the barrier. Puzzled, Ajay speculates that the sanctuary may be temporarily closed on account of the tusker's presence. Moving cautiously, we follow a dirt path through columns of trees until it descends steeply into a forested gorge.

While keeping an anxious eye out for the elephant, I forget to check my shoes for leeches until it is too late. At least a dozen of the bloodsuckers are inching their way up my shoes and pant-legs, while three have already latched onto my right ankle and calf. We have brought no salt with us, so I do my best to pick them off, though they stick to my fingers as I try to flick them away. My socks are soaked with blood and one of the leeches has climbed up to my waist, leaving a red stain on my shirt.

Sunset is still several hours away but the valley is cloaked in shadows. The last section of the path is like an uneven, overgrown staircase. When we reach the bottom there is a large, green pool at the foot of the falls, from where the stream flows out into the gorge. Using rocks at the water's edge as stepping stones, we cross over to the other side. Covered in algae and moss, the wet surfaces are as slick as ice. More than leeches or the elephant, I am worried about slipping and falling. Ajay leads the way, casually jumping from foothold to foothold, but I set aside any pretence of a graceful descent, moving like an arthritic crab over the treacherous rocks.

Stopping at a point where the stream sluices under a pair of boulders, Ajay directs his headlamp into the wet crevices until he finds the object of our quest. Seconds later, a male dancing frog leaps into view on a grey-green slab of rock, wet with spray from the stream. This small, seemingly nondescript creature is about the size of my thumb and almost the same colour as the rock, a brindled, ruddy green. Its hind legs are tucked into its sides and its forelegs are braced on the rock like a sprinter waiting for a starting pistol. As we move about, trying to get the right angle for a photograph, it jumps again, onto the top of another boulder overlooking the stream. With a pointed, upturned nose, it eyes us suspiciously. As with most frogs, the female is larger, but she is nowhere in sight and the male doesn't seem to be in an amorous mood.

The frog's so-called 'dancing' is actually a breeding display. Scientists refer to it as 'foot-flagging'. The male stretches out one hind leg and splays his webbed foot in a seductive pose to attract female frogs. Its behaviour also resembles a martial arts kick and is sometimes used to fend off other males. This is not the right season for this frog to give us a demonstration but I've seen plenty of videos online. Dancing frogs have attracted a lot of attention in recent years since fourteen new species were identified in the Western Ghats.

Also known as 'torrent frogs' because they inhabit streams that flood during the monsoon, this diminutive genus has evolved in the Sahyadri over a span of 80 million years, from around the time India broke free of Madagascar. Its life story is still being written by researchers who are studying these rare amphibians that live within isolated pockets of rainforest and are threatened by pollution and habitat loss.

Despite its rarity, I have to admit that I am initially unimpressed. We have braved bull elephants as well as bloodthirsty leeches, and I have almost fallen and broken my neck on the slippery rocks only to find a small brown frog that doesn't even live up to its name. Watching this creature doing absolutely nothing—neither dancing nor singing—but simply sitting on a wet rock by a swift mountain stream, I wonder what its round, unblinking eyes see in us and in its immediate surroundings. The frog's world is confined to this narrow gorge, where direct sunlight never enters. It does not make a sound, though I've been told that when the vocal sac in its throat inflates like a miniature balloon, it emits a high-pitched chirping that resembles the call of a bird.

But as I watch the frog after lowering my camera, I realize that I am projecting human expectations upon this creature. My indifference is a result of my desire to see the frog perform in the same way that we expect cobras or even elephants to dance for our amusement. To say the frog is doing nothing, is to fail to understand the subtle nuances of life. Whatever may be going on inside its moist, amphibian skin—neurons firing, organs pumping, glands excreting, muscles flexing—it is alive. Its eyes register light and shadow, sending signals to its brain. Simply because the frog does not behave as I would like it to, doesn't mean that it hasn't fulfilled its purpose on this planet.

Wanting animals to replicate human behaviour is a common error of observation. Even the most dispassionate naturalist tends to see a reflection of herself or himself in the wild species that she or he observes. Yet, the frog has an existence all its own, which I will never be able to fully appreciate, research, describe, or photograph. It lies beyond my limited powers of comprehension and the flawed conceit of metaphors and names that I might use. Here, in this moment, I have to accept that I matter less to the frog than it matters to me.

2

LOST JUNGLES

The Bhagavata Purana contains the story of Kaliya, a fearsome naga or serpent deity who inhabited the Yamuna at Vrindavan. He was a giant cobra with multiple heads whose venom polluted the river. The snake tormented the villagers of Gokula, where Krishna lived as a child. Kaliya's only enemy, Garuda, the sacred raptor of Vishnu, had been banished from Vrindavan by a sage's curse. For this reason, the great naga lived unchallenged in the Yamuna with his many wives—the enchanting naginis. On the riverbank, beneath the shade of a flowering tree, with spreading branches and perfumed blossoms, the young Krishna played with his friends. One day, a ball that they had been tossing back and forth fell in the river. Krishna plunged into the Yamuna to retrieve it. Immediately, Kaliya rose out of the current and wrapped his coils around the boy. Krishna wrestled with the snake and freed himself, then leapt atop the cobra's hood and began to dance, revealing his supreme powers. Stamping on each of Kaliya's heads with his nimble feet, he subdued the giant naga through the rhythm of his dance, forcing the snake to bow his head and vomit up venom. Afraid that Krishna would kill their husband, the naginis emerged from the Yamuna and pleaded for mercy. Krishna then spared Kaliya's life and banished him to Patala, the lowest realm of the underworld, where nagas have their kingdom.

This allegory of good and evil is one of the most popular episodes in the mythology of Vrindavan. As the historian D. D. Kosambi has noted, 'The Naga was the patron deity, perhaps aboriginal cult-object of the place. The trampling down of Kaliya instead of killing indicates the obvious survival of Naga worship.' Many paintings and sculptures depict the giant cobra with Krishna dancing on his head, holding the serpent's tail with one hand. In classical dance traditions, like Bharatanatyam and Kuchipudi, this scene is re-enacted in a performance known as the Kaliya Mardana. Taking on multiple roles, a dancer lifts her arms above her head signifying the cobra's hood. Then, holding a flute to her lips, she portrays Krishna with one leg raised as he leaps victoriously upon Kaliya's menacing crown, ridding the Yamuna of the naga's toxic presence.

∽

A rickshaw driver takes me to Kaliya Ghat, which lies along the riverfront in Vrindavan. It is the fourth day of the month of Shravan, at the peak of the monsoon, in early August. The swollen waters of the Yamuna splash over the top steps of the temple ghats, a broad, swift current reflecting the grey colour of the clouds which threaten rain. Riverboats are tied up along the shore and the air is warm and muggy. Thousands of pilgrims are circling the parikrama, a twelve-kilometre circuit of the town. One man prostrates himself on the ground, measuring the distance with lengths of his body. The humid atmosphere is infused with religious fervour, celebrating Krishna's divine compassion.

An image of Kaliya, carved out of a black rock, with his hood unfurled, stands beneath a sandstone pavilion. Coins and flower petals are scattered on the pedestal. To the right of this shrine is an enormous tree with outstretched branches that twist and turn in all directions. Most scholarly texts and treatises on Krishna identify the trees he played under in Vrindavan as kadamb (*Neolamarckia cadamba*). Yet, the ancient tree at Kaliya Ghat, which priests insist has stood here since the time of Krishna's childhood, bearing marks of his games on its gnarled limbs, is actually *Mitragyna parvifolia*, commonly known as kaim. The two species have similar flowers, shaped like pale, yellow balls, with protruding white styles that give them a furry appearance. The blossoms on both trees emit a sweet, pervasive fragrance. But the leaves and bark are entirely different. 'This is a case of mistaken identity. *Neolamarckia cadamba* is native to moist forests in Northeast India and would not survive unaided in the hot, dry Brindavan area,' writes Pradip Krishen, the eminent conservationist and arboreal authority. 'Kaim is not only native to the (remnant) Brindavan forests but is their dominant tree. Clinchingly, everyone in Brindavan calls kaim "kadamb". Time to revise some of those old books!'

The tree at Kaliya Ghat is worshipped by pilgrims and the lower branches are wrapped in red and saffron scarves that contrast brightly with the round green leaves. Its roots descend deep into the mud along the Yamuna's riverbank. Vrindavan's name means a forest or grove full of holy basil (vrinda in Sanskrit or tulsi in Hindi). An idyllic sanctuary of nature, this is where Krishna and his consort Radha grew up together and came of age, a pristine forest that sheltered their innocent love play. The Puranas tell us that Krishna's youth was spent as a simple cowherd playing a flute, though he often revealed his supernatural powers, even as he engaged in mischievous pranks and flirtations. His association with sacred cows is a central part of the devotional stories that emphasize his pastoral heritage. Several gaushalas are located in Vrindavan, where stray cattle are given shelter and fed through charitable endowments.

Except for the venerable kaim, the original forests that once grew by the Yamuna have vanished and the only tulsi plants I see are being sold in flowerpots. Vrindavan is now a crowded pilgrim town full of ashrams and temples. The marble spires of Prem Mandir lie within a walled enclosure and are surrounded by landscaped lawns and flower beds. Most of Vrindavan's markets are a clutter of food stalls and shops selling religious souvenirs. At the International Society for Krishna Consciousness (ISKCON) temple, a troupe of European devotees in pastel-coloured dhotis and saris are ringing cymbals and dancing as they perform the ecstatic worship of Krishna. Minutes later, the heavens open and a monsoon deluge drenches the town, sending pilgrims running for shelter. Lightning flashes and thunder rumbles as the clouds release their life-giving moisture.

The Yamuna is one of India's most polluted rivers. Though its sources lie in glacier-fed streams of the Himalaya, and its waters remain relatively clean until they leave the mountains near Kalsi, the Yamuna quickly becomes a conduit for all of the industrial effluents and sewage from towns and cities along its banks. By the time it flows past Delhi, the river is a poisonous, foul-smelling swamp. India's capital adds its wastewater and other pollutants to the Yamuna, flushing it on downstream to Vrindavan, Mathura, and Agra. During winter and summer, when water levels drop, the Yamuna becomes even more toxic and whatever aquatic life it supports is wiped out or severely threatened. Rafts of dead fish, deprived of oxygen and poisoned by chemicals, float on its surface as the river glides past the Taj Mahal, underscoring the careless, criminal indifference of manufacturers and municipal authorities. Even the venomous Kaliya could not have defiled the Yamuna as thoroughly and deliberately as human beings have done over the past century or more. During the monsoon, when water levels rise, there is some reprieve, though the pollutants are simply washed downriver towards the Yamuna's confluence with the Ganga at Prayagraj, formerly Allahabad.

Early the next morning, I hire a boat from the temple ghats in Mathura, 12 kilometres downstream from Vrindavan. The sun is just striking the ornate facades of shrines and havelis overlooking the river. Clumps of water hyacinths float by on the flooded current. A motorboat crosses ahead of us, carrying schoolchildren from villages on the opposite shore. Worshippers are conducting prayers and bathing in the murky water. As a boatman rows me upstream, marigold petals and an assortment of empty plastic bottles, as well as the discarded foam seat cover from a scooter, drift past. Several open drains debouch bilious streams of wastewater into the sacred river. A small sewage treatment unit is situated nearby, but it seems hardly adequate for the densely packed neighbourhoods that extend in a warren of narrow streets behind the ghats.

The boatman points out various temples and religious landmarks as he struggles to make headway against the strong current. 'For twenty years, I've been serving the Yamuna,' he tells me in Hindi and proceeds to recount fragments of the story of Krishna's birth, how he was the eighth avatar of Vishnu and entered the womb of his birth mother, Devaki. He also describes how Krishna's father, Vasudeva, carried him across the Yamuna to save him from the tyrant Kamsa who was intent on killing the child. 'The Yamuna rose up and touched Krishna's feet,' the boatman explains, 'as Vasudeva struggled to cross over.' Ultimately, another serpent, Vishnu's Shesh Nag, helped ferry them to the other shore where the newborn Krishna was left in the care of Nanda and Yashoda, who became his foster parents and raised him in the village of Gokula. This region, along both banks of the Yamuna, is known as Braj Bhoomi, the sacred homeland of Krishna. His birthplace is marked by a large temple complex in Mathura and the entire landscape is invested with myths and lore that are part of the Krishna Leela, the life story of the divine cowherd who symbolizes love and devotion, protecting the earth from destruction through his benevolent powers.

Mathura is an ancient city, with archaeological evidence of urban habitation going back more than two millennia and probably several centuries before that. It is mentioned both in the Mahabharata and Ramayana, as being the capital of the kingdom of Surasena. But earlier still, at the uncertain juncture of history and myth, it was originally called Madhuvan, which means a forest full of honey. The trees that grew here were felled by Prince Shatrughana, who cleared the forest and built the city on the banks of the Yamuna. The name, Madhuvan, from which Madhura or Mathura evolved, has been appropriated by other towns in different parts of the country.

India's lost forests play a significant role in mythology and religion, as a source of everything from medicinal herbs to spiritual wisdom. The Sanskrit word 'van' (or 'ban' as it is also spelled) means a forest but can be translated as a grove or a wooded thicket. It is the root of many other words like 'vanya', which means wild. 'Vanaspati' are plants found in a forest and 'vanara' is a word for monkey, from which the common name, bandar, is derived. Another synonym for forest in Sanskrit is 'aranya' which also means a wild place or wilderness, home of the forester and woodsman.

As we consider the many ways in which mythology and natural history intersect, it is important to understand how India's linguistic and religious heritage recalls and venerates those ancient forests that disappeared centuries ago but remain alive in our spiritual and cultural imagination. Classical poetry, folklore and myths, as well as sculpture and other forms of art, evoke a nostalgia and deep-rooted longing for wild places and a desire to reclaim, even in an illusory manner, something of those vanished forests full of flowering kaim trees and venomous cobras.

∽

The fifth day of Shravan is celebrated as Naga Panchami, a festival in which cobras and other snakes are worshipped by Hindus, Buddhists, and Jains. It commemorates the mythological date when Astika Muni intervened and stopped the Sarpa Satra, a snake sacrifice initiated by a king named Janamejaya to avenge the death of his father Parikshita, who died of snakebite. A huge firepit, or yagna kund, was set alight and through the powerful prayers and mantras of priests, snakes from all corners of the earth were drawn into the flames. Astika, whose mother was a naga queen, Manasa, persuaded Janamejaya to halt the sacrifice, rescuing cobras and other serpents from extinction.

Until recently, live cobras were worshipped on Naga Panchami, as well as naga images in temples. Snake handlers brought captive cobras to sacred sites and shrines, often near a peepul tree, where devotees offered milk to the snakes and performed rituals, praying for protection and prosperity. In some places this practice persists but it has largely been stopped by state forest departments and animal rights groups. Nevertheless, the festival is celebrated throughout India, with many local traditions such as the Nagdwar Yatra pilgrimage in Pachmarhi. In Varanasi and other towns in Uttar Pradesh, wrestling akharas give special prominence to the Naga Panchami festival. The cobra represents kundalini energy that lies dormant, like a coiled serpent's at the base of the spine, which is released through yoga and physical exercise. Essentially, this festival recalls the importance of ancient naga deities, a pantheon of early demigods rooted in animistic traditions and forest worship that predates contemporary faiths.

India's wildlife protection laws forbid the capture and public display of snakes. The Sapera community, popularly referred to as snake charmers, are a nomadic caste in North India. Traditionally, they moved about from village to town, exhibiting cobras and pythons, while collecting coins from whatever audience they could attract. Using a reed instrument called a been or pungi, made from a dried gourd, with two protruding flutes, they created an illusion that their captive cobras were performing a swaying dance in time to the hypnotic music. The snakes had usually been defanged and the glands that produce venom removed.

Their 'dance' was simply a defensive display in which the cobra raised its head and extended its hood. Instead of moving to the music, which cobras cannot hear because they are deaf, the snakes followed the rocking motion of their captor. An exotic cliché, popular with tourists, snake charming is no longer permitted in India. Efforts have been made to settle and rehabilitate Sapera communities, encouraging them to find other employment. Nevertheless, a few Saperas surreptitiously continue their ancestral way of life and are still called upon to remove cobras and other snakes that enter people's homes.

After my boat ride along the ghats, I wander through the narrow back lanes of Mathura. It is still early in the morning, though pilgrims are making their way to temples by the river. Street vendors are selling aloo poori and kulcha chole for breakfast. A theka bhang shop has just raised its shutters. At this hour of the day, troops of rhesus macaques outnumber human devotees. Descendants of the vanara that lived in ancient forests, these monkeys have successfully adapted to urban life and live off handouts from pilgrims, as well as food scraps and waste. They also snatch bags and other belongings from unsuspecting passers-by. When challenged, the macaques can be aggressive, but most of the time they sit and wait expectantly like docile beggars, depending on the generosity of those who believe they acquire merit by feeding animals. Packs of stray dogs compete with the macaques for leftovers from the food stalls. A woman offers withered vegetables to a roaming bull while pigeons flock the rooftops of Mathura, feasting off scattered handfuls of grain. Further on, another woman is crumbling batasha, a white sugary confection, and feeding ants that scurry about busily near her toes.

Turning a corner, I catch sight of an elderly man in a faded red shirt, wearing a yellow headscarf. He has his back to me but as I approach I can see that he is holding a cobra in his hands. The snake is about a metre long, coiled up in the crook of his arm, its head slithering through his fingers. Another man, middle-aged and well dressed, is seated on a ledge next to a locked doorway. As I stop to watch, the Sapera drapes the cobra around the man's neck like a scaly grey garland. The serpent is sluggish but lifts its head as the man holds up his mobile phone to photograph himself with the cobra. He then hands me his phone and asks me to take his photograph, posing proudly as the snake encircles his neck. On a ledge nearby, the Sapera has placed a round basket, in which he keeps the snake. A small crowd has gathered and people throw coins into the basket and fold their hands. A woman comes out of her house and gives the Sapera a ten-rupee note. Turning to me, she explains that it is Naga Panchami and urges me to make an offering. After I add another ten rupees to his earnings, the Sapera deftly coils the snake into the basket and covers it with a lid.

Looking nervously over his shoulder, the snake handler quickly vanishes down one of the side lanes. If the police were to catch him, he could be arrested or fined and the cobra confiscated, but it is early enough in the day to avoid detection and those rules are easily broken. The entire encounter takes no more than five minutes, an illicit transaction that conjures up old myths and makes me recall the cobra's symbolic nature, how the shedding of a serpent's skin suggests immortality and the regeneration of life. The cobra embodies our primal fears and fascination, the awe and horror with which we perceive deities and demons within the natural world.

A ten-minute rickshaw ride from the ghats brings me to the Mathura Museum. Its extensive collection of sculptures was excavated from in and around the city. Some of these artworks date back to the third century BCE, though most of them are from the first to ninth centuries of the common era. Many of the sculptures reflect Greek influences passed on from the remnants of Alexander's dominions, as well as the Kushana empire, which controlled most of northwestern India during the first and second centuries CE, when Mathura was an important centre for commerce and art. The Mathura School of Sculpture is usually associated with the refined and stylized features of Buddha images, clad in pleated garments delicately carved out of red sandstone.

The museum was started in 1874 by the district collector, F. S. Growse, an Orientalist scholar. The current building was completed in 1930 and is circular in shape, with both inner and outer galleries, as well as a garden in the centre. The collection is remarkable for many reasons but primarily because it reveals a complex synthesis of Buddhist, Jain, and Hindu iconography. The hundreds of different pieces of art on display provide a historical perspective on Indian culture as it evolved during the first millennium and on into the medieval period. These statues show how mythological narratives can be traced back to a shared heritage and aesthetic principles grounded in nature. Early yaksha cults, which venerated forest spirits, nymphs, and animal deities, were gradually co-opted into mainstream traditions. The sculptors who produced these works of art were prolific in their use of flowers, trees, birds, and mammals and they constantly integrated these wild species into the iconography of the images they produced.

Naga figures are prominently represented in the Mathura Museum and they were clearly an important part of the mythology of those early times. In many statues, naga gods and goddesses are carved in human form but framed beneath a cobra's hood, so that the deity and the serpent are seen as one. In most of these images the cobra has multiple heads. A life-sized figure of a nagaraja from the second century appears to be dancing beneath the cobra's splayed hood as its coils encircle his limbs. This iconic motif is then adapted to other deities, such as a Jain Tirthankara, Parshvanatha, also from the second century, who sits in meditation beneath a cobra's hood.

Among the numerous artworks on display, one sculpture that conveys, more than any other, a close connection between nature and spirituality, is a badly damaged fragment from the first or second century CE that depicts a naga queen and her two nagini attendants. The three female figures have a sinuous grace, with large, pendulous breasts. Their arms are adorned with bracelets and they appear very similar to the yakshis or tree sprites in other sculptures from the same period. Sadly, the queen's face and the cobra canopy that surrounds her is broken, but the back of the snake's hood is mostly intact. Here the sculptor has decorated the reverse side with intricately carved leaves and flowers of an Ashoka tree. This floral imagery provides a subtle contrast to the voluptuous figures on the front, though the foliage and branches mirror the naginis' serpentine curves. In a playful gesture, the artist—who was also an observant naturalist—has added a five-striped palm squirrel perched on one of the tree's upper limbs.

Almost every period of art represented in the museum contains naga figures, from a first century image of Garuda with a nagini clutched in his beak to a carved panel from the medieval period, possibly the fifteenth century, depicting Vishnu resting upon the coils of the Shesh Nag, whose hood shelters the deity in his eternal repose. Seeing these sculptures evokes a sense of cultural continuity and underscores the way in which nature permeates human dreams and desires. The mysterious, and sometimes threatening, presence of snakes both attracts and repels us in ways that are best explained through the artful imagery of myths.

∽

If we try to picture what the original forests of Madhuvan and Vrindavan must have looked like, and what trees and plants they contained, the landscape would have been entirely different from what exists today. Most of the region on either side of the Yamuna is now an expanse of irrigated fields and orchards interspersed with villages and towns. Even the few patches of uncultivated land that can still be found are overgrown with mostly non-native species and the mix of trees is nothing like the wild growth that would have been here two or three hundred years ago, let alone three thousand. All that remains of the original forests are remnants of indigenous species that have survived in isolated pockets. Like the statuary in the Mathura Museum these are living relics that provide clues to the arboreal past.

The honeybees that gave Madhuvan its name would have been attracted to the flowers of kaim, as well as palash or dhak, amaltas and possibly bauhinias like jhinjheri or kachnar. Undoubtedly, giant semal trees towered above the forest canopy, their rubbery red blossoms pollinated by bats. In drier parts of the forest the predominant trees would have been acacias like khair, ronjh, and babool. Wild fruit trees probably included ber, amla, jamun, bael, and possibly mangoes. Nearer the river, where the water table lay close to the surface, different varieties of figs, including peepul and banyan, must have put down their roots. And where the forest ended and the shifting course of the Yamuna left broad margins of sandy soil, it is likely that tall white plumes of munj grass fringed the riverbanks.

Though we can only speculate about the composition of those lost forests that were cleared to make way for temple towns, the terrain and climate would have been similar to Delhi, 130 kilometres upstream along the Yamuna. In his book, *Trees of Delhi*, Pradip Krishen lists four 'ecotones' or micro-habitats of the capital, using traditional terminology adopted from the 1887 Gazetteer of Delhi. 'Kohi', the rocky escarpments of the Aravalli, are not relevant to Mathura, which lies to the east of this primordial mountain range. However, the other three ecotones would apply to Krishna's Braj Bhoomi. 'Bangar' describes arable high ground, mostly flat, with fertile soil that would have been the first to come under cultivation. 'Khadar' refers to a belt of marginal land, where the river shifted course and its banks were cut through by ravines. 'Dabar' are the lowest areas that flood during the monsoon, parts of which remain marshland for much of the year.

Spreading westward from the relatively moist, riparian terrain along the Yamuna, the landscape would have quickly grown drier, and the broad-leafed trees must have thinned out into dry deciduous forests of dhok and other hardy species like jhand and bistendu. Sometimes referred to as 'monsoon forests' these arid woodlands contain species that shed their leaves in the dry season to reduce evaporation and conserve moisture, regaining their foliage after the rains begin. Interspersed with grasslands, this is the typical forest cover that extends from Western Uttar Pradesh and Madhya Pradesh into Rajasthan and Haryana. Ironically, though often considered wasteland, these are the true jungles of India.

Hobson-Jobson, Henry Yule and A. C. Burnell's dictionary of Anglo-Indian words and usage, first published in 1886, traces the word 'jungle' back to the Sanskrit, 'jangala', which they note 'occurs mostly in medical treatises'. They cite the *Sushruta Samhita*, a foundational text for Ayurveda, composed in the ancient, indeterminate past by the sage and surgeon, Sushruta. The original meaning of jangala was arid land covered with thorny trees and sparse brush.

> The native word means in strictness only waste, uncultivated ground; then such ground covered with shrubs, trees or long grass; and thence, the Anglo-Indian application is to forest, or other wild growth, rather than to the fact that it is not cultivated. A forest; a thicket; a tangled wilderness. The word seems to have passed at a rather early date into Persian, and also into use in Turkistan. From Anglo-Indian it has been adopted into French as well as in English.

The acceptance of the word into English vocabulary is acknowledged by Fitzedward Hall in his *Modern English* in 1873: 'Jungle, derived to us, through the living language of India, from the Sanskrit, may now be regarded as good English.' The poet and essayist Algernon Charles Swinburne used it metaphorically in 1867 referring to 'jungles of argument', suggesting language and thought that it is tangled and unintelligible.

British colonial writers, particularly hunter-naturalists, changed the meaning of jungle completely. Instead of the dry, unirrigated high ground referred to in Sanskrit, the English word now implied dense, humid forests full of bamboo and rampant lianas. This wet, impenetrable labyrinth of foliage was infested with leeches, fever-inducing insects, and bloodthirsty predators. It was a dangerous, hostile environment in which courageous white hunters pursued wildlife for science and sport. The jungle epitomized everything in nature that was exotic and unknown. More than anyone, Rudyard Kipling, in his Jungle Books, permanently etched this meaning upon our modern consciousness.

Francis Zimmermann, a French anthropologist, has published a provocative book titled, *The Jungle and the Aroma of Meats,* which explores the idea of wild environments as they relate to medical tradition in India. He focuses primarily on the *Sushruta Samhita* as well as other Ayurvedic texts. Going back to the root meaning of jangala, Zimmermann explains how these dry, uncultivated lands contrast with another Sanskrit term, 'anupa', signifying low, marshy wetlands. A middle ground also exists, known as 'sadharna', where the jangala and anupa meet. Rainfall is the primary factor in determining the kind of vegetation and dominant species of trees. Broadly speaking, jangala prevailed from the Yamuna westward, towards the Indus, while anupa extended along the Ganga and further east. Using this system of classification, different species of plants and animals were associated with each environment. For example, blackbuck and other antelope were found in the jangala, whereas buffalo, elephants, and rhinos inhabited the anupa.

According to Zimmermann, this 'bioclimatic polarity' served as an organizing principle for ancient Indian taxonomy, driven primarily by the medical uses of flora and fauna. Ayurvedic pharmacists divide our bodily humours into three categories: vata (wind–air), pitta (bile–fire), and kapha (phlegm–water). To ensure health and well-being, each of the humours must be kept in balance. Illness occurs when one or more of them become 'deranged'. In scholarly, postmodern prose that sometimes merits Swinburne's analogy, Zimmermann connects geography, climate, and forest cover to the human body. This synthesis of biogeographical elements guides the Ayurvedic physician while performing his primary function, which is 'the continuation of life'.

At the same time, Sushruta cautions his readers about simply accumulating knowledge without cultivating a deeper understanding of life: 'A foolish person who has gone through a large number of books without gaining any real insight into the knowledge propounded therein, is like an ass laden with logs of sandalwood, that labours under the weight which it carries without being able to appreciate its virtue.'

One of the conventions of Sanskrit literature is the listing of names, which includes classification of everything from erotic gestures to catalogues of wild flora. The *Sushruta Samhita* contains numerous lists of plants that Ayurvedic healers were instructed to cultivate in pharmaceutical gardens from which they gathered fresh ingredients for their medicines. At the same time, Sushruta recognizes that these plants originate in the wild and are best known to people who are familiar with the forest.

> All medicinal herbs and substances should be used as fresh as possible, excepting Pippali, Vidanga, Madhu, Guda, and Ghritam, (which should be used in a matured condition i.e., not before a year).... Medicinal herbs and plants should be recognized and identified with the help of cowherds, hermits, huntsmen, forest-dwellers, and those who cull the fruits and edible roots of the forest.

To take just one of the names on this list, pippali is a common vine that is used in Ayurveda to treat a variety of ailments from coughs to epilepsy. Both the roots and the fruit are dried and powdered. The Latin name for this species is *Piper longum* and the common English name is long pepper. It can be used as a spice in place of black pepper. The name pippali hasn't changed for at least two millennia and a Google Search will call up an online link where we learn that, 'Rubbing a paste of Pippali powder along with honey on the gums and teeth reduces pain and inflammation in the teeth due to its Kapha balancing nature.'

The consistency with which Ayurvedic pharmacology identifies botanical species is remarkable when we think of how many successive generations of philosophers and physicians have commented on these plants. Yet, exactly the same name used by Sushruta applies to this plant today. *Hobson-Jobson* informs us, once again, that the English word 'pepper' originated from the Sanskrit pippali. Both long pepper and black pepper (*Piper nigrum*) are indigenous to India, though chilli peppers, which belong to the genus *Capsicum*, came to the subcontinent from South America.

Sushrutha's materia medica does not confine itself to plants but also includes the therapeutic value of consuming meat from both wild and domesticated beasts.

> Now I shall describe the properties of the different species of edible meats. The flesh of animals such as those which are aquatic in their habits (Jaleshaya), or frequent marshy lands (Anupa), or dwell in villages (Gramya), or are carnivorous in their habits (Kravyabhuja), or are possessed of unbifurcated hoofs (Ekashapha), or dwell on high ground (Jangala), is generally used as food. Of these each succeeding kind is superior to the one immediately preceding it in the order of enumeration.

Among the lists of venison and other wild meats, are several surprising animals. 'The flesh of the Elephant tends to produce a state of extreme parchedness in the system, and is liquefacient and heat-making in its potency,' Sushrutha opines. 'It vitiates the Pittam and has a palatable acid and saline taste, and destroys the Vayu and Kapham.' He also includes several mythical beasts and monsters in his catalogue of edible meats, which suggests that some of his prescriptions are more theoretical than practical.

During the period that Sushruta was writing there were few restrictions on non-vegetarian foods, most of which hunters provided. Of course, within our current cultural context, wherein a vegetarian diet is considered healthier and eating meat, especially beef, is taboo, these chapters in the *Sushruta Samhita* seem almost heretical. Nevertheless, cooking meat, perhaps spiced with pippali, is appreciated for its aroma as well as its savour, which is linked to the habitat in which the animal lived. Antelope are given the highest therapeutic value because they are found in the jangala; the healing properties of their flesh are linked to the arid lands they inhabit. In particular, Sushruta's catalogue of meats identifies the flesh of blackbuck (ena) and the four-horned antelope (kuranga) as being particularly palatable and nutritious.

Defining a jungle is not as easy as it might seem, though the monsoon forests that once extended across northwestern and central India certainly conform to the Sanskrit term, jangala, and represent key features of the early ecology of this region. Not only are the trees distinctive but also the wildlife. Nilgai, the largest of India's antelopes, proliferate in this kind of habitat, along with chinkara and blackbuck, whose numbers have decreased as the forests and grasslands have disappeared. Instead of tigers, which prefer dense cover, lions would have been the dominant predators here. Cheetahs were also at home in the open-canopied forests and grasslands, preying on swift antelope and gazelle. The disappearance of these two species from this region is a clear consequence of the lost jungles—the true jangala—that disappeared as the land came under the plough.

∽

The Mahabharata contains a disturbing story about the destruction of the Khandava forest, which was located near the banks of the Yamuna. Anthropologist Irawati Karve has explored this episode in her Sahitya Akademi award-winning book *Yuganta: The End of an Epoch*. She tells us that the Khandava forest lay at the edge of the kingdom ruled by the blind king, Dhritarashtra, father of the Kauravas. This large tract of jungle was situated along a small tributary of the Yamuna called Ikshumati, which means 'full of sugar cane'. When the sons of Pandu were given their share of the kingdom, Dhritarashtra kept the capital, Hastinapur (the elephant city), for himself and his sons, assigning the town of Khandavaprastha to the Pandavas. When Yudhishthira and his brothers settled there and began to develop and expand the town, it was renamed Indraprastha.

At some point, during this period of relative peace, Arjuna and Krishna went for an 'outing to the forest near the city'. As Karve tells the story:

> In the party were Krishna, Arjuna, their wives and servants. They ate, they drank, they sang and danced. All the time the shade of the great trees protected them from the sun. Krishna and Arjuna sat a little apart from the others, discussing all possible subjects, telling each other of their conquests in war and love. While they were seated there, a Brahman approached them and said, 'I am hungry. I have a great appetite which has no bounds. Satisfy my hunger.' When they started to offer him food he appeared in his true form as Agni, the god of fire, and said, 'Give me the Khandava forest as food. Let me burn it. Every time I start to burn it Indra sends rain and defeats my purpose.' Krishna and Arjuna consented to help him, provided that Agni supplied them with superb chariots and weapons. To Arjuna he gave a divine chariot, white horses with the speed of wind, and the great bow Gandiva. To Krishna he gave the discus and other weapons. Then Agni started devouring the forest. As it burned, Krishna and Arjuna guarded all sides so tightly that the creatures fleeing from the blaze found not a single chink to escape through... Indra came with a host of gods to save the forest, but was quickly routed by the two heroes. Enraged, Indra wanted to

> fight further, but the gods pointed out that his friend Takshaka, a resident of the forest was safe because he had gone away, and urged Indra to retire. The forest continued to burn for a week... Finally, having consumed the flesh and fat of every last creature in the forest, Agni went away satisfied.

Fire would have been the easiest method of clearing ancient forests and it was used by many indigenous communities, who practised shifting cultivation, slashing and burning the jungle, so as to plant crops in the ashes. More than likely, Prince Shatrughana used fire when he cleared the Madhuvan forests to build his capital in Mathura, setting the trees alight rather than cutting them down. Karve and other scholars have suggested that the burning of the Khandava forest represents a historical conflict between pastoral communities and forest dwellers. Takshaka and the nagas can be interpreted both as symbols of prehistoric serpent cults but also as indigenous inhabitants, who worshipped cobras and made their home in the jangala. As these narratives suggest, our nostalgia and cultural yearning for lost forests is complicated by the need to clear land for cultivation, which raises ethical and moral questions that are as relevant today as they were at the time of the Mahabharata.

3

TERAI ELEGY

As we arrive on the outskirts of Palia Kalan, a long line of tractors, hauling trailers piled high with sugar cane, blocks the road. The farmers are queued up in front of a sugar mill, waiting to unload the freshly cut stalks and have them weighed. Earlier, driving north from Lucknow, via Lakhimpur Kheri, we passed several villages along the highway where cane syrup was being boiled in large, open vats to make gur. The sickly-sweet smell of molasses and woodsmoke filtered into our car, even with the windows closed and the air-conditioner running. At roadside markets, vendors were hawking gur shaped into balls or disc-like cakes, piled up in orange heaps on handcarts. Others were squeezing fresh sugar cane juice and selling glass tumblers full of the frothy green liquid to eager children and adults. Some were simply chewing on the sweet stalks, stripping away the tough skin with their teeth.

Most varieties of sugar cane planted today are hybrids of *Saccharum officinarum*, which is originally from Papua New Guinea. Several sweetgrasses belonging to the same genus are native to South Asia, where sugar was processed from cane as early as the eighth century BCE. References to sugar cane, called ikshu (from which the Hindi word ikh is derived), are found in the Atharva Veda and other early Sanskrit and Pali texts. Greek visitors to India during the time of the Maurya empire, around the third century BCE, refer to 'reeds that make honey without the agency of bees', and Chanakya's *Arthashashtra*, from roughly the same period, lists the methods for manufacturing sugar from cane. Today these tall, perennial grasses are one of the largest cash crops in India.

The Terai region, a belt of lowlands that stretch along the base of the Himalaya, is particularly well suited to growing sugar cane because there is a plentiful supply of water. Until the beginning of the twentieth century, much of the Terai was covered by extensive grasslands and forests, as well as ponds and marshes where numerous rivers from the mountains flooded the plains during the monsoon. Most of the Terai forests were uninhabited because of the prevalence of malaria. A few tribal communities like the Tharu, who had developed immunity to this disease, lived and hunted in the Terai, but it was seen as a dangerous, inhospitable place, 'infested' with mosquitoes, tigers, and elephants. At the same time, the Terai is the birthplace of Gautama Buddha, who is believed to have been born in a sacred grove of sal trees at Lumbini, 200 kilometres east of Palia Kalan and across the border in Nepal. The Buddha's mother, Maya, is often depicted in sculpture as a yakshi, or forest sprite, one arm entwined like a creeper with the branch of a sal tree, while the Buddha himself takes the form of an elephant descending into her womb.

Until the middle of the eighteenth century, the central part of the Terai, along the southern border of Nepal, remained one of the largest surviving tracts of old growth forests in the subcontinent. The destruction of this verdant wilderness began with the felling of sal trees by the British, who used the timber for sleepers to anchor railway tracks that were spreading across the land. A slow-growing hardwood resistant to termites, *Shorea robusta* is the dominant tree of the Terai forests. While this was certainly the beginning of the end, the final blow came in the 1940s and 1950s, with the widespread use of Dichlorodiphenyltrichloroethane, better known as DDT, a toxic pesticide that promised to 'eradicate' mosquitoes.

Suddenly, the threat of malaria in the Terai was seen as manageable and much of this fertile land was handed over by the government to refugee farmers from the Punjab who had been displaced during Partition. They quickly began to clear the Terai of its jungles and cultivate wheat, rice, and other crops, especially sugar cane. Where earlier, wild species like bhabar grass, kunai, munj, and kans had flourished, fields of hybrid *Saccharum* were planted and took over. To irrigate the land, canals were dug that diverted water from rivers like the Sharda, which flows out of the mountains and serves as the border between Western Nepal and Kumaon. By the 1960s, the entire landscape of the Terai had changed dramatically as villages like Palia Kalan were connected by motor roads and bridges. Only a few patches of jungle remained, under the jurisdiction of the Uttar Pradesh Forest Department. The tigers, elephants, and other wildlife were isolated in these reserves, where poaching was rampant.

Eventually, our vehicle squeezes past the traffic jam of tractors delivering sugar cane to the mill and we pass through the centre of Palia Kalan, which has grown from a village into a small town. Signs of prosperity are everywhere—motorcycle showrooms and elaborate wedding points—but also hints of discontentment. Half a dozen emigration consultants have posted signboards promising visa services for people who want to relocate to the United States, Canada, and New Zealand. The grandsons and granddaughters of Punjabi farmers who first cleared and worked the Terai have become restless in this rural backwater and see the promise of a better future abroad.

About a kilometre and a half beyond Palia Kalan, we turn off onto an unmarked dirt track that takes us through sugar cane fields, where men are harvesting the stalks with sharp cleavers. Five minutes later, we arrive at the entrance to a forested estate surrounded by fields. This is the former home of the renowned conservationist, Kanwar Arjan Singh, known to his friends and admirers as Billy, who settled here in 1945, acquiring 750 acres of land adjoining the north bank of the Sharda. He named the property Jasbirnagar, in memory of his father, Kanwar Jasbir Singh, who belonged to the royal family of Kapurthala. Billy soon set about clearing the land, which was covered in grass and scrub jungle. Living in a thatch hut for several years, he built the farmhouse in 1948.

Shaminder Boparai, our host, and the current owner of the property, greets us when we arrive. Accompanying me is Ajay Mark, a close friend I've known since childhood. He introduces me to Shaminder and his son, Armaan, who is in his early twenties. As soon as we sit down in the shade of the deep veranda, Shaminder tells us that a farm labourer cutting sugar cane was killed by a tiger two days ago, less than a kilometre from the house. On his mobile phone, he shows us a video of a pair of forest department elephants flushing the tiger from a partially harvested thicket of cane. It appears to be a large male, accompanied by a smaller female. According to Shaminder, the two tigers must have strayed out of Kishanpur Wildlife Sanctuary, on the other side of the Sharda, then taken cover in the fields. When the victim started cutting cane, the tiger attacked him, killing the man instantly but leaving the body where it lay. This suggests the tiger is not a man-eater but simply became aggressive when the labourer accidentally disturbed him. Shaminder tells us that the forest department has installed camera traps all around his property to monitor the tigers, which are still roaming nearby.

Ajay and I listen intently, disturbed but intrigued by this news. We have come here to observe wildlife in Dudhwa Tiger Reserve, which lies about 10 kilometres north of Palia Kalan, and extends up to the border with Nepal. One of the pioneers of wildlife conservation in India, Billy Arjan Singh was responsible for having Dudhwa notified as a wildlife sanctuary in 1968 and a national park in 1977. By then, he had given away much of his original farm to the tenants that worked on the land and acquired another property adjoining Dudhwa's forests, which he called 'Tiger Haven', named for his brother, Jaswant, an Air Force officer, whose nickname was 'Tiger'.

Though the estate surrounding the farmhouse at Jasbirnagar isn't a wild forest, it covers about 2 hectares (5 acres) and is densely wooded with several enormous trees including an *Alstonia scholaris*, or scholar's tree, that Billy's mother planted in the front yard. By far the largest of this species I've ever seen, it towers close to 30 metres over the house. Several arjuna trees are almost as tall. One of these has a pair of collared scops owls living in a hollow of its trunk. They are perfectly camouflaged against the bark and we wouldn't have noticed them if Shaminder hadn't pointed them out. Dozing in the early afternoon, they occasionally open one eye to check on us. Tufts of feathers on either side of the owls' heads make it look as if they have horns. A flock of red junglefowl also wander about the yard. The roosters are handsome-looking birds, their fiery red feathers accented with black. All of them were hatched from wild eggs, using domestic brood hens, and they behave no differently than their tame descendants, pecking at handfuls of grain that one of the staff scatters on the ground. A peacock named Mohan also wanders about. He too was born in a henhouse. In addition to these creatures, there are horses and dogs on the premises. Being the only jungle in a sea of sugar cane, the estate attracts a variety of wildlife, including leopards, jackals, and wild pigs. On one side of the property, Shaminder has dug a large pond, where kingfishers and other birds congregate. As much as the renovated house, the presence of these animals honours the legacy of Billy Arjan Singh.

∽

A colourful and controversial figure, Billy fought tirelessly to protect what little remained of the Terai forests in North Kheri District. As a young man, he had been an enthusiastic hunter, killing his first leopard at the age of twelve and his first tiger at fourteen. After settling in Jasbirnagar, he continued to hunt, partly for sport but also to protect his fields from wild pigs and other animals that raided the crops. Eventually, though, he gave up shikar and devoted himself to protecting wildlife and their habitats.

Billy's books, *Tiger Haven*, *Tara: A Tigress*, *Prince of Cats*, *Tiger! Tiger!*, *Eelie and the Big Cats*,and *The Legend of the Maneater*, tell the story of his close relationship with tigers and leopards, several of whom he adopted as cubs and attempted to rehabilitate in the Dudhwa forests. His passion and persistence, as well as his personal ties with Prime Minister Indira Gandhi, helped save a corner of India's lost jungles and its wildlife, though he was often thwarted by forest department officials, self-serving politicians, and neighbouring farmers who felt threatened by the predators he reared on his land.

Geoffrey C. Ward, in his book *Tiger-Wallahs: Encounters with the Men Who Tried to Save the Greatest of the Great Cats* (co-authored with Diane Raines Ward), describes meeting Billy in the 1980s at Tiger Haven.

> I asked him once just what it was about tigers that so gripped his imagination. In answering, it seemed to me that Billy was describing not only the qualities he most admired about the tiger but also those he has labored to develop within himself. 'The tiger is a symbol of power,' he said, 'unbridled, elemental. Then of course there's the fact that he's maligned. He's got a finer character than the lion, doesn't quarrel over kills. And he lives alone, unblemished, unmarred. The more you know about him, the more he gets into your imagination.'

In Ward's biographical account of Billy's upbringing, his indifferent education, and unsuccessful career in the army, he comes across as something of a misfit and a loner. His childhood was spent in the princely state of Balrampur, about 200 kilometres east of Dudhwa, where his father was appointed by the British as 'special manager' for the young maharaja who was mentally challenged. Billy's mother, Mabel, was the daughter of an Englishwoman and an Indian police officer. She had a degree in education from the University of Indiana. Born in 1917, Billy was the second of four children. Though sickly as a child, he took up bodybuilding in his twenties and developed a powerful physique. Despite being well connected in the elite circles of Lucknow and Delhi society, Billy was happiest in the Terai forests, sharing the company of the animals he raised and released.

In a passage from one of his books that Ward quotes, Billy describes his first visit to the site where he eventually built Tiger Haven.

> I walked along the edge of the forest for a little way, exploring the area, and soon came upon an open space surrounded by forest on three sides. Standing there, facing south… (not) a single sign of human life disturbed the view. There were no electricity pylons, no road, no habitation of any kind. The only reminder of the outside world was the sound of trains trundling heavily down the tracks with their loads of sugar cane, seven miles away, a sound which reinforced one's sense of isolation…
>
> Behind me was the meeting point of two rivers (one the Soheli), the other a shallow and lazy stream called the Neora which flowed down from the hills of Nepal and meandered through the forest over sandbanks and dead logs. At the point where they met the rivers widened to form a pool, and here all day long brilliantly colored kingfishers flashed up and down between the water and the surrounding trees. On the far side the bank rose steeply to the plateau of the reserved forest; magnificent trees over a hundred feet tall, with long branches interlocking with each other, towered above the river and from there spread in an even roof to the Nepal border

> five miles away. Underneath, in an eerie landscape of bare tree trunks and creepers, was the home of the tiger, the leopard, the sloth bear and many other animals in retreat from man.
>
> It seemed to me then, standing beside the river and listening to the intense buzz of insects in the forest all around me, that I had found the place I was looking for. It was as far as I could go in that direction, right on the edge of the plain, and if civilization was bound to catch up in the end, at least it would take some time.

The experiments that Billy conducted at Tiger Haven, raising and rehabilitating leopards and tigers, would be illegal now. India's Wild Life Protection Act of 1972 forbids private individuals from keeping wild animals in captivity or as pets. But in the 1960s, the rules were not as restrictive and Joy Adamson's bestselling book, *Born Free*, had just been published, telling the story of how she and her husband raised lion cubs in Kenya, nurturing their natural instincts so that they could ultimately be returned to the wild.

After moving to Tiger Haven in the late 1950s, Billy owned two elephants and provided shelter for a menagerie of junglefowl, peacocks, monkeys, wolves, a fishing cat, and several chital, all of whom lived together in his care. In addition to these, he raised a succession of dogs, including Eelie, a tan female of uncertain pedigree, who served as a stepmother for the large predators that Billy adopted.

The first of these was named Prince, a male leopard, given to him as a cub by friends. Though reluctant at first, Billy took up the challenge of rearing a leopard. Within a year and a half, Prince was nearly full-grown and he had begun to hunt on his own, killing peacocks, monkeys, and porcupines in the forest nearby. He still made his home at Tiger Haven, wrestling and playing with Eelie. Though now a third of his size, the dog had asserted her dominance when the leopard was still a cub. Prince was also comfortable in the company of human beings and would nuzzle Billy affectionately, as well as some of his guests. However, the first of several tragedies occurred when Prince unexpectedly attacked the eight-year-old son of one of the elephant handlers, biting the child's head and fracturing his skull. The boy was rushed to a hospital but died a few weeks later. After this incident, Prince was caged for a while but eventually set free once again. He soon began to roam further and further afield. In May 1973, he stopped returning to Tiger Haven for visits and Billy never saw him again.

After this, two more leopard cubs arrived, presented to Billy by Indira Gandhi, who had received them as a gift. Both cubs were females and given the names Harriet and Juliette. They were also successfully raised by Billy under the watchful eye of Eelie, who was unafraid of these creatures, though leopards often kill dogs. By this time, however, villagers in the surrounding area had grown increasingly nervous about the presence of the large cats, afraid that they would prey on them and their cattle. Billy also had heated confrontations with farmers who let their livestock graze in the Dudhwa forest, of which he was now honorary wildlife warden. Out of either fear or retaliation, Juliette was poisoned. As Ward writes: 'Billy was devastated: Juliette had been the gentlest and most affectionate of his leopards. "The memory of her soft little grunts of welcome, now still forever, made me feel unashamedly as though I had lost a child," he wrote later.'

Harriet survived and, after reaching adulthood, she became pregnant. Billy was convinced that the father was Prince, whom he believed was still in the vicinity. Neither of Harriet's two cubs lived beyond three months; the first was killed by a wild tigress and the second drowned in the river. Then, in 1975, without warning, Harriet entered one of the employee's quarters at Tiger Haven and killed a twelve-year-old boy. Rumours began to spread that Billy was raising man-eaters on his farm. Ultimately, Harriet was also poisoned by villagers who had no sympathy for his radical methods of conservation.

But before Harriet was killed, Billy had already embarked on an even more ambitious project. With the prime minister's blessings, he imported a three-month-old tigress from the Twycross Zoo in England and brought her to Tiger Haven. Naming her Tara, Billy began raising the cub, with the goal of setting her free in the jungles of Dudhwa. He wanted to prove that a tigress bred in captivity could be introduced into the wild, as a means of increasing India's tiger population. It was a bold, some would say reckless, idea.

Tara became as devoted to Billy as he was to her. She was also welcomed by Eelie, who asserted her dominance once again. Harriet too accepted the cub as part of the family and the three of them wrestled and played with endearing exuberance. In 1977, a British film crew came to Tiger Haven and made a documentary about this unusual relationship. Footage of Tara, Billy, Harriet, and Eelie walking through the soft light of the sal forests creates a romantic, mystical aura that seems to blur the lines between species.

By the time she was two years old, Tara weighed almost 150 kilograms and her affectionate games often knocked Billy to the ground. She had also started hunting and successfully killed a variety of birds and small mammals. Soon enough, her presence along the margins of the jungle attracted the interest of wild males, who sought her as their mate. Tara began to spend more and more time away from Tiger Haven and, eventually, like Prince, she too vanished into the forest. Billy had succeeded in his quest to reintroduce a zoo-bred animal into the wild.

However, not everyone saw it that way. Officials of the Uttar Pradesh Forest Department were suspicious and jealous of Billy's efforts. He had alienated many of them by opposing the illegal felling of trees and grazing of livestock in Dudhwa, accusing the forest staff of corruption. Despite being notified as a national park, poaching continued at Dudhwa. Tiger skins and bones were easily smuggled across the border into Nepal and on to China. Meanwhile, Indira Gandhi had lost the general election in 1977 and she was out of power, which meant that Billy no longer enjoyed her patronage and protection. Some wildlife scientists had also begun to question his methods and approach, raising the issue of Tara's DNA. Bred in a zoo in England, she had traces of Siberian tiger in her lineage and Billy was accused of polluting the purity of India's tigers.

Regardless of the consequences of rehabilitating tigers and leopards in the wild, and the controversies that surrounded Billy's efforts at Tiger Haven, his most important contribution to conservation was the creation of Dudhwa National Park along with his ability and willingness to be an outspoken advocate for wildlife throughout India. At a time when conservation was neither appreciated nor understood, particularly in political circles, Billy raised awareness of the crisis in India's forests and used his influence to help save tigers and other wild species. In an interview towards the end of his life, he expressed a conviction that, 'The air we breathe and the water we drink stem from the biodiversity of the universal environment and its economics. The tiger is at the centre of this truth. If it goes, we go.'

His personal, hands-on intervention may not be consistent with wildlife rehabilitation practices today, which try to minimize human contact with animals that are going to be reintroduced in the wild. By giving Prince, Harriet, Juliette, and Tara their names, Billy was indulging in the kind of anthropomorphism that has fallen into disfavour. Today, wildlife scientists tend to identify individual animals by letters and numbers to avoid treating them like pets. He could even be accused of having valued the lives of his adopted predators over their human victims. One of the signs at Tiger Haven read: THE ANIMALS HAVE FIRST PRECEDENCE HERE.

Nevertheless, what makes Billy Arjan Singh's story so compelling and complicated is that he had a personal relationship with each of the animals he cared for, which crossed the boundaries between species. He felt a deep kinship with each of them, which motivated him to protect not just the tigers and leopards alone but also their wild habitat and all of the other creatures it contained, both seen and unseen. In fact, Billy's first efforts to save wildlife, were directed at protecting swamp deer, which are one of the prey species on which tigers depend. Ultimately, Billy Arjan Singh embodied, on a personal and intimate level, the larger debate about whether tigers should be given priority over people. He represented the kind of commitment and empathy that goes beyond either scientific or sentimental approaches to wildlife—a genuine love for species other than his own.

~

Having read Billy's books and after hearing about Dudhwa for years, I am excited to finally visit these forests for the first time. Both Ajay and I have observed wildlife together in other parts of the Terai, particularly at Rajaji and Corbett Tiger reserves. At half past two in the afternoon, we climb into an open jeep with our guide, Sudhir Kumar. A large contingent of police are present at the main gate, awaiting the arrival of a VIP, who enters the park ahead of us in a convoy of three vehicles. We are told that the daughter of Uttar Pradesh's governor is here to visit the tiger reserve. Aside from her, there is only one other jeep safari, in addition to ours.

An extended colonnade of sal trees frames both sides of the narrow forest road, which stretches ahead of us in a straight line, as far as we can see. The high canopy of foliage blocks most of the sunlight and green shadows enclose us. Half a kilometre on, Sudhir instructs the driver to turn off onto a sidetrack that is rougher and twists its way through a mixed forest, mostly teak and terminalia. Five minutes later, we come to an abrupt halt.

Immediately to our right, about 40 metres away, stands a greater one-horned rhinoceros. A full-grown male, with a prominent single horn, he is as large as our jeep. Both Ajay and I are startled by this sudden apparition, which neither of us was expecting. Rhinos were once plentiful throughout the Terai, but by the nineteenth century they had completely disappeared except for a small population in the lowlands of Nepal and a few survivors in Assam.

As we quickly focus our cameras, the rhino seems less surprised by our presence than we are by his. He is feeding on the leaves of a creeper, chewing contentedly, and eyeing us with a disinterested expression. In many ways, rhinos seem more geological than biological, as if they are massive boulders that have come to life. His thick hide folds over in large patches on his shoulders and haunches so that when he moves these shift like tectonic plates. The rhino's eyes and ears appear small in relation to the rest of his bulk, but his snout and mouth are enormous. Slowly, he turns and moves towards us, until he is about 15 metres away. His nostrils flare and his ears twitch as he studies us carefully.

It is only now that I notice the electric fence between us. The three thin strands of wire seem hardly capable of keeping this huge beast in his place. Adult one-horned rhinos can weigh more than 1.5 tonnes. Fortunately, this one doesn't seem aggressive and lowers his head to crop at the shrubs around his knees. Sudhir explains that he is one of about forty rhinos that are the result of a translocation project that began in 1984, when two males and three females were brought here from Assam. Another three females were released a few years later and, by 2015, their numbers had increased to more than thirty.

The World Wide Fund for Nature (WWF) and the Wildlife Trust of India (WTI) collaborated with the UP and Assam forest departments, as well as the forest service in Nepal, to bring the rhinos to Dudhwa. Electric fences restrict the animals to a section of the South Sonaripur Range of the park, which has extensive grasslands as well as marshes and ponds, the ideal habitat for rhinos. The project has been so successful that some of the rhinos were recently relocated to another area of the park, allowing them to continue multiplying without depleting the grasslands. Though they are still vulnerable to poaching, because of the illegal trade in their horns, the number of rhinos in India and Nepal has risen dramatically from roughly 200 in the 1970s to more than 3,500 today.

When I ask Sudhir if the rhinos ever escape, he nods but says that the electric fence is effective. The only problem is that wild elephants sometimes knock down trees that fall on the fence and break it. But generally, the rhinos don't seem to have any inclination to leave their new home.

After watching the rhino for twenty minutes or so, we drive on along the rough track. Though we come upon a few chital, the forest is quiet and feels deserted. As it is still early in the afternoon, I imagine that the animals are just beginning to shake off their midday torpor. Beneath the sal trees, the ground is carpeted with ferns, as well as a broad-leafed plant that Sudhir tells us is 'jungli haldi', wild turmeric. Though he says it isn't used for cooking, people apply its roots and leaves to injuries as a healing poultice.

Eventually, we emerge from the sal forest into a stretch of grasslands, the munj and imperata plumes rising to almost 3 metres above the ground, their thin stalks as dense as a field of sugar cane. A wild sow followed by a litter of piglets cross the road and immediately disappear into the grass on the other side. Soon afterwards, a couple of black francolins emerge and scuttle ahead of us for about 30 metres, along one of the two parallel wheel ruts in the track. The male is resplendent in his regalia, with a black head and white patches on his ears, a chestnut collar and black breast, speckled with pearl-like white spots. The grass attracts a number of smaller birds, warblers and prinias, that fidget restlessly, searching for insects. A flock of rose-ringed parakeets sail in overhead and land together abruptly with noisy shrieks, the slender stems of munj grass bending under their weight. Further on, a pair of grey-headed woodpeckers fly up in front of us and land on the trunk of a silk cotton tree. Their dull green wings blend in with the bark but the bright crimson cap on the male catches the late afternoon sun like a red flag.

We pass several small ponds, where Eurasian coots and white-breasted waterhens swim and wade through the algae that covers most of the surface. Eventually, we come to a watchtower overlooking a larger pond, most of which has been choked with grass. Other than egrets and pond herons, we see nothing here, though Ajay tells me that when he visited Dudhwa four years ago, they watched a herd of swamp deer browsing along the opposite shore and a fishing cat made an appearance just in front of the tower.

Suddenly, while we are standing there, a train goes by on the far side of the grasslands, rattling past us about half a kilometre away. This line connects Lakhimpur Kheri and Palia Kalan to Pilibhit Junction and runs through the park, with a branch line that goes up to the Nepal border. It used to be a narrow-gauge track, once used to haul timber. The trains on this line pose a risk to wildlife. A leopard cub from a second litter that Harriet gave birth to at Tiger Haven was killed by a train. Over the years, a number of different animals, especially deer, have died on these tracks. Three elephants were killed in 2003 when an engine knocked them off an embankment. And, in 2006, a young tigress was fatally struck by a train passing through the park. Restrictions on speed have been introduced but these are seldom observed or enforced.

As the sun dips below the tops of the sal trees and shadows darken, we head back towards the gate. Though seeing the rhino at the beginning of our drive was encouraging, both Ajay and I are disappointed at the lack of wildlife. Of course, spotting a tiger is always a matter of chance, but in most national parks there are plenty of other mammals, while Dudhwa feels empty. The forest itself is beautiful and there were plenty of birds in the grasslands but other than a handful of chital and wild pigs, we have seen little else.

Arriving back at Jasbirnagar in the dark, our vehicle triggers the flash on a camera trap installed to keep track of the tiger that killed the labourer cutting sugar cane. Later in the evening, before dinner, Shaminder shows us around the house, which he has restored and filled with photographs and memorabilia. The walls of the drawing room and dining room are covered in framed pictures of Billy's leopards and tigers, as well as copies of newspaper clippings and letters. Shaminder tells us that when he was a boy his family owned a farm nearby. He first met Billy at an early age and has idolized him ever since. Though Billy spent most of his time at Tiger Haven, he stayed at Jasbirnagar during the monsoon, when the Soheli and Neora rivers flooded. Later, Shaminder and his wife,

Rupeela, often visited Billy here towards the end of his life. He shows us a chair on the veranda, where Billy always sat and reminisced about Tara and the other animals he raised.

In 2011, a year after Billy died, Shaminder published an illustrated biography, *Billy Arjan Singh: Tiger of Dudhwa*, which contains many of the images that hang on the walls of the farmhouse. One of the most striking and poignant pictures is of Billy embracing Tara, who hugs him with one of her paws. Shaminder points out a series of photographs and newspaper clippings related to the final controversy surrounding Tara. After leaving Tiger Haven, she was seen in the company of two different males and, according to Billy's account, ultimately gave birth to four litters of cubs. In 1979, several human beings were killed by a tigress along the periphery of Dudhwa, near Tiger Haven. Forest department officials, who were opposed to Billy's efforts, promoted a theory that Tara had become a man-eater. Towards the end of 1980, this man-eater was shot by park director, R. L. Singh. Her skin was displayed in public and it was announced that Tara had been killed.

As Shaminder writes in his book, 'This was also the period when IUCN's Cat Specialist Group was highly critical of Billy's project for introducing a zoo tigress of mixed origins into the Indian gene pool, as this "would contaminate the Indian sub-species", a sentiment echoed by others as well. R. L. Singh went on to ridicule Billy by calling Tara a "cocktail tigress", and even suggested that her cubs be eliminated to contain the damage the Siberian genes might have on the Indian stock.'

Billy was naturally sceptical of the claim that Tara had become a man-eater and he felt that another tigress was responsible for the killings. As Shaminder recounts the story, he points out several pictures of Tara, who had a recognizable Y-shaped mark on her left cheek. He then shows us a photograph of the dead man-eater, which has slightly different facial markings. In his opinion, this vindicates Billy's belief that Tara lived on, helping to repopulate the park with tigers. He was convinced that she ultimately died a natural death sometime around 1992.

∽

The next morning, before daybreak, our guide, Sudhir, picks us up from the farmhouse and we drive to Kishanpur Wildlife Sanctuary, which is part of the larger Dudhwa Tiger Reserve but on the south bank of the Sharda. After a forty-five-minute drive, we reach the gate, after the sky has brightened. Swathes of mist lie over the sugar cane fields and other crops that encircle the reserve. One farmer is up early, ploughing his fields. A flock of egrets follow in the tractor's wake, plucking worms from the freshly dug furrows.

Kishanpur Sanctuary covers 227 square kilometres, while Dudhwa is more than twice its size at 490 square kilometres. Katarniaghat (400 square kilometres) is the third protected zone within this tiger reserve. Though the three areas are not contiguous, they lie close enough to allow some of the wildlife to move back and forth but a lack of protected corridors means that certain species remain isolated while elephants and tigers often come into conflict with farmers. Fragmentation of these jungles is a significant problem. As human habitation and agriculture continue to expand, along with highways, canals, and railway tracks, the animals are squeezed into increasingly compressed spaces with little or no opportunity to migrate.

The Kishanpur forest is similar to Dudhwa but not as dense, with plenty of sal and teak, as well as jamun and semal. As we enter the sanctuary, Sudhir focuses his attention on the sides of the unpaved road, looking for pugmarks. The soil is still damp with dew and within 500 metres we come upon a tiger's tracks. No other vehicles have passed along our route this morning and the pugmarks are fresh, like a block-printed border running along one side of the road. The tiger—Sudhir tells us it is a male—walked here less than an hour ago and as we drive on, all of us scan the margins of the forest ahead. After another 500 metres, the pugmarks turn off the dirt road and disappear into the grass. Here in Kishanpur, there seem to be many more chital than we saw in Dudhwa and we pass several herds, one of which is lying down in the undergrowth, only their heads and antlers visible. We listen for alarm calls, hoping the tiger is still nearby, but the forest remains quiet, except for the occasional crowing of red junglefowl and the shriek of a woodpecker.

After an hour of driving through the forest we come to a large lake with a watchtower. Morning sunlight is striking the golden feathers of tall grasses along the opposite shoreline and Sudhir points out a small herd of swamp deer browsing in the marshy shallows. They are about 300 metres away, and through my binoculars I can see that most of them are stags. Because of the twelve tines on their antlers, they are known as barasingha. A lighter brown than sambar and slightly smaller, swamp deer do not have the chital's spotted coat, though fawns are born with spots. One of the stags has a hayrick of water weeds stuck on his antlers. As their name implies, they prefer to live near wetlands, feeding on sweetgrasses and aquatic plants.

In a foreword to Shaminder's book, the famous field zoologist, George Schaller, describes visiting Billy Arjan Singh in 1965. At the time, Schaller was doing research for his book, *The Deer and the Tiger*, one of the first scientific studies of the relationship between predators and prey in India. He recalls setting out in these grasslands on elephant back.

> With a wave from Billy Arjan Singh, we moved slowly forward through the high grass, each elephant urged on by foot movements of the mahout perched on its neck. The elephants, the vast marsh, the dark line of forest on the horizon, seemed just the same as they were centuries past. I scanned ahead for the swamp deer, for which this place was famous. Suddenly, water churned and the grass shook as a large herd of swamp deer bolted. According to my journal, 'There were about 500, a brown wave bunched tightly, then strung out and splitting, only to join again.' I was exhilarated by this sight, the largest remaining such herd in existence.

Swamp deer numbers have diminished steadily because of the loss of wetlands, which have been drained and cleared for cultivation. From the watchtower, I can count only eight animals, a small group, nowhere near the size of the enormous herd that Schaller observed sixty-seven years ago. Three subspecies of swamp deer have been identified in India. Those found in the Terai belt, *Rucervus duvaucelii duvaucelii,* are the most plentiful. The IUCN Red List estimates only 1,800 to 2,400 surviving in India today and 1,650 to 1,800 in Nepal. Another subspecies *R. d. branderi* are only found in Kanha National Park in Madhya Pradesh and they number an estimated 500. Assam is home to the third subspecies, *R. d. ranjitsinhi*, which also has a population of roughly 500. All of these numbers, however, are from surveys done more than a decade ago, and in some places barasingha were last counted in the 1990s, so it is likely the populations have further decreased.

At this time of year, the lake attracts migratory ducks and several flocks congregate at different places on the water, feeding off aquatic plants. Many of them are northern pintails, which are easy to recognize when they put their heads underwater, revealing their pointed tail feathers, which protrude above the surface. We can also see a number of red-crested pochards and gadwalls amongst the nearest flock. Feeding together, they make contented, chuckling sounds like a chorus of frogs.

Heading on from here, we circle through the grasslands on the far side of the lake, near where the barasingha are feeding. Bay-backed shrikes perch on the tall stems of grass lining both sides of the road. The Sharda River lies just beyond a stand of trees to the north but we cannot see it. As we complete a circuit of the wetlands, we come upon three men walking towards us. They ask if we have seen any buffaloes. Three of their animals strayed in this direction and didn't return home last night. The village of Kishanpur lies within the boundaries of the reserve and their cattle are permitted to graze in sections of the forest. Several centuries ago, wild buffalo would have inhabited these wetlands, thriving on the same marshy habitat as the swamp deer. Today, their domesticated descendants do the same and sometimes fall prey to tigers.

Re-entering the forest, we pass between shafts of sunlight filtering through the open canopy of leaves overhead. This creates a magical aura, casting dappled patterns of light and shadow on the understorey. At one place, a stand of imperata grass, with delicately tapered plumes, catches the morning rays, as if it is on fire. We come upon another set of pugmarks, this time a leopard's, but all we find after following them is a sounder of wild pigs. One of the females, who has five young in tow, turns to face us and confronts the jeep with a belligerent stance, her bristles on end. The sow refuses to make way for us until her brood has safely crossed and entered the jungle on the other side.

Once again, though Kishanpur is a relatively well-preserved forest and we see more deer than we did at Dudhwa, it feels as if the wildlife has been depleted here and there is a confined sense of being hemmed in by fields and human settlements. These scant patches of wild habitat are the last remnants of the Terai jungles that once stretched for more than 1,000 kilometres, skirting the Himalaya from Punjab to Bengal. While the ecological memory of lost forests persists in pockets of wilderness like this, it also reminds us of those vast tracts of grassland and wild habitat that have disappeared forever.

Later in the afternoon, we drive to Dudhwa again for a second tour of the park. On the way, I ask Sudhir if we can stop and visit Tiger Haven, which lies a few kilometres off the motor road. He confirms what I've already been told; the forest department controls the dirt road that leads to Billy's old property and tourists are not allowed to visit the site. Tiger Haven is still owned by his heirs, but without prior invitation, entry is not permitted.

During our second drive through Dudhwa, we follow a different route, parallel to the Sarju River, a winding, muddy stream that runs through the southern edge of the park. On its banks, we can see a high-water mark, where the Sarju floods during the monsoon, spilling into marshlands on either side. Dead trees have toppled into the stream, diverting the sluggish current, which joins the Sharda a few kilometres south-east of Dudhwa. In turn, the Sharda flows into the Ghaghara, another large river from Nepal, which is a tributary of the Ganga. In this way, the rivers of the Terai form a network of arteries that once watered the wetlands and jungles that have all but vanished. Descending out of the Himalaya, these rivers bear silt from the mountains, both fertilizing and irrigating the plains of northern India before flowing on into the Bay of Bengal.

On our final circuit of the park, we spot a barking deer in the shadows, its white tail flashing as it darts for cover. From a high perch in a sal tree, a changeable hawk eagle surveys the forest floor for any sign of movement. A full-grown adult, it is dark brown, almost black, with a loose crest of feathers that dangle like a tassel from the back of its head. Further on, a grey-headed fish eagle keeps watch over a grass-rimmed pond. These raptors have sharper eyes than we do and can see creatures that are invisible to us. Just as it is beginning to get dark and we are about to leave Dudhwa, we hear the alarm call of a chital, a sharp falsetto cry that warns others of a predator's presence but by now it is too late for us to stop as darkness is closing in.

When we return to the farmhouse at Jasbirnagar, Shaminder meets us on the veranda and asks what we saw in the park. Then, with a smile, he says, 'You should have stayed back here. We had a visitor this afternoon.'

Around 4 p.m., the tiger appeared at the edge of the property on the other side of the bridge across the pond. Shaminder shows us pictures and videos of a large male, standing casually at the edge of the woods, next to a wooden bridge. Though the gardeners and other staff were terrified and ran for cover, the tiger did not cause any harm and soon retreated into the sugar cane fields. Imagining him prowling the margins of Billy's estate, I can't help but wonder if he might be one of Tara's descendants.

Our experience in Dudhwa, though disappointing, makes me think of some of the more innovative approaches to tiger conservation that have been articulated in recent years. Ullas Karanth, one of India's foremost tiger specialists, has proposed what he calls a Tiger Habitat Expansion Model, which essentially promotes the idea of converting agricultural lands into wildlife habitat, not through government intervention, but based on an entrepreneurial approach. Pointing out the proven economic potential of tiger tourism, he is essentially suggesting that farmers with land adjoining or near reserved forests could cooperate and convert their fields into jungle that would support the presence of tigers. This, in turn, would attract high-end tourism from which the farmers could benefit.

Karanth acknowledges the obvious obstacles, when he writes, 'Even if the economics works, the social management necessary to assemble a cooperative of dozens of feisty farmers will be a formidable challenge.' Nevertheless, he points to many examples of land use changes based on commercial calculations, such as rice paddies that have been converted into areca nut or coffee plantations to provide more income for landowners. The involvement of India's corporate sector in many agro-businesses like rubber, tobacco, bamboo, etc., shows that these kinds of changes and initiatives are possible.

The Dudhwa region would seem to be an excellent location for attempting this experiment, especially since many descendants of the original Terai farmers are now choosing to emigrate. If significant areas of sugar cane cultivation could be returned to the wild, reviving natural grasslands and jungles, both tigers and farmers would benefit. The promise of income from tiger tourism could help knit together wildlife corridors between Dudhwa and Kishanpur. As Karanth explains in his recent book, *Among Tigers*:

> I would argue that tiger tourism should be reinvented so that its economic power can be harnessed to expand tiger habitats and augment tiger populations outside government-owned reserves. If such a radical shift does not happen, tiger tourism will largely continue to be a mere nuisance confined to tiger reserves, rather than a game changer for national tiger recovery, which it can be.

For the tigers of Dudhwa this would mean having more freedom to roam and greater connectivity between fragmented and degraded areas of the reserve. Instead of wandering through sugar cane fields, where they come into conflict with human beings, the predators would have access to privately managed and rewilded conservancies, where prey species would also find forage and shelter. Private jungle lodges could promote Karanth's Tiger Habitat Expansion Model because it would mean that tourists could see wild tigers both inside and outside government reserves.

4

RETURN OF THE CHEETAH

Translocation of wildlife is a conservation strategy that has worked well for critically endangered species like the one-horned rhino. It has also been effective in augmenting the prey base in certain wildlife sanctuaries and national parks to support an existing population of large predators like tigers. Even elephants have been relocated from one region to another, in order to reduce human–animal conflict. But the translocation of African cheetahs to Kuno Palpur National Park in Madhya Pradesh has presented a more complex and controversial challenge.

Cheetahs became extinct in India roughly three-quarters of a century ago. The coup de grâce was delivered by Maharaja Ramanuj Pratap Singh Deo of the princely state of Korea who shot three cheetahs in December 1947, just five months after Independence. In his recent book, *The Story of India's Cheetahs*, Divyabhanusinh, former president of WWF-India, explains that there were several unconfirmed sightings after this, and a few surviving stragglers may have remained alive until the 1970s.

Over the years, a number of prominent wildlife experts have argued in favour of relocating cheetahs from outside India, to restore their presence here. As far back as 1955, the Indian Board of Wildlife officially endorsed this 'bold experiment'. Initial efforts were made to acquire cheetahs from Iran, which still has a small population of the same sub-species of Asiatic cheetahs (*Acinonyx jubatus venaticus*) that were once found in India. However, the Iranians were understandably reluctant to share their cheetahs, since these are critically endangered, with less than fifty surviving now. At one point Iran offered to exchange a few cheetahs for an equal number of Asiatic lions but India didn't want to part with an animal that was also facing extinction. By the 1970s, nothing had been resolved and between the political upheaval following Indira Gandhi's declaration of the Emergency in 1975 and the Iranian revolution in 1979, the cheetahs were largely forgotten.

Nevertheless, influential wildlife experts like M. K. Ranjitsinh continued to press for the introduction of cheetahs from Africa, where a different subspecies is still found in substantial numbers. Despite several false starts, bureaucratic delays, and legal challenges, this contentious project finally received a stamp of approval from the Supreme Court of India in 2020. Exhaustive planning and preparations for the relocation of cheetahs involved the Ministry of Environment and other central government agencies working with the state government of Madhya Pradesh, particularly its forest department, as well as scientists from the Wildlife Institute of India (WII) and foreign experts from Namibia and South Africa. Ultimately, all of this came to fruition on 17 September 2022, when Prime Minister Narendra Modi released two African cheetahs into a temporary enclosure at Kuno Palpur. These animals were part of a group of eight that had been airlifted from Namibia. Five of them were females and three were males.

Suddenly, what had been, until then, a long-running and somewhat arcane debate amongst conservationists of various persuasions, became headline news. These imported cheetahs were immediately transformed into a symbol of national pride during the seventy-fifth anniversary celebrations of India's independence. A second batch of twelve cheetahs, five females and seven males, arrived at Kuno Palpur on 18 February 2023, bringing the total number of imported animals to twenty.

Television channels and newspapers covered the events with breathless excitement, while social media dispersed patriotic homage to the cheetah's return. Headlines in the *Indian Express* focused on the prime minister's remarks following their initial release.

'Cheetahs are back; economy and ecology not in conflict: PM'
'Chance to restore link broken decades ago, we must not let our efforts fail.'

After so many years of discussion and debate, in which politics has always played a significant role, the arrival of the cheetahs was hailed as an ecological victory, perhaps as significant as winning a cricket world cup. Divyabhanusinh has been a vocal advocate for introducing African cheetahs into India. He praises this international conservation effort as a collaboration between 'three developing countries across two continents' and compares it to Project Tiger, which has saved India's national animal from extinction.

> The flourishing of these mega fauna preservation efforts and the protection of the respective landscapes is a result of our country's long-term commitment to conservation. These are laudable because they are taking place in the face of obstacles, such as the unrelenting increase in human, livestock and domestic dog populations and human-animal conflict,

> including predation by carnivores. In 1972, Indira Gandhi, the then prime minister, took a lead in tiger conservation. Half a century later, Prime Minister Narendra Modi has taken the lead in the cheetah introduction programme. The same level of commitment on the part of the authorities, together with the use of scientific advances in the field, should make this too an Indian success story.

Of course, it is much too early to gauge or judge the outcome of this project, which will require many years of hard work and sustained commitment on the part of government, conservation agencies, and individuals to ensure the cheetahs' survival in Kuno Palpur and fulfil the expectations that have been placed upon them. If anything, the publicity and national prestige associated with the translocation of cheetahs has only made the task harder.

In some ways, this experiment is reminiscent of Billy Arjan Singh's attempts to reintroduce leopards and tigers into the wild during the early 1970s, though the cheetah project is happening on a much larger scale. Billy did not have the vast resources, scientific expertise, and government machinery at his disposal, but he did have the support and blessings of Indira Gandhi. Some of the same criticisms about genetic purity that were levelled against him have been raised by conservationists who feel that the African subspecies is alien to India and should not be introduced. Other criticisms include the argument that money allocated for the cheetahs would have been better spent on indigenous species that are endangered, such as the great bustard or the caracal. Some have also questioned the choice of Kuno Palpur as the site for releasing the cheetahs, suggesting that the terrain may be unsuitable and the prey base inadequate. With the high-profile politicization of this project, the pros and cons of relocating these charismatic creatures has become a polarizing issue within the conservation community.

∽

Kuno Palpur lies about 150 kilometres south-west of Gwalior, a comfortable three-and-a-half-hour drive. At the end of April, the landscape along this route is dry and covered in degraded scrub jungle, with patches of fields wherever the low, rocky hills open out into stretches of level ground. Most of the rock is sandstone, which fractures into thick slabs that are used for building walls. After turning off the main highway between Gwalior and Indore, my taxi driver, Ravi, and I pass through forested hills and small villages, where flocks of goats as well as herds of cows and buffaloes block traffic on the two-lane road.

Reaching the small town of Pohri, we pass a forest department complex, with several signs depicting images of cheetahs. This is the headquarters of the Sub-divisional Forest Officer, Kuno South. One of the signs welcomes us to the park, though the main entrance is still some distance from here. A startled-looking cheetah, painted bright yellow and covered with black polka dots, stares out at me from another sign. Most of Kuno Palpur is currently closed to visitors so that the new arrivals won't be disturbed. Initially, the cheetahs were kept in quarantined enclosures, called 'bomas', after which they were released into larger fenced-in areas of 500 hectares (1,235 acres), where chital have been introduced as prey. Until the cheetahs are safely and comfortably settled in their new habitat, most of Kuno Palpur is off-limits to tourists, though I have arranged to visit one section of the national park that remains open.

As we pass through a buffer zone of the park, I get my first look at the forests of this region. The predominant tree here is *Anogeissus pendula*, locally known as kardhai, but also called dhok. A resilient species, kardhai flourishes on dry, rocky soil, where most other trees are unable to survive. This time of year, at the beginning of summer, its limbs are usually bare, with only a few withered leaves. Over the past three days, however, unseasonal rain has fallen and new leaf buds are appearing on the branches, like a pale green mist of foliage. Kardhai have small, simple leaves, tapered at both ends, no more than 2 centimetres long.

Kuno Jungle Resort, where I have booked a room, lies 15 kilometres beyond Pohri. Though it is late in the afternoon, a time of day when animals begin moving about, I see no deer or other wildlife, except for a jackal that has been run over on the road. While there isn't a lot of traffic, this route is used by trucks, both during the day and at night, which will eventually pose a risk for the cheetahs. We also pass the remains of two dead cows at the side of the road, which may have been hit by vehicles, though it's hard to tell. Thirty years ago, vultures would have picked these carcasses clean but now they slowly rot away, eaten by smaller scavengers and dogs, who aren't as efficient at disposing of carrion.

The resort is situated on a high bank overlooking the Kuno River. An old, two-room dak bungalow originally stood on this scenic site. Developed by the Madhya Pradesh Tourism corporation over a decade ago, the new resort is now leased out to a private company that has added an infinity pool facing the river. While the resort has five-star aspirations, a flash flood two years ago caused considerable damage and the facility suffered neglect during the Covid-19 pandemic. Regardless of these shortcomings, the accommodation is comfortable, and the staff are eager to please. Now that Kuno Palpur has become famous for its cheetahs there is likely to be a rush of tourists, once more sections of the park reopen for visitors.

After checking in, I set out for a walk along the riverbank to stretch my legs and get a sense of the landscape. At this point, the river is about 75 metres across because of a barrage just below the resort. Further upstream, the Kuno narrows to less than 5 metres, though it obviously fills up during the monsoon. A broad shelf of red sandstone extends along the near shore, like a natural promenade. The rocks are similar to those I saw earlier on my drive, fissured into layered slabs, formed out of sedimentary deposits that compacted and hardened millions of years ago. At several places, these multi-tiered strata have broken into what looks like a series of shallow terraces or stairs, revealing different periods of geological history. Each surface is embossed with the impressions of ancient floods that left wave-like marks when they receded. These fluid contours on the sandstone reflect the rippled surface of the river.

A few birds are about, mostly red-vented bulbuls and bank mynahs. A red-wattled lapwing is calling somewhere downstream and at the water's edge are a great thick-knee and a common sandpiper. Two houses stand on the opposite shore but beyond these, there is nothing but forest, for as far as I can see. Most of the land is rolling hills extending in all directions. While I can hear the occasional roar of a truck passing over a bridge nearby, it is a peaceful place that must have been full of wildlife at one time, before the dak bungalow was built and much earlier still, when these slabs of rock were being formed aeons ago. Most of the creatures from that era are now extinct.

Though I have no expectation of finding anything, I cast about to see if there might be fossilized footprints in the sedimentary rocks. Some of the sandstone slabs are pitted by erosion and contain impressions that look like the pugmarks of a large cat or a dog. Giving my imagination full rein, I wonder if it might be an ancient cheetah that walked here a million years ago. Most felids, like tigers or leopards, have retractable claws and they leave only the impression of their pads. A cheetah's claws are semi-retractable and remain extended when it runs, to give it more traction. As a result, its pugmarks look more like those of a dog or a wolf. Of course, when I examine these prints carefully, I can see that they have been caused by water, which has carved out round depressions in the rocks. But perhaps my speculation isn't so far-fetched. Dr Laurie Marker, director of the Cheetah Conservation Fund, has co-authored a paper titled 'A Brief History of Cheetah Conservation'. In it, she writes:

> The cheetah is a survivor; its challenging evolutionary history has shaped a unique physiology, optimized for speed. The first fossil records of cheetah (*Acinonyx*) date from approximately 4 million years ago and evidence of related species was retrieved in America, Europe, Asia, and Africa. Following a founder effect approximately 100,000 years ago, the cheetah

> escaped extinction in the Pleistocene, which left the species with both reduced numbers and diminished genetic diversity.

Dr Marker is an American zoologist who lives in Namibia. For the past twelve years, she has served as one of the advisers for the cheetah relocation project, working with colleagues in Namibia, South Africa, and India, including Dr Y. V. Jhala at WII, who led the project until February 2023.

∽

The origins of the cheetah in India are a subject of dispute. Though there is considerable and persuasive evidence that Asiatic cheetahs are native to South Asia, some naturalists have questioned whether there was ever an indigenous population at all. Conservationist and tiger expert, Valmik Thapar, is the most outspoken proponent of this theory, which he has articulated in a book titled *Exotic Aliens: The Lion and the Cheetah in India*, co-authored with Romila Thapar and Yusuf Ansari. Not only does he dismiss the cheetah as an alien species, Thapar also questions whether lions were ever native to India. He writes:

> I believe there was never an 'Asiatic cheetah'. Rather, this animal was an imported royal pet that escaped into the wild on several occasions and may, at times, have created small feral populations. The evidence that my co-authors and I have unearthed in the course of our research and study has duly underlined the basic premise that I began this book with—that the Indian (or Asiatic) lion and the Indian (or Asiatic) cheetah are not distinctive subspecies but are exotic aliens that live (or lived) in the land of the tiger.

Thapar backs up his opinions by pointing out the absence of any clear and consistent references to cheetahs in early historical and cultural sources, prior to the eleventh century CE. The use of cheetahs for hunting in India occurs only after the arrival of Muslim rulers. Akbar the Great Mughal is reported to have had more than 1,000 hunting cheetahs in his imperial menagerie. According to Thapar, these animals probably came from Persia or Africa. He argues that the first visual images of cheetahs in Indian art are Mughal miniatures and most of these paintings are of captive cheetahs. The majority of hunting scenes in which cheetahs appear, show them chasing and killing blackbuck and other animals inside stockades. These 'canned hunts', over which the emperor presided while on horseback or atop an elephant, were more spectacle than sport.

In addition to this, Thapar emphasizes that British colonial hunters, who were never shy about celebrating the slaughter they indulged in, listed numerous tigers and leopards amongst the animals they killed, though they seldom mention cheetahs and very few trophies exist. Following the decline of the Mughal empire, many of the maharajas and nawabs in different parts of India took up coursing with cheetahs and it became a popular and prestigious pastime. Thapar believes that not enough cheetahs were available in India and additional animals had to be shipped across from Africa. One of the main problems is that cheetahs rarely breed in captivity. For this reason, it would have been impossible to sustain a population within a menagerie and hunting cheetahs had to be captured in the wild.

Romila Thapar, Valmik's aunt and one of India's most respected historians, focuses her attention primarily on the lion and lays out arguments to suggest that it may not be an indigenous species. Compared to the images that appear in Egyptian, Assyrian, and Greek sculpture, she suggests that statues and other artwork in India display less familiarity with the anatomy and behaviour of lions. She also sifts through ancient textual references that leave her with doubts about the existence of wild lions in India.

As for the cheetah, Romila Thapar points out that Sanskrit texts use the words dvipi and chitraka, when referring to a spotted predator that is more likely to have been a leopard rather than a cheetah. Naturally, there has always been a certain amount of ambiguity in written accounts of leopards and cheetahs because their pelage is somewhat similar, though the former have black rosettes and the latter have spots. Adding to the confusion is the fact that cheetahs have often been referred to as 'hunting leopards', a name that appears even in S. H. Prater's *The Book of Indian Animals*, first published by the Bombay Natural History Society in 1948.

In part, both Valmik and Romila Thapar were responding to Divyabhanusinh's earlier books, *The End of the Trail: The Cheetah in India* (1995) and *The Lions of India* (2008). In his new book on cheetahs, which reworks much of the material from the first and includes an account of the relocation project up until February 2023, Divyabhanusinh has the opportunity to refute the Thapars' assertions. He presents carefully researched and convincing evidence that cheetahs were indigenous to India, including an illustrated manual from 1904 on the capture and training of cheetahs in the princely state of Ajaigarh, as well as several other manuals and documents from various royal archives. In addition, his book contains photographs of trapped cheetahs being trained. One of the interesting facts is that only adult cheetahs were captured because they already knew how to hunt. Their training was essentially a process of taming the animal, so that it became dependent on its handlers and could be recaptured after it was released. The hunting and killing of prey was entirely instinctual, as it is with a falcon.

Divyabhanusinh and wildlife scholar Raza Kazmi have also published an article in the *Journal of the Bombay Natural History Society*, detailing their research into historical reports of cheetah sightings in many different parts of the subcontinent and the existence of tribal communities who specialized in trapping and training cheetahs. Kazmi has also meticulously researched various accounts of lions in India and he makes a persuasive case that *Panthera leo persica* is an indigenous subspecies that was wiped out in places like Haryana, through hunting and habitat loss in the early nineteenth century.

Establishing the provenance of a wild species is difficult, especially when relying on cultural texts and artefacts. However, DNA analysis seems to have confirmed a genetic separation between Asiatic and African cheetahs, just as there is between the two subspecies of lions. Enough historical evidence exists to show that both of these predators were found in the wild in different parts of Central and Western India, as well as the Deccan. Equally clear is the fact that neither cheetahs nor lions were ever particularly plentiful in India, but simply because an animal is seldom seen doesn't mean it isn't there.

In any case, those who line up on either side of this debate should be able to agree that whatever the origins of the cheetah in India, it no longer exists in the wild. The other indisputable fact is that the African animals, recently imported, can never be considered indigenous, even if they breed and multiply here. The extinction of India's cheetahs is not something that can be reversed. Bringing a different subspecies from Namibia and South Africa to Kuno Palpur simply offers us a chance to see if the forests of India can still provide this remarkable predator with a suitable habitat to sustain its existence.

Covering 748 square kilometres, Kuno Palpur National Park lies within a larger area of buffer zones and reserved forests that extend over 3,200 square kilometres. This region was originally identified as suitable habitat for relocating some of the lions from Gir National Park. In 2013, after considerable controversy and legal challenges, the Supreme Court of India decided in favour of moving a limited number of lions from Gujarat to disperse the growing population in Saurashtra. As a result, twenty-four villages inside Kuno forest division, consisting of almost 1,500 families, were resettled on peripheral land outside the park. Extensive surveys of the flora and fauna were conducted by senior scientists from WII. They reported that Kuno's forests and grasslands were sufficient to support an adequate prey base of ungulates such as chital, sambar, and nilgai, on which the lions could feed. The translocation of lions, however, was stalled by the Gujarat government, which did not want to share this iconic species with any other state. As a result, all of the conservation efforts directed towards the introduction of lions remained unrequited, much to the frustration of the wildlife scientists and Madhya Pradesh forest officials.

In 2020, when the cheetah translocation project was given a green light, Kuno Palpur was again chosen as the most suitable location. One of the advantages of this park is that it currently contains no resident tigers, though individuals do wander in occasionally from Ranthambore, which is less than 100 kilometres away and connected by forest corridors. A primary concern has always been that the cheetahs might be killed by tigers. Leopards too are a potential threat, being the primary predator in Kuno Palpur. However, the cheetahs have shared territory with leopards in Africa and the hope is that once they establish their range, they will be able to avoid conflict with other predators, including wolves, jackals, hyenas, jungle cats, and foxes, all of which inhabit this landscape.

Another concern has been that the terrain and vegetation is obviously different from their original habitat in southern Africa. Everything will be new and unfamiliar for the cheetahs, whether it be the deer they kill and eat or the grass in which they hide. All of the smells and sounds will be unknown to them and the experience is bound to be disorienting and stressful. Even the seasons will be reversed, for they have come from the southern hemisphere to northern latitudes and their bodies will have to adjust to different cycles of daylight and darkness, temperature and climate. Ultimately, the success of this project depends to a very large extent on the cheetahs' ability to adapt to an alien environment.

This is not the first time that wild predators have been translocated from Africa to Kuno Palpur. Raza Kazmi has researched and uncovered fascinating details about the maharaja of Gwalior's attempts to introduce African lions into his forests, between 1900 and 1920. With the encouragement of the viceroy, Curzon, Madho Rao Scindia acquired ten lion cubs from Kenya and other parts of East Africa. (The nawab of Junagadh had refused to give any of his Gir lions to Gwalior.) The cubs were brought to India and after two years in captivity, pairs were released into the forests of Kuno at separate intervals. Unfortunately, the lions soon began killing cattle and became man-eaters, claiming a total of twenty-nine human victims. Scindia then ordered the head of his shikar department, a Frenchman named Auret, to recapture the lions. Kazmi describes how this difficult task was achieved:

> The Gwalior Shikar Department devised a unique plan to follow Scindia's orders. They pinned the lions down to the vicinity of the village where they had made their last kill and plastered innumerable extra-sticky flypapers

> across all the possible exit routes. As the lions tried escaping, the fly papers stuck to their feet. When they tried to scrape them off with their teeth, they ended up further plastering those flypapers onto their manes and faces. Eventually, they were covered in flypapers and could barely see. They were then netted and carted back to their former enclosures.

While this account seems somewhat exaggerated, if not entirely apocryphal, the lions were recaptured somehow. Soon afterwards, they were moved to a walled enclosure at a place called Dobekund, located within the current Kuno Palpur National Park. Kept there for several years, they were given live buffaloes to feed on. These lions also bred in captivity, their numbers increasing to twelve. One of Kazmi's sources is Colonel Kesri Singh, who succeeded Auret as the head of Gwalior's shikar department. In his hunting memoirs, he describes how the lions were released again in 1920. After they dispersed into Kuno's forests, one was killed in a fight with a tiger, while the rest seem to have survived and even bred in the wild. Gradually, though, they turned to man-eating and were shot one by one in various places, as far apart as Jhansi, Panna, and Pachwara.

∽

News reports on the cheetah relocation project have appeared regularly in the papers. At the beginning of November 2022, six weeks after their arrival, a pair of males from Namibia, named Freddie and Elton, were released from their boma into the larger 'acclimatization enclosure'. Within twenty-four hours, they had made their first kill and three days later they killed again. Madhya Pradesh's Chief Wildlife Warden was quoted: 'It is encouraging to learn about the "rockstars", Freddie and Elton, successfully hunting another spotted deer.... This proves they are in the best of health and agility conditions, even after the mandatory quarantine period.'

All seemed to be going well, as the South African contingent arrived in February but then, on 27 March, there was bad news. Sasha, a female from Namibia, had died of a kidney infection. Her death cast a shadow over the project, though two days later, on 29 March, mourning was replaced by jubilation, when another female, Siyaya, gave birth to four cubs. Union Environment Minister Bhupender Yadav tweeted: 'Congratulations, India! A momentous event in our wildlife conservation history during Amrit Kaal! (the 75th anniversary of independence)'.

The emotional pendulum soon swung back in the other direction when a second tragedy occurred. One of the South African males, named Uday, died suddenly on 23 April. An initial autopsy suggested that the cause was 'cardiopulmonary failure'—a heart attack. However, Professor Adrian Tordiffe, a wildlife veterinary specialist from the University of Pretoria and a project consultant, offered a different diagnosis. 'After speaking to the team of vets, at this stage it looks like a case of severe neurotoxins, most likely the botulinum toxin, released by bacteria. This toxin is often found in rotting meat. My assessment at this stage is that the cheetah ingested either an old carcass, or drank from a pool of water where there was a dead animal or bird. The toxin causes paralysis of the nerves, the animal becomes weak, can't even lift its head because the toxin has paralyzed its neck muscles—signs that we saw in this cheetah.'

This second death occurred four days before I reached Kuno Palpur and forest officials were clearly anxious that the experiment was not going entirely as planned. Though the area I was scheduled to visit lies on the opposite side of the river from where the cheetahs are being kept, I was worried that I might not be permitted to enter any part of the park.

Setting out at quarter past five in the morning, Ravi and I retrace our route through the buffer zone, heading for Ahera gate, one of three entrances to the park. In the half-light before dawn, I see a jackal at the side of the road, gnawing on the rotting remains of one of the dead cows we passed yesterday. Half an hour later, when we turn off the main road at a village called Bhatnawar, the sky has grown brighter, and a few people and cattle are moving about. After following a rough rural road for several kilometres, we come to a new road under construction that is broader but still unpaved. Access to the park is being improved, in anticipation of more tourists wanting to see the cheetahs.

A couple of kilometres before Ahera gate, we pass through two settlements, where people who once lived inside the forest have been relocated. The first is a complex of concrete quarters that look like barracks, with a patch of open ground in the middle where goats are grazing. A solar pump, attached to a borewell, feeds a PVC water storage tank, where women and children are lined up to fill buckets. Half a kilometre beyond this is another settlement of mud shacks covered in tattered plastic. Some of the people that were moved out of the park are from tribal communities, while others are herders who used to tend livestock inside Kuno Palpur. The settlements are a depressing sight, more like refugee camps than villages and the landscape around them is badly degraded. Only the sacred mahua trees haven't been lopped or felled, spared because they are a valuable natural resource for the villagers, who eat the flowers and also use them to make liquor. Growing more than 15 metres tall, with shaggy crowns, each tree can produce 300 kilograms of flowers in a single season. At this time of year, the mahua's new leaves have a coppery tint that makes them look as if they are glowing, even before the first rays of morning sunlight touch the trees.

At the gate, we are met by a group of five forest guards, who are just waking up. They seem surprised to see us and call the range officer to make sure it's okay for me to enter the park. Curious about where I've come from, they interrogate me in a polite but persistent manner, as if they suspect I am a spy gathering sensitive information on the cheetahs. Once they convince themselves of my innocence, Ravi and I are offered a cup of tea, while I fill out the necessary forms and pay my entry fee. No jeep safaris operate here, as they do in most other parks, but Ravi is allowed to take his taxi inside, as long as we are accompanied by one of the guards.

I'll change his name to Rajinder. In his mid-thirties, he has only been working at the park for three months and was probably hired because more experienced staff were required to deal with the cheetahs. It soon becomes clear that his knowledge of the forest is limited and he has no concept of how or why anyone would observe wildlife in a national park. The first thing he does is ask Ravi to turn on the radio. When I veto that, Rajinder takes out his mobile phone and begins to play film tunes as we drive along. After asking him several times to switch off the music, without success, I resign myself to experiencing Kuno Palpur with 'Daiyya! Daiyya! Daiyya re!' and other item numbers as an accompanying soundtrack.

When we spot a herd of chital, Rajinder points to a large stag and calls it a barasingha. Later, he identifies a group of female nilgai as sambar. Throughout our drive, he maintains a surly attitude of boredom and yawns loudly at regular intervals. When we stop at a forest camp, 7 or 8 kilometres inside the park, Rajinder goes off to chat with the other guards while we wait. At this point, I'm almost ready to drive on and leave him behind but I have no choice. Eventually, with a certain amount of cajoling and threats that I'll report him to the park director, I finally get him to silence his phone.

The landscape we pass through is a mix of dry deciduous forest and patchy grasslands. In this season the tall grasses are dry and don't offer much nutrition for herbivores. They also increase the risk of wildfires. Surprisingly, this area of the park has very little *Prosopis juliflora* or lantana, two of the most prolific invasive species, though one alien plant that does grow here is a kind of cactus or prickly pear (*Opuntia dillenii*) from South America. In an unpublished report from 2016, before Kuno Palpur was upgraded to a national park, Dr A. J. T. Johnsingh, one of India's most respected wildlife scientists, recounts how WII's survey teams identified a number of fodder grasses like *Apluda mutica, Sorghum halepense*, and *Saccharum spontaneum*, the last of which is a sweetgrass commonly known as kans.

The mix of trees is very different from other forests I've visited in Central

India. Kuno Palpur borders Rajasthan and the ecology reflects a more arid climate and poor soil conditions. In many ways, this is what I imagine the original jangala to be, as defined by early Ayurvedic texts. Instead of a humid, tropical 'jungle', it is a thorny, tenacious biome, with trees and plants that survive for long periods without rain. Kardhai is the most prominent species but there are also a number of acacias like khair that are leafless at this time of year and reonjha, which has intense green foliage that stands out vividly amidst the bare branches of other deciduous species. At a few places we come upon flowering amaltas, their dangling showers of blossoms a dazzling yellow. Predictably, there is also lots of ber and tendu, which is laden with fruit at this time of year but hasn't yet got its new leaves.

Rajinder tells me that a few days ago, when he was patrolling the forest with another guard, they came upon a sloth bear in a tendu tree, feeding on the fruit. Saying it is very sweet, he offers to pick some for us. Spotting a large tendu at the side of the road, with a lot of ripe fruit, he tells Ravi to stop. Climbing into the tree with ursine agility, Rajinder shakes the branches so that dozens of the round, orange fruit rain down on the ground. About the size of a plum, they have a leathery skin and large seeds, similar to a loquat. The pulpy flesh has a sweet, pleasant flavour, though the aftertaste is astringent.

Aside from chital and nilgai, the only other wild mammals we see are several troops of langurs. The park also contains large herds of feral cattle. In 2016, the WII team estimated that there were between 2,000 to 2,500 of these ownerless bovines, which were included in calculations of potential prey species for the lions. Leopards kill some of the smaller cows, but not the big bulls, of which there are many. At one place, we come upon the remains of a cow, just its head and hooves with some skin, hanging from the branches of a reonjha tree, where a leopard has stashed its kill out of reach of jackals and other scavengers. Cheetahs are unlikely to prey on feral cattle, except perhaps young calves. It isn't entirely clear where these cows and bulls came from but one explanation is that they were left behind in the forest by villagers when they were resettled outside the park.

The birdlife in Kuno Palpur is rich and varied. Never before have I seen so many golden orioles. It seems as if every few minutes one of them flies from tree to tree, its yellow plumage as bright as the amaltas flowers. Large coveys of grey francolins scuttle through the grass. Their Hindi name, teetar, comes from their call, which is repeated loudly in sharp, strident tones. Peafowl are also plentiful and an important prey species for smaller predators. It is very likely that the African cheetahs will soon acquire a taste for India's national bird. I also see a male Asian paradise-flycatcher with tail feathers 30 centimetres long, nearly three times the length of its body. These spectacular birds are almost entirely white, except for a crested black head. As it flies through the dense branches of kardhai trees, I can't understand how paradise flycatchers avoid snagging their tails.

After about an hour of driving, we reach a series of low, corrugated ridges with several prominent hills further on. In amongst the trees, I can see broken sandstone and brick walls—the ruins of a village. It is impossible to count how many houses there must have been here, because the site is overgrown with grass and shrubs, but the demolished homes appear to have been substantial dwellings, unlike the makeshift settlements outside the park. The only building still standing is a small temple. Though it looks abandoned, I can see a faded pennant on a bamboo flagstaff and a small idol, which has been freshly painted bright orange. Rajinder tells me that though the villagers have been removed from the park they are permitted to come and perform pujas on special occasions. In the middle of the ruined village is a tenti tree, about 3 metres tall. I recognize it from the mass of drooping, leafless stems that look like a pile of green thatch. Tenti fruit is edible but sour and usually made into pickle.

Less than a kilometre beyond the ruined village, we come to the Kuno River. Getting out of the vehicle, I leave Rajinder and Ravi to listen to their film music, while I walk down to the riverbank. On the far side of the expanse of still water is a magnificent fort, constructed of red sandstone with imposing bastions, ramparts, and watchtowers. Overlooking the river, it is built on layered strata of the same rocks that form its high walls. In the morning light, the abandoned fort looks almost like a geological formation, overgrown with trees and shrubs. The pale, skeletal branches of a kulu or ghost tree protrude from a gap in one of the ramparts. Several *Prosopis* have breached the walls and invaded the fortress, adding a delicate fringe of green foliage to the tiered rocks. Palpur Garhi was built in the eighteenth century. The royal family of Palpur, now settled in Bhopal, vacated the fort around the same time as the villages were relocated. However, the fort's former owners are now fighting a case to reclaim their property, arguing that they were forced out on the pretext that lions would be resettled here but now the cheetahs have been introduced instead. Next to the ruined citadel is a forest department rest house and the park headquarters, where the translocation project is based. Through my binoculars, I can see a cluster of buildings, several vehicles, and a communications tower.

The Kuno River is about 50 metres wide at this point and contains crocodiles, though I don't see any. From here it flows on to Morena, where it joins the Chambal. A white-browed wagtail loiters at the water's edge, bobbing up and down, while river terns sail by overhead on sharply tapered wings. We are forbidden to cross the river and, despite my curiosity, I reluctantly return to the taxi where Rajinder and Ravi are waiting. To the east, the sky has darkened with bruised rain clouds; a sudden storm is approaching.

Within ten minutes, as we head back towards Ahera gate, the first raindrops splash on the windshield. Soon, it turns into a downpour. The dry forest is drenched with rain and the clay surface of the road turns slick, our vehicle skidding from side to side. Feral cattle take shelter under leafless trees while a group of langurs hunker down in the ruins of an abandoned hut that has no roof. I wonder what the cheetahs make of this deluge and whether it reminds them of storms back home in Africa. Rajinder seems pleased with the rain and tells me that he and the other forest guards won't have to worry about wildfires for a while.

Half an hour later, the storm finally subsides, leaving the kardhai trees dripping and the tall grasses bent by the torrential rain. Rolling down my window, I can smell the sweet, musky scent of damp earth and wet foliage. This fresh, clean fragrance signals a brief respite from the impending summer heat, as well as the promise of regrowth and renewal.

∽

As of this writing, a little over a year after the first batch of cheetahs arrived in Kuno Palpur, a total of six adults and three cubs have died, leaving only fifteen remaining. While it was expected that some of these animals might not survive, the mortality rate is a serious concern. Some of the deaths appear to have been avoidable. One of the females was killed by two males when she was released into their enclosure in a misguided attempt to encourage them to mate. Unfortunately, a lot of confusing and contradictory information has been circulated about the status of the project, both by officials and media sources, making it difficult to know exactly what is happening. However, it seems that three cheetahs died during the monsoon because of infected wounds caused by the GPS collars fitted around their necks. Apparently, another cheetah went missing for several weeks after its collar stopped working. Fortunately, this animal was found and recaptured.

Until now, all attempts to reintroduce the cheetahs into the wild have been unsuccessful. While several males and females were released from their enclosures in April and May, allowing them to roam free in the park, they were eventually brought back into fenced-in areas after project officials feared that they were wandering too far afield. For the past few months, the cheetahs have been confined to large enclosures, where they are fed butchered meat to supplement any deer they might kill.

Whatever the ultimate outcomes and consequences of the cheetah translocation project may be, it can still provide an opportunity for a more comprehensive and integrated conservation strategy. As problems arise and lessons are learned, it is essential to rethink the future of not just the cheetahs but the ecology of Kuno Palpur as a whole. More than just relocating these swift predators from Africa, the entire landscape needs to be rehabilitated and restored. Having moved so many villagers out of the park, it would be a tragedy if the forests and grasslands were simply cordoned off to provide a caged existence for a single, exotic species.

Though tourism can certainly help sustain this effort, the primary objective should not be to create yet another venue for wildlife safaris. The cheetahs will undoubtedly attract plenty of visitors to the park and their presence can help support the preservation of other, less charismatic species, like hyenas, vultures, and pangolins. In this way, the high-profile publicity and political synergy can be redirected to create an ecologically sound and balanced conservation venture that also engages with and empowers the people who have been displaced.

If protected consistently and vigilantly, the kardhai forests, saccharum meadows, sandstone escarpments, and clear waters of the Kuno River will recover and flourish over time. Poaching has been a longstanding problem in the park and needs to be strictly controlled, as does the presence of feral cattle. Only then will a greater degree of biodiversity be restored. During my visit to Kuno Palpur, I saw no blackbuck or chinkara, which is ironic because they are the cheetah's preferred prey. These antelope and gazelle must have been plentiful here in the past, but their numbers have been depleted, largely because of poaching. Reintroducing blackbuck into the park would seem to be a logical approach to augmenting the prey base, as they breed prolifically in a safe and secure environment. Many other wild species can also benefit from the translocation of cheetahs, and one would hope that in addition to becoming a second home for these African exiles, Kuno Palpur will serve as a safe haven for indigenous flora and fauna. After all, this ancient, living landscape represents one of the few surviving tracts of India's true jangala.

5

RESILIENCE AND RECOVERY

Morning sunlight has yet to touch the earth, though the overcast sky has brightened. The horizon is hidden by shadowy silhouettes of acacia trees. Herds of blackbuck and nilgai are scattered across the plain, as motionless as figures painted on stone. At daybreak, colours are muted—the grasslands tinged a sooty gold and the distant trees a haze of blue and green. This could easily be a scene from several millennia ago, an uncontested landscape where nature balances the needs of every species in its domain.

The illusion persists for a few minutes longer as a lone raptor takes to the air ahead of us, rising just above the western rim of the plain. A feathered shadow against the sky, its wings move with a slow, almost languid beat as it circles out and around, then back again in our direction, passing no more than 2 metres above the grass. Gliding in to land, the bird settles on the ground, a stone's throw away. Seeing its pale nape and crown, Ram Singh, the forest ranger accompanying me, identifies it as a juvenile western marsh harrier, a winter visitor recently arrived from Europe.

We are driving along one of the dirt tracks that bifurcates Tal Chhapar Wildlife Sanctuary in Churu district of Rajasthan, near the edge of the Thar Desert. Ram Singh is at the wheel of an open-roofed Gypsy that rumbles and creaks as we move forward after the harrier has flown off again. No other vehicles are in the sanctuary, and it feels as if we are trespassing on the seclusion and stillness of the grasslands at dawn.

Yesterday afternoon, a late monsoon storm lashed Tal Chhapar and the ground is still muddy in places. The rain has also stirred up the amorous instincts of a peacock, who is performing for his mate. In a flamboyant display, his gaudy, iridescent tail feathers fan out as he struts in a circle. The peahen seems unimpressed as she searches the moist ground for worms and insects. Nature doesn't offer us many cliches, but the 'dancing' peacock is an image that we have appropriated through art and advertising to a point where it seems almost mundane. Yet, here in these natural surroundings, there is something profoundly beautiful, perhaps even romantic, in a peacock's courtship ritual.

As if to complete this idyllic picture, a male blackbuck stands nearby, his long, spiral horns diverging in a V, like the tines on a geometry compass, splayed at an angle of thirty degrees. The antelope is partly hidden in the tall grass, which comes up to his shoulders. With the sunrise behind him, he looks as if he belongs in a fairy tale, an imaginary creature conjured up to amuse an impressionable child. But this marvellous species is not a fantasy. Endemic to India, the blackbuck is as iconic as the peacock, and it is often represented in miniature paintings or sculpture. Hindu mythology tells us that these swift, graceful antelope serve as the vahana, or sacred mount, of Vayu the Vedic god of wind. Fleet-footed blackbuck are also said to draw Krishna's chariot, racing across the land.

Though the blackbuck watches us warily, he remains where he is as we pass by. Safe within the sanctuary, he is secure in his natural habitat. But despite the illusion of a primal paradise this landscape was not always as peaceable and protected as it is today. For much of the twentieth century, Tal Chhapar was badly degraded, almost devoid of grass, its soil crusted with salt and the native trees displaced by an invasive species. Only within the past thirty years have these grasslands been restored.

As its name suggests, Tal Chhapar was once a large, seasonal wetland that flooded during the monsoon. Whatever lake or marsh was here originally, must have dried up centuries ago, leaving a broad, shallow depression. The soil is saline, and annual flooding caused salt to rise to the surface. Even today, just beyond the south-western boundary of the sanctuary, commercial salt pans are still in operation. Most of this land was once a private game preserve of the royal family of Bikaner, where they hunted blackbuck, demoiselle cranes, and bar-headed geese. Maharaja Ganga Singh, who ruled from 1888 to 1943, built himself a palatial hunting lodge at the edge of the grasslands. This building, with its regal sandstone cupolas, has now been converted into a school.

In 1877, a fast-growing species of mesquite from Central America, *Prosopis juliflora*, was brought to India and introduced extensively in a disastrous scheme to reforest areas considered 'wasteland'. Mesquite thrives in arid conditions with poor soil, and it quickly spread across many parts of India, pushing out native species. Though *Prosopis* is not an acacia, the feathery leaflets and long thorns, as well as its rough, ridged bark, resemble the indigenous babool, also called keekar. The aggressive invader has proliferated so successfully in places like Rajasthan, Haryana, and Delhi, that it has become the predominant tree in many areas and is considered a botanical menace. Its local name is baavlia, which means 'the mad one' because it spreads rampantly and can't be controlled. Also referred to as 'vilayati keekar' (foreign keekar) or 'angrezi babool' (English babool), it produces seeds twice a year, which are spread by grazing cattle and other animals that eat the pods and disperse it through their dung.

Babool and khair, both native acacias, were edged out of Tal Chhapar, along with an indigenous mesquite, *Prosopis cineraria*, locally known as khejdi or jhand. Small herds of blackbuck and nilgai survived but they had to compete with village cattle and goats for sparse forage. Though the maharaja's hunting expeditions ended in 1966, when Tal Chhapar was declared a wildlife sanctuary, most of the damage had already been done. Added to the loss of habitat, the blackbuck and other animals fell prey to packs of village dogs that hunted newborn calves.

The ecological recovery of Tal Chhapar began in the early 1990s, under the direction of a visionary forest officer, Surat Singh Poonia, who had the foresight and commitment to bring these lost grasslands back to life. Working with a forest department team, Poonia began by uprooting all of the *Prosopis*, an enormous task that required repeated efforts because this invasive species is so prolific and persistent. At the same time, the 900 hectares (2,225 acres) of the sanctuary had to be completely fenced in to keep out cattle, goats, and dogs. Part of the cost of fencing was covered by the sale of baavlia wood, which is used for fuel. Poonia and his colleagues then reseeded the plain with indigenous grasses and sedges. Though Tal Chhapar is a relatively small sanctuary, compared to other national parks and reserves, the effort was monumental and the results are self-evident. Blackbuck have multiplied from approximately 800 animals when Poonia took charge to an estimated 3,200 today. The population has grown so abundant that the Rajasthan Forest Department has decided to expand the area of the sanctuary and relocate some of the blackbuck. Other mammals such as desert foxes, jungle cats, and black-naped hares have reclaimed their habitat too. When the grasslands were denuded, many migratory birds had stopped visiting Tal Chhapar but now most of them have returned.

No large predators reside in the sanctuary to help limit the number of antelope, which is part of the reason they have multiplied so successfully. The expression 'rewilding' as it is used by conservationists in Europe and North America, not only emphasizes the reintroduction of species that have become locally extinct but also requires the presence of 'apex predators' that help maintain a natural balance between herbivores and carnivores. By this definition, Tal Chhapar is not entirely wild, and the use of fences also creates an artificial enclosure. However, the limited area of the sanctuary makes it unfeasible to introduce leopards, wolves, or cheetahs. On the other hand, birds of prey are plentiful, and they fulfil their role in the food chain, feeding on smaller mammals, reptiles, insects, and birds. As for the fence, it may keep out stray cattle but the antelope have clearly found ways to escape, coming and going without hindrance. Tal Chhapar is by no means a safari park or zoo full of captive species, but a carefully managed ecosystem in which animals live almost as they would in the wild. For this reason, it provides a unique model for wildlife conservation in other parts of India where large tracts of forest no longer exist but smaller, viable habitats can be restored.

Looking out across the savanna, it appears to contain little biodiversity, but in fact the sanctuary supports a multitude of plants, many of them interdependent, their roots woven together into a living fabric that carpets the earth. A recent botanical survey, conducted between 2015 and 2017, identifies seventy-eight different species of flowering plants growing within the 9 square kilometres of Tal Chhapar. The majority of these are wild grasses, the most common of which are jargu, dabh, poolongi, and sevan or lilon. All of these species are indigenous and provide wild herbivores with plentiful forage.

As we continue on our circuit of the sanctuary, Ram Singh points out a laggar falcon perched on one of the wooden posts erected at intervals along both sides of the dirt track. This elegant bird is smaller than the marsh harrier, with grey-brown feathers on its back and wings, which darken towards the tips. The falcon's breast is a paler shade of mottled brown and it has a dark moustachial stripe extending from either side of its sharp beak, and framing white patches on its cheeks. When the falcon takes off, it has a swifter, straighter flight than the harrier, wings beating steadily as it sets course for another post 200 metres further on. Permanent residents at Tal Chhapar, laggar falcons feed on reptiles and small birds like larks and drongos, as well as grasshoppers and locusts that proliferate in the grass.

By now the sun is higher in the sky and it disperses a fresh yellow light on the scene. A solitary male nilgai stands in profile about 50 metres to our right, a common mynah perched on his rump. The nilgai, India's largest antelope, *Boselaphus tragocamelus*, has short, erect horns and a slate-grey hide with a bluish cast. The Hindi name, nilgai, means blue cow and in English it is often called a blue bull. *Hobson-Jobson* spells it as Neelgye or Nilghau and gives its Sanskrit name as risya or rishya, but there is considerable ambiguity surrounding this animal, which is also known as rohu or rojh. Part of the confusion comes from the nilgai's appearance. Its horns are similar to those of a cow and for this reason many Hindus consider it sacred and will not eat its meat. The nilgai's stature, however, is more like a horse. Large males stand almost 2 metres at the shoulder and are strong runners that gallop across the open plains. During the Mughal period, it was sometimes called nilghor, which means blue horse. First described for European science in 1766 by a German zoologist, Peter Simon Pallas, who never saw a live specimen, its Latin name is equally confusing. *Boselaphus* means 'cow/deer' and *tragocamelus* means 'male-goat/camel', all of which is anything but precise. This shows how scientific taxonomy can be highly subjective and open to the vagaries of language, whether it is Sanskrit, Latin, English, or any of India's many vernaculars.

Nevertheless, the nilgai is an imposing creature, with a prominent white patch on its throat. A sparse black mane extends along the back of its neck and humped shoulders, with a matching tuft of hair on its chest. Females are a dusty fawn colour and have no horns. Lying down, they blend into the tawny grass and at several places, as we drive by, they stand up suddenly, taking us by surprise. Nilgai are common throughout the plains of India and are often considered a pest because they feed on crops. Even at Tal Chhapar, many of them leave the sanctuary during the night to raid fields nearby.

More raptors appear, including several black kites, which are common residents and a migratory Montagu's harrier. We also see plenty of white-eyed buzzards, one of which is so absorbed in studying grasshoppers beneath his perch that he ignores our presence. The largest raptor we observe is a tawny eagle, grooming its feathers atop a babool tree. The smallest and prettiest bird of prey is a common kestrel. About 30 centimetres in length, it has a grey cap and a prominent moustachial stripe that would make any Rajput proud. Its breast feathers are a pale brown with dark streaks and its back and wings are chestnut, decorated with numerous brown bars that look like intricate marquetry patterns. The kestrel's tail feathers are brick red, with broad bars, almost black. This aerial hunter's flight is swift and it often hovers above its prey before plunging to earth.

Aside from raptors, a number of other birds are found at Tal Chhapar. The demoiselle cranes have not arrived yet, but Ram Singh says they are expected in another week or two. He identifies a Siberian stonechat that has recently flown in to spend the winter here. A small, rust-coloured bird, it seems hardly capable of such an arduous migration. Further on, a European roller is perched on a thorny branch. Though similar in shape and size to the Indian roller, this bird has pale turquoise plumage with a rufous back. A passage migrant, it stops over in western India on its long journey from Europe to southern Africa. The fact that the stonechat and roller converge on this small patch of grassland, after flying thousands of kilometres from different hemispheres, underscores the global reach of Tal Chhapar's restoration.

As the temperature rises, herds of blackbuck begin to move about the grasslands. Females do not have horns and are a light tan, blending into the grass. We watch a bachelor group of six males sparring with each other. Locking horns, they press their heads to the ground, trying to get their opponents to submit. The competition between them seems more playful than serious, as if they are practising for later contests. On the other side of the plain, a flock of egrets take off suddenly in a flurry of white wings, startling two bucks that run for several hundred metres, leaping through the grass with graceful bounds.

The warmth of the day also brings out a young Bengal monitor lizard, which we spot clinging to the fissured bark of a babool. About a metre long, including its tail, the monitor's head is flat and relatively small compared to the size of its body. Its wrinkled skin is a muddy grey, with a pattern of yellowish spots arranged in orderly stripes across its back and legs. The lizard's thin, clawed toes are also marked by white spots that give them a delicate appearance, though this reptile has a formidable grip. Legend has it that Maratha warriors used monitor lizards to scale the walls of besieged forts. This one may have been climbing the tree in search of a nest full of eggs or fledglings. Four species of monitors exist in India and the desert monitor, also found in this region, is the smallest. They are hunted for their skins, which are used to make drums, and their meat, particularly the male genitals, is considered an aphrodisiac.

Ram Singh points out several baavlia seedlings sprouting in the grass and explains that the forest guards have to be vigilant about uprooting them before they get too large and reproduce. Outside the boundaries of Tal Chhapar, these invasive trees are plentiful. Nilgai and blackbuck feed on the pods, reintroducing the seeds into the sanctuary through their dung. Within the grasslands, babool and khair have reestablished themselves in scattered groves, particularly near four artificial ponds that have been dug to provide animals with water. Ram Singh also draws my attention to a khejdi tree, growing on its own. *Prosopis cineraria* resembles the acacias, as well as baavlia, but it is a unique species, revered in desert regions of Rajasthan because of its many uses. Growing mostly in dry, sandy soil, its roots can extend 10 metres beneath the surface. The pods look like long beans, and are cooked as a nutritious vegetable. Khejdi has rough, grey bark that is prescribed for various medical conditions including skin ailments. The bark can also be ground into coarse flour. Famously, it helped many villagers survive the great Rajputana Famine of 1868–69.

The Bishnoi community, who live along the margins of the Thar Desert, worship the khejdi tree and have protected this species for generations. One of the earliest conservation movements in India is associated with khejdi. In 1730, a group of Bishnoi women in a village near Jodhpur resisted the orders of Abhay Singh, the maharaja of Mewar, to cut down a sacred grove of khejdi. He had planned to use the timber to build a new palace. According to Bishnoi tradition, these women hugged the trees and were killed by the maharaja's soldiers. Altogether, 363 Bishnois were martyred while protecting the grove until Abhay Singh relented and spared the trees. This incident is often cited as an inspiration for the more recent Chipko movement of the 1970s, when village women in Garhwal hugged trees to protect them from timber contractors.

Bishnois espouse a philosophy of non-violence and respect for all forms of life. Their spiritual founder, Guru Jhamboji (1451–1536), outlined twenty-nine guiding principles for his followers. (The word 'Bishnoi' means twenty-nine.) Most of these are commandments forbidding the use of tobacco, alcohol, opium, and other intoxicants, as well as societal injunctions, including a rule that women must be secluded for thirty days after childbirth. Two of the principles dictate that Bishnois must not cut green wood and that they should protect wildlife. In the past, these beliefs often put them at odds with the maharajas, who hunted birds and mammals for sport. In an arid environment, where only the hardiest forms of life survive, the compassionate ethics of the Bishnoi community have helped preserve endangered species.

The wildlife sanctuary is located next to the village of Chhapar. Over the years, the Bishnois who live here have protected blackbuck and other species, even when the grasslands were denuded. In 1980, the naturalist and author, M. Krishnan, visited Chhapar and praised their conservation practices and ethos:

> It is only around Bishnoi settlements that one suddenly finds blackbuck, chinkara, peafowl, partridges and other shy, fugitive wild animals being quite confiding and unafraid of men—proof positive of the potency of a strict policy of non-interference towards the local wildlife.... if you want to know how conservation can be really effected successfully in the field without all this fuss and bother, by illiterate rustics through dedicated and sincere effort and faith in the policy of leaving well alone, go to Tal Chhapar.

Many naturalists have heeded Krishnan's advice. Chhapar has several homestays that cater to birdwatchers and wildlife photographers. The forest department also maintains a rest house here, where visitors can stay. After our morning safari, Ram Singh drives me across to the eastern side of the settlement. This area is known as Gaushala or Gauchar, which means a place where cows are set loose to graze on common land. Unlike the sanctuary, this open space is not managed or protected by the forest department and cows, camels, and large flocks of goats wander about. Several dogs lie asleep in the dust. The grass is sparse and plenty of baavlia grows here. In many ways, this must have been what the sanctuary looked like before restoration—bald patches of ground, frosted with salt. A few nilgai and blackbuck mingle amongst the cattle and goats.

This area is also home to a large colony of Indian spiny-tailed lizards, which burrow into the hard, saline soil and emerge every morning to bask in the sun. Dozens of these reptiles are scattered across the dry pastureland. Smaller than the monitor, they are no more than 30 centimetres in length. Their blunt heads look somewhat like a turtle's face, with small, orange-rimmed eyes that study us intently. The lizards' mottled grey-brown skin has a rough texture like sandpaper. The tail is a sturdy appendage, ringed with multiple ridges covered in small, rasp-like spikes. Spiny-tailed lizards use their tails for self-defence, lashing out at predators.

Mostly vegetarian, these skittish reptiles feed on desert plants and grasses. They are a favourite prey for laggar falcons and other raptors. For this reason, the lizards remain close to their burrows, and at the slightest hint of danger, they slip out of sight, with their armoured tails blocking the hole.

More than fifteen different species of spiny-tailed lizards are found in South Asia, the Middle East, and North Africa. They have become locally extinct in many parts of India and are now restricted to semi-desert landscapes in the western regions of the country. These ancient creatures have inhabited the earth for roughly 20 million years. Having survived catastrophic events and dramatic changes in climate, spiny-tailed lizards now face their greatest threat today, from the spread of human settlements and agriculture, which destroys their habitat. Hunted for their meat and for oil extracted from their tails, they are also sold as exotic pets. While these lizards may not have the speed or grace of a blackbuck, or the colourful plumage of peacocks, they are no less important than other, more photogenic species. Having survived three epochs, from the Miocene until today, it would be a tragic loss if, on our account, their existence ended in the Anthropocene.

∽

Two hundred and seventy kilometres southwest of Tal Chhapar, Mehrangarh looms above Jodhpur. Built in 1459 by Rao Jodha, a Rathore chieftain, the fort stands on a hilltop that overlooks the city. Successive rulers expanded the fort, adding walls, gates, temples, and palaces. This huge sandstone citadel is spread over 486 hectares (1,200 acres) of rocky terrain, enclosed by a perimeter wall more than 5 kilometres long. It was from this desert stronghold, in 1730, that Maharaja Abhay Singh gave orders to cut down the khejdi trees for which the Bishnois sacrificed their lives. Two centuries later, his descendant, Maharaja Umaid Singh, decided to grow *Prosopis juliflora* throughout his kingdom, including on the slopes of the hill surrounding Mehrangarh. Umaid Singh was an enthusiastic aviator, who owned a fleet of aircraft and built landing strips all over Rajasthan. During the early 1930s, he broadcast quantities of mesquite seeds from the air in an ill-advised effort to add green cover to this dry, unyielding landscape.

'I imagine that he must have been dressed like Biggles—with leather headgear and goggles—flying low over the desert in his Tiger Moth biplane, scattering baavlia seeds wherever he went,' says Pradip Krishen, with a smile.

Though Umaid Singh died of an appendicitis in 1947 while on a tiger hunt, the alien mesquite took root in the crevices of rocks and flourished, eventually covering most of the hill around the fort. In 2006, supported by the Mehrangarh Museum Trust, Pradip and his team began an ambitious project to restore the natural ecology within the outer walls of the fort. The result is the Rao Jodha Desert Rock Park, which covers an area of 70 hectares (175 acres). Most of the hill consists of a hard igneous rock called rhyolite as well as some welded tuff and breccia, which are also volcanic in origin. The native species of trees and plants that originally grew here had been overwhelmed by *Prosopis* and the first challenge was to remove it completely.

'When we started, we had no idea how to dig out the baavlia roots, which had penetrated deep into fissures in the rocks,' Pradip tells me. 'We didn't want to use herbicides, of course. Someone suggested dynamite but that didn't sound like a good idea. Eventually, we recruited a group of Khandwaliyas, who are traditional stone miners. They use only a hammer and chisel.'

To eliminate the *Prosopis* it was necessary to excavate the rocks to a depth of almost a metre. Striking the brittle rhyolite with their hammers, the Khandwaliya stone workers were able to gauge what lay underneath and where to begin cutting into the rock, simply by listening to the sound. Through a painstaking process that extended over seven years, the invasive trees were uprooted one at a time, after removing sections of rock. These cavities were then filled with soil and planted with indigenous desert flora. Meanwhile, the fort's outer walls were repaired to keep out stray cattle and goats. Today, more than eighty lithophytes and other desert plants grow in the park. Some were already here but many were reintroduced and had to be collected from areas surrounding Jodhpur.

Rao Jodha Desert Rock Park opened to the public in 2011 and it remains an ongoing project that needs continuous monitoring and maintenance. In 2021, Pradip retired as director but he is still actively involved. My visit coincides with a conference held at Mehrangarh organized by the Ecological Restoration Alliance, a group of conservationists from different parts of India who are united in their efforts to protect, revive, and replant degraded habitats.

As a prelude to the conference, Pradip and the new director, Somil Daga, take the participants on a tour of the park. It is mid-September and our walkabout starts at 6.30 a.m., when the air is still relatively cool. The main fort rises above us and catches the first light, its ruddy sandstone walls fired by the sun's radiance. Mehran is a derivation of 'Mihir', the solar deity, and garh means fort. Outside the ancient, crenelated walls, we can see the rooftops of Jodhpur, spreading into the distance like a mosaic of concrete.

Just beyond the park entrance is a set of xeriscapes, laid out as small, raised beds, each about a metre square. Somil explains how these unirrigated plots were created by collecting bags of surface soil containing seeds. Each plot is filled with earth from a different landscape and when the monsoon rains arrive, they sprout with whatever grasses and other plants are specific to that particular ecology. To begin with, not all the plots were successful but over the years these microhabitats have been tested and tweaked until they have become a lush, wild garden, harbouring an array of desert flora.

From here, Pradip leads us down a rough, stone staircase into a man-made gorge. Hewn from the rocks, it serves as a storm drain to carry rainwater to a reservoir below the fort. This gulley is known as Hathi Nahar, the elephant canal, and it was excavated 500 years ago when the fort was first built. Because of recent rain, water has collected at places and we make our way over stepping stones. A few liverworts are growing on the rough walls and a gecko has laid three tiny white eggs in a niche in the rocks. As we duck under dangling creepers, Somil tells us that two cobras were seen here yesterday.

One of the most distinctive desert plants in this region is a large euphorbia called thhor. It grows as a dense thicket of tall, erect stalks, covered in small thorns like a cactus. To retain moisture, thhor remains leafless for most of the year and photosynthesis occurs through its fleshy green limbs which sprout small leaflets only during the monsoon. Thhor favours rocky terrain and provides shade and shelter for a variety of smaller plants, as well as rodents, birds, and reptiles. One species that grows at the base of this hardy spurge is a root parasite called missi or cowpea witchweed. With no leaves or roots of its own, it depends entirely on its host for moisture and nutrients. Missi produces pink flowers at the end of the monsoon before it disappears for another year. Farmers consider it a noxious weed because it attaches itself to wheat and millet plants, stunting their growth, though it seems to do no damage to the thhor.

Each of the desert plants and shrubs have evolved traits that allow them to survive in harsh, arid conditions. Several bloom and are pollinated only at night to preserve moisture, like vajradanti, which has white tubular blossoms that open after dark and wither at dawn. Many plants like bui, also called desert cotton, have hairy white flowers and leaves that reflect sunlight and provide insulation. Bui's soft, fluffy florets are used by villagers in Rajasthan to stuff pillows and mattresses.

Desert flora grow much more slowly than plants and trees in other biomes but after sixteen years of careful nurturing, several species have grown tall enough to offer some shade. A small stand of kaim trees, the same Krishna kadamb I saw in Vrindavan, seem to be thriving, rising to more than twice my height, with a verdant crown of round leaves. Next to them is a familiar-looking tree, at least 4 metres tall. Sargooro is a desert relative of the common drumstick tree, sonjna, but its long, slender fruit is bitter. To help visitors identify species in the park, Pradip has published a pocket field guide, featuring forty-two trees, shrubs, herbaceous plants, and climbers. Illustrated with photographs, the booklet gives common, scientific, and local names, some of which suggest intriguing associations from folklore such as 'geedar tambaku' (jackal's tobacco) and a thistle known as 'oont kaantalo' (camel thorn).

Four different trails circle through the park, ascending and descending the rugged contours of the volcanic hill. Everything has been done to keep the landscape as natural as possible and at places the rocks are bare. Rather than being a carefully planned and cultivated garden, the approach that Pradip adopted was to assist nature in reclaiming the land on its own terms. One of the gratifying results is that many of the plants are now self-propagating. At the same time, a lot of research and experimentation was required to provide wild species with the correct type of soil, exposure, and access to moisture. Most of these plants have never been tended before and the only way to find out how they grow is by trial and error. The monsoon is the season for planting and also the time of year when the park is at its best, with lots of green foliage. In another few weeks, this enormous rock garden will start to turn brown and gold. During the driest months of winter and spring, many of the shrubs and trees shed their leaves while others will flower, like the endangered rohida or Marwar teak, which blooms in February–March with extravagant orange and yellow blossoms.

At the visitors centre, we are shown a display of rocks from different regions of Rajasthan, illustrating the geological diversity of this desert landscape. In addition to rhyolite, which we have just walked over, there is a whitish pegmatite embedded with large crystals and a darker gabbro, their differing colours and textures a result of the minerals they contain but also the conditions under which the molten magma cooked and cooled. Both dolerite and dolomite are on display as well as banded chert, each with its own origin story, recounting different episodes of the earth's formation.

Pranay Lal, author of *Indica*, is participating in the conference and he gives us an off-the-cuff lecture on different types of sandstone, which is Jodhpur's best-known rock, quarried throughout Rajasthan as building material. Explaining that the various shades of red and pink are a result of the mix of silica and oxides, he also points out a large trace fossil on a slab of sandstone found in a quarry 2 kilometres from here. The delicate outline of an aquatic plant, much like kelp, is preserved on the surface, reminding us that even as these sedimentary rocks were being created the first forms of multicellular life were also evolving, 635 million years ago.

Two hours later, about fifty participants gather for the first session of the conference, which is held at Chokhelao Mahal, one of several palaces within Mehrangarh. In his opening remarks, Pradip explains some of the history and challenges they faced while restoring Rao Jodha Park and he makes the point that projects like this are 'both symbolic and educational'. While demonstrating the possibility of bringing degraded landscapes back to life, the park also helps visitors of all ages understand and appreciate the unique features of the desert, from rocks and soil to botanical communities as well as insects, birds, and animals that share this space. It also proves that human beings can be responsible stewards of nature and preserve wild spaces, even within the confines of an ancient city that has stood here for half a millennium.

Noting that the Ecological Restoration Alliance represents a disparate group, with many different approaches and motives, Pradip jokes that they might be described as a 'lunatic fringe' taking on what may seem to be impossible projects. He also emphasizes the need to acknowledge that we have an imperfect understanding of how nature works. Restoring a landscape requires patience and a willingness to learn both from science and from the many ways a wild environment expresses itself.

Over the course of the next three days, many of these themes are explored by the different speakers, each of whom shares his or her experiences, ranging from a botanical rescue centre for endangered plants in the rainforests of Kerala to large-scale projects in which strip mines and industrial sites have been restored in Tamil Nadu and Maharashtra. One of the repeated refrains is that only the most degraded and abused landscapes are likely to be designated for ecological restoration.

The discussions include issues of land rights and community involvement, as well as relations with state forest departments and forest-dwelling communities, many of which have been displaced. One of the participants is undertaking a project to protect and revive the breeding habitat of hornbills in Arunachal Pradesh. Another is restoring wildlife corridors in different parts of the country that allow elephants to roam freely between one reserve forest and another. Some members of the alliance engage with village communities to restore small parcels of common land, which have been badly polluted and deforested. A few of the participants work as consultants to private landowners and corporations that want to create wild spaces on their properties.

Listening in on the conference as an independent observer gives me a fresh perspective on various approaches to environmental conservation and the debates surrounding complex ecological issues. It also makes me think about the meaning of wild spaces and the nuances of protecting and nurturing threatened habitats. Altogether, despite enormous challenges, the presentations and discussions leave me encouraged and cautiously hopeful, mostly because of the passion and commitment of individuals who have dedicated their lives to restoring and preserving our wild heritage.

∽

Following the success of Rao Jodha Desert Rock Park in Jodhpur, Pradip Krishen and his team were invited to undertake a similar restoration project in Jaipur. The municipal authorities initially proposed several sites, most of which were existing parks with formal flower beds, lawns, and ornamental trees. All of these were rejected and instead a neglected area of sand dunes was selected, in a northern suburb of the city. These 'obstruction dunes' were created years ago when sand blew in from the desert and was then blocked by a low line of foothills. Forming a series of corrugated ridges, with eroded troughs in between, the dunes were eventually covered with both native and invasive species, including the ubiquitous *Prosopis*. Before work on the park began, this area was used as a garbage dump, where pigs and other animals scavenged amidst heaps of refuse. Today, Kishan Bagh Sand Dunes Park is a verdant oasis within the city and the original ecology has been reestablished, enabling native species to reclaim the land.

'Roee' is a traditional Marwari term for this kind of habitat, an arid scrub jungle and mixed grassland that borders the true desert, which is referred to as 'thad' (from which the name Thar is derived). These colloquial expressions, still used by villagers today, were identified by Pradip and his team, as they tried to find descriptive names for marginal ecotones, often dismissively and generically referred to as 'wasteland'. Reviving indigenous names for threatened biomes is almost as important as restoring the native species that grow there.

I arrive at Kishan Bagh just as the sun appears over the Aravalli Range, some of the oldest mountains on earth. Three hundred kilometres north-east of Mehrangarh, this is a very different landscape. Dinkar Samore, a naturalist and guide, is waiting for me and we set off immediately, along the main trail, passing an interpretation centre thatched with kheemp, a tough desert plant with thin broom-like branches. Accompanying us is Mirchi, one of the resident dogs, who has a personality as peppery as her name. She leads the way and looks back at us impatiently when we pause along the trail. Our route is paved with slabs of rock that mark different stages of geological history—pale cream limestone progressing on to roseate shades of sandstone.

Dinkar shows me several local grasses that have been planted at Kishan Bagh, one of which is munj, with beautiful plumes that wave in the breeze, as white as egret feathers. On one of the long blades of munj grass, a bagworm has built its cocoon, using spines from a babool tree. This ingenious construction, which looks like a bundle of matchsticks, is made by caterpillars of the Psychidae family, which emerge as moths. The grass and shrubs host many insects, from grasshoppers to butterflies, which in turn attract birds. We see two species of bee-eaters, green and blue-tailed, as well as black drongos, and plenty of plain prinias. Eurasian collared doves are everywhere, as are common mynahs. Flocks of dusky crag martins skim through the air overhead. Mirchi, our canine escort, flushes a covey of grey francolins that burst out of the grass with a stutter of wings.

To protect the dunes from crumbling underfoot, raised stone walkways and wooden staircases have been constructed. These also allow small mammals and reptiles safe passage beneath. At one point, we see the tail of a grey mongoose disappearing into the grass as it ducks out of sight. Dinkar also spots an Indian fringe-fingered lizard, about 10 centimetres long, with black and yellow stripes on its back that extend along its tail. Watching us from the branches of shrubs are several Oriental garden lizards, the colour of sand. Kishan Bagh contains cobras, sand boas, and checkered keelbacks. Descending into the eroded channels between the dunes, we follow a dirt trail marked by numerous footprints, including those of jackals and jungle cats. Dinkar mentions that they sometimes find the pugmarks of leopards that live along the margins of the city.

One of the trees growing in Kishan Bagh is called kumatiyo, or the gum arabic tree. In addition to being a native species in Rajasthan, it grows throughout the Middle East and North Africa. Kumatiyo has finger-length clusters of white flowers and delicate, compound leaves. Its thorny spines are different from those on other Indian acacias, growing in groups of three, two of which point upwards, while the third, shaped like a raptor's talon, faces in the opposite direction.

Most of the trees in Kishan Bagh are still relatively small because restoration work began only five years ago, though there are a few larger trees that were here before, including one about 10 metres tall, with dense, dark foliage. Dinkar tells me it has two Hindi names—bandar ki roti (monkey's bread) and chudail papadi (witches' biscuit)—both of which refer to its round, flat seedpods, that turn a toasted brown when they are dry. Also known as the Indian elm, it has a shadowy, haunted appearance, even on a bright September morning.

Kishan Bagh opened in 2021 and Dinkar has been working here as a naturalist for only ten months. Before that, he was employed at WWF and at other conservation organizations. His home town is Alwar, 150 kilometres north-east of Jaipur, and he has always had a keen interest in nature and the outdoors. 'I enjoy working here,' he says, 'because it's not "species specific" conservation.' Instead of protecting natural habitat, merely because it supports an endangered animal, restoration projects like this take a more holistic approach in which every species matters. Kishan Bagh covers 64 hectares (158 acres) with several winding trails. Within an hour of dawn, the sun is intense and the temperature has risen by at least five degrees. In this season of rain, the folded contours of the dunes are deceptively green. During most of the year the grasses and shrubs turn subtle shades of gold and brown, the characteristic colours of a roee landscape.

In these surroundings, the city of Jaipur feels much farther away than it actually is. Open spaces like this inspire us to appreciate nature, not as a controlled and cultivated environment, but as an unrestrained and interconnected community of living things. The pale green foliage of the kumatiyo trees and the munj grass that fringe the dunes with white plumes—along with so many other plants that grow here in wild profusion—defy anyone to call this a wasteland.

6

THE WHITE BABBLER OF BANDHAVGARH

Forests are sometimes described as magical places but the true mysteries and marvels they contain are often commonplace things. After two hours of driving through Bandhavgarh Tiger Reserve, on an early January morning, we stop at a midway halt with food stalls, operated by local villagers, selling tea, Maggi noodles, samosas, and omelettes. We are at the western edge of the park, in Khitauli Zone, one of three areas open to tourists. At this point the trees give way to grasslands, beyond which lies a ragged patchwork of millet and mustard fields, fenced in with thorns and flimsy bamboo stockades, hardly adequate to keep wildlife from raiding the crops. The temperature is a few degrees above zero and tourists, drivers, and guides, bundled up in woollen hats, coats, and blankets, hurry across to order tea and breakfast. Remains of a twig fire smoulder near the stalls and several of us try to warm ourselves from the meagre heat rising out of the ashes. Winter mist cloaks the landscape though the sun is trying to break through.

When I get my tea in a clay kulhad, I hold it with both hands, hoping that some of the heat will escape into my numb fingers and revive circulation. About 20 metres away, a flock of jungle babblers are feeding on something that's been scattered on the ground, perhaps the crumbled remains from a packet of instant noodles. These birds are often called either seven sisters or seven brothers, but at least fourteen of them have congregated here. A mix of males and females, it is impossible to tell them apart as they squabble and swear at each other like a tetchy brood of irritable siblings. Jungle babblers are one of the most common birds in India's forests, but I've always been fascinated by their scruffy, gregarious behaviour and the seemingly menacing looks in their yellow-rimmed eyes. Evolution has deprived jungle babblers of bright plumage; they are a smudged, grey-brown, as if dusted with soot. As the flock fights over scraps on the ground, hissing at each other and flexing their wings in threatening gestures, I suddenly notice a very different bird in their midst.

The same size and shape as the others, its behaviour is equally quarrelsome but instead of having drab, grey feathers, it is almost entirely white. The contrast with the rest of the flock is so striking that I assume it must be a different species. But the bird is close enough for me to observe without binoculars and there's no mistaking *Turdoides striata*. A mutation in the babbler's genes, known as leucism, has turned its feathers a pale cream instead of the normal pigmentation. It is like seeing a phantom in the middle of the flock, something mysterious and inexplicable, conjured up by nature's sleight of hand. Retrieving my camera from the jeep, I take a few hasty pictures before the bird flies off on stubby, fluttering wings, disappearing amongst the lower branches of a sal tree and into the forest beyond.

So called, 'freaks of nature' have always intrigued and enchanted human beings. One of the ironies of our fascination with wildlife is that amidst a panoply of pigments in the jungle what captures our imagination, more often than not, is the absence of colour, whether it is the black coat of a melanistic panther or the white hide of an albino stag.

Bandhavgarh is one of the oldest national parks in India, established in 1968. Formerly a hunting preserve of the maharaja of Rewa, it lies in the eastern part of the Vindhya Range in Madhya Pradesh. In 1951, Maharaja Martand Singh, the last ruler of Rewa, learned of a white tiger cub in his forests and had it captured. This tiger, named Mohan, was raised on the palace grounds and became the progenitor of an extensive line of white tigers that were bred in captivity and are now found in zoos in many parts of the world. The recessive gene that turned Mohan white was passed on through various tigresses with whom he mated.

Despite popular misconceptions, white tigers are not albinos and they have black stripes but instead of being a fiery orange, their coats are the colour of snow. Leucism does not affect a tiger's eyesight, though their irises are a pale blue, green, or amber colour with black pupils. Because of inbreeding, many white tigers suffer from genetic infirmities. By some estimates there are more than 200 white tigers in captivity around the world. The German–American magicians and entertainers, Siegfried and Roy, were famous for featuring white tigers and lions as part of their extravagant nightclub act in Las Vegas. Eventually, though, one of the tigers grabbed Roy by the neck and dragged him off stage. The magician was severely injured but survived, though this incident brought down the curtain on their show.

In many ways, it seems almost inevitable that Mohan's descendant, several generations removed from Rewa's jungles, would respond in this way to the stress and indignities of being paraded in front of an audience, night after night, and forced to perform unnatural acts for the amusement of human beings.

Showmen like Siegfried and Roy have turned white tigers into a grotesque spectacle that inflicts human fetishes and fantasies on these rare and beautiful creatures. Seeing the white babbler in Bandhavgarh, I am spellbound by its unique colouration but, at the same time, I remind myself that there is nothing inherently mysterious or magical about this bird. It is only a genetic quirk that makes it appear so different.

~

Hashim Tyabji is my host in Bandhavgarh, where he has a home in the village of Pathor, on the periphery of the tiger reserve. We have known each other, off and on, for roughly fifty years, since 1973, when our two schools competed in athletic meets in Dehradun and Mussoorie. Hashim often likes to recall that he 'thrashed' me in the 400 metres, while I maintain a somewhat different memory of that race. Nevertheless, we both share a keen interest in wildlife and wild places, though Hashim has spent many more years than I have in close proximity with tigers and other forest creatures.

His house in Pathor is a simple yet elegant bungalow on about 2 hectares (5 acres) of land. A grove of stately sal and mahua trees grow on the property, as well as a tall haldu in front of the house, while thickets of bamboo enclose the backyard. The spacious veranda overlooks a large field of wild grass, mostly kans, some of which has been cut for thatch. In the flower beds next to the house, a couple of common tiger butterflies have settled on a rattlepod plant that has gone to seed. Common tigers share the same rich, russet colouring and black stripes as their feline namesakes. Hashim explains that tigers, like most brush-footed butterflies, ingest alkaloids from *Crotolaria* and similar plants. These chemicals give them a bad smell and taste that repels predators. At the same time, male butterflies also use the alkaloids to generate pheromones to lure their mates. In this way, the host plants provide the butterflies with both a means of protection and procreation.

In the distance, through winter haze, I can see the ruins of Bandhavgarh Fort, silhouetted on a broad hill at the centre of the tiger reserve. As the sun dips towards the horizon, Hashim and I set off for a walk along the edge of the forest. Red-rumped swallows and dusky crag martins are dive-bombing insects in the knee-high grass. Heading out the gate, we follow a dirt track running parallel to a wooded ridge that is technically part of the core area of the reserve, though it is used by villagers for grazing cattle and collecting firewood. Just beyond the boundary of his property, Hashim shows me where a tiger killed a cow three years ago. Not far from the path is a shallow, rocky ravine in which the victim's bleached skull remains.

'I put up an expensive trail camera on that tree over there, to try and get a shot of the tiger,' Hashim says, pointing with his stick. 'He approached the kill from this side and when the flash went off, the tiger must have attacked the camera and ripped it loose. I don't know what he did with it. Though I searched everywhere, I never found it.'

Most of the forest here is sal. Much of it is degraded and full of invasive lantana, which chokes out native plants, especially after there is a fire. Though the trees themselves look healthy, Hashim predicts they may not survive because the average rainfall here has dropped from 1,000 millimetres a year to roughly 800 millimetres, which means a greater risk of wildfires and less possibility that seeds will germinate and take root.

Continuing along the dusty path, we can see an assortment of tracks, mostly chital and wild pigs, but also tiger and leopard pugmarks. Hashim puzzles over one set of prints, wondering if they are dogs or maybe wolves. Another, with an elongated pad and small, splayed toes, looks as if it might be a porcupine or possibly a ratel. Many of the tracks have been obscured by the hooves of goats and cattle, as well as human footprints. At night, once the villagers and their livestock have retreated, this path becomes a thoroughfare for nocturnal creatures.

By now, the setting sun has turned the western sky a brassy ochre. Simultaneously, a near-full moon rises through a cross-hatching of branches. The temperature has dropped noticeably and the shadows of the sal trees coalesce into deeper darkness. A red junglefowl is crowing somewhere up the ridge as we turn around to head back home, after having walked a couple of kilometres. Minutes later, to our right, a langur gives an alarm call, a hoarse cough that is repeated several times. The monkey may have spotted a leopard or jungle cat but the only animals we meet are a sounder of wild pigs, one of which snorts at us belligerently, as it moves off.

Returning to the house, we settle down by a fire outdoors, the flames providing both warmth and light but also drawing us into a circle of stories. Hashim recounts how he first came to Pathor, thirty-four years ago, while conducting a bird survey in Bandhavgarh. As soon as he saw this place, he knew that he wanted to settle here.

'I had very little money at the time, so after purchasing the land, I planned the house carefully, calculating everything down to the last rupee. I was architect and engineer, as well as one of the labourers too,' he says. 'When I finished, less than a hundred bricks were left over.'

Hashim is one of the pioneers of wildlife tourism in India. Straight out of university, he joined Tiger Tops and Mountain Travels, working in Nepal, Kashmir, and Ladakh. His first visit to Bandhavgarh was to help create a tented resort for the fledgling Bandhavgarh Jungle Camp, which occupied the maharaja of Rewa's hunting lodge and its extensive grounds. The former rulers of Rewa were inveterate hunters and they believed that each heir to the throne had to shoot 108 tigers (being an auspicious number). But after Independence, Maharaja Martand Singh persuaded the government to turn Bandhavgarh into a national park.

'When I first came here in the 1980s, there was nothing, except for a tea shop and the old lodge, which only had four guest rooms. Now there must be seventy tourist resorts and homestays in Bandhavgarh. The whole place is unrecognizable.'

After working for several years as head of operations for Tiger Tops India, Hashim ventured out on his own, forming a company with partners and building two jungle resorts—Baghvan in Pench and Forsyth Lodge near Satpura Tiger Reserve.

'People said those projects would never succeed because Pench and Satpura had very few tigers at the time. Tourists will only go where tigers can be seen,' he says. 'But both places had a good prey base and after we and Madhya Pradesh Tourism built our lodges, the number of visitors grew and tiger numbers increased.'

One of Hashim's firmest convictions is that wildlife tourism, if conducted responsibly, supports conservation by creating employment and commercial opportunities for local people. Providing them with a strong financial stake in the business of conservation mitigates the 'cost of conservation' that local communities bear. Forest department officials also realize the benefits of tourism and inevitably the national parks are protected and managed with greater commitment and consistency. Both Pench and Satpura are now designated tiger reserves, each with a healthy population of large predators. Of course, Hashim is the first to acknowledge that tourism must be contained within strict guidelines and community involvement is only part of the conservation equation. He believes that India's success in saving its tigers is primarily the result of the Wild Life Protection Act of 1972, and the launch of Project Tiger in 1973, both of which were driven by Indira Gandhi's commitment to wildlife conservation. This nationwide effort was supported by extensive scientific research, as well as advocacy and lobbying by NGOs, and the efforts of many individuals and institutions.

'Ultimately, the original nine tiger reserves were created and sustained through the heroic field protection of forest department staff in the face of intense local hostility,' Hashim declares.

When I ask him whether some of the wildlife resorts need to be as luxurious as they are, with swimming pools and other five-star amenities, he shakes his head impatiently.

'You're asking the wrong question,' he says. 'The problem isn't whether it's high-end or low-end tourism. It's the approach you take and the attitude of the tourists that you bring here. If they're genuinely interested in wildlife and understand how to behave in the forest, then there's nothing wrong with giving them a swimming pool to cool off in during the middle of the day. But if they just want to party and picnic, like many of them do, then we shouldn't cater to them.'

Aside from being ecologically responsible, Hashim's projects are based on the underlying premise of creating employment opportunities in the local community, so that conservation becomes part of the culture. Though he now claims to be semi-retired, Hashim is still actively involved with the Snow Leopard Lodges at Ulley and Mangyu in Ladakh. He and his partners have also taken up the management of a resort in Gujarat near the Wild Ass Sanctuary in the Little Rann of Kutch.

Though he travels constantly, Bandhavgarh remains home for Hashim and it is these forests that provide him with a sense of personal sanctuary. For a number of years, he was the honorary wildlife warden at Bandhavgarh, which gave him the freedom to enter the reserve whenever he wished. He still knows many of the forest guards by name and keeps track of what is happening in the park. In 1994, he published a pocket guide to Bandhavgarh, which includes a list of flora and fauna found here. Being the grand-nephew of Salim Ali, Hashim has always been a devoted birdwatcher, and something of a purist. He laughs when he tells me a story about going to see monal pheasants in Uttarakhand. A number of other birdwatchers were there, at a place called Chopta. Most of them were armed with cameras, while he was carrying only a pair of binoculars.

'We were clearly not on the same page. None of them could understand why I wasn't taking photographs,' he tells me, then adds. 'Most people think of birdwatching as something you do occasionally. But, for me, I'm watching birds all the time!'

Of course, wildlife photography is a form of observation but to really understand and recognize a bird or animal fully, we must study it closely over time and acquire not just a nice photograph but knowledge of its morphology, behaviour, and habitat. When I mention that I recently read that he once helped Billy Arjan Singh get a photograph of Tara, the tigress raised at Tiger Haven, Hashim nods and smiles.

'I was in Nepal, at Tiger Tops, in those days. Chuck McDougal (his boss and an authority on tigers) sent me to Dudhwa with one of his cameras. It was an old Nikon F1 with a motor drive that made a lot of noise, so we covered it with a tea cozy to muffle the sound. I spent four weeks sitting up in a machan with Billy over buffalo baits. We got pictures of a tigress, but it wasn't Tara. Her markings were different.'

In some ways, Hashim's house in Pathor is similar to Tiger Haven, being situated at the edge of a national park where the boundaries between human habitation and wild spaces become blurred. He often hears tigers and leopards calling at night and sees them along the edge of his property. Wild pigs and chital regularly pass through, as well as rarer creatures. Hashim recounts how he and one of his friends were sitting exactly where we are now, in the front yard of the house, when suddenly a small Indian civet appeared and circled in front of them, unconcerned by their presence.

As much as he feels a part of the forest, Hashim also connects with the people of Pathor. Many of the villagers are members of the Gond community, as well as some buffalo herders that were resettled here after being moved out of the tiger reserve. Hashim employs a man named Rakesh as a caretaker for the house. He explains that when he first came to Pathor, Rakesh's grandfather started working for him.

'Gulab Singh was originally from this area but his family had migrated to Assam to work on a tea garden. When he retired, he returned to Pathor. Gulab was a Gond Thakur and considered something of a medicine man with a healing touch. His specialty was backaches and joint pains and he cured several of my guests.'

Gazing into the fire for a moment, Hashim continues.

'When Gulab Singh died, one of the strangest things happened. I had built quarters for him behind the house, at the back of the property. He got sick while I was away travelling somewhere. Lying on his deathbed, Gulab Singh kept saying that he had to give me the key to the house. "Hakim ko chabbi dena hai." Having worked in the tea gardens, that's what he called me, "Hakim". Anyway, he died at about three in the afternoon and while the villagers were preparing his body for cremation, a large tiger suddenly showed up and sat down about 30 metres from Gulab Singh's quarters. This tiger was the dominant male in the area and usually kept his distance from human settlements. But there he was! I was told about it later and the villagers were convinced that when Gulab Singh died, his spirit entered the tiger who guarded the house until I returned.'

∽

The forest department headquarters in Bandhavgarh is located at Tala and all of the jeep safaris must get their entry permits from here, as well as a GPS monitor that is used to keep track of any vehicles entering the reserve. At 6.30 a.m., the complex is busy despite heavy fog and bitterly cold temperatures. At least forty

Maruti Gypsies are lined up, as if for the start of a rally. Altogether, 280 vehicles are licensed by the forest department as safari vehicles, though less than half that number are permitted to enter the park at any one time. The total area of Bandhavgarh is 1,161 square kilometres, including the core and buffer zones, but tourists are only allowed in about 100 square kilometres, divided into three separate zones.

This morning my safari is in the main Tala Zone. Just after 7 a.m., I set off with a driver named Rajkumar. My guide is Sadhari, a young woman who has been working at the reserve for only three months. Trained by the forest department, she has memorized a standard fact sheet, informing me that Bandhavgarh has the highest density of tigers in India, with more than 110 animals altogether. As we pass through the gate, she also explains that there are three kinds of deer in this forest—spotted deer or chital, sambar, and barking deer. When we cross a shallow stream, Sadhari tells me that this water flows down from the hill, where the fort is located. 'Bhagwan ke charan choo ke aati hai (It comes here after touching God's feet),' she says. The springs that feed this stream emerge near a reclining statue of Vishnu, popularly known as Shesh Shaiya because the deity's head is shaded by a multi-headed cobra's hood. Archaeologists estimate that the idol is more than 1,000 years old, dating back to the time of the Kalachuri dynasty. Water from the spring collects in a tank in front of the statue, which is roughly 12 metres long. When filled to the brim it appears as if Vishnu is floating on the water. Recently restored by the Indian National Trust for Art and Cultural Heritage (INTACH), this statue lies within Tala Zone but when I ask Rajkumar if we can see it he explains that a tree has fallen across the road and the site is currently closed to tourists.

The presence of archaeological sites inside Bandhavgarh isn't surprising because this region was obviously inhabited for almost a millennium and served as an artery for commerce. From the eighth century, the fort was controlled by the Kalachuri dynasty, until it passed on to their successors, the Vaghelas, who ruled from the thirteenth to the early fourteenth centuries. Just as wildlife is protected within these forests, so is human history preserved in abandoned caves and ruined temples which now provide shelter for tigers and other animals, including bats, snakes, sloth bears, and wild dogs.

The first part of our drive takes us through hilly terrain, the rough forest track climbing over rocky ridges and descending into moist ravines, full of ferns and creepers. Though we see fresh tiger pugmarks, there is no sign of the predators themselves and no alarm calls can be heard. We come upon scattered herds of chital, a few wild pigs, and langurs, but no other mammals.

Eventually, the hills give way to open grasslands, where a group of langurs and chital are basking in the sun. By now the mist has begun to dissipate and the slanting rays illuminate the pale fur on the monkey's heads, as if they are crowned by halos. Some of the chital stags have velvet on their antlers. This peaceable, harmonious scene appears as if in soft focus, two very different species mingling with each other in the welcome warmth of a new day. Sadhari is moved to tell me that, 'Chital and langurs are good friends. They help each other. The langurs feed in the trees and drop fruit on the ground for the deer.'

One of the remarkable sights in the forest are large strangler vines, known as gulhari that grow in amongst the sal trees, spreading from one to the next. These woody lianas wrap themselves around the tree trunks like pythons. As the host species grows, it chokes itself and eventually dies. Many of the vines must be well over a hundred years old and the sal trees they killed have long since disappeared, leaving the gulhari dangling in elaborate, sinuous shapes.

When we cross a rocky outcropping, Sadhari points out the stark white trunk and limbs of a ghost tree. Locally known as gum karaya, its sticky sap is used as a binder to make laddoos and other sweets, though it is also believed to have medicinal properties and serves as a laxative. Much of this area is covered with a single species of bamboo, *Dendrocalamus strictus*, commonly known as male or Calcutta bamboo. The most widespread species in India, it is used for construction and manufacturing paper. Like all bamboos, these giant grasses die after they bloom and only regenerate from seeds. Calcutta bamboo undergoes a gregarious flowering every thirty to forty-five years, though not all of the clumps die at once. Some of the bamboo in the reserve has recently flowered but most of the thickets are green.

Tala Zone has plenty of water and sections of the lowlands are marshy, where several streams flow down from the Bandhavgarh plateau. There is also a spring in the middle of a broad meadow where water seeps out of the soil to form a shallow pond. At one place, we pass an ancient cave shelter, hewn out of sandstone. Known as the Badi Gufa, or large cave, this shelter lies near a turnoff leading up to the fort and the Shesh Shaiya sculpture. Now that the mist has evaporated, I can see the enormous flat topped hill rising 374 metres above the lower forests and grasslands. The plateau where the fort is situated covers 94 hectares (232 acres). To the west, is a second, smaller ridge almost as high, separated by a gap of about a kilometre.

On the steep cliffs below the fort, Rajkumar points out white streaks on the rocks where a few slender-billed vultures are nesting. As the air grows warmer, we see a pair of them wheeling overhead in search of carrion below. In his guidebook, Hashim describes the history and mythology of this landscape.

> 'Bandhavgarh' literally means the fort of the Brother and one of the most intriguing questions confronting one is the curious fact of its existence in this remote wilderness, famous through the centuries only as a place for hunting. Legend has it that Lord Rama, seeking to secure his southern borders after his triumphal return from Lanka climbed to the top of the highest hill in the region and, stamping down upon it, created both the plateau of Bandhavgarh as also the surrounding marshes. This he then proceeded to hand over to his brother (Bandhu) Laxman to guard and to protect thus earning the fort its present name.

After leaving the grasslands behind us and entering a moist forest, with a meandering stream to our right, we come upon a stand of tall Arjuna trees which share their name with the hero of the Mahabharata. A sacred tree, these terminalias are mentioned in the Rig Veda. The name Arjuna means 'bright' or 'white', which may be a reference to the pale cream colour of its flowers. The smooth, buttressed trunks which rise 30 metres overhead, are a ruddy grey colour. Arjuna's bark is used for medicinal purposes, primarily to treat heart and liver diseases.

Though we have seen relatively few animals, our drive through the forests of Tala is memorable for the variety of terrain and habitats—dry, rocky escarpments, grass-fringed swamps and mixed forests of sal and other trees. By eleven o'clock, we exit the reserve and Rajkumar drives me across to a homestay near the main gate which is owned by Satyendra Tiwari and his wife, Kay Hassall Tiwari. They have invited Hashim and me for brunch. After the bone-chilling drive in an open Gypsy, it is a relief to sit in the sun in their courtyard, where a pair of scaly-breasted munias are nesting amidst the magenta blossoms of a bougainvillea vine.

Satyendra, a naturalist and photographer, has been here since 1990 when he started leading tours in Bandhavgarh. Kay joined him in 1993. A wildlife artist, she paints wonderfully life-like watercolours of tigers and other animals. Her artwork illustrates Hashim's guidebook. The Tiwari's homestay caters mostly to nature enthusiasts and photographers from abroad. Tomorrow a group of nine guests are arriving from the UK and they will stay for ten days, going out on safari every morning and evening.

When Hashim joins us, the conversation turns to the white tigers of Rewa. Though it is often said that Mohan, the first white cub, was found in Bandhavgarh, I learn that he was actually captured in another forest to the east, in what is now Sanjay-Dubri Tiger Reserve. Satyendra tells me that he once researched the export of white tigers from India and discovered that in the 1950s the maharaja was shipping them to America for ₹10,000 apiece. The other story he recounts is about Marshal Tito of Yugoslavia, who visited India in the 1960s, when he and Jawaharlal Nehru were leaders of the non-aligned movement. Nehru was eager to show off a white tiger, recently acquired from Rewa for the Delhi Zoo. When he took Tito across to have a look at it, the Yugoslav president was so impressed he immediately said that he wanted to take the tiger back home with him. Despite this awkward request, diplomacy prevailed and another of Mohan's white offspring was subsequently shipped to Belgrade.

In his book, *The Wild Life of India,* E. P. Gee has an account of the white tigers of Rewa and describes how he visited Govindgarh, a summer palace where the tigers were kept and bred. Mohan mated with several captive tigresses and the resulting litters were a mix of white and ordinary cubs. Eventually, feeding the tigers a diet of fresh mutton put a strain on the maharaja's budget and he was eager to sell them to support the project. Gee describes how the government and Rewa had protracted negotiations regarding permission to export the cubs. At one point, in frustration, the maharaja threatened to release the white tigers back into the jungle. Finally, it was agreed that the government and Rewa would share the costs of maintaining and breeding white tigers, as well as the revenue from their sale abroad. A pair of white tigers were housed in Delhi Zoo and two others were sold to the Calcutta Zoo, while Mohan and another female remained in Govindgarh. Since then, breeding white tigers has become a profitable enterprise, both in zoos and private menageries. However, efforts to reintroduce them into the wild remain restricted to a White Tiger Safari Park set up near Govindgarh.

~

Wild elephants disappeared from most of Central India two or three centuries ago, though they feature in many of the wall paintings in rock shelters at places like Bhimbetka. It is difficult to say definitively why they left but it was probably on account of habitat loss with the spread of agriculture. Climatic or ecological changes like a drought or possibly the mass flowering and death of bamboo could also have been the cause. Under pressure, the elephants probably migrated to large tracts of forests that now lie within the states of Chhattisgarh and Jharkhand.

In 2014, however, elephants returned to the Vindhya Range for the first time in recent memory, entering Bandhavgarh as well as Kanha and Sanjay-Dubri Tiger Reserves. Altogether about fifty animals arrived unexpectedly, taking up residence here and causing considerable damage to nearby farms. Though a few earlier instances of elephants straying through the region had been reported, these new arrivals seem to be here to stay. More than likely, they have moved back into Central India for the same reason they originally left, because of deforestation and conflict with villagers in their former home territory.

Elephas maximus is a restless species that requires plenty of space to roam. As forests shrink, herds are forced to migrate from one region to another. The primary strategy in elephant conservation today is to preserve and restore corridors that allow herds to migrate between one protected area and another. The Wildlife Trust of India has initiated a National Elephant Corridors Project dedicated to identifying, protecting, and restoring the ecology in marginal lands that elephants traverse. This project, operating mostly in Assam and Kerala as well as Uttarakhand, also provides assistance and reimbursement to villagers whose crops and homes are damaged by transient herds. One of the challenges of elephant conservation is that when a forest becomes degraded, the elephants are forced to wander further and further in search of forage and water. In a well-protected jungle, their home range can be as little as 250 square kilometres but in fragmented and badly denuded forests, they can cover as much as 3,500 square kilometres. A precarious balance also exists between the number of elephants in a particular region and the supply of vegetation. If herds increase beyond the carrying capacity of a forest, elephants can decimate the trees, shrubs, and grasses on which they depend.

Bandhavgarh, with its wetlands and bamboo jungles, is obviously an attractive habitat for displaced elephants. However, their presence poses a dilemma for the Madhya Pradesh Forest Department which has never had to manage these large herbivores until now. It also creates an added burden on farming communities that already have to contend with crop damage from smaller species like wild pigs and deer. Hashim estimates that roughly seventy elephants are now living in this part of the state.

My second morning in Bandhavgarh, we come upon the wreckage left by solitary tusker, currently living in Khitauli Zone. He has ripped apart a thicket of bamboo to get at the tender shoots and leaves, casting aside whatever he finds unappetizing. His footprints are clearly visible at the side of the road, large saucer-like impressions in the dust. Fibrous clods of dung also mark his passage and at one place he has torn a branch off an amla tree and tossed it in the middle of the road, so that our Gypsy has to make a detour. My guide this morning is Mahadev, an experienced man in his forties, who tells me that this elephant is known to confront vehicles and become aggressive. A short while later, we meet another jeep coming in the opposite direction. The driver and his excited passengers tell us that they saw the elephant a short while ago and he mock charged them before moving off into the forest. Our driver, Chintu Yadav, immediately takes us to the place where the elephant was seen but all we find is more dung and broken branches.

The fog is even thicker than it was yesterday, and visibility is no more than 50 metres. Nevertheless, we see plenty of chital and sambar, including a hind and her young fawn that stare at us from within the shelter of a bamboo grove. At a crossroads, Mahadev points out a large mahua tree that has been clawed by tigers, its bark raked with deep gashes about 2 to 3 metres off the ground.

Further on, we crest a low hill where broad margins of grass and ber bushes extend along either side of the road. Here the fog is even more dense because of a waterhole nearby. The parallel tyre tracks ahead of us fade into a bleak white cloud. Suddenly, to our left, we hear the alarm call of a sambar—a sharp, honking sound. I cannot see the deer, which is hidden in the trees. Chintu stops the jeep and we wait expectantly, until the sambar calls again.

A faint movement is visible on the road ahead of us, a shadow in the mist.

Seconds later, I see the blurred outline of a large animal come into view. A tiger is walking towards us. He is an adult male in his prime. Standing at the back of the vehicle, I hold my breath. At first, the tiger appears colourless in the fog, black stripes on his face and forelegs framing a white forehead as well as a pale patch on his chest. As he draws closer, the smouldering orange of his flame-coloured fur becomes visible. The tiger can obviously see us in the middle of the road but he doesn't break stride, lifting one huge forepaw after the other and advancing steadily towards us, less than 20 metres away.

'Back up,' Mahadev tells Chintu, who puts the jeep in reverse and glances over his shoulder to steer as we retreat along the rutted road. Untroubled by the noise of the engine, the tiger keeps coming, his watchful eyes fixed on us.

Moments later, the huge animal moves to his right, stepping from one tyre track to the other, before leaving the road to stop and sniff the lower branches of a ber bush. After this, he appears to snarl, curling his lips and revealing sharp canines as well as his rough, pink tongue. Though his expression looks menacing, it is not a sign of aggression. This behaviour is known as a flehmen response. Like cobras and many other animals, tigers use a vomeronasal organ, located on their upper palate, to help them analyse a scent. This allows them to process a variety of information, such as the identity of other tigers that have marked their territory with a spray of urine and, if it is a tigress, whether she is in oestrus or not. While it is impossible to know how much a tiger can comprehend about a potential challenger or mate from its scent, he clearly relies on it to heighten his awareness and guide his instincts.

After the tiger turns and sprays the bush with his own urine, I expect him to move away from the road and into the forest. Instead, he returns to the tyre tracks and proceeds towards us once again. As soon as he comes within 10 metres of the jeep, Chintu reverses another 50 metres, while the tiger keeps on coming. Fortunately, no one is behind us, and no other jeeps are in sight. This manoeuvre is repeated at least ten times.

By now, the sambar has stopped calling and forest is silent, muffled by the fog. The grass and leaves are wet with dew and the tiger makes no sound at all as he advances towards us. It is like watching a prolonged pantomime. At one place, Chintu has to back up a low hill and manoeuvre around a sharp turn at the top. The vehicle rocks from side to side as we negotiate the incline. For a moment, I worry that the Gypsy might tip over into a ditch but Chintu keeps us on track. Meanwhile, the tiger continues pursuing us without any sign of hesitation or impatience.

The big male has been following us persistently for more than fifteen minutes. Though his behaviour isn't overtly threatening and the expression on his face remains impassive, I begin to feel anxious. Each time he comes closer, I can see the amber colour of his eyes punctuated by black pupils. The markings on his face are symmetrical, like delicate arabesques tattooed above raised eyebrows, with a wishbone stripe on either cheek. His forehead is daubed with black lines, like broad brush strokes, and the white patches above his eyes give way to a saffron crown. As he flicks his ears, I can see two white spots on the back of each. The stripes on his shoulders seem to ripple as the muscles under his taut hide flex with each step he takes.

Finally, after we have reversed for almost a kilometre, the tiger casually steps off the road once again, striding to our left. As he passes less than 10 metres away, we get a clear view of his striped flanks and long tail before he vanishes into the mist, a bold and confident predator who betrays no further interest in us.

Seeing a tiger like this at close quarters, for an extended period of time, is unusual and exciting, even for Mahadev and Chintu. They tell me that this is the dominant male in Khitauli. He is called 'Chota Bhim' (Small Bhim) because his father, a legendary Bandhavgarh tiger, was named Bhim, after the largest and most powerful of the Pandava heroes in the Mahabharata.

We have been fortunate to spend more than a quarter of an hour alone in the company of this magnificent creature. For the most part, the tiger seemed to ignore us, though I could tell he was intensely aware of our presence, even if he didn't recognize us as a threat. From a young age, he must have become habituated to the sight, smell, and sound of safari vehicles in his domain. The tiger's bold and purposeful manner proves that here in this reserve he has nothing to fear. Though India's tigers remain an endangered species, they are no longer facing imminent extinction, thanks to the vigilant efforts of forest department officers and staff, along with conservationists, who have been fighting to protect this species for the past fifty years.

7

CARBON FOOTPRINTS

Long ago, I remember reading a story about how oil was discovered in Assam. Though probably apocryphal, there was an appealing simplicity to the tale, as if it were a children's fable. One day, a working elephant wandered off into the forest near a lumber camp where it was employed moving heavy logs with its trunk and tusks. Eventually, when the elephant returned, after having shirked his duties for most of the day, the handlers noticed that his feet were coated in a black, tar-like substance. Not knowing what it was, they retraced the path that the tusker had taken through the jungle and discovered a large quantity of crude oil oozing out of the ground.

Driving into Digboi, I can smell the sooty, sulphurous odour of the oil refinery well before its chimneys come into view. The birthplace of India's petroleum industry, Digboi is a small yet busy town along the railway line between Tinsukia and Ledo on the border with Arunachal Pradesh. This remote corner of Assam has significant deposits of carbon fuels that were first exploited by the Assam Railways and Trading Company in the late nineteenth century. More than likely, the allegorical elephant mentioned above was laying sleepers for a broad-gauge line that was being built to extract coal from open-cast mines near Ledo. After oil was discovered, the first well was dug in 1889 and the original refinery was commissioned at Digboi in 1901.

While it doesn't feel like a boom town any more, there was a time when Digboi would have attracted all kinds of prospectors searching for black gold. Today, it is more like a corporate township, with walled compounds and bungalows set amidst the lush green hills of north-eastern Assam. A sign outside the gate of the Digboi Club announces that it is celebrating its centenary and I can easily imagine tea planters and oil men from the past, sitting down together in the evenings for a generous dose of quinine, laced with gin, to keep malaria and other fevers at bay.

Digboi's refinery is one of the oldest still operating, anywhere in the world, though it now processes far fewer barrels of crude oil a day than it did at the height of production, in the 1940s. Nevertheless, Oil India Limited (OIL), the government corporation that oversees production, is clearly expanding operations. As we set off from Digboi for Dehing Patkai National Park, I can see that a new pipeline is being laid alongside the road. Much of Assam's oil and coal still lies buried beneath its forests. And in case anyone needs reminding, these finite energy reserves, formed out of vegetation that decomposed millions of years ago, are now the primary source of greenhouse emissions that cause climate change. At the same time, the shrinking rainforests serve as carbon sinks, absorbing carbon dioxide (CO_2) from the atmosphere. The disturbing ironies of our dependence on fossil fuels and what this means for conservation, particularly in an oil-and-coal-producing region of Assam, suggests a discouraging cycle of destruction and a bleak future for the few wild spaces that remain. The moral of this fable is that if an elephant steps in it, there will be serious consequences.

∽

Manash Pratim, the naturalist accompanying me on my travels in Assam, is a genial, soft-spoken young man of twenty-nine, with a neatly trimmed beard and attentive eyes. Born in Tinsukia, 50 kilometres north-west of Digboi, Manash is exceptionally knowledgeable about the birdlife of this region. While studying geography at Tinsukia College, he was inspired and mentored by Professor Ranjan Kumar Das, an ornithologist who specializes in grassland birds. Hooked on birdwatching, Manash began working as a freelance guide for several years. Then, in October 2022, he and four partners, including Binanda Hatibaruah, one of the foremost birders in the region, formed a company called Wild Feathers, specializing in birdwatching tours. They operate mainly in Assam and Arunachal Pradesh, where avian enthusiasts from all over India and other parts of the world come to see rare species found nowhere else on earth. Wild Feathers runs a rustic resort near Tinsukia, with four cottages, called the Maguri Eco Camp. Runap Gogoi, the manager, joins us on the trip and is learning to be a guide. The third member of our party, also a birder, is Pallul Hazarika, who drives the vehicle I've hired.

Dehing Patkai is one of India's newest national parks and was only notified in 2021. Before that it was designated as a wildlife sanctuary and elephant reserve by the Assam Forest Department in 2004. Its name comes from the Dehing River, which flows through the Patkai Hills along the edge of Arunachal Pradesh and Myanmar. Roughly 230 square kilometres in size, Dehing Patkai contains sections of the largest surviving lowland rainforest in Northeast India. Abundant in birdlife, it serves as a refuge for wild elephants, clouded leopards, and primates like pig-tailed macaques, capped langurs, and hoolock gibbons.

At Soraipung forest village, next to the park gate, we meet our guide, Bijay Panika, a local resident and experienced birder. After driving a short distance into the park, we get down from our vehicle and enter the jungle through a tunnel of creepers. Bijay leads the way into a humid green sanctum, where I can almost feel the plants growing in around me. No direct sunlight penetrates the thick layers of leaves. Reaching a narrow clearing, we can hear birdcalls from all sides, though each of these songsters is hidden from sight.

A loud cackle, about 30 metres away, signals the presence of a grey peacock-pheasant. These large birds, slightly bigger than a chicken, are relatively common but virtually impossible to see. On earlier visits to the Northeast, I have spent frustrating hours pursuing their calls, without spotting a feather. Though not as brightly coloured as its namesake, the male peacock-pheasant's tail and wings are ornately patterned with oval ocelli, or eyespots, of iridescent purple and green. Females are a brownish grey with similar but muted markings. A tufted crest droops forward over their beaks. Bijay whispers that this is a place where he has seen pheasants many times before. Though we wait silently for twenty minutes, the cackling grows fainter as the bird moves away through the rainforest's matted undergrowth.

For most of the morning, we continue birdwatching on foot. Along the corridor formed by the forest road we spot more than fifty species, including a red-headed trogon that flies furtively through the lower branches of trees from one sheltered perch to the next. Its crimson head and pink belly stand out brightly in the leafy arcades. Small niltavas, chestnut-bellied nuthatches, pygmy blue flycatchers, rufous woodpeckers, and scarlet minivets, appear and disappear faster than Manash and Bijay can identify them. One of the most spectacular birds is the sultan tit with its black jacket, bright yellow crest, and matching underbelly. It joins mixed flocks of other small birds that hunt for insects in an agitated feeding frenzy.

At several places, I notice fresh clods of elephant dung on the road but when I ask Bijay if there is any danger, he seems unconcerned, saying it is only the solitary males that we need to worry about. The herds of females and young will move off into the forest if they hear us coming. There is plenty for them to feed on, including wild bananas and thickets of bamboo as well as otenga trees, which are laden with lumpy, round fruit, known as elephant apples. Another tree that Bijay identifies, with clusters of round fruit, is called bandar dima, which means monkey's eggs. A short while later, we hear a branch snap above us and Bijay points out a capped langur high up in the canopy. It is difficult to see, even with binoculars, because the foliage is so thick.

One of the tallest trees in these rainforests is hollong, which is the state tree of Assam and Arunachal Pradesh. It grows to a height of 30 metres with a straight, unbranched trunk and a high crown of broad leaves. Manash shows me one of the hollong seeds lying on the ground, about the size of a marble with long, propeller-like wings. Hollong is considered sacred by some communities in Assam and its wax-like resin is collected and used to make oil and soap. Manash says that the timber is not particularly valuable, though it was used for railway sleepers in the past and is sometimes cut into planks or beams for house construction. More often, hollong is turned into plywood.

Having grown up in these jungles, Bijay knows the local names and uses for many of the rainforest flora. Pointing out a hingoli tree, with delicate sprays of white flowers, he explains that its seeds can be roasted and taste like almonds. Another tree that he identifies as khukan is shaped like a large parasol with pendant leaves and clusters of fruit that attract hornbills. Gaan khoshu, an elephant ear plant, has edible roots like taro. Breaking off a piece of a large leaf, he crushes it between his fingers and gives it to me to smell. The sweet fragrance is similar to a ripe mango. Bijay also shows me three kinds of wild paan leaves, their creepers growing up the trunks of different trees. The smallest and most delicate of these grow flat against the bark of a tree, as if they've been glued in place. Paan is closely related to black pepper. Plucking the heart-shaped leaf from another creeper, Bijay gives it to me to taste. It has a clean, spicy flavour, which is more intense than most leaves used by paanwallas. Both Bijay and Pallul are carrying chopped areca nuts and other ingredients, including lime paste and tobacco. Picking leaves from the wild creepers, they prepare neatly folded mouthfuls of paan, to chew as we walk along.

Further on, we come upon more piles of fresh dung and several broken branches where a herd of elephants have recently crossed the road. Bijay tells me that the best place to see elephants is a natural salt lick on the other side of this forest, towards the main road.

'When there is a full moon,' he says, 'many elephants come to that spot at night because the salt bubbles out of the ground in the moonlight.'

When I ask what the name for elephants is in Assamese, Manash answers. 'Outside the forest, we call them hathi, just like in Hindi, but when we are in the forest, we always refer to elephants as "baba", out of respect, because we worship them.'

The relationship between human beings and wild elephants in Assam is complex and ambivalent, ranging from veneration to hostility. Though considered sacred animals, associated with the deity Ganesh but also revered through tribal lore and mythology, elephants decimate crops and damage property. Conflict between humans and elephants often ends in death. Recently, the forest minister of Assam reported that an average of seventy people are killed by elephants in Assam every year, while approximately eighty elephants die because villagers strike back when herds raid their fields, often poisoning or electrocuting them. At the heart of the problem is the loss of adequate forest habitat and the lack of connecting corridors that would allow elephants free passage.

Bijay repeats what he said earlier about the greatest danger being lone males that wander out of the forest, raiding crops and vandalizing homes on the periphery of Dehing Patkai. He tells me that the worst offender is an elephant that the villagers of Soraipung call 'Tempu' because of his vicious temper. One theory is that Tempu originally came from Myanmar and wandered into Assam. He is somewhat shorter and stockier than most of the local elephants, with a brownish hue to his hide.

'Tempu has killed thirty people,' Bijay says. 'Just a few weeks back he attacked a man who was working on the oil pipeline. Tempu broke his back and would have killed him, except the man fell into a deep ditch where the elephant couldn't reach him. The victim is still in the hospital, paralysed from the waist down.'

Listening to these stories, I'm struck by the way in which wild elephants that remain in the forest are revered and accepted, while those that stray outside are feared and hated. The idea that Tempu is a foreign creature, an intruder from beyond the borders of Assam, also plays into a narrative of competing identities that has been politicized. Over the years refugees from Bangladesh and Myanmar have settled in Assam, which has created tensions with indigenous communities. In this way, our conflicts with wild species are often interpreted according to adversarial relationships with other human beings.

After hearing about Tempu's violent behaviour, we retreat to our vehicle and drive on to a forest camp nearby. Bijay explains that it is known as Baint Camp because a lot of cane or rattan grows in this area. The baint vines weave in amongst the other foliage, looping together in elaborate, thorny skeins that don't seem to have any beginning or end. Their green bark is covered with sharp, needle-like spines. Cane is used for making furniture because of its flexibility and strength. Related to palms there are many different species of rattan found in India and Southeast Asia.

Baint Camp consists of a small, two-room building standing on reinforced concrete stilts. Painted a pale green, it lies empty and nobody seems to have stayed here for a while. Manash explains that though Dehing Patkai has been notified as a national park, the forest department doesn't have adequate resources or manpower to guard and patrol these jungles. The only other visitors we have met this morning are three birdwatchers from Tezpur but they turned back earlier and we now have the forest to ourselves.

As soon as we get out of the jeep, Bijay points to the trees at the edge of the clearing. In the foliage, I can just make out a black shape, hanging by one arm—a male hoolock gibbon. He swings across to another branch and then turns to look at us with an inquisitive expression, exaggerated by his prominent white eyebrows. Lower down, in another tree, a female gibbon cradles a baby in her arms. Both the mother and infant are a dusty fawn colour with white circles around their eyes. The baby clings to the thick fur on its mother's belly as she clambers across to a tangle of creepers in the trees 15 metres above the ground. Hoolock gibbons have no tails but are equipped with exceptionally long arms that they use to swing from branch to branch with acrobatic ease. Brachiation is the scientific term for this form of arboreal ambulation, which allows gibbons to travel through the trees at speeds above 50 kilometre per hour.

Settling into the green rigging of vines, the female reaches out to pick a fresh tendril from a creeping fern which she nibbles appreciatively. The hoolock family don't seem alarmed by our proximity, a reassuring sign that they feel safe in this forest. We watch them for half an hour as they move about in the treetops without making any effort to hide from us.

Observing this wild pair and their newborn offspring, feeding peacefully in the upper storey of a rainforest, gives me a deep sense of fulfilment. One of my strongest childhood memories is of hoolock gibbons in the Delhi Zoo, where I used to be fascinated by the way in which they swung back and forth in their cage making loud hooting calls that my brothers and I tried to imitate. At the innocent age of eight or nine, I felt these gibbons were everything an ape should be—agile and loose-limbed, noisy and rambunctious. Yet, even though I was fascinated by them, their captivity and confinement troubled me. It was obvious they were used to swinging wildly from limb to limb through the jungle, instead of being imprisoned in a cage. The wire mesh enclosure where they lived had only a single dead tree in it, on which they could perch, looking down at us accusingly with their wide eyes and white eyebrows. Descending to the ground, they walked on their hind legs, with their arms raised over their heads, as if surrendering to their captors. More than any other animals in the zoo, these were the ones I wanted to help escape.

The family we watch doesn't make a sound, though I'm tempted to hoot at them and see if they will respond. Some sources, including the Oxford Dictionary, claim that the name 'hoolock' comes from Assamese but Bijay shakes his head when I ask.

'Here, people call them "hello monkeys" because they can't remember their name.'

Altogether, twenty different species of gibbons live in different parts of

Southeast Asia. In India, there are just two species, the western and eastern hoolock gibbon, which are virtually identical in appearance and differentiated mostly by their distribution. Western hoolock gibbons are listed as endangered, primarily on account of habitat loss but also because of hunting, while the eastern species, which is also found in Myanmar and Bangladesh, is listed as vulnerable.

~

After a successful morning of birdwatching, followed by a lunch of pork curry, vegetables, and rice, at a village homestay in Soraipung, we set off to look for elephants in the afternoon. Just as we're passing the main gate of the park, Bijay gestures for Pallul to stop the vehicle and we all pile out. On a bare branch, at the top of a tall tree, is a tiny raptor, smaller than a dove. Manash confirms that it is a pied falconet, a compact little bird of prey that is black above and white below with a black patch surrounding each eye. Through my binoculars, I can see that the falconet is feeding on something, but I can't make out what it is. The answer comes from a farmer's hut nearby, where a hen is squawking anxiously, mourning the loss of one of her chicks. Despite its diminutive size, this tiny raptor has a lethal beak and rapacious talons.

Leaving the bird to finish its meal, we drive on to a temple at the side of the road, where a path leads into the forest. A couple of villagers pass by carrying huge palm fronds balanced on their heads. Bijay explains that these will be used to thatch the roofs of their huts. He then gestures for us to be quiet as we walk single file along the overgrown path, which leads to the salt lick. I can see plenty of evidence of elephants. Bark has been stripped off several of the trees and branches have been torn apart. Five minutes' walk from the temple, we come to a large clearing at the centre of which is a shallow pond, no more than a few centimetres deep. All around the water is a muddy area with fresh elephant footprints. Their round, flat pads have sunk into the mud and the impressions of toenails are clearly visible. We stop and listen for several minutes but they seem to have moved off into the forest beyond, probably less than half an hour before our arrival. The salt lick is quite different from what I expected and there is no evidence of salinity in the mud, though some if it is a greasy, green colour that looks as if it might be mixed with oil seeping out of the ground.

Sunbeams filter through the high branches of hollong trees and I can easily imagine the shadowy forms of elephants gathering here in the moonlight. A flock of green imperial pigeons watch us from a grove of trees on the far side of the pond, their pale grey heads cocked to one side and their dark green wings tinged with a metallic sheen.

After visiting the salt lick, we explore some of the peripheral areas of the park and come upon several old oil wells that have been capped. Square concrete platforms support steel plugs that protrude a metre above ground. Some of the oil has leaked out and collected in black puddles. We also pass a storage facility with large, cylindrical tanks, surrounded by high walls topped with barbed wire. New technologies are now used to extract residual deposits of oil from wells that went dry years ago. At a couple of places, teams of men in hard hats are working on the new pipeline which cuts through the forest, parallel to the paved road. JCB earthmovers have dug up the ground which is mired in mud. At another place, we watch a JCB moving huge logs with its steel shovel just as a working elephant would have used its tusks and trunk. These motorized, mechanical beasts have replaced the labouring giants of the past.

Most of the birds don't seem to be bothered by the disturbance. Whenever we get down to walk for a stretch, we come upon more and more species that I've never seen before. Unlike in other parts of India, where I might find one or two birds that are new to me, here in this corner of Assam virtually every species is a surprise from red-breasted parakeets to orange-headed thrushes. Even the bulbuls are different—black-headed and ashy—while in the streams that trickle through overgrown ravines, we spot both black-backed and white-crowned forktails. Though I am not a compulsive birder and don't keep a life list, I find myself consciously noting new species, which I can now boast that I've seen.

One of the birds that Bijay and Manash are keen to show me is the white-winged duck, which is the state bird of Assam. An endemic species, it is usually found in forest ponds surrounded by jungle. We visit five different waterbodies, two of which we approach on foot, stalking through dense cover, but the ducks are elusive and like the peacock-pheasant they remain out of sight. The largest pond is about 100 metres from end to end and half that width, its shores thickly wooded and fringed with tree ferns. A bright green film of algae covers the water. Next to the pond is a walled compound with a large gate and signs forbidding entry. When I ask what it is, Bijay replies, 'a bomb godown', where explosives are kept that are used when prospecting for oil.

Though the white-winged ducks have wisely avoided this area, we see a Pallas's squirrel on a tree near the gate oblivious of the danger nearby. This arboreal rodent is about 35 centimetres long, including its bottle-brush tail. Also known as a red-bellied squirrel, it is mostly a dusky brown colour with dark vermilion fur on its stomach and under its legs. Pallas's squirrels are named after Peter Simon Pallas, an eighteenth-century German naturalist and author of *Spicilegia Zoologica*, who worked in St. Petersburg, Russia, for most of his career under the patronage of Catherine the Great. Pallas never visited India or any other parts of Asia, though he described hundreds of species based on specimens that others had collected. As the squirrel studies us from its perch on the branch, the name it bears seems incongruous. Several other species in India are named after Pallas, including a fish-eagle, a wild cat in Ladakh, a long-tongued bat, and a viper, none of which were ever seen alive by the taxonomist they commemorate.

So much of what we think of as knowledge is nothing but names. Just because I can remember what someone else called a particular animal, or look it up in a field guide, doesn't mean that I know what it is. To actually begin understanding that species, I must learn where it lives, what it eats, and other aspects of its behaviour, including the sounds it makes or when and where it breeds. There is no end to how much I can discover about a bird or mammal—its anatomy, its genetic make-up, and its relationship to other creatures. In most cases, the name is simply a marker that helps us hold an image in our minds until we can identify and observe a species more completely. On the other hand, I've always been fascinated by both common and scientific names. They are an essential part of our appreciation of nature and allow us to classify species and place them in comprehensible categories. Names also provide mimetic cues that trigger our memories and sometimes even the most obtuse binomials can be wonderfully inventive or playful.

As the sun descends, birds become more active. Bijay takes us to an overgrown track that leads to another abandoned oil well. The surrounding forest is alive with greater necklaced laughingthrushes, blue-bearded bee-eaters, and white-rumped shamas. In addition to birds, we also come upon a variety of insects. This isn't the season for butterflies but Manash identifies a one-spot grass yellow. To my inexperienced eye, it doesn't look any different to other grass yellows, whether 'common', 'three-spotted', or 'spotless', though I'm sure a lepidopterist could point out the distinguishing features. Elsewhere, we see an army of red ants that are building a nest out of leaves, swarming up and down the stem of a tall plant with industrious teamwork. What species they are, none of us can say. We are also unable to identify a large, bronze-coloured dragonfly with white spots at the ends of its wings that remains so still, it looks as if it is made of stained glass. Later, I learn from entomologist Vivek Sarkar that it is called a fulvous forest skimmer.

Encircling the old oil well is a patch of open ground, much of which has been colonized by *Ageratum houstonianum*, an invasive plant with small blue flowers. Originally from Central America and related to asters, this exotic weed has spread throughout the world. Sometimes called floss flower or blue maudlin, in Assamese it is known as gendali-bon. While the flowers are an attractive colour, *Ageratum* has replaced native plants that were cleared when the oil well was dug. Another invasive species from South America, which has spread around the globe, is *Mimosa pudica*. Growing close to the ground, it is known as the sensitive plant, shame-plant, or touch-me-nots because its feathery pinnate leaves fold together for a couple of minutes if anything brushes against them.

Stopping suddenly, Bijay points to the wall of vegetation on our left. Several creepers have been ripped aside and a broken branch hangs by a frayed strip of bark where an elephant emerged from the forest and crossed the clearing. Anxiously scanning the ground, we find a single footprint about 150 centimetres in circumference. The general rule of thumb when calculating an elephant's height, based on the size of its foot, is to double the circumference. A full-grown male elephant can stand over 3 metres tall at the shoulder.

'Tempu!' Bijay exclaims, under his breath.

About 20 metres away, on the other side of the clearing, I can see where the elephant re-entered the jungle. All of us are suddenly alert and tense, though we hear no telltale sounds of snapping branches or rustling foliage. Moments later, Manash nudges my arm and points at the ground. Just beyond the elephant's footprint, several stems of sensitive grass have closed their leaves. Tempu must have touched the plants, as he passed through the clearing, no more than two or three minutes ahead of us.

Twenty years ago, when I was able to run much faster than I can today, I wrote a book about elephants. Having spent a good deal of time in pursuit of these majestic animals, the largest of all terrestrial megafauna, I gained a healthy respect for their ability to move silently and swiftly through the jungle, as well as an appreciation for the severe damage they can do with their trunks and feet. Elephants are not just large; they are also highly intelligent and often temperamental. Even captive male elephants that are ordinarily gentle in the presence of human beings can become aggressive and unpredictable when they go into musth, a condition caused by hormonal changes connected to their breeding cycle, similar to the rut of a stag. The expression 'rogue elephant' often refers to the period of musth which can last for weeks and months. At the same time, certain males, and a few females too, simply don't like human beings and will attack them on sight. If you are on foot, and one of these elephants turns against you, there isn't much chance of escape. We are lucky that Tempu keeps moving in the opposite direction, as we quickly retrace our steps and get back into our vehicle, deciding that we've done enough birdwatching for today.

∽

The following morning, when we return along the same road at dawn, a lone elephant suddenly crosses the road in front of us, near the turn-off for the abandoned oil well. He is a tuskless male, or makhna, with a stocky build and a bulging forehead. Though this elephant doesn't stop to look at us, we drive forward cautiously and catch sight of him again just inside the first line of trees, a looming shadow behind a curtain of leaves. For a couple of minutes, he studies our vehicle as we watch him, but the makhna seems to have no quarrel with us and soon vanishes into the forest.

About 40 per cent of male elephants in India do not have tusks. In some places, like Assam, the proportion of makhnas to tuskers is much higher. The primary reason is that hunters and elephant catchers in the past targeted male elephants for their ivory and left makhnas alone. As a result, tuskless males multiplied in the wild and were able to pass on their genes more frequently. This is an example of how human beings have affected a wild species, influencing not only its numbers but its physical characteristics as well. There was a time in Assam, when a hunter who shot a tusker was required by the forest department to kill a makhna, too, in a futile attempt to redress the balance. Shooting an elephant has been illegal since 1972, though poaching has continued in parts of Assam and tuskers are now extremely rare.

When we pick up Bijay, near the park gate, he confirms that the elephant we encountered was probably Tempu who is a makhna. Over the past few days, this bull has been seen several times near Soraipung village. Though elephants can wander over large tracts of jungle, they will often remain near one place for several days or weeks, if adequate food and water are available.

This morning, we plan to return to the core area of Dehing Patkai, searching for peacock-pheasants and other species that live in the dense understorey of the rainforest. Once again, we are surrounded by birdcalls most of which I do not recognize. Some are as loud as a ringtone while others are as soft as a needle striking a thimble. The rainforest is a richly orchestrated soundscape, as layered and tangled as the vegetation, with shrill whistles, shrieks, warblings, trills, and chatter. Each bird communicates its presence while crying out to others of its kind. These high-pitched queries are answered by a mate or rival. Practised birders can often identify a species more accurately by its call than from a fleeting glimpse of blurred feathers. But even the most experienced ornithologist can only guess at what these sounds actually mean, and what specific responses they elicit. While each species has distinctive calls, some with a purpose that can be inferred, the vocalization of birds is much more complex and enigmatic than the simple notes registered by human eardrums.

Inaudible frequencies and subtle harmonics are part of an avian chorus that we will never be able to fully appreciate. The cries of birds can vary from one place to another, like dialects, with unique tonal patterns. Using audio recordings, researchers have shown how a birdcall from one region may not receive a response from the same species when played back in another location even a few kilometres away. It has also been shown that birds are much more likely to respond if they hear their own recordings played back at them, presumably because they recognize their own calls. At one point, Manash and Bijay locate a streaked wren babbler twitching about inside a snarled thicket of shrubs and ferns. Its call is so faint, I can barely hear it, a reedy sigh, but for this bird and others of its species that sound must be intensely audible, full of nuance and meaning.

Birds understand and interpret calls that have no significance for us, aside from being a pleasing sound. To my ear, the loud crowing of a peacock-pheasant this morning sounds exactly like the same bird we followed yesterday, though it could easily be any one of three or four others that are calling within a radius of half a kilometre. More than likely, inside their own territory, these shy, yet garrulous creatures can recognize each individual's call, and also identify an outsider's voice.

While birds generally communicate amongst themselves, their alarm calls will alert other creatures to the presence of predators. In this way, a certain element of interspecies discourse takes place. On the other hand, predators also use the calls of birds and animals to locate their prey. Dehing Patkai has no resident tigers but both leopards and clouded leopards are found here, as well as several smaller cats. These are rarely visible, however, because of the thick foliage. Bijay tells me that he has only seen clouded leopards twice. One was dead, mauled to death by a leopard that must have found it scavenging on its kill. The other crossed his path soon after sunset, five years ago. He spotted its eyes in the beam of his torch, after which he recognized the bold patterns on its coat—an irregular mosaic of tan and grey medallions edged with black. This beautiful pelage serves as perfect camouflage within the leafy shadows of the rainforest, where clouded leopards spend much of their time in trees, hunting for monkeys and other small mammals, as well as birds like peacock-pheasants.

After wandering about on foot for a couple of hours, we drive on to Baint Camp where we saw the hoolock gibbons yesterday. From there we take another track that leads to a second camp. This route is much narrower than the main forest road and our vehicle brushes against the foliage on either side. About half a kilometre into the forest, a huge grey shape lumbers in front of us, crossing from left to right.

Pallul brakes, then edges forward cautiously. The elephant is standing in a clearing, about 30 metres away, with his back to us. Immediately, he wheels around and charges. An enormous makhna, well over 3 metres at the shoulder, with a domed forehead and dark grey hide, he is clearly annoyed by our presence.

Bijay anxiously urges Pallul to drive on and get away from him as fast as we can. The elephant flaps his ears and sways his trunk belligerently, blundering onto the track and following us at an aggressive pace. Pallul tries to put some distance between us, but broken branches are strewn on the road and other obstacles force him to slow down, while the elephant keeps gaining ground. At one point, the makhna is no more than 5 metres behind us. Bearing down on our vehicle, his enormous bulk fills the rear window.

Fortunately, after chasing us for half a kilometre, the elephant finally stops and lets us go on. In our relief and excitement, all of us begin speaking at once. Runap asks if it was Tempu and Bijay shakes his head, telling him that this is another lone makhna called Laden, who has also killed a number of people. Named after Osama bin Laden, he terrorizes villagers on the periphery of the park.

The narrow track finally ends at Premier Camp, about 3 kilometres on ahead. Another two-room building on concrete stilts stands empty in a clearing ringed with tall trees. As we nervously get down to stretch our legs, each of us keeps an eye out for any sign of movement. Though the elephant probably wouldn't have done anything to us or our vehicle, while we were inside, it was a close encounter, and the forest feels suddenly threatening. Even the birds have fallen silent and there is an ominous hush. We wait for half an hour before returning along the same route. When we climb into the vehicle, Bijay hands Manash two firecrackers and a cigarette lighter, in case we come upon Laden again. Thankfully, the bull is nowhere to be seen. Driving to a safer section of the park, we continue birdwatching until noon, when it is time for us to depart.

After dropping Bijay at his village, we head back to Digboi. Entering the outskirts of town, the sooty petroleum odour of the refinery assails us. Once again, I think of that fabled elephant that wandered into the jungle so many years ago. For him, the crude oil he stepped in would have had no special significance or value. As his feet sank into the black ooze, he probably sniffed it and may even have dipped the tip of his trunk in this strange, sticky substance. Touching it to his tongue, the greasy, bitter flavour would not have appealed, and he must have backed away in disgust. Little did he know that these ancient carbon deposits, the denatured remains of primaeval rain forests and swamps from aeons ago, would soon change the future of his world and ours.

INTERLUDE

THE SPARROW AND THE HORNBILL

The closest I ever came to meeting Salim Ali was at the Royal Bombay Yacht Club, where I was staying as a guest, sometime around 1981 or 1982. Getting into the elevator one morning, I saw an elderly, white-bearded gentleman approaching, and I held the door open until he stepped aboard. Recognizing him instantly, I was too surprised and tongue-tied to mumble anything more than 'good morning'. He returned my greeting with a nod and a distracted smile. The antique elevator rattled and creaked as we slowly descended to the ground floor where we both got out and went our separate ways. I sometimes wonder what I might have said to him—words of admiration, of course, or a question, perhaps—but I knew that whatever came out of my mouth would sound foolish and trite, like an ardent fan gushing over a Bollywood star. Salim Ali would have been in his mid-eighties at the time, a slight, frail-looking man but with a firm, steady stride.

Five minutes' walk from the yacht club lies Hornbill House, headquarters of the Bombay Natural History Society (BNHS), an organization with which Salim Ali was associated for most of his life, serving at different times as honorary secretary, editor of the society's journal, and president. The traffic circle outside Hornbill House is named Salim Ali Chowk and during his lifetime he received countless prizes and awards that recognized his enormous contributions to Indian ornithology and conservation. Perhaps his greatest legacy lives on in the work of so many dedicated naturalists that followed his lead and continue to explore, document, and preserve India's wild heritage.

~

On a muggy October morning, I enter the main gate of Hornbill House and head upstairs to meet Dr Bivash Pandav, the current director of BNHS. An engaging and energetic wildlife scientist with a wealth of experience in the field, Bivash is on deputation from the Wildlife Institute of India in Dehradun where he is a member of the faculty. Originally from Odisha, he spent his childhood observing waterfowl along the Mahanadi River and has studied a variety of wild species, from sea turtles and swamp deer to tigers and elephants. On the wall above his desk is dramatic black and white photograph of a large tusker silhouetted in the mist.

'That was taken in the winter of 2020, along the Ganga below Haridwar,' Bivash replies, when I ask about the picture. 'This elephant was the dominant male in a bachelor herd that used to cross the river every night to feed in the fields. I took this picture just after dawn when they were returning to the forest. He was always the last elephant to enter the river, making sure that all of the others got safely across. We radio-collared him to monitor the herd's movements, to avoid any conflict with pilgrims during the Kumbh Mela in 2021.'

Studying large mammals can be an unpredictable occupation, especially when wild elephants immerse themselves in the same sacred river with millions of human devotees. Fortunately, for the duration of the Kumbh, the troop of elephants remained safely downstream from Haridwar.

Though he is happiest wandering about in the forest, Bivash clearly relishes the opportunity to direct a historic institution.

'At WII, our primary mission is to train wildlife scientists,' he explains. 'But here at BNHS the emphasis is on research that supports conservation.'

He describes how one of the projects they sponsor identifies and protects the nesting sites of Indian skimmers and black-bellied terns along the Chambal River. These birds lay their eggs in shallow depressions in the sand, usually on riverine islands, and are highly vulnerable to predators, especially feral dogs and jackals. Parveen Sheikh, a conservation biologist, has set up a research project, funded by the BNHS, to erect fences on the islands and hire villagers to guard the nests of skimmers and terns. Among other initiatives, the society also actively supports ongoing efforts to understand the catastrophic drop in India's vulture population and try to save them from extinction.

Founded in 1883, the BNHS began as a fraternity of eight colonial naturalists, united by the shared goals of 'exchanging notes, exhibiting interesting specimens and otherwise encouraging one another'. Their first official meeting took place at the Victoria and Albert Museum (now called the Dr. Bhau Daji Lad Museum). Among the founding members was Herbert Musgrave Phipson, whose family were wine merchants in Bombay. Phipson made one of the rooms in his shop at 18 Forbes Street available to house the society's collections and as a place where the group could meet. Later, when more space was needed for an office and collection room, Phipson provided the BNHS with a larger space in another property at 6 Apollo Street. The society's headquarters remained there until

1958, when the building was torn down. Nearby, the Prince of Wales Museum (now the Chhatrapati Shivaji Maharaj Vastu Sangrahalaya), housed a natural history section where Salim Ali had worked as a guide-lecturer in the 1920s. Years later, as president of the BNHS, he was able to persuade the museum and the Government of India to build new headquarters for the society on one corner of the museum's property which is where it now stands.

'We pay one rupee rent a year to the museum,' Bivash says with a laugh.

In his memoir, *The Fall of a Sparrow*, Salim Ali recounts the well-known story of his first encounter with the BNHS, in 1908, when he was twelve. His uncle was one of the society's first Indian members and after Salim, armed with a BB gun, shot an unusual-looking sparrow, with what looked like 'a curry-stain' on its throat, he went to the society's headquarters to have it identified. He describes this fateful event:

> I remember the feeling of nervousness—almost of fear and trembling—at the prospect of meeting a full-grown sahib face to face with which I entered the quaint old single-storeyed building through its magnificent solid teakwood portal. After due checking of my bona fides I was led up the shallow coir-carpeted steps by a supercilious khaki-liveried sepoy, the flanking walls covered with mounted heads of shikar trophies in terrifying profusion. Upstairs, in a corner of the wooden-floored room chock-a-block with desk showcases displaying seashells, butterflies, birds' eggs and miscellaneous natural history bric-a-brac, the walls were still more crowded with skulls and mounted heads of tigers and leopards staring glassily down at the intruder, or snarling with bared fangs more ferociously than they ever did in life. I was piloted to the sanctum sanctorum through this welter of animal remnants, stumbling over stuffed crocodiles and hoofs of sambar floor-rugs. In a corner of this congested junk shop, which was the Society's museum in those days, and partitioned off by swing doors, sat, leaning over his desk, the genial bald-headed Walter Samuel Millard, the Honorary Secretary.

Far from being the forbidding burra sahib that young Salim had imagined, Millard turned out to be gentle and encouraging. He identified the bird as a yellow-throated sparrow, igniting the boy's interest in ornithology and setting the course of his illustrious career. This story, like many others, has become part of a rich compendium of lore, legends, myths, and anecdotes associated with the BNHS. Another famous bird is the great hornbill that appears on the society's logo, and after whom the society's headquarters and journal are named. This hornbill was a four-month-old chick when it was presented to the BNHS by a member from Karwar in 1894. Kept in a cage on the premises of Phipson's wine shop it grew very tame and was named William. Fully grown, the hornbill was 1.3 metres long. In 1897, Phipson wrote an account of the hornbill in the society's journal, describing how he subsisted on a diet of plantains and figs as well as lizards, scorpions, snails, and centipedes. Though suspicious of strangers, he was affectionate with those he recognized and even tried to feed them treats in the same way that male hornbills feed their nesting mates. William was also extremely playful and enjoyed catching tennis balls in his beak. Phipson recounts how the bird groomed himself several times a day by rubbing his huge casque on a 'uropygial gland on its back, at the root of its tail' and then smearing the yellowish secretions on his feathers. Sometimes referred to as 'the office canary', William was obviously a novelty and a pet but also a source of scientific information for those who observed his behaviour.

When the society was formed, and throughout much of the twentieth century, the accepted approach to studying wildlife was by collecting and preserving specimens. Shooting and stuffing wild animals and birds was seen as the only way to confirm the identity of each species and examine its morphology—the appearance, shape, and dimensions of a creature and its various parts. Butterflies and other insects were caught in nets and placed in killing jars containing ether or chloroform. The dead specimens were then carefully mounted on pins with their wings extended for display. Snakes and other small reptiles or amphibians were caught and killed, then preserved in bottles filled with formaldehyde. Larger reptiles like crocodiles were skinned and stuffed, as were most mammals. In this way, the dividing line between hunting trophies and scientific specimens was often blurred. Most of the collections at natural history museums in places like London or New York were supplied by big game hunters who donated the remains of lions, tigers, and other species to science.

During the eighteenth and nineteenth centuries, when European nations were acquiring colonies in far-flung corners of the globe, there was a concerted effort to collect and catalogue specimens of flora and fauna from all over the world. Anything that caught the attention of wandering naturalists, from birds' eggs and feathers to fossils and seashells, was crated and shipped back to Europe. Among wealthy patrons, who funded these natural history expeditions, maintaining private collections or 'cabinets of curiosities' became a craze. Many naturalists like Alexander Von Humboldt and others supported themselves by selling exotic specimens upon their return to Europe.

In many ways, the BNHS is rooted in the mouldering traditions of nineteenth century taxonomy and like all venerable institutions it has become something of an anachronism in an age when most biologists are focused on genetic research, computer modelling, and biotechnologies. At the same time, the BNHS is hardly irrelevant. Its library and collections are an invaluable resource for scientists today, and its emphasis on fieldwork and close observation of individual species and ecological communities harks back to the extensive field surveys that Salim Ali conducted throughout the country.

When I was in high school, in the late 1960s and early 1970s, I was taught how to skin and mount bird specimens. It is a messy, time-consuming process in which the bird is cut open from its vent to the breastbone and then, essentially turned inside out, like removing a sock from your foot so that the body can be separated from the skin. The bones on the legs and wings, as well as the base of the spine, are cut and any adhering flesh removed. The most delicate part of the operation is peeling back the skin on the bird's head and making a triangular incision at the back of the skull to extract the brain. The skin is then dusted with borax, to dry and preserve the specimen. Finally, a slender length of bamboo, wrapped around with cotton wool, is inserted inside the hollow skin to give the dead bird some semblance of its original shape.

Fortunately, the Wild Life Protection Act of 1972 put an end to the indiscriminate killing of fauna in the name of science. Salim Ali was certainly part of a generation that believed in the importance of collecting specimens, but he too felt there needed to be limits.

> I do not enjoy the killing, and sometimes even suffer a prick of conscience, but I have no doubt that but for the methodical collecting of specimens in my earlier years—several thousand, alas—it would have been impossible to advance our taxonomical knowledge of Indian birds—as the various regional surveys have done—nor indeed of their geographical distribution, ecology and bionomics. However, I believe a stage has now been reached when the *ad hoc* collecting of Indian bird specimens is no longer essential, except for special studies such as moult, or in the case of a few little-known species that are rare in museum collections. There is sufficient research material available in the BNHS, the Zoological Survey of India, and the great natural-history museums abroad, for solving most taxonomical problems.

The research that Salim Ali undertook resulted in a prodigious list of publications, beginning with his first field guide *The Book of Indian Birds*, which was published in 1941, followed by *Birds of Kutch, Indian Hill Birds, Birds of Kerala, The Birds of Sikkim*, and *Field Guide to the Birds of the Eastern Himalayas*. All of these were a prelude to the exhaustive ten-volume *Handbook of the Birds of India and Pakistan*, which he and S. Dillon Ripley completed in 1976. In addition to these books, Salim Ali wrote and published a number of scientific papers on ornithology and contributed regularly to the BNHS journal. He also gave talks that were broadcast on All India Radio, in an effort to popularize birdwatching and promote conservation amongst the wider public.

~

Vithoba Hegde has worked at the BNHS for forty-two years. A soft-spoken, bespectacled man in his mid-sixties, he is a senior zoological assistant in collections and knows where every specimen is kept. When Hegde joined the BNHS in 1982, Salim Ali was still an active presence at Hornbill House. From one of the many green steel cabinets, he produces a yellow-throated sparrow, collected in 1948 by Salim Ali—the same species that a nervous young boy carried to the BNHS forty years earlier, wanting to learn its identity. Since then, the yellow-throated sparrow's common name has been changed to the chestnut-shouldered petronia.

More birds emerge from the line of cabinets, assorted specimens neatly arranged on rectangular examination trays. A western tragopan, its breast feathers a rich crimson, flecked with numerous white spots, lies next to a Himalayan monal, also known as an Impeyan pheasant, which has iridescent purple and green plumage with a terracotta-hued tail. Two other Phasianidae share this tray, a grey peacock-pheasant, its ornate feathers the colour of tarnished silver, and a blood pheasant with streaks of grey, green, and white on its breast and belly, splashed with red. Each bird is carefully labelled with a tag that gives the date and place it was collected, as well as the collector's name and a reference number. Bivash shows me another specimen of a Sclater's monal from Arunachal Pradesh, which is similar to the Himalayan monal, except that it has a white tail. Ornithologists can consult this collection to compare with birds they have observed or photographed in the wild.

'We also permit researchers to take DNA samples, if required,' Bivash explains. 'BNHS has about 150,000 specimens altogether, representing more than 35,000 different species of birds, mammals, amphibians, reptiles, insects and invertebrates.'

The next tray I'm shown contains two large ducks and a smaller bird with cream and tan plumage, about the size of a mynah but with longer legs.

'Pink-headed ducks,' Bivash confirms my suspicions, 'and Jerdon's courser.'

By the middle of the twentieth century, both of these species were assumed to be extinct. The last pink-headed duck was shot by a hunter in 1935, in Bihar, after which no reliable sightings have been recorded. A resident of northern India, it was never common but occasionally found in the Terai, frequenting wetlands along the foot of the Himalaya as far east as Assam. In one of his popular radio broadcasts, Salim Ali described it as follows: 'Known in Hindi as ghulab-sir, it is about the size of the domestic duck, blackish brown overall with a quite distinctive rose-pink face, head, and hind neck. The colour has been well likened to that of new blotting paper.' Salim Ali also had an opportunity to see a captive flock in the UK. 'Some of the last pink-headed ducks—a batch of eleven said to have been obtained in Goalpara district—were exported to London in 1929 or thereabouts and lived for several years in captivity but all efforts to breed them proved unsuccessful.'

The rose-coloured feathers on the two specimens' heads have faded to a dusty cream and there is only a subtle hint of pink on the napes of their long necks. The dark back and wing feathers are dishevelled, as if from a shotgun blast. Knowing that these are among the last, lifeless remnants of an extinct species makes them seem all the more tragic. Efforts at conservation, including a total ban on shooting pink-headed ducks, instituted in the 1950s, came much too late.

Jerdon's courser was first described in 1848 by Thomas Caverhill Jerdon, an East India Company surgeon, who took a special interest in ornithology and published *The Birds of India* in 1862, listing 1,008 different species. Even at the time, the courser that bears his name was one of the most elusive birds on the subcontinent. Found only in the scrubby plains of what is now Telangana and Andhra Pradesh, it was entirely nocturnal. Jerdon only found it with the help of tribal hunters, who caught the bird with snares. After he collected a specimen and described it for science, it was seldom seen. During the first half of the twentieth century, while conducting bird surveys in the princely state of Hyderabad, Salim Ali tried unsuccessfully to find this bird. Then, suddenly, in 1986, an ornithologist named Bharat Bhushan made the astonishing announcement that he had rediscovered Jerdon's courser in the possession of a tribal hunter. The tag attached to the specimen tells the story succinctly: 'Trapped at night by local trapper on 14th Jan. Died on 17th Jan. 1986.'

Salim Ali was ninety years old when the news broke.

'As soon as he heard that the bird was alive, he tried to go and see it,' Bivash tells me. 'But by the time he got there, it had died.'

The next year, on 20 June 1987, Salim Ali himself passed away.

Compared to the two pink-headed ducks, the specimen of Jerdon's courser is in much better condition and the distinctive, double-collar of grey and dark brown, on its upper breast and neck, has not faded. From its shape and long legs, it's easy to see why Thomas Jerdon first called it a plover. Though this specimen is as lifeless as the other birds in the collection, there is something encouraging in its story. Perhaps even the rarest of birds, unreported for almost a century, might possibly be found again. Another sighting of Jerdon's courser, in 1996, was reported by Aasheesh Pittie in his book on Indian birds, *The Living Air*, in which he describes locating one in Cuddapah (now Kadapa) district in Andhra Pradesh.

Examining the bird skins is a bit like rummaging through a mortuary, but many of the colours are still as bright as when the specimens were first collected. The feathers on a fairy bluebird are a vivid ultramarine, while a Nicobar pigeon is a dark metallic green with coppery hackles. Among the oldest birds in the collection is a white-throated kingfisher found in Sindh in 1879. The smallest is a fire-breasted flowerpecker collected in Bhutan in 1967.

From birds, we move on to reptiles, crossing over to the opposite side of the room. Hegde opens a fireproof cabinet that contains an assortment of holotypes. These are the original specimens that were used to describe a new species or subspecies. *Coelognathus helena nigriangularis*, a subspecies of the common trinket snake was found in 2016 in a limestone cave near Gupteshwar temple in Koraput district of Odisha. The specimen is coiled up in a plastic bin full of alcohol with the intricately patterned black and white stripes on its grey body. Another holotype is *Dendrelaphis girii*, a new species of bronzeback tree snake from the Western Ghats, named after Varad Giri, who was curator of the herpetological collection at the BNHS for a number of years. Seeing the dozens of bottles of alcohol with their precious contents, the fireproof cabinets make sense. They contain enough flammable material to set Hornbill House ablaze.

We examine several more cabinets stocked with jars full of pickled frogs and toads, including one bottle containing ten or twelve *Bufo himalayanus*, the most common toad in the Himalaya. Bivash then tells me that Vithoba Hegde has a species of rock gecko named in his honour and we persuade him to bring out the specimen. *Hemidactylus hegdei* is about 10 to 12 centimetres long and a mottled grey colour. It was found in the highlands of Tamil Nadu by herpetologists Saunak Pal and Zeeshan Mirza and described in 2022. Hegde obliges us by posing for a photograph with his namesake, a tribute to a lifetime spent caring for these collections. He says that the alcohol in the bottles must be regularly changed to make sure the specimens remain in perfect condition. Researchers who wish to examine the reptiles are able to study them here in this wet lab after removing them from the bottles and placing them in trays containing alcohol.

When I ask to see a king cobra, Hegde takes out a huge bottle, with a ten-litre capacity. The snake is not a large specimen, but it is so tightly coiled up inside that I can't make out which end is the head and which is the tail. All I can see are the broad ventral scales on the underside of its body. As I'm puzzling over this Gordian knot, Hegde places a smaller bottle on the table. It contains the severed head of a large king cobra, about the size of my fist, floating upside down in alcohol. One milky eye stares out of the glass with posthumous omniscience.

Once again, I feel an oppressive sense of morbidity in the room, the presence of so many dead creatures killed and preserved for science. Biology may be the study of life, in all its abundant diversity, but much of the research on which our knowledge is based relies on lifeless specimens like these. Just as medical students practise surgery on human cadavers and learn how to save lives by dissecting the dead, conservation scientists study the preserved remains of rare and endangered species in order to protect those that still survive in the wild.

The BNHS has an extensive collection of insects, all of which are kept in wooden cabinets with shallow drawers. Rows upon rows of moths, butterflies, and beetles are preserved under glass, like a jewellery display. These are some of the most fragile specimens and can be easily destroyed by humidity or even an infestation of other insects that might cannibalize their own kind. Bivash points out that many of the cabinets are sealed with tape to protect them during the monsoon.

'This collection room used to have climate control,' he says, shaking his head ruefully and pointing to the open windows through which the sounds of Mumbai traffic enter. 'But some years ago, the air conditioners were removed because BNHS couldn't pay its electricity bills. Now, I'm trying to find donors that will help us install a new air-conditioning system to control temperature and humidity. We'll also need to raise funds to cover the electricity and maintenance costs.'

Mammals are represented in the collection too, many of which are old shikar trophies donated by society members, like the mounted tiger head that greeted us with a silent snarl as we entered the repository. Antlers adorn some of the walls, the most impressive of which belong to a hangul or Kashmir stag and a Schomburgk's deer which is now extinct. Atop one of the steel cabinets sits a stuffed pangolin, with its long nose and claws, as well as an armour plating of scales. Many of these animals are victims of the illegal trade in animal parts, most of which can be traced to China, where tiger bones, deer antlers, and pangolin scales are used to manufacture traditional medicines.

Just before I take my leave, Hegde produces the skin of a cheetah collected in Afghanistan, in 1917. This specimen, more than a hundred years old, isn't mounted but the hide is mostly intact, with black spots like spattered ink dispersed over its yellow pelage. Touching the fur, it feels soft yet brittle, like dry grass. The pattern and size of the spots is irregular, unlike a leopard's rosettes. Folded up in an examination tray, this isn't just a physical relic of natural history but also a symbol of impermanence, from a time when this animal still had open spaces to roam and hunt as it was meant to do. In 1917, the human population of India was roughly 250 million, while today, a little over a century later, more than 1.4 billion *Homo sapiens* inhabit the same territory. Estimating cheetah numbers from the past is little more than guesswork, but some writers have placed the population in 1920 at about 200, some of which were probably African cheetahs imported for hunting blackbuck, which had escaped into the wild. Nevertheless, there is no doubt about the number of Asiatic cheetahs surviving in India today—it is zero.

Edward Hamilton Aitken, known to his readers as EHA, was one of the founding members of the Bombay Natural History Society. During the last two decades of the nineteenth century, and until he retired to Scotland in 1906, EHA wrote a regular column on wildlife for the *Times of India*. These pieces were collected and published as a series of books that included *Tribes on My Frontier, A Naturalist on the Prowl*, and *Common Birds of Bombay.*

At a time when most nature writing in India consisted of shikar stories, EHA offered a very different perspective. Instead of bloodthirsty tales of shooting man-eating tigers and rogue elephants, his books focused on less intimidating creatures such as lizards, crabs, mosquitoes, ants, crows, and bats. His prose was lively and full of a wry sense of humour, but his observations were precise and accurately described. One of the first pieces he wrote was about rats and this short passage gives a sense of his style and voice:

> There is the black rat, the brown rat, the field-rat, the tree-rat, the bandicoot, and so on, to the lovely fawn-coloured Jerboa rat, with its satin-white breast and tufted tail, which wrought such ruin to the crops two years ago. Two of these, *Mus rattus,* the black rat, and *Mus decumanus* (from *decumanus,* a tax collector), the brown rat, have attached themselves to man, and how to detach them is a question which all the ingenuity the world has produced, from Archimedes to Mr. Edison, has left unanswered.

EHA's books remain enjoyable and informative more than a century after he wrote them. They were admired and emulated by nature writers who followed in his footsteps, including Salim Ali, M. Krishnan, and more recently, Ruskin Bond, who wrote the introductions for new editions of EHA's books, reissued by Penguin in 2007.

Though he was not a scientist by training, EHA was more than just an amateur naturalist. Unlike most of his European contemporaries, he approached India's forests and open spaces not as an arena for blood sport or commercial exploitation, but as an intensely fascinating community of wild species, both great and small, whose stories he sought to tell. Part of the reason for his sensitivity and understanding undoubtedly came from the fact that India was his birthplace. In his introduction to *The Tribes on My Frontier*, Bond explains how the biographical facts we know about EHA are as abbreviated at his initials.

> (He) was born in 1851 at Satara, in what was then the Bombay Presidency. His parents were Scottish missionaries. The boy received most of his early education from his father, who must have been an outstanding teacher, for when young EHA was sent to Bombay University he had no difficulty in securing a 'first' with honours. For the next six years he taught Latin at the Deccan College, Poona, and then entered the Customs and Salt Department of the Government of Bombay and was stationed in Kharaghoda....

EHA renamed Kharaghoda, 'Dustypore', which is the setting for his early stories. After his promotion to customs supervisor, he moved to the Western Ghats on the border between Goa and what was then known as Upper Kanara, a very different landscape from the dry, salt flats of Gujarat. More than likely, he is the BNHS member who presented William Phipson with the great hornbill chick that became the society's mascot. After this posting, EHA eventually moved up the coast to Bombay where he obviously enjoyed the company of fellow naturalists and focused his attention on the birds and other creatures that shared his semi-urban backyard.

A Naturalist on the Prowl begins with a sentence that sums up EHA's approach to observing wildlife: 'I have always felt a strange pleasure in seeing without being seen.' Several lines later, he expands on this idea with a tongue-in-cheek criticism of other naturalists, who approach their subjects quite differently, from narrower perspectives. More than likely, he was nudging some of the other founding members of the BNHS.

> I wander into the jungle, where 'things that own not man's dominion dwell,' and there I prowl, climb into a tree, sit under a bush, or lie on the grass and watch the ways of my fellow-creatures, seeing but unseen, or, if seen, not regarded; for beasts and birds and creeping things, except when they fear man, ignore him, and so they go about their various occupations, their labours and their amusements, without affectation and without self-consciousness. This is the way to read the book of nature, and after all there is no book like that. It never comes to an end, and there is a growing fascination about it, so that when once you have got well into it, you can scarcely lay it down.
>
> I speak of reading the book. There are many who busy themselves with it but do not read it. There is your doctor of nomenclature, who

> devotes his laborious life to the elucidation of such questions as whether you shall call the common crow *Corvus impudicus* or *Corvus splendens*. He is an index-maker. Then there is a host of commentators and editors, who toil to shed such light as they may on the text, or oftener, on each other. Lastly, there is your collector, who makes extracts. I esteem all these laborious men and feel grateful to them and rejoice that I am none of them, for I hold with Matthew Arnold, that the best use to which you can put a good book is to read and enjoy it.

EHA admits that collecting specimens was a necessary part of being a naturalist in the 1880s, when he was writing. 'Without a collection, a man's knowledge of natural history becomes nebulous and his pursuit of it dilettante. I am sorry it is so, for in spirit I am a Buddhist. But, alas! Not every Buddhist is a Buddha.'

Despite EHA's claim to being a Buddhist in spirit, his prose echoes both the cadence and moral surety of his Scottish missionary father delivering a sermon. Even as he playfully compares the hoot of an owl to the sacred syllable Om, he is laying out a clear and compassionate philosophy of nature, which would have contradicted the beliefs and actions of his fellow colonials. In many ways, Aitken was carrying on the tradition of most of the great naturalists in the West, from Aristotle to Darwin, who considered themselves to be natural philosophers and historians, rather than scientists.

Reading EHA's books, it is difficult not to keep quoting him at length because of the eloquence of his language but also the provocative ideas that he spins out of his observations in the wild. Pondering how a butterfly perceives the world, he writes: 'Has a butterfly ears? No. Can it hear? Yes. If you doubt me, tread on withered lives, or break a twig, as you are stalking a *Fuonia*. Perhaps the delicate expanse of its wings is sensitive to the slightest concussions of the air....' Carrying on like this through all five human senses, he speculates on a butterfly's consciousness of the world it lives in and, at the same time, underscores how little we understand of an insect's perceptions of us and other things. 'What are the antennae of a butterfly? "Feelers" they are called in English, but to overawe the unlearned, we men of science write of them as antennae, which means the yards of a ship. Under either term we know as much about them as the butterfly knows why I carry a walking stick.'

Another prominent writer-naturalist, and an active member of the BNHS, was Edward Pritchard Gee (1904–68). In 1969, at the age of twelve, I was given his book, *The Wild Life of India*, as a Christmas present from my mother. This paperback volume is still with me, though the binding has come apart at several places because I have read and referred to it so often. E. P. Gee was also a keen wildlife photographer, and the book contains a selection of his pictures, including one of a bull gaur that appeared on a ten-naya-paisa postage stamp.

A tea planter by profession and a bachelor by choice, Gee was born and educated in England but spent most of his adult life in different parts of Assam. After four years of service in the Indian Army during World War II, he eventually retired to Shillong, where he tended a large collection of orchids before dying suddenly at the early age of sixty-four. Many of his articles were published in the BNHS Journal and he was one of several influential conservationists who expressed concern for the protection of wild fauna following Independence. Serving on the Indian Board of Wildlife, he advised the government on conservation policies and was a vocal proponent of creating national parks in different parts of the country. In 1959, he visited Nepal at the behest of the Fauna and Flora Preservation Society in the UK and the IUCN. Chitwan National Park was created on his recommendation. Gee is also famous for having discovered a new species of primate, the golden langur, in submontane forests between the Sankosh and Manas rivers, along the borders of Assam and Bhutan. This monkey was named in his honour—*Trachypithecus geei*.

An amusing description of Gee comes to us from the diary of Loke Wan Tho, the Singaporean ornithologist and friend of Salim Ali, who quotes Tho in his memoir:

> (Gee is) a fairly heavily built man, balding, and wears tortoise-shell covered spectacles. Like Browning's thrush he repeats everything twice over, the second phrase tumbling out after the first, 'peeneka pani hai, peeneka pani; He got fed up, he got fed up, so he shot himself, so he shot himself.' Gee is rather hard of hearing, and this may be the reason for the trick of repetition. Salim too is pretty deaf, and when he and Gee talk to each other, the one in his high piercing voice and the other in his lower monotone, the world does not have to strain its ears to hear what they are saying!

Gee's book is a personal account of his visits to a long list of wildlife sanctuaries and national parks in various parts of India, ranging from Kaziranga in the east, Bandipur in the south, Gir in the west, and Dachigam to the north. He writes without the rhetorical flourishes and wit of EHA but casts a clear and sympathetic eye on the creatures he observes and brings them to life on the page. At the end of the book, Gee looks ahead with a certain amount of pessimism but also a good measure of hope.

> Imagine the year 2000, with the only wild life consisting of those creatures which can adapt themselves easily to thickly populated areas, such as jackals, rats, mice, vultures, pariah and Brahminy kites, crows and sparrows!... If the spectacular tiger, the proud peacock and all the other splendid denizens of the forests and grasslands were to cease to exist, then how dull life would be!... The existence of a sound nature and wild life conservation organization in a country is a reliable indication of the stage of the country's progress and development. There is a very good chance that the leaders, planners and people of India will see 'the writing on the wall', and they will not fail today in their duty of preserving the country's heritage of forests and fauna for those of tomorrow.

Even as India's wildlife policies have progressed and considerable success has been achieved in protecting species like the tiger, it is always useful to look back on the context and concerns of conservationists in the past. Both Salim Ali and E. P. Gee, as well as most of their contemporaries, believed that if wildlife sanctuaries were to be effectively protected it was imperative to remove human settlements and livestock from within their boundaries. While this has been shown to be true in many places, particularly where larger megafauna require extensive areas of undisturbed forest to be able to survive and multiply, it is not always the case. When Bharatpur Bird Sanctuary in Rajasthan was created in 1976, and later became Keoladeo Ghana National Park in 1982, Salim Ali and Gee argued that domestic buffaloes released by villagers into these wetlands for grazing had to be excluded.

This policy triggered protests in 1982 and when police opened fire on an agitating crowd, eight people were killed. The tragedy at Bharatpur marred the creation of this important refuge for migratory birds. Subsequently, it was discovered that the exclusion of livestock from the wetlands led to the proliferation of water hyacinths, which the buffaloes fed on. With the uncontrolled spread of these invasive plants, water levels dropped and many of the lakes became choked with weeds, reducing the total area where birds could congregate and feed. In this way, sometimes a certain level of disturbance actually helps preserve an ecological balance.

∽

> At times a profound truth is embodied in a jocular saying, and the classic definition of a virgin forest as a tract where the hand of man has never set foot is such a saying. Provided they are of adequate area, all manner of wildlife tracts in our country have the potential to recoup if left strictly alone, even if now heavily depleted.

> If only 10 percent of our total land area... can be effectively saved from the hand of man setting foot on them, the future of our national integrity and character can be perpetuated to generations of Indians yet unborn, and provide them with an authentic Indian setting and identity and a vital interest in life that can compensate for most ills.

M. Krishnan (1912–96) wrote these lines in an essay titled 'Ecological Patriotism'. He argues that the preservation of India's wild spaces is essential for preserving the nation's character, ideals, and identity. Being of the same generation as Salim Ali and E. P. Gee, though a few years younger, he firmly believed that the best way to preserve a forest was to restrict human access and then leave it alone, allowing nature to manage its own affairs. Krishnan was a fierce opponent of exotic trees and plants, especially when used for afforestation, and in one of his essays he compares the spread of invasive lantana to the insidious proliferation of colonial rule.

Without a doubt, India's finest nature writer to date, Krishnan was also an exceptional artist and photographer. Many of his images—pen and ink or watercolour sketches, as well as photographs—accompanied his essays in publications like *The Hindu, Illustrated Weekly of India*, and *Sanctuary*. He also wrote a fortnightly column for *The Statesman*, 'The Country Notebook', which appeared regularly for forty-six years, until the day of his death. I remember reading Krishnan's pieces when I was in high school. Both his stories and his black and white photographs of elephants and other wildlife left an indelible impression on my mind. Though he specialized in concise, tightly written pieces, Krishnan published several books, including *India's Wildlife, 1959-70*, which was written after he received a Jawaharlal Nehru Fellowship. A confirmed freelancer by nature, Krishnan lived mostly in Madras (now Chennai) but was employed intermittently in various capacities, particularly in the administrative service of the princely state of Sandur, where he had ample opportunities to observe wildlife in the surrounding forests. He was suspicious of most institutions and organizations, though he served on the Indian Board of Wildlife, alongside Salim Ali and E. P. Gee.

Krishnan's essays are marked with a sharp sense of detail and a critical eye, but they also contain flashes of gentle humour and irony. In one piece, he observes an elderly cobra sunning itself each morning, coiled up on the flagstones near a temple, and he wonders if it might suffer from lumbago. In another, he describes an encounter with a sloth bear in the Nilgiris. Instead of turning around to look at him, the bear lowers its head and looks backwards between its legs. The tribal tracker accompanying Krishnan is puzzled and asks, 'Would we have seemed upside down to the bear?' Though his prose is less flamboyant, Krishnan's writing is reminiscent of EHA, partly because he often focuses on lesser species but also because he sees things that nobody else would notice. As a columnist, he set a high standard for contemporary nature writers who have followed his lead.

E. P. Gee praised Krishnan for his skills as a naturalist and as a writer, while commenting on his eccentricities:

> One of the best naturalists of present-day India… He is an artist also, and an expert wild life photographer. 'Every hair' must be his motto, for his pictures show the finest detail of the coats of gaur, sambar, chital and the like, and every wrinkle on the skin of a wild elephant.
>
> The camera I once saw him using in Guindy Park, Madras, was a large, composite affair, with the body of one make and the tele lens of another, and other parts and accessories all ingeniously mounted together by himself. I cannot swear that I saw the proverbial bootlace used to fix them all together, but I am sure there must have been some wire and hoop iron somewhere!
>
> His results, even when greatly enlarged, are very good. His activities, I think, are restricted to south India. He is a bit of a 'lone wolf' and does not care for meetings or advisory boards, but as a naturalist he has no equal as far as the wild life and sanctuaries of that part of India are concerned.

Ramachandra Guha, who edited a collection of Krishnan's essays, writes that, 'His character is, I think, nicely revealed in the technical apparatus of his photography.' Krishnan jokingly referred to his jerry-rigged camera as a 'Super Ponderosa'. The body was a Pentacon Six, made in East Germany. It used 120 roll film, which allowed him to make high quality enlargements. Guha recounts how the camera body finally stopped working and Krishnan was forced to track down a replacement, which involved numerous letters to suppliers, who didn't want to sell the body without an accompanying lens. He also had to apply for a customs permit to import a new camera body from beyond the Iron Curtain. And then, after all of this wrangling and red tape, Krishnan discovered that the P-6 was no longer being produced. Eventually, though, he was able to get a replacement through friends in England, who procured it there.

In his book, *Nature and Nation*, environmental historian Mahesh Rangarajan writes: 'Krishnan represents the voice of the unrelenting preservationist. In this role his eloquence has not been matched. There is no dearth of zealous wildlife protectors now, but no one has the same literary flair, that eccentric ability to convey the lived quality of life in the wild and the imperatives of keeping it alive.'

In Krishnan's descriptions of birds and animals there is a keen awareness of the species' morphology and behaviour but also a sense of its presence and place in the wild. A few examples will suffice, beginning with *Ardeotis nigriceps*.

> The Great Indian Bustard is a bird of the open country and very large, so that its presence anywhere is not hard to locate. It is a big fowl, nearly forty lbs when full grown (a prodigious weight for a flying bird) and four feet tall on its thick, yellow legs. It takes off with some difficulty and after the manner of an aeroplane, with a long run assisted by flapping wings. Once launched in the air, it gains height with lubberly beats of its sail-like wings, then soars on their stretched spread with surprising ease. However, it comes down to earth after a while, for it is essentially a ground bird... (which) runs far more readily than it flies, and at a fair pace.

In an essay on black kites, a raptor once known by the disparaging name 'pariah kite', Krishnan explains that they are not always scavengers.

> I know a lake in such a place where I have seen kites fishing. They sail low over the water and clutch at the slippery prey on the surface with their talons, often without success. Here they are awkward apprentices in comparison to the many expert fishermen around, birds equipped with long, stabbing beaks or long, wading legs, other specialized features or at least the boldness to plunge headlong into the water. Elsewhere, I have seen kites chasing maimed quarry or flapping heavily among swarming termites, which they seized ponderously in their grappling-hook feet.

Krishnan also describes a bandicoot rat, which most human beings consider repulsive, though he offers a somewhat sympathetic and even admiring portrait of this much-maligned rodent.

> Such is the bandicoot. His nocturnal habits, his profound distrust of traps and baits, his incredible cunning—all these make him an exceptionally difficult creature to deal with. And still he is clubbed to death in the streets and flattened out beneath the tyres of passing cars on the roads. For the bandicoot is anything but agile. He is inordinately fond of the ditch and gutter and will come out after dark, mooching around the garbage heaps and dustbins. And in the open, away from burrows and convenient nooks and corners, he is more or less defenceless. His gait is a slinking hobble and when hard-pressed he accelerates into an intoxicated lurch, but at all times his speed is negligible... Not that he is a coward. He will fight desperately when cornered. I have seen a bandicoot escape from between the jaws of

> a Poligar dog, biting and clawing his way to safety in a nearby drain. His thick body with its cover of loose hide and coarse, straight hair gives little purchase to canine jaws, and it takes a powerful dog to hold and kill him.

While Krishnan may use the occasional anthropomorphic adjective or metaphor, his descriptions of wild species are neither sentimental nor condescending. His essays convey a considerable amount of information, though he is not a scientist cataloguing behavioural traits and taxonomical details, but essentially a storyteller whose protagonists are the birds and animals he observes. Acutely conscious of the role that wildlife plays in Indian culture, Krishnan was, in a sense, rewriting the parables of the *Jataka Tales* and *Hitopadesha*, for readers in the twentieth century and beyond. The birds and animals in his stories don't talk or behave like human beings. Instead, they are living, breathing creatures in the wild, though they do have lessons to teach us.

II

TRACING THE EDGE

Rivers–Coastlines–Wetlands

1

AFTER THE FLOOD

The boatman squats in his wooden skiff, using a plastic scoop to bail out water that has seeped through cracks in the hull. At 6 a.m., thick fog obscures everything beyond the prow of the boat. We are standing on the bank of the Dibru River, a tributary of the Brahmaputra, in north-eastern Assam. The grey current licks the sand but barely seems to move, merging with the opaque stasis of the fog. Stepping awkwardly from the muddy shoreline into the flimsy boat, I topple over while trying to settle myself on the narrow strut that serves as a seat. We almost capsize, though the water is shallow, and the stern is wedged in the sand. Manash Pratim, my guide, and the boatman help me up and I brace myself, feet spread apart, hands gripping the gunnels on either side.

Using a long bamboo pole, our boatman steers us into the void. The air is cold, motionless, and damp. There seems to be nothing ahead of us and I feel as if we are drifting through an infinite cloud. Pleated ripples diverge from either side of the prow. Feeling somewhat steadier, I reach into the water with my right hand and find that the river is warmer than the air. The boat rocks gently each time the boatman plunges his pole into the stream, propelling us through the fog. Bits of flotsam drift by, sticks and stray water hyacinths, as well as clumps of oily foam, evidence of pollution. Glancing over my shoulder, I can see that the shore has disappeared. It seems as if we have passed beyond the edge of the earth.

Eventually, a low sandbar appears ahead of us like a shadowy seam where the water joins with the land. There is no sky, only the enveloping fog. Having lost all sense of direction, I try unsuccessfully to reorient myself as we step onto shore. The boatman immediately turns around to ferry the third member of our party across and we wait in silence. There is nothing to say.

Ten minutes later, Runap Gogoi, Manash's colleague, joins us and the boatman disappears again without a word. I am accompanied by the same team that guided me around Dehing Patkai National Park. Together, we set off across the sand, which is firm underfoot but embossed with delicate patterns of receding floodwaters, a ruffled expanse of miniature dunes where the swollen current once lapped the riverbed. We skirt around scalloped troughs formed by whirlpools boring into the sand. A desolate, lifeless landscape surrounds us, blanketed beneath a cloud, and I imagine that we are walking on the surface of a barren planet other than our own.

Manash seems to know the way, leading us across unmarked terrain. We follow no path or footprints, only the undulating edge of a sandbar that was once submerged and sculpted by cross-currents. Fifteen minutes later, we come to a stagnant pond rimmed with algae, the first sign of life. Beyond this, a higher sandbank rises a couple of metres above us. Through the fog, I can just make out a fringe of grass growing along the top.

'This island was formed only last year,' Manash tells me, as we circle the pond. 'It appeared after the floods in July.'

During each monsoon, the river reshapes the land, carving out a new course for itself while depositing huge quantities of sand and silt. Flying into Dibrugarh, four days ago, I could see the broad floodplain of the Brahmaputra with its interlacing streams, exposed shoals of sand, and scattered islands. From the air, the river looked like an enormous rope unravelling into different strands, diverging and converging as it flows out of the Himalaya through the fertile lowlands of Assam.

Climbing the sandbank, we wade into the grass which is wet with dew and waist high, a few prodigious stems rising over our heads. It grows thickly in places between bare patches of crusted silt. Only one species of grass has established itself here. Runap tell me its local name—ekora. Prevalent throughout Assam, especially in places like Kaziranga National Park, it is often referred to generically as elephant grass, though its scientific name is *Saccharum ravennae*, a wild relative of sugar cane. Ekora quickly colonizes these shifting sandscapes which are known as a char or chapori in Assamese.

'This grass grows fast. I was here only two weeks ago and now it is already this much higher,' Manash says, measuring 20 centimetres with his hands.

All around us, I can see where the ekora is spreading, sending out runners or adventitious roots from which new tufts of grass emerge. The seeds could have been washed here and germinated once the floodwaters receded or clumped strands of roots and rhizomes may have been carried along with the silt, taking hold on new ground. I can see a few other plants, including a casuarina bush, but the chapori is dominated by ekora. Closer to the ground a spidery fern has found purchase in the soil, alongside a small seedling with dark red leaves.

The idea that we are standing on land that wasn't here six months ago is unsettling but also strangely reassuring. When a flood occurs, it disassembles the soil upriver and then reassembles it downstream, an annual process of regeneration. And then, in a short space of time, no more than a season, life takes root and spreads. Ekora is a pioneer species, claiming the island for itself but also preparing this nascent ecosystem for other life forms. Its long, coarse blades have a sharp edge that can cut a person's skin like a razor, though at this stage the grass is still relatively soft.

The youngest landscape I have ever traversed, this island has a history as old as the river. We have stepped into a world that has just been created, the ground beneath my feet newly formed—a fresh, unnamed place beneath an ancient sky. During the last century, this entire region of north-eastern Assam has changed dramatically.

On 15 August 1950, one of the most severe earthquakes in human memory (8.6 on the Richter scale, with several aftershocks above 6), violently shook this region of Assam. The epicentre was in the Himalaya, north of the Mishmi Hills of Arunachal Pradesh, then known as the North-East Frontier Agency. More than 1,600 villages were completely destroyed as were towns like Digboi. Official estimates put the death toll at more than 1,500 victims, though the actual number was probably much higher. Widespread destruction of homes, railway lines, bridges, and tea gardens disrupted life in Assam for years afterwards and the physical features of the Upper Brahmaputra Valley were changed forever. The earthquake immediately shifted the course of the rivers, which were in spate at that time, almost doubling their width. Millions of tonnes of sediment from landslides in the mountains were carried downstream, while in many places the ground became a fluid whorl, a phenomenon known as liquefaction. This catastrophic earthquake, and an earlier temblor in 1897, were caused by the sudden shifting of continental plates where India connects with the rest of Asia.

Dr Anwaruddin Chowdhury, an eminent conservationist and retired IAS officer, has written about the ecological effects of this tectonic event.

> Dibru-Saikhowa was once a rainforest but during the great Assam earthquake of 1950, a large part of the area sank by a few metres, resulting in regular flooding. The natural vegetation then gradually changed to tropical deciduous forest with salix swamps.... By the late 1990s, a major stretch of the Lohit river was diverted, which eroded a large chunk of landmass stocked with trees. Soon villagers lured by timber smugglers caused more damage by hacking down most of the remaining trees! By the first decade of the present century, the 30 m. wide Dangori river and 50 m. wide Dibru river turned into 700 m. to two kilometre-wide rivers (at

> places)—an example of 'river capture'! The entire park is now dominated by tall grass and degraded woodland with some salix swamps. But the large salix swamps with mature trees have almost vanished.

The new chapori we visit is just one small part of an ever-changing landscape where nature's resilience is being tested and proved as it rewilds itself. With the grass come insects, tiny flies that land on my glasses and crawl along the frames until I flick them off. They have migrated here and multiplied. Between the blades of grass, miniscule spiders with round bodies like gold beads have constructed their webs to catch these flying specks of chitin. The insects, in turn, attract birds to this island—endemic grassland species like the swamp prinia as well as migrants from as far away as Europe. The common reed bunting has travelled thousands of kilometres to winter here. Though a relatively common migrant in western India, it was reported in Assam for the first time, exactly a month ago. Manash is delighted because we observe two individuals on the ground and then perched atop tufts of grass. The male has a black head with a white moustachial stripe and the female is tan and brown. At a distance they could be mistaken for house sparrows, but their presence adds to a sense of newness and discovery. For a serious birdwatcher like Manash it is a rare, auspicious encounter.

Among other avian species we see a Jerdon's babbler clinging to a tall stem of ekora that bends under the bird's slight weight. Through my binoculars I can see the babbler opening its beak to emit a faint trill as the sun finally begins to disperse the fog. This morning, we encounter a dozen birds I've never seen before, including a golden-headed cisticola. While its plumage is not as dramatic as its name suggests, it is a lively, khaki-coloured bird with dark streaks on its back and wings. Males sport a gold crest during the breeding season. We also see a white-tailed stonechat, with distinctive pied markings, though most grassland birds have relatively dull colouring.

In the distance, I can now see a line of tall trees a couple of kilometres away that marks the edge of Dibru–Saikhowa National Park and Biosphere Reserve. These protected wildlands consist mostly of chapori that extend over 765 square kilometres. Adjacent to this are the Koliapani grasslands and Maguri marshes which have both been designated as Important Birding Areas by the IUCN.

The new island, which Manash says is about 2 hectares (5 acres) in size, also attracts small mammals from the forests nearby. We find fresh prints of jackals, civets, and jungle cats, as well as dry scat containing feathers and bones. The surface soil is a chalky grey colour and still bears the marks of flowing water. It also preserves the prints of birds that landed here soon after the floods receded, mostly waders with long, splayed toes, as well as the webbed impressions of ducks' feet. These marks have dried and hardened upon the brittle crust of silt, like recent fossils that have been preserved along with the rippled fingerprints of the flood.

∽

Maguri–Motapung Wetlands takes its name from an indigenous catfish (*Clarius magur*) found in these waters. Manash explains that the local name, magur, is a reference to the shape of its head, which is similar to a mugger crocodile, though the catfish seldom grows larger than 30 centimetres. Its mouth is lined with small teeth that add to its menacing appearance. Sometimes referred to as a walking catfish (or Asian catfish), it is able to breath oxygen from the air when it is out of the water and its strong pectoral fins are used to drag itself over patches of dry land, slithering from one waterbody to another. This allows it to survive in shallow channels choked with weeds as well as polluted ponds and streams. However, the magur's ability to remain alive out of water, as well as its flavourful flesh, has led to its popularity in fish markets, where it can be sold alive. Because of overfishing, this species is now classified as endangered on the IUCN's Red List.

Around half-past two in the afternoon, we board another boat, similar to the one in which we crossed the Dibru River. But here we set off along a narrow channel, hardly 5 metres wide. The sun is already descending behind us, for it rises and sets more than an hour earlier in Northeast India than it does in the central and western parts of the country. Beel is the Assamese name for a lake or wetlands. Maguri Beel covers roughly 10 square kilometres, with areas of open water, as well as intersecting channels, marsh, and grasslands. This varied habitat supports an eclectic array of birdlife, particularly migratory species that cross the Himalaya, following flyways along the Siang or Brahmaputra Valley. For many of these birds, Maguri is one of the first stops after their exhausting journey and the wetlands provide an abundance of aquatic plants and animals on which they feed. Though it is not part of a national park or wildlife sanctuary, Maguri Beel is a protected area, popular with birdwatchers and photographers. Fishermen from nearby villages also cast their nets here for catfish and other species.

Manash and Runap board the skiff with me, along with a young boatman who poles us slowly through the shallow waterways. Though I recognize a number of familiar birds, from ruddy shelducks to citrine wagtails, there are many species I've never seen before. Manash points out a rosy pipit on the near bank and further off, a Pacific golden plover. In the distance, we can hear flocks of ducks emitting gossipy, muttering calls as they feed. One common resident in this part of Assam is the Asian openbill, a relatively small, compact stork with a large bill that has a noticeable gap between its upper and lower mandibles which meet only at the tip. I've seen openbills before but never this close and they eye us warily, though we are able to approach within a few metres. Standing on long pink legs, most of their bodies are a greyish white and their wings are black. They feed on fish and snails, as well as other crustaceans, reptiles, and amphibians. Though it looks as if it might be an evolutionary mistake, their unusual bill allows them to scoop food from the shallows and strain out water. Like most storks they make very little noise, except for soft grunts and hoots. Generally monogamous, openbills gather as pairs at communal nesting sites during the breeding season in early spring.

Most of the wetlands are covered in water hyacinths, an invasive species brought here from South America by the British, as an ornamental plant. Despite its attractive mauve flowers, this weed is a severe environmental threat throughout India because it spreads rapidly and reduces water levels, choking out all other forms of life. At Maguri, the channels and some ponds have been cleared by fishermen. Further off is a wall of high grass that encloses one side of the wetlands like a stockade. A purple heron and a lesser adjutant stork are standing sentry near the perimeter, while a flotilla of ducks—mostly red-crested pochards and gadwalls—are feeding along the far edges of a pond. A pheasant-tailed jacana picks its way gingerly over a raft of water hyacinths and with our binoculars we identify greylags and bar-headed geese huddled in the grass along the shore.

After an hour, we get down on a spit of land that separates two marshes. Immediately, our clothes are covered by swarms of tiny white bugs that look like flecks of lint. Barn swallows and plain martins skim overhead, feeding on these and other insects attracted to the beel. By now the sun has dropped closer to the horizon casting the wetlands in bronze. Fishermen are pulling in their nets, some in boats like ours and others wading through the waist-deep water.

As we turn back, we meet another group of birdwatchers in three boats. Most of them are wearing camouflage uniforms and are armed with assault rifles, though they wave and greet us with friendly smiles. Shadowing the boats along the shore are six commandos in full battle gear. When I react with alarm, Manash quickly explains that they are from the Central Reserve Police Force (CRPF) post in Tinsukia. He recognizes the local commandant, a woman, who is a keen birdwatcher. In one of the boats is a tall Sikh officer, in a khaki uniform, with stars on his shoulders and a badge on his turban. The bodyguards are obviously here to protect him. Assam has had a long history of political unrest and insurgency and the CRPF is deployed in large numbers. Though the peaceful surroundings of Maguri Beel seem to harbour no threats, they are obviously taking no chances

The greatest danger here is oil, which is being pumped out of the ground from wells near the wetlands. About half a kilometre away from Maguri, near the edge of Dibru–Saikhowa National Park, is the site of the Bhagjan blowout, a gas fire and oil spill that occurred in August 2020. The blaze continued for five months before it was finally put out and the well was capped. During that time huge quantities of oil seeped into the wetlands and the Dibru River killing more than 25,000 birds and animals. Showing me the site of Well No. 5, which has now been sealed and surrounded by a high barbed wire fence, Manash explains that the ecology of the wetlands was badly affected and the water is still polluted, impacting virtually every species that lives here, including river dolphins. Nevertheless, despite the catastrophe, other oil wells continue operating near Maguri.

Balancing the country's demands for hydrocarbons with environmental concerns is a difficult and complex challenge, especially when seismic activity, annual floods, and political unrest all add to the instability of this region. Geographically, Assam has served as a bridge for many species that began to migrate here from other parts of Asia roughly 50 million years ago, when the two landmasses came in contact with each other. As a result of this tectonic collision, which still reverberates from time to time, a whole range of new creatures entered the subcontinent from tigers and elephants to catfish and cobras. It represents an ecological frontier where European migrants come in contact with Oriental species. Despite constant change and upheaval, the rivers, grasslands, and forests of Assam provide vital habitat for both transient and resident species, all of whom live on the edge—geographically, biologically, and metaphorically.

As the sun goes down, we pull over at the side of the road near Maguri, next to a small pond hemmed in by tall grass. Runap explains that the predominant species here is known as khagori in Assam, and elsewhere as kans. Mature stalks rise to almost twice my height with large plumes like feather dusters turning gold at sunset. Growing about 2 metres from the edge of a pond, the khagori forms a dense barricade of thatch. Along the shoreline, two swamp francolins are feeding at twilight. With binoculars, I can see their tan plumage which is heavily barred on the back with white streaks on the breast. Endemic to this part of Assam they are a 'target species' for birdwatchers, Manash tells me.

After circling the pond, we spot a greater painted snipe standing motionless against the grass. It is completely camouflaged, though once I see it, the white belly, russet throat, and spectacle-like markings on its face are hard to miss. Meanwhile, at the same place, a brown-cheeked rail emerges furtively from the grass, its feathers mottled with rich shades of rust and ochre. Moments later, a ruddy-breasted crake appears half a metre away, partly hidden within the shadows of khagori stems. All three species are similar in shape, each about the size of a small partridge, with stubby tails, plump bodies, and long, delicate legs. In the fading light, we watch these three birds as they pick their way along the muddy strip of shoreline between the grass and the pond. Timidly, they skulk amidst the darkening shadows as fading daylight blurs into night.

~

To get some sense of the different species of fish that live in the wetlands and rivers, I ask Runap and Manash to take me to the local fish market at Guijan Ghat, the main river port on the Dibru River. Runap's home is in the neighbouring village of Natun Gaon and he tells me that the fishermen arrive with their catch at 5.30 a.m., 11 a.m., and 2 p.m. A local cooperative organizes the auction, with retailers purchasing fish that they resell in the bazaars of Tinsukia and other neighbouring towns.

When we arrive at Guijan Ghat, just before 11 in the morning, everything is quiet. Under the rusting metal sheets of an open shed hangs a large set of scales. Next to this is a table where three bored-looking men are seated with open ledgers and a calculator. Even the flies that hover seem to be sluggish at this time of day. The auctioneer is middle-aged, with rheumy eyes and a grizzled, unshaven face. Preparing a paan for himself, he smears the leaf with lime and adds betel nuts and tobacco, then stuffs it in his mouth before taking his seat on a cracked plastic chair by the scales. Several buyers are hanging about but no fishermen have arrived. I notice a stack of aluminium basins, with holes in the bottoms, like giant sieves.

Finally, a man on a bicycle pulls up with a large plastic shopping bag suspended from the crossbar. As he unties his load and carries it across to the scales, the buyers gather around. A slurry of tiny fish, no bigger than my fingernails are poured into the aluminium basin. This small species, which looks as if it belongs in an aquarium rather than a fish market, is known as puthi. Later, I learn its Latin and common English names—*Puntius saphore*, the spotfin swamp barb. A common river fish, it is cooked whole in curries, with the head, fins, and scales intact.

The auctioneer shakes the basin to strain out the water before placing it on the scales. He calls out the weight, just over five kilos. Two of the buyers make an offer, followed by a third. Within a minute the bid is accepted, a hurried transaction that seems to satisfy the fisherman. His name and the weight of the catch are noted down by the accountants, while the third man at the table collects the payment and adds it to a wad of cash he holds in one hand.

'These fish sell here for as little as twenty rupees a kilo,' Runap tells me, 'but in Tinsukia, the price can go above a hundred. Sometimes the fish merchants mark up the price eight or ten times.'

By now, several more fishermen have arrived. One of them empties his catch into another basin, revealing a dozen or more eels coiled together. Though I cannot make out the heads or tails, they are still alive, writhing in slippery knots. Mostly dark green, they have yellow underbellies. Kuchia is the local name, Runap says, and they will fetch a good price. The eels sell for more than ₹200 per kilo, though the auctioneer speaks rapidly and signals with his hands, which makes it difficult to understand exactly what is being transacted.

I had hoped that one of the fishermen would arrive with magur, the catfish for which Maguri Beel is named, but today none of them are brought to the market. As each species is emptied into the basins, Runap and Manash recite their names. The Asian needlefish is known as kokila and has a thin beak almost half again as long as its body. None of the fish brought to the market today are bigger than 20 centimetres and most are much smaller. A bottom feeder called goroi is an olive-green colour with dark vertical stripes. Another is called boroli, which seems to attract a lot of interest from the buyers. Each time the auctioneer accepts a bid, he helps himself to one or two fish, which he slips into a basin under his chair as part of his commission.

Most of the fish are dead on arrival but one of the fishermen brings in a plastic bucket that looks as if it is full of oil. When he dumps the contents into a basin, I can see more than fifty small black bodies squirming about as water pours out of the sieve. My first impression is that they must be leeches, about 6 centimetres long, though when I look closely, I can see they are a small catfish with prominent whiskers.

'Don't touch them,' Manash warns me. 'They have a painful sting.'

These are called singhi or xingi. Known as the Asian stinging catfish, their pectoral fins have venomous spines. This species is found in many parts of South Asia, including Bangladesh and Sri Lanka as well as Myanmar. They are said to have medicinal properties and are used to treat diseases like malaria. Also called fossil cats, singhi are popular with aquarists who keep exotic freshwater species.

Within half an hour, the auction is over; both the fishermen and the buyers have dispersed. All of the fish that were caught and sold this morning at Guijan Ghat are wild species taken from ponds and flooded ditches, marshes, and rivers. As much a part of the ecosystem as birds and animals, they also have a commercial value. Larger fish, like catla and rohu, sold in town markets are now raised in farms but these smaller species don't lend themselves to aquaculture. Watching the wholesale trading in wild fish, I wonder how much longer human beings can continue to harvest nature's dwindling abundance. The wetlands, where these small creatures thrive, are already severely threatened by oil slicks, invasive plants, and human encroachment.

~

Stories of floods are as old as humankind. In different traditions, torrential storms and rising waters that inundate the land signify some form of divine retribution as well as the renewal of life. In essence, either God or nature passes a moral judgement on human society and wipes out everything on earth in order to begin the process of creation all over again. European naturalists struggled for centuries to reconcile Biblical accounts of the great flood with their discoveries of fossils and emerging theories of evolution. A variety of antediluvian narratives were proposed to explain the existence and extinction of dinosaurs and the changes that have occurred in different genera over millions of years. The idea of a sudden, apocalyptic deluge that destroys all living things, except for a few chosen survivors that are carried to safety on higher ground, suggests that the natural world is governed by vengeful forces that administer environmental justice.

At the heart of these stories lies a fatalistic sense of despair that, somehow, we have failed to live up to the expectations of our creators. For early inhabitants of river valleys, from the Nile to the Euphrates and the Indus to the Brahmaputra, annual flooding of fields and pastures, homesteads, and forests was an accepted pattern of life. But when extreme weather made the waters rise to catastrophic levels it was interpreted as an unprecedented, supernatural event. Within these cultures it became part of their collective memory, both a climatic and a climactic moment in history and legend, suggesting that life is not continuous but can be wiped out and that we human beings are responsible for nature's destruction and incapable of restoring it on our own.

Folklore in Assam and Arunachal Pradesh contains many stories about rivers and floods. From the Mishmi Hills, immediately to the north of Dibru–Saikhowa, comes a tale about the origins of the Brahmaputra River which was once confined to a large lake high in the mountains. Without access to its waters, the creatures of the lower hills and plains suffered from severe droughts. One day, a worm burrowed through the soil into the lake and quenched its thirst. Out of this thin channel seeped a trickle of moisture that caught the attention of a wild cat who made the channel wider with its claws so that it could drink its fill. The river that flowed out of the channel then followed the cat as it wandered across the mountains, which is why the tributaries of the Brahmaputra meander through the hills on their way to Assam.

In other folk tales, collected by the ethnographer Verrier Elwin from different tribal communities in the Northeast, the source of a primal river is guarded by a serpent who holds the water in its coils. One story recounts how a bird pecked out the snake's eyes while it was asleep. As the serpent writhed in pain, water gushed forth and formed a great river. The Kaman Mishmi tribe, in the Lohit Valley, have a myth in which their deity, Kharane, tells a man named Brassa that the first rain will fall on the earth when migratory birds arrive near his home. Brassa selfishly keeps this information to himself and when the birds appear, only he has prepared his fields to grow crops. But because of Brassa's greed, a limited amount of rain falls, which is quickly used up. Brassa then begs Kharane to send more rain. This time there is a deluge and the land is flooded. When others discover what Brassa has done, they beat him to death and cut his body into small pieces that are scattered over the land, bringing fertility to the soil.

In another story told by the Wancho tribe, the water deity, Namwang, takes the form of a wild buffalo. When hunters kill and eat the buffalo, Namwang sends a great flood to destroy humankind. The only survivors are a woman and her daughter who did not feast on the buffalo's flesh. The daughter is then impregnated by the wind and gives birth to the Wancho tribe.

∽

In January, when I visit north-eastern Assam, the level of the rivers has dropped to their lowest point, leaving the highwater mark several hundred metres from shore, separated by an expanse of sand. At Guijan Ghat, four large ferries are anchored a few metres offshore. We make our way down to the water's edge where a smaller country boat is tied up. About 6 metres long, it is partly covered with a blue plastic tarp stretched over a bamboo frame to create a tent-like shelter. The boatman, his head wrapped in a scarf, is bailing out water from the stern near a diesel engine that looks as if it has been salvaged and rebuilt several times over. The boat is old and battered, as if it has ridden out numerous floods.

Manash introduces me to Hiren who has organized our trip to the southern part of Dibru–Saikhowa National Park. Though Hiren owns one of the large ferries, he has rented the smaller boat and hired the boatman, explaining that the water level is too low for us to use his vessel today. He is armed with a dao in a beadwork sheath slung over one shoulder and across his back. Including the wooden hilt, this broadsword is about three-quarters of a metre long, most of which consists of a flat steel blade sharpened on one side. Daos are standard equipment in the Northeast, used for everything from cutting bamboo to clearing grass and thorns, or chopping firewood. It can also serve as a weapon.

The engine starts with a black cloud of diesel smoke as we push off into the murky water. Unlike the silent fishing craft that we rode through the Maguri wetlands, this boat roars and vibrates like a floating stone crusher. Our pilot sits atop an elevated bench at the back, operating the rudder and throttle. He can see over the top of the blue plastic roof, keeping an eye out for sandbars and other obstructions.

We are travelling downstream, towards a confluence where the Dibru joins a branch of the Lohit and the Brahmaputra. All around us, I can see evidence of floods. Protruding from the current at several places are dead trees, their skeletal branches entwined with accumulated debris—sticks, grass, and various forms of plastic trash. A tea garden extends along the eroded riverbanks. Floodwaters have gouged out sections of the land, leaving the roots of tea bushes and shade trees exposed. At a few places, sandbags have been stacked up to fight the current but it is a losing battle. The factory buildings, where the tea is processed, are also in danger of being swallowed up by the river, their rusting, derelict sheds standing barely a metre from the edge.

Travelling downstream with the engine running, we make good time but the moving air is bitterly cold and I huddle in a plastic chair with my hands tucked under my armpits. The river broadens to half a kilometre or more, a featureless expanse of water and sand. Occasionally, a flight of white egrets or black cormorants pass by, winging their way through the monochromatic mist. The sun has risen behind us but it is a weak yellow disc, barely visible through low-lying clouds. The only other birds we see are a grey heron standing sentinel on a sandbar and darters that perch on dead branches near the shoreline with long, serpentine necks and chisel-like beaks. We also pass a great crested grebe that is paddling upstream, a handsome bird with a russet head and black cockade.

Suddenly, the smooth expanse of water swells up in front of the boat's prow, about 30 metres to my right, and I see a Ganges river dolphin breach the surface. Visible for only a moment, it has a sleek grey shape, the same colour as the water. Hiren signals to the boatman to ease up on the throttle and a few minutes later, we spot the dolphin again, rolling over on the surface. This time I can see its long, toothed beak though it appears for no more than a couple of seconds. After breaching a third time, further off, it disappears. These brief glimpses are a reassuring sight, for the river shows signs of pollution, particularly clots of oily foam floating on the surface. Nevertheless, the presence of the dolphin means that the Dibru is still clean enough to support these sensitive, aquatic mammals.

Further downstream, near the confluence, we come upon two more dolphins that rise to the surface at regular intervals. When the boatman cuts the engine, they seem to circle around us, breaching more than a dozen times. Ganges river dolphins are called sisu or hisu in Assamese and shushuk in Bengali. Virtually blind, they can distinguish only shades of light and darkness. Living in the silt-filled waters of the Ganga and Brahmaputra, dolphins emit high frequency sounds that help them locate the fish on which they feed.

One of the oldest mammals on earth, they are related to the smaller Indus river dolphin found in Pakistan. Their ancestors once swam in the Tethys Sea, more than 50 million years ago, before the Himalaya were formed. As the mountains ascended out of the sea, these ancient cetaceans adapted to life in the great rivers. With the emergence of the Himalaya, the climate changed gradually and the monsoon became part of annual weather patterns, resulting in floods and erosion that impacted the river dolphins' habitat. Nevertheless, their species survived these turbulent conditions. Today, they are endangered not by floods or erosion but by human indifference and waste.

An hour and a half later, we pull over to shore on an island at the southern end of a riverine archipelago, most of which is part of Dibru–Saikhowa National Park. Hiren leaps ashore carrying a bulky anchor that he plunges into the sand to hold us fast. Two smaller boats are tied up here and beyond a thicket of casuarina, I can see thatch huts and buffaloes. A large ber tree also marks the spot, its leafy branches laden with green and reddish-brown fruit. Still numb with cold, I stand with my back to the sun which has finally burned through the mist and gilds a strip of tall grass on the far side of the huts. Unlike the new chapori we visited yesterday, this island has obviously been here for some time, though the sandbanks along the shore crumble like chunks of ice calving off a glacier where the current of the Brahmaputra cuts into the shore.

After a hurried breakfast, we stop by the herders' camp. About forty buffaloes of all ages are tethered here, though several of the young males are loose and get up aggressively to challenge us. They are handsome, imposing bulls, with dangerous-looking horns. The herdsmen warn us not to get too close. Three thatch huts serve as home for these hardy pastoralists who live a rough life with their animals. One of the elders is a short, gaunt man with white bristle on his chin and a woollen scarf wrapped around his head. He insists we take photographs of him and his prize buffalo, a blonde female named Bhogimati, which means white pearl. She also has a calf that is light brown but not as pale as its mother. The rest of the herd is mostly black and dark brown.

Domesticated buffaloes in different parts of India show considerable variations in size and shape, though they are all descended from wild herds that were once common in many parts of the subcontinent. Assam is one of the few places where wild buffaloes are still found in significant numbers and they often interbreed with livestock. When I ask the herders if their animals ever mate with wild buffaloes, they confirm that this happens, saying that it is usually wild bulls that cross with tame females. Dibru–Saikhowa has a sizeable population of wild buffaloes. Yesterday, in the early morning fog, we saw a group of four near the Maguri wetlands. From a distance, they looked no different than the animals tethered here, except that their horns appeared larger.

The tame herds are let loose to graze in the grasslands and as we walk from one side of the island to the other, we come upon a number of animals that have been allowed to roam free, including several females with newborn calves. Manash tells me that the herders spend only part of the year on this island, arriving after the floods recede and remaining until the onset of the monsoon. They collect milk and take it across the river by boat to sell on the mainland. At this point, the river is almost a kilometre wide. When I ask how the herds get to the island and back, the answer is simple—both domesticated and wild buffaloes are strong swimmers. The herdsmen and their animals move from one shore to the other according to the seasons and the rise and fall of water levels. In this way, the rhythm and pulse of the river sets migration in motion.

We see few birds on this island, other than flocks of common cranes that have flown here from Russia and Central Asia. They are shy and take to the air when we approach, though they circle overhead in loose formations calling out with hoarse trumpeting cries. The grass cover on the island has been severely degraded by the buffaloes. One area is nothing but a field of dry tussocks, though dense stands of ekora and khagori survive in other sections. We also come upon two small cultivated patches with huts, where families have settled and are growing vegetables. Hiren tells us that one household lost three members in the floods last July.

My main purpose in coming here is to see Dibru–Saikhowa's feral horses. Several accounts I've read suggest that these animals were released at the end of World War II by British troops stationed in Assam. However, it seems improbable that the Indian Army would have abandoned their horses after the Japanese were defeated. More likely, though I have no evidence to prove this, the horses were set loose on the islands earlier in the war, when a Japanese invasion seemed imminent, and the allies were retreating. The same was done with elephants used for logging by the Bombay Burmah Trading Corporation Limited. Those elephants lived out the war in the jungle and were later reunited with their handlers once the fighting ended. It's possible that the horses were released at the same time, though they were never retrieved and rehabilitated. The great earthquake of 1950, five years after the end of World War II, would have further displaced and isolated these herds. Today, they continue to roam free in the park, having survived on their own for almost eighty years.

One of the herdsmen agrees to help us find the feral horses and we set off on a stiff march through the grasslands, circling the island for almost an hour before doubling back towards the buffalo camp and our boat. Just when I begin to think that our luck has run out, we come upon a herd of eleven horses standing in the shade of a bamboo grove. A mix of mares and stallions, with no foals among them, they are all a dark chestnut brown. Allowing us to approach within 30 metres, the horses watch me with dark, equine eyes, cautious but not alarmed. They appear healthy and well fed. Their thick tails and manes look as if they've been recently groomed, though these animals have never been stabled and must be the fourth or fifth generation to live in the wild.

After I've taken photographs, Manash approaches the horses from the other side. They soon become skittish and break into a run. Until now, they could have easily been a group of polo ponies enjoying a day off but as they canter away from us with their manes flowing and hides rippling in the sunlight, it is obvious that these graceful creatures have never been ridden by human beings. For all intents and purposes, they are wild, though they do not figure in the official schedules of the Wild Life Protection Act.

Feral animals can cause a lot of damage to fragile ecosystems and equids set loose in other places like Australia, which has an estimated 400,000 horses living in the wild, and more than a million feral donkeys, have become serious pests. They destroy natural pastures through overgrazing, deplete waterholes used by other wildlife, and cause severe erosion because of their hard hooves. Without any predators to control their numbers, Australia's feral herds have proliferated to the point where they must be culled.

Though a proper survey of the feral horses in Dibru–Saikhowa has not been conducted, rough estimates put their numbers at approximately 300, broken up into small herds like these. Though tigers are seldom found in the park, it has a healthy population of leopards, which prey on the horses, augmenting their more traditional diet of hog deer, muntjac, and sambar. Annual floods also help control numbers and weaker animals are often washed away when the rivers rise, while most of the herds find higher ground. Over the years, attempts have been made to capture some of the horses. In 2020, six of them were confiscated from smugglers who were transporting them to a private polo club in Guwahati, presumably for breeding. Not knowing what else to do, the Assam Forest Department re-released the animals back onto the Dibru–Saikhowa islands.

As we follow the feral horses on foot through the grass and scrub, they mingle with the herdsmen's buffaloes. Living without support from human beings, in isolated habitat, they represent a puzzling paradox. The chapori grasslands sustain large numbers of domesticated buffaloes but few, if any, wild ungulates, other than the horses. Whatever the origins of these feral herds, their story suggests an element of resilience—abandoned warhorses that now live in relative peace, on islands whose contours shift with the seasons. Drawing neat lines between domesticated and wild species is often more difficult than it might seem, and I feel a confusing ambivalence, when it comes to these creatures that are not native species but have established themselves here along the uncertain, uncharted margins of rivers.

2

DENWA BACKWATERS

At dusk, the verdant colours of the forest are subdued. But the leopard's coat, with its pattern of black rosettes on a field of gold, seems to glow like embers amidst the ashen shadows of the trees. Rising from a crouch, he climbs the embankment near a waterhole, gliding away from us without a sound. An adult male, the leopard is well over 2.5 metres long, including his luxurious, white-tufted tail. He was drinking at the forest pool when our arrival interrupted him. Reaching level ground, no more than 30 metres from our jeep, the leopard pauses and turns to look in our direction, his features expressing more annoyance than alarm. The amber eyes with coal black pupils could easily be part of the dappled markings on his fur and it seems as if his body is covered with dozens of eyes, all of them staring directly at me.

Nothing compares to the beauty of a leopard's pelage, not even the stripes on a tiger, or the iridescent hues in a peacock's tail. The dark spots, grouped mostly in clusters of five, cover virtually every part of his body. Beneath these rosettes, the underlying colour varies from a golden tan to different shades of yellow and white, though the overall effect is like a fierce blaze of sunlight filtering through the silhouettes of leaves. This provides the predator with the camouflage he needs to prowl the jungle unseen.

Yet here he is, completely visible and unobscured, like a startling image projected on a twilit screen. His powerful, agile body is poised, as if preparing to bound away out of sight, though the leopard remains completely still for thirty seconds before he moves again, betraying no urgency at all. As he turns broadside and his tail sways from left to right, we watch him for several long minutes, mesmerized by the patterns on his coat and the wild intensity of his gaze. Eventually, he slips away, passing through a stand of trees before disappearing into the darkening forest beyond.

We are driving through the buffer zone of Satpura Tiger Reserve, where night safaris are permitted. The leopard has appeared less than a kilometre from the gate, long before my guide, Khet Singh, has switched on his spotlight. Accompanying me and driving the jeep is Arpita Dutta, a naturalist from Forsyth Lodge where I am staying. A short distance beyond the waterhole we come upon two other jeeps blocking the single-lane road. Minutes earlier, they had spotted a tiger crossing in front of their vehicles but it has vanished into a thick belt of lantana. We wait for a quarter of an hour, hoping it might reappear. Though we listen for alarm calls, the jungle is silent, and the tiger has either stopped to lie down or moved off across a low ridge.

By the time we drive on, darkness has fallen and the headlights of our jeep flash against a colonnade of teak trees bordering the unpaved track. Khet Singh shines his torch from side to side, hoping to catch the reflection of an animal's eyes. After turning off the main route, we come upon a large wild boar rooting in a ditch by the side of the road. He ignores us with his head lowered, intent on digging up a tuber or whatever his callused snout has smelled beneath the ground. The stiff black bristles on his back are raised like hackles and his strong shoulders thrust forward with determined energy like a bulldozer excavating a building site. When he finally looks up, his two small eyes shine in the torchlight and his face is caked with mud.

Further on, Khet Singh picks up a glint in the trees and spots a crested serpent eagle perched on a branch. After that we see two nilgai at some distance, their long necks shying away from the light, both females without horns.

After circling through the buffer zone for another hour, we stop at a forest department complex equipped with toilets. Solar lamps are the only source of light, emitting a chalky glow. A captive female elephant, tethered to a tree stump, ignores the tourists who approach her as she feeds on a pile of leaves. This elephant is used to patrol remote areas that are inaccessible by jeep, particularly during the monsoon. Satpura Tiger Reserve has no wild elephants, which disappeared from these forests centuries ago. Two female blackbuck with baleful eyes and slender legs that seem almost too thin for their bodies sidle up to me and nuzzle my hand, hoping for treats. Arpita explains that they were rescued when young and adopted by the forest guards.

From the camp, we carry on for several kilometres and drive up a rough track to a high point on a ridge where Arpita stops the jeep, turning off the engine and headlights. Khet Singh also switches off his torch and none of us speak. The night is moonless and it feels as if we are parked on the rim of the world, beneath a dazzling canopy of stars. Arpita tells me that several prehistoric rock shelters lie nearby that have paintings on the walls. As I look up at Orion, the celestial hunter with his hound, and other constellations arranged above us, I realize that the light from many of those stars is much older than the rock art left behind by stone age wanderers. Some of the distant galaxies are billions of light years away. Time loses all meaning amidst the infinite scale of the cosmos while the vast reaches of outer space suggest a strange sense of intimacy in this lonely place as if I might be able reach out and touch those pinpoints of light. The forest around us is invisible but I can feel the living presence of the trees and the nocturnal creatures that are beginning to move about under cover of darkness. As my eyes adjust to the starlight, I can just make out the faintest contours of the land and the blurred outline of the Satpura Range where the glittering sky is blotted out by hills. We often think of darkness as being empty and devoid of life, but here on this ridge, I am aware of the vibrancy of the night. Though the jungle may not be visible to my eyes, it is no less real or alive than it is during daylight hours.

Eventually, Arpita restarts the jeep and its headlights illuminate the rocky profile of the ridge. We turn around and head back down the track, with Khet Singh shining his spotlight into the bushes. The roar of the engine and the shafts of electric light penetrating the darkness seem all the more intrusive now. Just before the road levels off, we encounter a second leopard standing in a clearing, about 10 metres to our right. Two large, bright eyes return the glare of the torch beam. This animal is probably a female, smaller than the male we saw earlier at dusk. In the artificial light, the colours of her coat are muted, reduced almost to black and white, but the rosettes are just as striking. Every leopard has a different arrangement of spots, as distinct as fingerprints. Experienced naturalists can identify individual animals by the unique patterns on their fur. Khet Singh follows the leopard with his spotlight as she turns away with a dismissive whisk of her tail, stepping lightly through the grass before springing out of sight.

Though we see very few deer during our night drive, the buffer zone of the park contains enough prey for the leopards and tigers that hunt in this part of the forest. According to Arpita, the chances of sighting large predators in these peripheral forests is almost as good as it is in the core area of the reserve. At one point, a sambar hind crosses the road in front of us and we spot a few more nilgai before returning to the park gate, which closes at 8 p.m., allowing the animals some peace for the rest of the night. From here we drive back to the lodge through scattered settlements and fields.

Near a small village, Khet Singh shines his light into an open area of scrub. His torch picks up a pair of eyes and Arpita brakes. A small feline is eating something in a shallow depression and it takes a few minutes for us to realize it is a domestic cat from one of the village homes. Further on, we catch sight of its wild cousin, a jungle cat, which stands much taller on longer legs, marked with dark lateral stripes. The rest of its fur is a dusty brown. Larger than most house cats it has prominent, pointed ears with black tufts at the ends. Just before we reach the lodge, Khet Singh spots another creature. At first, it looks like a mongoose scurrying through the underbrush but when it comes out into the open and lifts its head, we can see it is an Indian fox. A sooty grey colour, with dark legs, it has a bushy, black-tipped tail. These smaller mammals live along the margins of the tiger reserve, retreating to the protection of the park during daylight hours but hunting and scavenging near human habitation during the night.

∽

The next morning, I wake up to slaughter.

At 5.30 a.m., one of the staff at Forsyth Lodge knocks on my door to make sure I am ready for a jeep safari. He then shows me a horrific scene outside my room. A green keelback has killed a common toad and is trying to swallow it whole. The snake is not very large, just over half a metre long, but the toad is the size of a cricket ball. During the night, it was obviously hunting for insects attracted to the outdoor light and, in the process, the toad fell victim to the snake. Keelbacks are not venomous though they have sharp teeth. This one has bitten the toad a number of times and blood is smeared all over the tiled floor. As a defence mechanism, the victim has urinated copiously, leaving a large puddle mixed with blood that makes the scene look all the more gruesome.

As its name suggests, the green keelback is the colour of bamboo with white and black streaks on both sides of its upper body. The head is slightly darker, marked by a flash of blue behind its jaws, which are stretched wide in a futile attempt to devour the toad. Having begun feeding from the rear, it has only been able to get one hind leg into its mouth. After half an hour, before I leave for my safari, the keelback has switched ends and part of the toad's head is lodged in its throat as the snake's jaws expand in a gaping yawn. Much later, when I return to my room, around noon, the snake is gone and the bloodstains have been mopped up. The staff tell me that the keelback was moved to a patch of jungle nearby, where it successfully ingested the toad, though I am sceptical and suspect the snake abandoned its meal.

Forsyth Lodge, named after Captain James Forsyth, the British hunter–explorer who visited these forests in the mid-nineteenth century, is a luxurious wildlife resort surrounded by 16 hectares (40 acres) of private jungle. In addition to keelbacks and toads, the dense scrub and trees provide refuge for a variety of small mammals, wild pigs, and deer. I am told that two years ago, during the pandemic lockdown, a tiger killed a cow less than a hundred metres from the lodge. The cow belonged to one of the villagers in a neighbouring settlement and the tiger remained near its kill for several days, within sight of the lodge.

With the increasing popularity of wildlife tourism in India, more and more resorts like Forsyth Lodge have been built near the entrances of national parks. While Satpura is one of the least crowded tiger reserves in the country, at least six jungle resorts are located on the park's perimeter, offering guests accommodation and meals, along with facilitating entry permits, guides, and jeep safaris. Though the forest departments in each state regulate the number of tourists that can enter core areas and buffer zones, high-end establishments catering to wealthy foreign and domestic visitors, provide exclusive access. Wildlife viewing has become an expensive pastime and cheaper options are hard to find. For the majority of young nature enthusiasts, the cost of visiting a national park becomes prohibitive, unless they are able to make bookings at forest department facilities, which are limited, very basic, and often poorly maintained.

Most jungle resorts like Forsyth Lodge employ naturalists to accompany guests on safari and help interpret the experience. For anyone who enjoys working in the wild and has some expertise in identifying birds and other animals, it can be a rewarding career, though the majority of parks and lodges close from mid-June to mid-November because of the monsoon and there isn't much job security. Arpita, who is from West Bengal, has worked with wildlife in different capacities over the past twenty years. She has been actively involved with education and community development projects related to wildlife, in addition to volunteering her time for animal rescue and rehabilitation. Most recently, over the past two years, she was hired as a researcher and conservationist on a project studying turtles and other reptiles in Northeast India.

'A lot of my time was spent in an office, writing reports and doing paperwork,' she tells me. 'But I really wanted to get back into the forest, which is why I took this job, so that I could recharge my batteries.'

Though her family, particularly her father, urged her to follow a more secure and practical profession, wildlife has always been Arpita's passion. She obviously cares deeply about conservation and wants to inspire others to do the same. When so many forces are arrayed against nature, it is encouraging that dedicated young naturalists like Arpita are working on the frontlines, actively engaged with preserving endangered species and promoting an appreciation for India's wild heritage.

The core area of Satpura Tiger Reserve lies to the south of Forsyth Lodge, on the other side of the Denwa backwaters, which were created when the Tawa Dam was completed in 1978. The tail end of the reservoir, where the Denwa River used to flow, is about 400 metres wide at this point. As the dawn sky brightens over the foothills, we board a motor launch and are ferried across to Madhai Gate where jeeps are waiting. In addition to the driver, the forest department requires that a trained guide accompany each vehicle. Vimla, a woman in her early thirties, who started working as a guide only six months ago, is assigned to our jeep. The driver's name is Vicky, an experienced veteran of these forests. Arpita knows him well and says that he is 'one of the best'.

The sun is just coming up as the four of us set off along the jungle track on a cool morning in late winter. Just beyond Madhai, flame of the forest or palash trees are blooming. Their orange-red blossoms attract a swarm of purple sunbirds that flit and hover as they draw nectar from the flowers. At the top of the tree, a black-winged kite sits alone and motionless, watching for any movement on the ground. This pale grey raptor with black eye patches and dark epaulettes on its wings is a graceful aerialist that swoops and dives while pursuing its prey.

A few chital are grazing at the edges of an open grassland but when we enter the trees it feels as if the jungle is still waking up after a late night. Early mornings are always a good time to see predators returning from their nocturnal pursuits but before the sun burns off the mist and dew, the jungle has a hollow stillness. The only sounds are birdcalls—barbets and mynahs mostly but also the mournful wail of a peafowl descending from its roost. We have already decided not to focus on seeing a tiger unless a clear opportunity arises. Too often drivers and guides on jeep safaris ignore other species until a tiger has been spotted, which means driving around in circles without fully appreciating the diversity of forest life. I have explained to Arpita and the others that my interest is in smaller mammals, as well as sloth bears, which are relatively common in the reserve.

Our first stop is a rocky escarpment overshadowed with sal trees. Arpita tells me that a pack of wild dogs, or dhole, have made their den in amongst the rocks above us. Only a few days ago, she and some other clients were able to watch a litter of pups playing near the mouth of a small cave. We scan the rocks with our binoculars but there is no sign of the dhole and Arpita suggests the adults may be out hunting at this hour, leaving the pups securely hidden out of sight.

From here, we continue further into the forest which grows thicker and more varied. One of the trees that catches my eye is ghiriya, also called bhirra. In English it is known as satinwood and the timber is prized for its pale lustre and fine grain which is used in marquetry and furniture making. At this time of year, in late February, the ghiriya's foliage turns a bright yellow which makes it stand out in the forest, as if each leaf has been gilded before it falls. Once the limbs are bare, the tree flowers in March with clusters of white blossoms that are almost as dramatic as the turning colours of the leaves. But perhaps the most recognizable feature of this tree is its bark which has a cork-like texture with ridges and furrows extending the length of its trunk. Ghiriya's thick bark serves as a fire retardant and protects the tree if the forest burns. It is also used by sambar and chital stags that rub their antlers on its rough surface to remove the velvet from their new tines. Many of the trees we pass show evidence of this, with smooth yellow patches about a metre and a half above the ground where the deer have scraped away the outer bark.

After crossing a low rise, we descend into a broad valley with meadows on either side of a shallow stream. Grazing on the dew-damp grass is a herd of fifteen gaur. In the early light, their bulky black profiles stand out against the mist like giant boulders. The uniform dark colouring of their hides and their white puttees, which extend from hocks to hooves, make it look as if the gaur are dressed for parade, though they stand at ease, scattered about the natural pasture. Both cows and bulls have impressive, symmetrical horns curving up from a grey-brown boss and tapering to sharp points that hook inward. The largest males have huge, muscular humps above their shoulders giving them a top-heavy appearance. Some bulls weigh as much as a tonne. Because of their size and the protection of the herd, gaur face few threats, except from tigers that occasionally prey on calves. Watching them feeding in the meadow, they seem as tame as village cattle and I almost expect to see a herdsman seated nearby

Gaur thrive in the hilly terrain and moist deciduous forests of the Satpura Range, though they are distributed across Central India in flatter, drier regions as well. Generally, with a few exceptions, they don't venture north of the Narmada. Herds are common in the submontane forests of Karnataka, Kerala, and Tamil Nadu. A separate population extends from Assam into neighbouring states of the Northeast. Though these wild cattle are seldom domesticated, cross-breeding has produced semi-feral livestock like the mithun in Arunachal Pradesh. In Sri Lanka and Bangladesh, gaur have become extinct but they are found in Myanmar and Malaysia. British shikaris like Forsyth referred to gaur as 'bison', which is a misnomer. Nevertheless, many writers still use this name even if scientists have determined that a gaur is quite different from an American bison, which themselves are often wrongly called 'buffalo'. In this way, colloquial usage tends to muddle the orderly categories of scientific taxonomy.

These large herbivores require a steady diet of grass and other plants as well as leaves from low-hanging branches. Their forest habitat provides them with large quantities of biomass on which the gaur's survival depends. Eating almost constantly, both at night as well as during the day, they consume and digest a significant portion of the jungle in which they live. Yet an ecological balance exists, allowing the gaur to grow as large as they do without destroying the forests that give them shelter and sustenance. Considering all of the wild creatures, from ants and caterpillars to deer and elephants, that feed on botanical species, India's forests are under constant pressure, not just from man. These wild tracts of jungle must continually regenerate themselves to keep up with the insects, birds, and mammals that devour their foliage.

Not far from where the gaur are feeding, we startle a herd of sambar. Most of the deer are females, along with a couple of fawns and one stag whose large, six-tined antlers look as if they have recently been polished on the bark of a ghiriya tree. Like the gaur, sambar depend entirely on plants for their survival while they, in turn, provide tigers with their favourite prey. In this way the continuum of life in the forest and the interrelationships between flora and fauna creates an ongoing cycle of supply and demand.

Though spotting wildlife on safari is usually a matter of luck, my driver and guide, as well as Arpita, are familiar with all the roads through the forest and know exactly where certain birds and animals are found. As we take a sharp turn, Vimla points out a collared scops owl nesting in the hollow of a ghost tree. The bird's mottled feathers are perfectly camouflaged within the peeling bark and it would be difficult to see the owl if Vimla didn't already know it was there. Further on, I am also shown a much larger Indian eagle-owl, which frequents a stand of jamun trees just above the road. A magnificent, regal bird, more than 50 centimetres tall, it has two feathered tufts on its head that look like horns.

Vicky is intent on showing me a sloth bear and he takes the jeep along a track where the bears regularly cross over at this time of day. We stop at several points where I can see a game trail entering the underbrush, which Vicky says is their 'pugdundee' or footpath. Though we circle about in pursuit of *Melursus ursinus*, none seem to be moving about. Several termite castles have been dug up, where the bears have been feeding, and we spot their elongated prints in the dust with distinct marks from their sharp claws.

Eventually, after I have given up any hope of seeing a sloth bear, Vimla and the others spot one on the far side of a densely wooded ravine. It is moving quickly through heavy cover, a shaggy black blur passing in and out of bamboo thickets and high grass. Vicky immediately reverses the jeep before heading down a side-track that takes us to the bottom of the ravine where the bear is headed. For a few minutes, all we can see is movement in the grass but then the bear appears directly in front of us, pausing for a minute to sniff at the ground with its long snout, before emerging from cover at a slow but deliberate pace. A sloth bear's hair is much longer than the coat on Himalayan black bears and it collects twigs, dead leaves, and burrs as the animal shoulders its way through the forest. While I have always assumed that this species' name reflects its slovenly appearance and shambling gait, Arpita informs me that an eighteenth-century zoologist, George Shaw, originally called it a 'bear sloth' because of its long claws and unusual teeth. They have smaller molars than most bears and a gap between their incisors that allows them to suck up ants or other insects. It also has the longest tail of any bear.

To my surprise this female has two cubs with her. One of them is riding on her back, clinging to its mother's matted coat, to keep from falling off. The other cub tumbles to the ground and quickly picks itself up, trying to scramble back onboard before stopping in the middle of the track and looking at us. No bigger than a small dog, it is covered in black fur with beady eyes and a puzzled expression of innocence on its face, though even at this age the cub's claws look dangerous. Arpita explains that these are the only bears that carry their young on their backs.

Sloth bears can be aggressive, particularly a mother with her young, but this one seems more intent on finding something to eat. She stops about 10 metres off the track and begins digging in the mud. Though she is hidden by tall grass, we can hear her snuffling about, having discovered something that satisfies her appetite, possibly termites, which she sucks up onto her tongue through leathery lips.

Though seeing the animals and birds provides most of the excitement, the landscape itself is equally compelling. From the Denwa backwaters, a series of low, folded scarps ascend into pleated foothills from where the higher ridges, creased with valleys and gorges, lead on to lofty summits. Beyond these mountains lies the Pachmarhi plateau. The entire topography is clad in heavy forest, like a variegated fabric, dyed different shades of green. Amidst this verdure, the yellow leaves of the ghiriya trees look like gold embroidery.

A forest track circles up into the foothills, and we stop for a packed breakfast by the side of a stream that flows through tiered shelves of rock. Worn smooth by monsoon torrents, the polished sandstone strata contrast with the wilder, chaotic shapes and textures of the surrounding jungle. Basking on a spit of sand beside the stream is a mugger crocodile, approximately 3 metres long, with a fretted tail and armoured hide. Being the same colour as the rocks, it looks like a giant fossil lying motionless at the water's edge. Not far away, an Indian flapshell turtle is sunning itself, its naked, tapered head and neck protruding from beneath a bulging carapace. These two creatures are survivors from the Mesozoic age of reptiles, which ended 66 million years ago. Their presence gives the place an ancient ambience, as if this valley exists outside the margins of time, recalling a primal epoch, long before hominids began to walk the earth.

One of the books I carry with me on my visit to the Satpura forests is Hugh Allen's *The Lonely Tiger*, written in the 1950s. It describes the author's experiences and adventures near the headwaters of the Denwa, at a farm called Mandikhera, adjacent to what is now the tiger reserve. Allen arrived in India at the end of World War II, recovering from a serious head wound, which had erased his memory for almost a year. In the mid-1940s, he and his sister, Babs, who had recently lost her husband, bought Mandikhera, a large estate, which included four villages and extensive tracts of forest. Against the advice of friends, they settled in Central India at a time when most of the British were packing up to leave. The Satpura forests and foothills provided this brother and sister with a refuge and retreat from the traumas and tragedies they had endured.

Allen was an avid hunter and recounts the pursuit of tigers and other wildlife. Ultimately, though, his book is an ambivalent elegy to shikar. Most of the animals he killed, in and around his farm, had been wounded by other hunters and he describes how the decade immediately following Independence was a period of unrestrained slaughter. Poachers with muzzleloaders and farmers who acquired guns to protect their crops began to shoot deer and antelope indiscriminately, selling venison in the market. Hugh and Babs rescued and adopted a number of wounded and orphaned animals. Under the British Raj, strict forest regulations favoured colonial hunters, though poaching had always occurred. After 1947, independent India had yet to formulate and enforce new rules about gun ownership and shikar. As Allen writes:

> The change came fast and its effects were noticeable at once. Indeed, looking back now it seems as though the animals disappeared over night. All of them, of course, had not been shot. It was just that they were not seen about so often, and when they were seen, there was something about the way they fled that showed them sensible of the constant threat now abroad both by day and night.

Allen begins his book by referring to the library in his home, which was well stocked with volumes on shikar. He observes how the earliest British hunters encountered plentiful game and one army officer, in 1858, shot ninety-eight tigers, four leopards, and twenty-five bears during a single summer furlough. Much later, a few years before Allen came to India, another shikar writer described himself as fortunate to have shot two tigers and a leopard during roughly the same span of time. The decimation of India's wildlife began under the British and despite urgent calls for conservation by some hunters and naturalists, the issue was never effectively addressed.

Though he was initially an enthusiastic shikari, after the first few years at

Mandikhera, Allen's views began to change. 'The urge to go hunting was still as strong as ever, and whenever I was out the old thrill of stalking an animal was just as fierce. Yet something now was different, though just what it was still escaped me. I went on wondering until one day I realized that the thrill of hunting vanished the second after I had pulled the trigger.' Over time, he became disillusioned with shikar especially when most hunters, faced with a dwindling number of animals, began to shoot them at night from jeeps, using spotlights. He also decries the shikar companies, operating in the 1950s and 1960s that brought wealthy hunters from abroad, particularly America, to bag tiger trophies.

Hugh Allen, who died in 1968, wrote only one book. *The Lonely Tiger* follows the format and style of shikar literature, though in many ways it is the last testament of that genre. An evocative storyteller with a poetic sensibility, Allen complains that the process of writing was difficult. '...my old idea that a writer's life was one of idleness and ease was rudely shattered the moment I took up my pen. Of all the forms of self-torture this is the most exquisite.'

The title story of his book is a poignant account of a young male tiger that Allen first encountered as a newborn cub. In the company of his mother and sister, the tiger spent the first year of his life in a secluded cave on the Mandikhera estate. Allen's account of the cub contains echoes of his own tragic struggles. In the beginning, he describes the pleasure of watching the young family of three tigers drinking together at a forest pool near their cave, both during the day and by moonlight. But eventually, this idyllic scene is destroyed when the mother is shot and killed by a truck driver along the highway to Jabalpur. Allen identifies her skin 'stretched out on the concrete floor of a garage'. Miraculously, the two cubs survive, though he wonders if they are old enough to hunt. After searching for them, he is reassured when he finds the brother and sister feeding on a peacock they have killed. Not long afterwards, however, he discovers the body of the female cub bearing fatal buckshot wounds. She has been killed by a poacher sitting up at a waterhole.

The male cub is now orphaned and alone. Allen keeps an eye on him as he grows up but eventually the tiger disappears and it seems that he too has been killed. However, after a year or so, he reappears, now as a full-grown adult. Though Allen is obviously pleased to see him, the tiger's return is marked by sadness and a troubling premonition of his fate. A passage in which Allen describes the tiger lying by the forest pool where he grew up distils the author's feelings.

> ...as he lay by the water's edge.... I saw that he was staring intently at a leaf that was blowing over the surface and drifting towards him. When it

> came within reach he started to dab at it with his right front paw, but with a touch so gentle that his pad was the merest caress on the tiny tip of the curled-up sail. From that moment, I always called him the Lonely Tiger. His expression was so forlorn that there flashed into my mind the vision of a small boy pondering the cruel fate that had killed first his mother and then his sister, and so condemned him to the heartache of loneliness and unexciting games played on his own.

The end of this story is profoundly moving and contains an incisive moral judgement on the ethics of shikar. Rereading *The Lonely Tiger* while visiting Satpura Tiger Reserve, I am struck by the historical context as well as Allen's vivid descriptions of wild landscapes along the Denwa River. The book serves as a rear-view mirror, looking back to a time before the Wild Life Protection Act became the law of the land, when the tiger had reached the tipping point of extinction and the jungles of India were about to fall silent.

∽

Walking through a forest you aren't likely to see as many mammals as you might on a jeep safari but everything else comes into focus. Most animals shy away from humans on foot, recognizing our scent and growing suspicious of our motives. Yet, being at ground level, it is easier to appreciate the jungle from the perspective of wild creatures, aligning my field of vision with theirs. Though it may not be possible to see as far as I can when standing at the back of an open vehicle, everything else around me becomes more visible, the sharp thorns on a wild ber bush, the delicately woven filaments of a funnel web spider's web hidden in the grass, or a skink that darts out of sight beneath a dead branch. These are the elements of the jungle that are often ignored, especially when larger wildlife is around.

Satpura Tiger Reserve permits walking safaris, within a limited radius surrounding Madhai forest camp. Crossing the backwaters again on the final morning of my visit, I see flocks of bar-headed geese on the banks of the reservoir. This migratory species flies all the way to and from Tibet and Central Asia, ranging as far south as Tamil Nadu. Herons, egrets, and stilts congregate along the shoreline and a large ficus tree on the near bank is full of yellow-footed green pigeons.

Two guides, Aadhar and Vinod, escort Arpita and me. Both men are employed by the tiger reserve and come from local Adivasi communities. They are armed with bamboo staves, though there is little risk of being attacked by wild animals. After disembarking from the motor launch, Aadhar leads us along a dusty path into the forest. Two chital are grazing in a clearing ahead but they race away as we approach. We also see a sambar hind that moves off into cover as soon as she spots us. The trees are full of birds—Oriental white eyes, small minivets, and common woodshrikes. Aadhar is carrying binoculars, suspended from a harness he has fashioned with rope made of sabai grass, which is used by tribal people for a variety of fibre crafts. As we walk along, he points out a clump of sabai. Picking the long, slender blades, Vinod demonstrates how it is twisted into rope.

A short distance ahead, we come upon a khair tree that has shed its leaves at this time of year. One of its branches is broken and the innermost wood is a dark red colour. Extracts from this wood are used for making katha, Vinod tells me, the scarlet paste that is smeared on paan leaves. Our guides also point out the claw marks of a bear on the trunk of a terminalia tree, the bark raked into deep grooves. At another place, we see where a tiger has sharpened its talons at almost twice the height, well over my head. The tree that he mauled is a tendu, leaves of which are used as wrappers for bidis which are filled with tobacco. Unexpectedly, we smell smoke and soon come to a smouldering tree stump. At this time of year, when the jungle is still moist, the forest department burns stretches of grass to help control wildfires during the dry season.

'Earlier, most of the fires were lit by villagers. They burned the grasslands to improve the next year's growth, for cattle to graze on. It also made it easier for them to find antlers shed by deer. These used to be sold for medicine but now it is illegal,' Aadhar tells me, 'and the villagers are gone.'

This area of the forest used to be inhabited by tribal communities that were resettled after the tiger reserve was created. Several villagers were moved to the other side of the Denwa backwaters, where they were given land and money to rebuild their homes. In most cases the compensation paid was inadequate and social activists are still fighting to get them a fair deal. Vinod tells me that his family was resettled in 2014. He was twenty-one at the time and until then he had grown up in the forest. When I ask if the people from his village resisted being moved, he shakes his head.

'After the Tawa Dam was built years ago, the reservoir cut us off from villages on the other side. Earlier, people could wade across the Denwa in most seasons but now they had to wait for a boat. It was inconvenient and difficult, especially if someone got sick,' Vinod says. 'After being resettled we have electricity, doctors, roads, and schools. It is better this way but, unfortunately, people have forgotten their forest knowledge.'

'With the next generation it will be gone,' Aadhar adds. 'Children don't know the names or the uses of plants. Everything has changed, even the food we eat.'

'Earlier we used to collect edible fruit and berries from the jungle,' Vinod explains. 'Also wild yams as big as my arm.'

'Now, young people don't even know what wild yams taste like,' says Aadhar.

'Are people allowed to come back to this side of the reservoir and visit the sites where their villages used to be?' I ask.

'Only to worship at old shrines,' Aadhar answers. 'The forest department allows villagers to conduct pujas on special occasions, though people are even forgetting their forest gods.'

'Have the gods forgotten them?'

'No, of course not,' Vinod replies with a smile.

The Satpura Hills are full of sacred sites, where tribal people have propitiated forest deities for thousands of years. Some of these shrines are no more than a stone placed at the base of a tree, while others are cave temples and sacred groves maintained by the Gond, Korku, and Mawasi tribes. Many of these are located within the Pachmarhi Biosphere and Satpura Tiger Reserve. The forest deities have names like Budhadeo (the elderly god), Baghdeo (the tiger deity), Nagdeo (the cobra deity), and Bari Mata (the great mother). After the forest dwellers were relocated outside the national park, they often set up new shrines in the buffer zone or in other peripheral jungles close to their settlements.

Aadhar and Vinod point out a hilltop in the mountains above us and tell me that the deity worshipped there is very popular. He is known as Chutkideo, (the god who pinches or snaps his fingers) because he grants people's wishes immediately.

'When our people lived in this part of the jungle, they walked up there to offer prayers,' says Aadhar. 'During the Mahadeo festival in Pachmarhi, villagers from here would go on foot, a journey of two or three days.'

The natural history of this region, as interpreted by tribal culture, includes both practical knowledge as well as spiritual significance. Often these two elements are combined, particularly when it comes to medicinal herbs. Sacred groves are believed to contain rare and powerful species that grow within a sanctified space. The deity that presides over the grove is usually a guardian spirit who answers prayers for protection—from dangerous snakes and tigers, or other outside forces that might threaten a village. In return, the supplicants protect the guardian's wild grove, fulfilling a cycle of conservation.

Both Aadhar and Vinod are expert trackers. They identify the spoor of various animals in the dust along the forest path, including the tracks of sambar, chital, and wild pigs, as well as the dung of a sloth bear. Arpita points out the termite heads in the dung that glisten like bits of mica. It also contains plenty of dirt and seeds of wild ber, locally known as reni. Reversing my binoculars, we use them like a microscope, magnifying and studying the half-digested remains of the sloth bear's diet.

When we arrive at a jeep track that circles a pond, Aadhar leans down and examines the hard ground. To my eye there is nothing to be seen, but he tells me that a tiger has passed this way. Twenty metres ahead, where the track turns to soft dust, the pugmarks are clearly visible.

'A male. He came straight from the pond this morning,' Aadhar says, indicating where drops of water fell from the tiger's coat, leaving tiny clumps of mud near each print.

The pugmarks are fresh and, at one place, we can see where the tiger's tail dragged on the ground, leaving a distinct mark like a brushstroke, the outline of each hair visible in the dust. Further on, a second set of prints appear. These are slightly smaller. Vinod and Aadhar examine them closely. A female has joined the male and the pair of tigers continues along the jeep track, walking side by side. We follow cautiously, keeping an eye on the forest ahead for any sign of movement.

A hundred metres further on, we come to a place where one of the tigers has scent-marked the trunk of a tendu tree, leaving a sharp feline odour. The other has urinated nearby, a damp patch of soil at the side of the track. A few drops of urine still cling to blades of grass. The tigers passed this way only a few minutes ago. For the first time, my guides look nervous, though we keep following the tracks until they eventually disappear into a thicket of lantana. Scanning the brush with my binoculars, I can imagine the two tigers watching us, though we see no sign of them and hear no alarm calls.

Aadhar decides it is best to cut short our walk and head back towards the reservoir. The excitement and anxiety of the past half hour, while we followed the trail of the tigers, has now eased. We stop to identify a bird perched on a dead branch, an Indian roller, which flies off with a blue flash of its wings. Arpita points to a series of conical depressions in the dust, where ant lions have burrowed into the ground, creating death traps for small insects. These minute predators are the larvae of lacewings, a genus similar to dragonflies. Just like the pugmarks we followed, these tiny declivities in the dust signal the presence of a hunter in pursuit of its prey. Meanwhile, in the sky above us, a green bee-eater is chasing a winged insect.

As morning sunlight filters through the foliage overhead, the feathery leaves of an amla tree come into focus. Searching about at my feet, I discover one of the pale green fruits on the ground where it fell from a branch. Brushing it on the sleeve of my shirt, I take a bite. It has a sharp, sour flavour, with a mildly sweet aftertaste. At this moment, being in a forest on foot, seeing birds and hearing their calls, smelling the fragrance of the earth still damp with dew, while holding the smooth, round amla and tasting its tartness, all five of my senses are attuned to the jungle that surrounds us.

3

WATER DOGS AND FOREST BABIES

A smooth-coated otter surfaces midstream in the slow, green waters of the Kaveri. The river appears almost motionless, except where it ripples around polished boulders that protrude from the current, some as large as elephants. The otter glides toward the riverbank then pauses on a submerged stone, only its head and shoulders visible. As it swivels about, rings of water radiate outwards, encircling this amphibious creature. The otter seems part of the river and every movement it makes has a fluid grace. Sleek brown fur is plastered to its face and neck, button ears tucked back. Only its drooping whiskers are out of line with the tapered silhouette of its lithe body and long tail, most of which remains underwater.

Turning, the otter looks in my direction, having already sensed that it is being watched but betraying no alarm. For several minutes, we observe each other, eyes meeting at a distance of 30 metres. The otter makes no sound though it communicates with others of its kind through soft grunts and squeaks, as well as chirps, whistles, and a loud scream if it senses danger. This otter's expression is alert and attentive but when I reach for my camera it yawns as if already bored by our interaction. Its mouth is pink, equipped with white incisors that catch and hold the fish it hunts. With a webbed forepaw, the otter scratches behind its left ear, sharp claws raking wet fur.

I am seated on the riverside terrace of a tourist rest house at Srirangapatna, overlooking one branch of the Kaveri, which bifurcates to form a large island. This was once the fortified stronghold of Tipu Sultan of Mysore. Defeated by the British in 1799, he was killed not far from where I sit. History presides over the heavy stone walls of Tipu's citadel, which was bombarded by British guns, as well as his pleasure palace, Daria Daulat Bagh (the garden of river treasures), with its formal flower beds, stucco arches, and colourful frescoes.

Tiger Tipu, as he is still remembered, was a fierce adversary of the East India Company army, many of whose officers and soldiers are buried in a cemetery near the rest house. Following the siege of Srirangapatna and Tipu's death, Arthur Wellesley, later the duke of Wellington, carried off cartloads of loot from Mysore, including a mechanical tiger made of painted wood. Hidden springs and gears animated this striped predator as he devoured a hapless redcoat. This gruesome novelty is now on display at the Victoria and Albert Museum in London.

After Tipu's defeat, the British installed the Wodeyar dynasty of Hindu maharajas on the throne. Mysore's royal crest has a mythical, two-headed bird, the Gandaberunda, at its centre, flanked by a pair of rampant Yali, with the bodies and heads of lions and the trunks and tusks of elephants. The princely state of Mysore (now Mysuru) was renowned for its jungles and wildlife, particularly tigers, elephants, and gaur. G. P. Sanderson's classic, *Thirteen Years Among the Wild Beasts of India*, published in 1878, describes his exploits in the forests of Mysore, where the author worked in the state's irrigation department. The Wodeyars were generous hosts for colonial dignitaries who flocked to Mysore to hunt big game. In 1922, the Prince of Wales, who later became Edward VIII, shot a tiger here, while touring India. Mysore was also famous for its kheddahs during which wild elephants were driven into stockades and captured. These annual events attracted an eager audience of VIPs who observed the kheddahs from specially constructed viewing stands. Most of the kheddahs were held in forests bordering the Kabini River near the village of Kharapur. Captured elephants were then tamed and trained for the maharaja's stables.

In the 1890s, a Dutch expatriate named Eugene Van Ingen moved to Mysore and set up shop as a taxidermist, catering to the numerous hunters who shot tigers and other wildlife in the maharaja's domains. His business rapidly expanded and by the early part of the twentieth century, Van Ingen & Van Ingen had become the premier taxidermists in India, patronized by hunters from all parts of the subcontinent. Viceroys and maharajas shipped the skins, skulls, antlers, and horns of animals they killed to Mysore, where these were mounted in life-like poses, with fierce glass eyes and snarling teeth. Eugene had four sons and the Van Ingens became so successful that their factory employed more than a hundred workers with an assembly line that produced dozens of trophies a day, including two of the last three cheetahs shot in 1947. After Independence, the company continued to operate but the demand for hunting trophies eventually tapered off and ended altogether in 1972 with passage of the Wild Life Protection Act.

In 1973, Mysore state became Karnataka. The Wodeyar's royal hunting grounds are now national parks and tiger reserves. Both Bandipur and Nagarhole are part of the Nilgiri Biosphere Reserve, the largest expanse of protected forests in India, extending across sections of Karnataka, Kerala, and Tamil Nadu. The wild heritage of this region is not limited to tigers and elephants but also includes endangered species of trees like sandalwood and rosewood, for which Mysore is famous. The Kaveri River and its tributaries, like the Kabini, as well as Mysore's numerous wetlands, attract large numbers of migratory birds. Three kilometres upriver from Srirangapatna is the Ranganathittu Bird Sanctuary, home to hundreds of different species including painted storks and pelicans that roost along the shore and on islands in the river.

Kaveri is one of the seven sacred rivers of India. Revered as a mother goddess, she was the wife of a great sage, Agastya. When the world was threatened by drought, Kaveri turned herself into liquid which the sage poured into his kamandalu (a round water vessel) for safekeeping. But while Agastya was performing his ablutions one morning, the kamandalu was knocked over by a crow. Kaveri flowed out across the parched land and restored the forests and fields with her life-giving waters.

The otter is unaware of human history or myths and lore. Its focus is on the fish that dart through sunlit shallows or lurk in the dark, deep pools. Schools of small mahseer swarm amongst the rocks, their gold and silver scales glinting like sequins sewn into the ruffled stream. These fingerlings are no more than 10 to 15 centimetres long though mahseer can grow to more than a metre, weighing as much as 35 kilograms. The Kaveri, or Cauvery as British anglers used to spell it, produces enormous, humpbacked mahseer that once lured sport fishermen from all over the world.

A liminal species, otters exist both on land and in water. They inhabit the shorelines of rivers and lakes as well as coastal mangrove jungles and tidal marshes. Sociable creatures, they live as pairs and family groups with four to five offspring. Otters burrow into mudbanks, beneath tree roots, and within hollow spaces under piles of river rocks. From a distance, without binoculars, it is virtually impossible to tell the difference between the male and female of this species. Smooth-coated otters grow close to a metre in length and weigh less than 10 kilograms. Being diurnal, they are active in the morning and late afternoon, resting during the midday heat. Aside from fish, they consume an eclectic, carnivorous diet of snakes, crabs, lizards, and rats. Family groups, known as pods, maintain communal latrines called spraints, defecating in a designated place a short distance from their dens. A pungent odour of rotting fish marks the spot.

While this otter seems to be hunting alone, others are probably close at hand. The collective English noun, a romp of otters, suggests the playful, undulating movement of their bodies and the way they tussle with each other. Smooth-coated otters often hunt as a team, attacking from opposite directions and disorienting the fish, which sometimes leap out of the water attempting to escape. Herons and egrets take advantage of the confusion and try to steal the otter's prey. In parts of Bengal, villagers trap and tame otters, using them to drive fish into their nets. S. H. Prater's *The Book of Indian Animals* describes how the Mohana (Muhana) river dwellers of Sind used otters as 'decoys' on the Indus to catch river dolphins.

Here in Karnataka, the local Kannada name for otters is niru nayi, which means water dog. Its Latin name, *Lutrogale perspicillata*, shares the same root, 'spicare', with the word perspicacious, which means to look attentively. Sharp-sighted, both above and beneath the surface of the river, this aquatic mustelid has a perceptive awareness of the world it inhabits. Living close to human habitation, the otter has probably encountered many more of my kind than I have seen of its species. At the same time, it is wary of my presence since poachers hunt the niru nayi for its pelt. Though smooth-coated otters are classified as vulnerable on the IUCN Red List, they are more common than Asian small-clawed otters, which also live along the Kaveri.

While otters may appear to be gentle, timid creatures, they are fierce predators and can become aggressive, particularly when protecting their young. Rare accounts of otters attacking human beings have been recorded, including a case in 2019, when a labourer who had gone to bathe in a small lake in Rajasthan, near the Chambal River, was ambushed by a family of seven otters. He was badly bitten on his legs and arms. The death of a fisherman in the same area was also blamed on otters. Similar reports have been verified by wildlife officials in Kerala in 2010 and 2011. In North America, river otters have been known to overturn kayaks and giant otters in South America, which can grow as big as 2 metres in length, often attack boats that get too close to their dens.

The otter I am watching displays no aggression, though it studies me attentively with sharp, intelligent eyes. After a few minutes, it slips off its perch and disappears into the green river. Webbed feet and a strong tail propel it through the water. My imagination follows, as I picture it swimming beneath the surface, enveloped by the liquid embrace of the goddess, diving down to the rock-strewn riverbed where Agastya's kamandalu lies alongside British cannon balls, submerged in the Kaveri's timeless undercurrents.

∽

Many wild creatures have adapted to life in or around towns and cities, occupying the green margins of urban spaces. A hundred and twenty-five kilometres north of Srirangapatna, in Bengaluru, our headlamps search the domed canopy of a gulmohur tree, focused beams of light illuminating a scaffolding of branches and foliage 15 metres overhead. A yellow glimmer of eyes betrays the hidden presence of an animal. Vidisha Kulkarni identifies it as a flying fox, roosting upside down within the clustered shadows of leaves. Earlier in the evening, we watched hundreds of these giant bats setting out at dusk on their nocturnal sorties in search of whatever fruit is now in season. Flying just above the treetops, their black wings beat slowly with a steady, ponderous rhythm.

Tonight, we are in pursuit of a very different creature, the grey slender loris, a tiny, furtive primate with large, observant eyes. Here on the campus of the Indian Institute of Science (IISC), Vidisha estimates there are about twenty lorises, though the last count was done several years ago. A reclusive, nocturnal animal, the slender loris is about 15 to 25 centimetres long with grey-brown fur and thin, supple limbs. Flexible fingers and toes allow it to grip stems and branches while climbing about in the upper storeys of trees. The loris's round, close-set eyes are a rich amber colour, framed by circular facial markings that make it look as if it is wearing oversized spectacles. A reflective membrane behind their retinas equips them with acute night vision, allowing them to hunt in the dark. They feed on insects, bird's eggs, and small reptiles, as well as leaves, fruit, and seeds. In Karnataka the slender loris is known by its local Kannada name, kaadu paapa, which means forest baby.

Lorises, like lemurs and tarsiers, are considered the most ancient form of primates that separated from the ancestors of *Homo sapiens* and other apes, somewhere around 60 million years ago. *Loris lydekkerianus* is a species found in South India and Sri Lanka. It is related to the Bengal slow loris of Northeast India, as well as other similar species distributed throughout Southeast Asia.

Vidisha and her husband, K. S. Seshadri, who accompanies us, are both affiliated with the Centre for Ecological Sciences (CES) at IISC. We are also joined by Professor Kartik Shanker who works on the evolutionary ecology and biogeography of various terrestrial and marine animals. Kartik has written a children's book about a slender loris titled *Lori's Magical Mystery*, which traces the adventures of a loris, a drongo, and an owl. Vidisha leads us on foot through the 178-hectare (440 acre) campus, which is thickly wooded with both native and non-native trees. At this hour of the evening, the roads inside IISC are empty, except for an occasional scooter and there are no streetlights. In the distance, we can hear the rumble of traffic from the surrounding city.

Vidisha is one of the founding members of a Citizen Science Project that was launched in Bengaluru in 2014, to investigate the urban population of slender lorises and promote their conservation. Initiated and led by Dr Kaberi Kar Gupta, an ecologist who did her PhD research on slender lorises, the project officially ended in 2016 though Vidisha continues to monitor and observe lorises on the IISC campus.

'We had a core team of about ten members who are not all scientists by profession but extremely enthusiastic citizens of Bangalore,' she explains. 'Over the two years that the project was active we had approximately 200 volunteers to attend the surveys and help conduct outreach programs for schools, colleges, and the public. Unfortunately, the project is no longer active as we ran out of permits to study these animals.'

Suddenly, somewhere in the darkness to our right, Vidisha hears a muted cry, between a whistle and a wail, which she recognizes as the call of a loris. Though often solitary, they sometimes move about in pairs or groups of three to four and tend to socialize just after sunset. Crossing the road, we direct our headlamps upwards into the leafy crown of another gulmohur. At first, there is no sign of the creature but then, after a minute or two, we see a small, agile shape like an acrobat in the spotlight, moving slowly along a high branch. The loris stops for a moment and looks down at us, its eyes reflecting the light, like two orange beads in the darkness. Seconds later, it scuttles out of sight.

'They have a one-note, two-note, and a three-note call,' Vidisha explains. 'But not much is known about their behaviour or the purpose of these calls. From what little we've observed, they call mostly at dusk when they leave their sleeping places and head out to forage. Phases of the moon may have something to do with the calls. The intensity of the calls is higher during the new moon and it decreases towards a full moon.'

When I ask what threats they face, she says the most serious problem is loss of habitat. Since lorises live and hunt in the treetops, rarely descending to the ground, they need an interconnected canopy of branches and foliage to move about. For that reason, when tree cover is diminished or cut through by roads or power lines, they cannot cross into adjacent woodlands. The problem is particularly acute in Bengaluru, which was once famous for its extensive parks and urban forest cover. However, because of recent infrastructure projects like the new metro and flyovers, contiguous areas where lorises used to live have been broken up or denuded.

IISC's campus is one of the few institutional spaces in the city that still has the kind of habitat where lorises find adequate food and shelter. Unfortunately, it is unlikely to remain this way much longer. The institute recently accepted large donations to establish a medical school and build an 800-bed research hospital on the campus, as well as several other buildings, all of which will mean that a substantial number of trees will be cut. Students and faculty have protested but these projects are moving forward.

Circling through the campus, we approach the main heritage building at IISC, a grand, double-storey structure with a sloping roof and a tall belltower.

After nightfall, it looks like a gothic mansion, framed by the leaning silhouettes of Araucariaceae trees— an exotic Australian conifer planted in parks and gardens throughout Bengaluru. Facing the building is a statue of Jamsetji Nusserwanji Tata, the industrialist who conceived of the institute and provided funds for its endowment. With his conical hat, flowing beard, and voluminous robes, he looks more like a medieval prophet than a modern business tycoon. Most of the land for the institute was donated by the maharaja of Mysore. Founded in 1909, IISC is one of India's most prestigious universities and a centre for research in all fields of science, including ecology.

Lurking about the darkened building, we could be mistaken for burglars, and I half-expect one of the security guards to challenge us. Just then, Seshdari picks up a set of eyes looking down at us from a tree about 20 metres away. As all of us point our headlamps at the creature, we can see it is an Indian palm civet perched halfway up the tree trunk. Unlike the loris, it doesn't try to escape, and remains where it is for several minutes, an inquisitive look on its face. The civet's dark, mottled fur and long tail give it a cat-like appearance though its face is more like a fox.

Kartik tells me that civets are rarely seen at IISC and this is an encouraging sight. Among the other small mammals found here are jungle cats, grey foxes, and smooth-coated otters. Plenty of reptiles, including cobras, also live within the confines of the campus. Beyond the main building is a densely forested patch of jungle with intersecting dirt paths. A number of young sandalwood trees are growing here along with other indigenous species like ziziphus. Most of the trees lining the main avenues are gulmohur, rain trees, and other exotic ornamentals.

Dense stands of bamboo grow near a building that used to house the Centre for Ecological Sciences, though Kartik and his colleagues have now moved to another site on campus. He points out an enormous liana coiling its way through the branches of trees nearby, its thick vines like twisted power cables. A couple of dogs begin to bark at us but Vidisha whistles to them and they retreat. Moments later, she spots two lorises in the tree overhead. One of them peers down at us, eyes glowing like miniature headlights. The other darts for cover, its delicate limbs and nimble feet propelling it through the branches. Kaadu paapa have a hunched, elfin appearance, stooped forward, with their knees and elbows folding into their furry torsos. Unlike lemurs, lorises do not have tails. Aside from large eyes, which dominate their features, they have small, round ears and an upturned nose.

Catching glimpses of these elusive animals, as they clamber about, taking cover in the leaves and trying to escape the intrusive beams of light, I wonder how many people in this city know of their existence. The forest baby's haunting cries could be mistaken for a bird. During daylight hours they hide and sleep out of sight in the hollows of trees or tucked inside thickets of foliage.

Altogether, we see five different lorises during our evening's excursion, each of them high up in their arboreal world where they seem to exist on another plane, separated from us on the earth below. While most primates, like the bonnet macaques that are common residents of the IISC campus, descend from the trees and scramble about the rooftops, these distant cousins of monkeys have little to do with human beings, though they live in the midst of the city. Squeezed into smaller and smaller pockets of green cover, the slender loris has every reason to hide.

'Sometimes raptors or crows will attack them and they fall from the trees,' Vidisha explains. 'People find them lying injured on the ground and take them to animal rescue centres. If they survive and recover, they are released back where they were found.'

Total population numbers for slender lorises are unknown, though they are listed under Schedule I of the Wild Life Protection Act, and considered endangered. Poaching is a serious threat and many lorises are caught in the wild and sold as exotic pets. Kartik tells me about a story that appeared in the newspapers several years ago reporting that a man was caught by customs in Mumbai trying to smuggle three lorises out of the country by hiding them inside his pants.

Kaadu paapu are also used in occult rituals. For this reason, Vidisha tells me, the Citizen's Science Project did not publicize the locations where lorises were found living in the city. Tantrics and folk-healers promote the misguided belief that these animals possess medicinal properties and magical powers. Being nocturnal creatures that seem to haunt the forest at night, emitting eerie cries, slender lorises are often associated with supernatural forces, simply because they are unknown to us and evoke unsettling emotions. As a result, they are subjected to human fetishes and superstitions.

Smitha Gnanaolivu, a wildlife biologist affiliated with the University of Mysore, has conducted extensive research on cultural practices surrounding slender lorises. In collaboration with other conservationists, she spent six years investigating how slender lorises are used for medicinal purposes and black magic rituals. The study covered four states—Andhra Pradesh, Tamil Nadu, Karnataka, and Kerala—all of which contain widely dispersed populations of *Loris lydekkerianus*. In July 2022, Gnanaolivu and her colleagues published their findings in the British Ecological Society's journal, *People and Nature*. Though it is a scientific paper, full of charts, statistics, and citations, it reads like a grim horror story, documenting the vicious treatment meted out by human tormentors on this innocent, misunderstood animal.

Gnanaolivu's research includes references to early Tamil sources, which reveal that lorises have been part of cultural narratives and practices in South India going back more than two millennia.

> Historical records suggest that slender lorises have been used in practices driven by cultural beliefs since 300 BCE. King Vel Pari, a chieftain leader of tribal clans of the ancient Parambu region, who lived in the Pachchai malai region, believed that the slender loris was the spirit of a Goddess. Lorises were thus venerated and protected in their natural environment. During festivals, his subjects would offer fruit baskets as holy offerings to lorises; the consumption of the holy offering officially marked the beginning of festivities. The exploitation of slender lorises is believed to have begun when kings of the Pandya dynasty discovered that a slender loris, when on the ground, was always facing the northern direction. The Pandya king and his court then used the loris as a compass to sail abroad and harness riches, after which he grandly delivered these riches to his subjects.

Today, kaadu paapa are occasionally kept in homes as tokens of good luck and they are sometimes worshipped as manifestations of forest deities. At the same time, others consider them evil omens and kill them on sight. Itinerant fortune tellers often keep captive lorises, using them to select cards or coloured threads that predict the future. In Sri Lanka, the tears of a loris are supposed to be the active ingredient in love potions. The inner organs and other body parts of dead lorises are used in traditional nostrums, supposedly to cure leprosy, eye problems, and joint pains.

But the most horrific revelations in Gnanaolivu's paper concern the use of slender lorises as living effigies like voodoo dolls that are tortured in order to inflict pain and suffering on human targets of evil spells. By physically abusing and maiming the animal, practitioners of black magic believe that its injuries will be transferred to the person they wish to harm. In other instances, the loris's fingers and limbs are broken in the perverse belief that a human patient's aches and pains will be cured. After being tortured, lorises are buried alive or left by the roadside to die.

Gnanaolivu collected a considerable amount of data from animal rescue centres in Bengaluru. She and her colleagues recorded 179 cases of lorises being brought to animal shelters in Karnataka, of which 139 were in Bengaluru. Of these, fifty-eight victims clearly exhibited injuries inflicted in black magic rituals, while an equal number were very likely victims of these same rites. The study examines the increased frequency of cases during the dark phases of the moon and certain seasons of the year associated with occult practices. Gnanaolivu's precise, clinical descriptions detail the atrocities committed.

> For 30 of the 58 reported cases directly linked to black magic, it was possible to detect fresh wounds linked to rituals that veterinarians estimated to be as recent as 2 days old. In some cases, we reported multiple fresh wounds in the same individual. We identified five mechanisms to inflict wounds to the body—burning (11 wounds), hitting (4), piercing (49), breaking (12) and cutting (2). Wounds occurred all over the body (mouth, head, eyes, limbs, spine, anus) and to the internal organs (heart, kidney). The most common wound was piercing the forelimb arm.

These gruesome rituals represent the darkest side of anthropomorphism, in which human attributes are assigned to a surrogate creature in order to project malevolent intent on other human beings. Gnanaolivu makes it clear that one of the primary reasons slender lorises are tortured is because they bear some resemblance to us. 'As primates with large forward-facing eyes, long limbs and no tails, lorises are often attributed human properties, which may help understand their extensive association with medicines and rituals,' she writes. 'Slender lorises are often regarded as small humans or human babies, which provide a link to their use as effigies.'

The most prominent feature of a kaadu paapa, particularly when seen in the dark, are its large, watchful eyes with dilated pupils. For this reason, slender lorises are said to possess supernatural vision. In other parts of India, similar associations are made with owls, which are also subjected to sadistic, sacrificial rites. In another bizarre ritual, reported by Gnanaolivu, a dead loris's eyes and other parts of its body are burned and the charred remains are made into a black eyeliner that tantric shamans apply to their eyelids to induce a hypnotic gaze or perceive the paranormal.

Instead of being outdated practices from the past, the persecution of slender lorises continues today in the twenty-first century. As Gnanaolivu writes, 'The number of cases related to black magic and the number of cases classified as trafficking within Bengaluru increased steadily between 2002 and 2020....' The fact that these illegal and brutal rituals occur in one of the largest, most technologically advanced cities in India, shows the persistence of cruel superstitions in which harmless, wild creatures fall victim to human ignorance and depravity.

4

THE GODDESS AND THE TIGER

The 'Royal' Bengal tiger is an outdated epithet, assigned by colonial naturalists in much the same way that the British empire bestowed honorific titles upon loyal maharajas, who reciprocated by allowing European dignitaries to slaughter wildlife in their princely domains. In 1867, the British zoologist, John Edward Gray, changed Linnaeus's original binomial, *Felis tigris*, to *Tigris regalis*. Around that time, most shikar literature and Kipling's Jungle Books portrayed tigers as kings of the Indian jungle, even if a dwindling cohort of Asiatic lions still vied for that distinction. In 1929, Reginald Innes Pocock, another British taxonomist, reclassified the tiger, giving it the Latin name that we currently use—*Panthera tigris*. Today, most self-respecting naturalists have dropped any references to royalty. Nevertheless, these apex predators remain the national animal of two modern republics—India and Bangladesh.

On either side of the border in Bengal, the few surviving tigers live mostly in the Sundarbans, an archipelago of riverine islands where the Ganga, Brahmaputra, and Meghna rivers converge and flow out into the Bay of Bengal, through a constantly shifting labyrinth of distributaries. The total area of the Sundarbans is roughly 40,000 square kilometres, about the size of Haryana. Three quarters of this delta lies in Bangladesh, while 9,630 square kilometres are part of West Bengal. About half of this area, somewhat larger than the size of Goa, consists of uninhabited islands and waterways that have been designated as the Sundarban Tiger Reserve.

Altogether, more than 200 tigers live here, though it is extremely difficult to ascertain exact numbers. The World Wide Fund for Nature estimates the global population of wild tigers to be roughly 5,500, about two-thirds of which are found in India. In 2021, West Bengal's Forest Department declared that 96 Sundarbans tigers are resident in Indian territory, though they frequently swim back and forth across the fluid border. Despite this relatively prolific number, mangrove jungles and tidal marshes are not the ideal habitat for these large cats and the prevalence of tigers has more to do with the absence of human settlements and agriculture, rather than the suitability of forest cover or an adequate prey base. Over time, tigers have been exterminated or pushed out of most other areas of Bengal and are now marooned on these forested islands, as ecological castaways.

Tigers in the Sundarbans are notorious for killing and eating human beings. An estimated 80 to 100 villagers fall victim every year on the Indian side of the border. Most of them are fishermen, crab catchers, honey gatherers, and woodcutters. Man-eating tigers are generally assumed to be elderly or infirm animals that consume human flesh only because they are unable to successfully hunt deer and other wild animals. However, in the Sundarbans it seems that most tigers will readily attack human beings because of a need to be opportunistic in their diet. No sambar or swamp deer are found on the islands, though there are limited herds of chital as well as wild pigs. Because of a shortage of prey, tigers are forced to feed on an eclectic assortment of species, ranging from crocodiles to crabs. When a boat full of fishermen drifts close to shore, it offers an easy target for tigers that lie in wait, hidden within the dense mangroves along the water's edge. Honey gatherers and woodcutters take even greater risks, entering the forest on foot and exposing themselves to the very real possibility of ambush. Sundarbans tigers are strong swimmers and have been known to cross wide estuaries and carry off victims from villages on the opposite shore.

Both tigers and human beings in the Sundarbans share a precarious existence in this inhospitable environment. A single cyclonic storm can kill more than 20,000 people, as well as uncounted numbers of wildlife, when tidal waves inundate the low-lying islands. Just as the tigers are marooned here, most of the human inhabitants arrived in the Sundarbans under desperate circumstances. Landless migrants and refugees from East Pakistan settled here after Partition in 1947 and subsequently during the wars between India and Pakistan, in 1965 and 1971. They struggle to subsist off fishing and forest resources, while cultivating rice paddies that are regularly destroyed by flooding and erosion. The Sundarbans have a reputation for being a lawless place, where poachers and pirates operate. Fractious politics and inequitable hierarchies of power lead to hostile relations between the islanders and government authorities.

While many people in the Sundarbans believe that their fate is tied to tigers, for better or worse, this is not always understood by outsiders. As anthropologist Annu Jalais has written in her perceptive book, *Forest of Tigers: People, Politics & Environment in the Sundarbans*: 'If in the literature of the region a rather crude opposition is built between tigers and humans it is because the two have never been studied together.' She goes on to argue that there is a close, entangled relationship between *Panthera tigris* and *Homo sapiens* in the Sundarbans, not just because they occupy the same ecosystem but because their narratives are entwined. Some islanders believe their two species possess some of the same traits.

> If the harsh environment of the Sundarbans is to be blamed for their 'cantankerous' nature argued the islanders, it is also this environment which brings about an element of 'complicity' between people and tigers, and by extension, people and people. This connivance is expressed in the way tigers are seen to be invested with human attributes (emotions, feelings, thoughts) and in how Sundarbans islanders see themselves as sharing the 'bad temperedness' of tigers.'

At dawn, in mid-November, the jetty and shoreline from where we depart are shrouded by a gauze-like mist. It is high tide and the reflections of mangrove trees growing along the bund create a penumbral illusion, smudging the separation between water and land. Our boat is the only vessel in sight with no horizon ahead of us. Because of the mist, the broad estuary merges seamlessly with the sky, as we head south-east across an open channel, more than a kilometre wide. Standing at the prow of the boat, I feel like a character in a Joseph Conrad novel setting off into uncharted territory.

After a quarter of an hour, we approach a large island downstream, its banks a phalanx of foliage. The alluvial flow of the rivers has carried sediment from as far away as the Himalaya to create these islands which are constantly being reshaped by erosion. As the sun burns through the mist and lights up the treetops, I notice that we are being observed. Perched like a sentry atop a mangrove, a rhesus macaque watches us pass by. Unlike others of his species, who have adapted to life amidst human habitation, this monkey lives in the wild, though, for a moment, he looks as if he is waiting to be rescued and returned to civilization.

All the islands that lie ahead of us to the south are part of Sundarban Tiger Reserve. A nylon mesh fence has been installed along the shoreline. Ostensibly, it is meant to keep the tigers from leaving and swimming across the river, but also to stop people from entering the forest. Constant erosion defeats the purpose of this flimsy barrier and at several places the mesh has been washed loose or collapsed. This area is easily accessible for fisherman from neighbouring islands upstream. Honey gatherers and crab catchers enter the narrow tidal channels to collect what they can, eluding forest department boats that patrol the waterways.

A flock of egrets fly ahead of us, their white wings churning just above the river, as if guiding us into a maze of saltwater creeks and forested islands. Core areas of the Sundarban Tiger Reserve are as close to being a wilderness as any place in India. Yet, the main rivers of the delta provide a busy passage for boats and ships, from small fishing launches to huge cargo vessels carrying fly ash from the power plants at Kidderpore, outside Kolkata, to Bangladesh and beyond.

Maa Ganga, our boat, is relatively large, about 20 metres from bow to stern, with an upper foredeck where I can lounge on a throne-like divan with an unobstructed view of the passing forest. This vessel is embarrassingly comfortable and spacious, with a crew of four, including a cook who prepares breakfast and lunch during our day-long cruise. For overnight voyages, four beds are available below deck. The captain and owner, Bapi, steers the boat from a glassed-in wheelhouse behind me. As in most national parks, the forest department requires that a guide accompany us. His name is Nirmal Mondal, fifty-two years old, a soft-spoken man whose home is on Bally Island where I am staying at a lodge called Sundarban Jungle Camp. Prasun Majumdar, a naturalist affiliated with the lodge, is also on board. A youthful forty, Prasun has spent a good deal of time in the Sundarbans, though he also works at other national parks, including Tadoba in Maharashtra.

The tide is beginning to recede, and I can see a sandbar emerging from a tapered headland on an island 200 metres downstream. Bapi knows these waters well and confidently navigates through the tidal shoals. In the distance, Eurasian curlews are calling—an eerie, mournful cry that echoes their name. A few minutes later, Prasun points out a pair on the shore. The birds' mottled grey-brown feathers blend into the mudflats that are littered with shells. A curlew's long, curved beak is like a surgical instrument that extracts invertebrates from the tidal muck. Wimbrels, common redshanks, and greenshanks, as well as Terek sandpipers wade along the water's edge, intent on finding worms and snails where the tide has pulled away from the shore. Lesser sand plovers scurry about, their jittery movements punctuated by brief interludes of stillness. All these birds have similar, long-legged profiles that have evolved with the ebb and flow of coastal waters. Perfectly adapted to this liminal world, they pick their way fastidiously along the wet margins of mud, flying briefly on restless wings parallel to the riverbank. Their lives comprise a daily commute within the limits of the tide.

Nirmal explains that the highest tides occur during the full moon and new moon when the water level can rise more than 2 metres. High ground in the Sundarbans lies only 6 or 7 metres above sea level which means that even the treetops of the tallest mangroves are no more than 20 metres above the waterline. Terrestrial and avian species inhabit this narrow band of forested habitat, much of which can be quickly submerged during cyclonic storms. As we pass through the tidal creeks that intersect the islands, mangroves hem us in on either side, stitching the soil to the current with their roots. Though the branches of these trees interlace with one another and the foliage is an indecipherable mass of green, the roots of different species help distinguish one from the other.

Prasun identifies a mangrove called gorjon which has an elaborate scaffolding of stilt roots that lift it out of the water, forming what looks like a cage. He also points out one of the most common species, genwa, its serpentine roots like a nest full of pythons. Another common mangrove is bain, which has thin snorkel-like roots called pneumatophores that protrude from the mud. These 'breathing roots' allow the tree to absorb oxygen from the air and filter out salt from tidal currents.

Where the mangroves give way to a muddy beach, a saltwater crocodile is sprawled on the shore, seemingly oblivious of the curlews and other birds that dart back and forth in front of its snaggle-toothed jaws. Soaking in the early warmth of the sun, this massive reptile is almost 4 metres long, lying flat on its belly. The crocodile's ridged and shingled hide is the same grey colour as the mud. Just as tigers feed on human beings, saltwater crocodiles are also responsible for a number of deaths. Particularly vulnerable are women who collect prawn seed, tiny hatchlings about 3 to 5 centimetres long. These are sold to fish farms that raise tiger prawns. The most common method of gathering prawn seed is for women to wade through chest-high water while dragging a fine-mesh net behind them. This makes them highly vulnerable to crocodile and shark attacks.

Not far away from the lounging reptile stands a lesser adjutant stork. From a distance, the bird's stance suggests a stooped dignity. Almost 1.5 metres tall, it has dull, black wings and a dusty brown breast. As we approach, my binoculars reveal its oversized beak and pale forehead. The bird has a balding scalp with scruffy tufts of feathers and a long, yellow neck. Walking with a slow, formal gait, the stork's shoulders appear hunched. There is something almost human about the stork's ugliness that is strangely endearing. Yet, when it takes to the air, tucking in its long neck and flapping its large wings, this ungainly bird is suddenly transformed into a graceful, elegant creature.

As our boat manoeuvres through the waterways, I can see chital grazing along the shore, their hooves sinking into the mud. *Porteresia coarctata*, the only grass found here, is known locally as dhani because it looks like rice plants. Growing under saline conditions, it excretes salt through its leaves and survives even when the tide washes over its roots. Chital feed on dhani grass, as well as the leaves of certain species of mangroves, particularly genwa, but there is limited forage. Prasun tells me how the forest department, in an attempt to increase the prey base for tigers, tried to relocate chital from forests on the mainland but they found that the outsiders could not adapt to this harsh habitat.

The chital that were introduced became malnourished and diseased because of the saline conditions.

Wild pigs are also feeding along the shoreline, rooting about in the mangroves. They too have adapted to a meagre diet of whatever tubers and fallen fruit are available, though they also scavenge dead fish and reptiles as well as crustaceans and molluscs. While ponds of rainwater are found on most islands, where animals can drink, these sources are usually brackish. Prasun lists several small mammals found in the Sundarbans, including smooth-coated otters, fishing cats, and leopard cats, though we are unable to spot any of these species. Leopards are not found here, probably because they have an aversion to water. At one time, rhinos and wild buffalo inhabited northern parts of the delta but they disappeared a couple of centuries ago.

Cruising slowly through the tidal jungles, we encounter plenty of birdlife, including six different species of kingfishers—common, pied, collared, white-throated, black-capped, and brown-winged. They perch on branches of mangroves overhanging the river, waiting patiently for fish to swim near the surface. When our boat disturbs them, they fly off, emitting irritable shrieks. In one stretch of shallows, we watch a pond heron catch a small mullet. He skewers it with his beak and then retreats up the shore, shaking his head furiously to dislodge his impaled victim, so that he can swallow it whole. The only raptors we see are brahminy kites and a lone eagle, probably a grey-headed fish eagle, though it is too far away to identify clearly. Other birds are more accommodating, including a green-billed malkoha that flies above the treetops, landing every 50 metres or so, staying just ahead of our boat. We follow this bird for half an hour. Malkohas are related to cuckoos and this one is about the size of a crow with dull green feathers and a long, white-trimmed tail.

Once the tide has dropped to its lowest level, Bapi steers us towards the entrance to Dobanki forest camp where a concrete jetty and a flight of steps lead up to the gate of a large, fenced-in enclosure. The guard on duty is slouched in a plastic chair, talking on his mobile phone and obviously unconcerned about man-eating tigers. Before we enter the camp, Prasun and Nirmal point out a swarm of fiddler crabs in the mud near the jetty. They are bright yellow and red, about the size of my thumb. Males have a large claw on their right foreleg, from which they get their name because it looks vaguely like a violin. Two males are duelling, snapping at each other with their pincers. Prasun shows me a red flower that has fallen from a mangrove known as kankra, which means crab, because the splayed petals of the flower resemble claws. Fiddler crabs use these fallen flowers to hide from birds and other predators. In this way, their bright hue serves as camouflage, one species imitating the shape and colour of the other. Fiddler crabs burrow in the mud around the roots of mangroves, aerating the soil and helping the trees access nutrients. They also feed on dead foliage, assisting with the process of decomposition. Kankra have unique seed pods shaped like sharpened pencils. When they fall from the branch, the pods penetrate the mud, effectively planting themselves.

Also on the exposed bank near the jetty are dozens of mudskippers. These odd-looking creatures are amphibious fish belonging to the Gobioid family. They can survive out of the water for extended periods of time and move around on land using leg-like fins. When I ask Nirmal if they are edible, he says that the larger ones are caught and cooked while the smaller ones are used as bait. The mudskippers themselves feed on insect larvae and small invertebrates. Just offshore in the shallows, we also spot a school of several dozen archerfish, each one no more than a couple centimetres long. A creamy white, with prominent black spots, they hover near the surface. Their name comes from the unusual way in which they hunt, spitting jets of water at insects perched on foliage and roots near the shore. When an insect falls in the river, after being struck by the water, the archerfish quickly collects its meal.

Dobanki is one of several forest department camps in the Sundarbans, where guards and range officers can stay in the field. To monitor the tiger reserve, they also have houseboats and motorized launches for patrolling the waterways. Entirely fenced in with sturdy steel mesh, to prevent tigers from entering, Dobanki contains a nursery for propagating mangroves and a captive breeding centre for endangered river terrapins. The other attraction for tourists is an elevated walkway, about 12 metres above the ground and extending half a kilometre through the treetops. From our boat, we are unable to see anything beyond the thickets of foliage barricading the shoreline and this is the only place where we get a glimpse of the interior of an island.

Prasun tells me that there are eighty-four different species of mangroves in the Sundarbans. This includes a number that aren't 'true mangroves' because their roots are not submerged in water. Nevertheless, each of these species is able to flourish in saline soil. The only other trees and shrubs that grow here are a few hardy species of palms. Prasun points out a mangrove known as sundari. Its name means beautiful, the same root word for Sundarbans. This tree can grow up to 15 metres tall and has hard, fine-grained wood that is used for making furniture. Because of illegal timber extraction, both in India and in Bangladesh, it is severely threatened in many areas.

Nirmal identifies another mangrove growing next to the canopy walk—keora. He gathers a handful of green fruit, some of which has fallen onto the walkway. 'Fishermen collect keora fruit and carry it with them when they go out in their boats,' he tells me. 'If they run out of drinking water, this quenches their thirst.' Choosing one of the round fruit, about the size of a marble, I take a bite. It has a sour flavour and a chewy texture that is not unpleasant. Nirmal says that villagers also use it to make chutney.

From the elevated walkway, I can see that some areas of the forest are not as dense as the riverside margins, though most of the mangroves grow close together, their leathery round leaves forming a layered canopy of foliage. A large waterhole has been dug about 30 metres beyond the camp's fence. At one edge of this pond sits a water monitor. The lizard's tail is submerged but the rest of its body and head are visible. About 2 metres long, its hide is a mottled grey, though it appears black because it is wet and silhouetted against sunlight reflecting off the water. Through my binoculars, I can see the monitor's forked tongue licking the air to gather information on potential prey, a receptive mate, or imminent danger. The lizard can see us on the walkway and after a minute or two it decides to move off, slowly backing into the pond and swimming away from shore. Its long, sinuous tail whips back and forth, propelling this giant reptile through the water.

Asian water monitors are the second largest lizards in the world, after Komodo dragons. They can grow more than 3 metres long and the hide on their backs is extremely tough, armoured with bone-like deposits called osteoderms. These give the lizard's skin a pebbled appearance. Perfectly suited to the mangrove-lined waterways of the Sundarbans, they feed on a wide range of fish, snakes, and amphibians, as well as crocodile eggs and carrion. Having strong, sharp claws, they are adept at climbing trees. Because water monitors are hunted for their meat and skins, they are extremely rare in India, though more plentiful populations can be found in Thailand and other parts of Southeast Asia.

At the far end of the walkway, before the forest officers' quarters, we come upon a small shrine, constructed of bamboo and recycled sheets of plastic. It contains four clay figures, each about a metre tall, painted bright colours and adorned with tinsel garlands. These are the main characters in the myth of the forest goddess, Bonbibi, who is seated at the centre of the tableau. Dressed in a red sari and wearing a gilded crown, she has a benevolent expression on her face and raises one hand in a gesture of blessing. To the left of Bonbibi is her brother, Shah Jongoli, with a trimmed black beard. On the other side of the goddess, stands a young boy, Dukhe, and behind them is an image of a tiger, the fearsome Dokkhin Rai (Lord of the South).

Bonbibi is a Muslim goddess who saves islanders in the Sundarbans from the depredations of man-eating tigers. Fisherfolk, honey gatherers, crab collectors, and woodcutters who enter the mangrove forests seek Bonbibi's protection. Her stories are read aloud as a form of worship, while folk theatre performances re-enact her mythology. Prasun explains that villagers take on the different roles, wearing masks and colourful costumes. The story of Dukhe is one of the important episodes in the myth. His name, which means sorrow, reflects his tragic fate. The boy lives with his widowed mother who is destitute. One day, Dukhe is taken to the forest by a wicked uncle who forces his nephew to work on his boat. When they enter the Sundarbans, Dokkhin Rai confronts the uncle and demands that he hand the boy over, promising plenty of honeycombs in return. Tempted by the tiger's offer, the uncle abandons Dukhe in the forest. When the predator appears, ready to devour him, Dukhe calls out to Bonbibi, who immediately appears and drives Dokkhin Rai away.

Scholars like Annu Jalais have documented and analysed this myth which is a core narrative of the region. Obviously, one of the unique and seemingly paradoxical elements of Bonbibi's story is that she is worshipped by both Muslims and Hindus. A booklet containing a verse narrative titled *Bonbibi Johuranamah* was published at the end of the nineteenth century by a writer named Abdur Rahim. Though written in Bangla, the book is read from back to front like an Arabic text. A key theme in the myth is the shared experiences of people from different communities. Dokkhin Rai is described as an avaricious Brahmin with magical powers who claims all of the land in the delta and transforms himself into a tiger to frighten others away. His mother, the goddess Narayani, initially fights with Bonbibi. When neither is able to defeat the other, they suspend their hostilities and work together to protect people of different faiths.

Jalais explains how Bonbibi herself was abandoned in the forest as an infant and suckled by a doe, who became her surrogate mother. Out of compassion for the suffering of islanders in the delta, Allah dispatched Bonbibi and her brother to the 'land of the twelve tides' (another name for the Sundarbans) to defeat Dokkhin Rai. Though the myth includes violence and confrontation, the conflict between the goddess and the tiger ends in compromise and conveys a message of conservation. Dokkhin Rai is banished to the southernmost islands which are uninhabited. Though the tiger is subdued by Bonbibi, he remains dangerous and attacks those who enter the forest with impure and destructive motives. As Jalais emphasizes, a strong ecological ethic lies at the heart of this myth, which instructs those who collect honey, wood, crabs, and other produce from the jungle to take only as much as they need and ensure that the sanctity and natural beauty of the islands is not despoiled.

The forest is seen as a sacred place and considered part of 'the realm of Islam'. Even the mud is said to be holy because Bonbibi and Shah Jongoli travelled to Medina before their confrontation with Dokkhin Rai and brought handfuls of earth from Arabia, mixing it with the sedimentary soil of the islands. In much the same way that sacred groves in other parts of India are revered as sanctuaries for wild plants and animals, the Sundarbans are considered 'pobitra' or pure. Anyone who desecrates the forest and threatens the multitude of species it contains, risks the wrath of the tiger, as well as crocodiles, sharks, and cobras that lurk in the water. Jalais writes: 'The idea that the forest is a sacred place is especially upheld by the crab and honey collectors and the woodcutters through the imposition of minutely elaborated rules pertaining to the forest. The imperative for them is to follow such rules when entering the forest to prove their goodwill to the forest deity Bonbibi.' This is part of 'the ethos of the forest' which must be respected and preserved.

As Jalais explains, the Sundarbans are considered an egalitarian space, owned by no one but governed by Muslim sensibilities and traditions which shun caste and class divisions. Part of the reason for this may be the history of the delta, northern parts of which were first settled by Sufi pirs and their followers, beginning in the thirteenth century CE. Though some Muslim clerics decry the idolatry of Bonbibi as heretical, she represents a mystical, unorthodox interpretation of Islam, which is closely tied to the forest, where Sufi mystics and saints found shelter and inspiration.

One of the interesting aspects of the social hierarchies within communities that live and work in the Sundarbans is that those who are landless have a greater moral claim on the collection of forest produce. Based on her extensive conversations with villagers, Jalais explains that owning land is considered a form of acquisitive greed that jeopardizes an individual's safety in the forest. For this reason, the poorest, most disadvantaged residents of the Sundarbans are more likely to enjoy the protection of the goddess. Dispossessed and dislocated peoples, who settled here at different periods of history, find this logic reassuring and it has become an underlying refrain in the stories that islanders tell. For example, Jalais found that many people in the delta believed that tigers were not always aggressive and it was only because they were forced to escape persecution and exiled to the Sundarbans that they became angry and dangerous, reflecting the dislocation and resentment of human migrants.

When honey gatherers and others enter the forest, they are usually accompanied by 'tiger-charmers' who have been blessed by visions of Bonbibi and have learned magic spells to ward off man-eaters. These individuals, who are credited with being able to sense danger, are the first to step off a boat onto a forested island and the last to climb back on board. They offer prayers of intercession, often recited in Arabic. Just as they cast protective spells upon entering the forest, they remove these spells when they depart, so that the predators and other wildlife can resume their natural way of life. Through faith and ritual, a shared sense of destiny and kinship is established between human beings and other species. At several places during our cruise through the Sundarbans, Prasun points out red scarves tied to the branches of trees. These mark the locations where tigers have claimed victims and the fluttering red flags signal danger but also offer homage to the goddess.

While the mythology of Bonbibi and Dokkhin Rai expresses the close yet fraught relationship between tigers and people in the Sundarbans, scientists have also tried to explain why so many man-eaters inhabit these forests. Some of their speculation, rather than being rational hypotheses that can be tested through scientific observation and experiment are as fanciful and far-fetched as folklore. One German PhD scholar in the mid-1970s, who did his field work in the Sundarbans, proposed that the tigers had a predilection for human flesh because of its 'sweetness', which counterbalanced the salinity of the brackish water the animals drank. Another naturalist suggested that tigers strayed outside the reserve and entered human settlements, killing people and cattle, because the constant erosion of the islands washed away the scent markings that tigers use to establish their territory. In all this speculation, the overriding assumption has been that the violent behaviour of the Sundarbans tigers is somehow 'unnatural' and not a result of the limited presence of prey or the pressure of human activity in the forest.

As conservationists and forest department officials have struggled to stop the depredations, they have come up with several imaginative but ultimately futile solutions. Electrified human dummies were placed in the jungle so that when tigers pounced on them they received a low-voltage shock that was supposed to deter any future attacks. At the same time, plastic masks were distributed to fisherfolk and other islanders with instructions that these should be worn facing backwards. The supposition was that tigers always stalk their victims from behind and man-eaters would avoid preying on two-faced humans with eyes on the backs of their heads. The story of these masks, which bear the caricatured features of a fierce-looking, moustachioed man, has been eagerly picked up by journalists and it is now part of the popular lore of the Sundarbans. Ultimately, though, the tigers were not fooled by either the mannequins or masks.

Many islanders that Jalais interviewed felt the government and conservationists from organizations like WWF were conspiring against them. Their fears led to rumours that the 'old tigers', which they claimed were not as aggressive, had been replaced by a new generation of zoo-bred 'hybrids' that were much more likely to kill people. All of this was seen as a plot by the forest department, which had banned islanders from hunting and gathering in the tiger reserve. Residents of the delta complained that wildlife advocates view tigers as being more important than people and that villagers, particularly fisherfolk, crab catchers, and honey gatherers have been reduced to little more than 'tiger food'.

Islanders in the Sundarbans have good reason to be suspicious of government authorities and there is a long history of conflict with the forest department. The most violent example was the 1979 massacre of villagers on Marichjhapi island. Almost all of them were Dalit Hindu refugees from Bangladesh. Accused of illegally occupying forest land, they were ordered to leave the island. When they resisted and fought back, police fired on them, killing a large number—some claim as many as a thousand, though the casualties were never counted.

Amitav Ghosh has explored this tragedy in his novel, *The Hungry Tide*, which is set in the Sundarbans. A multi-layered story, the book revisits the inequities and violence of the delta islands and their settlers, as well as the natural history and lore of this riverine world. One of the characters, a young man named Kanai, visits the islands after his uncle Nirmal's death. Kanai inherits a journal that recounts the story of Nirmal's life as a social activist in the Sundarbans. It also records the fate of the people of Marichjhapi, as well as Nirmal's reflections on Rainer Maria Rilke's poetry. Meanwhile, a separate thread of the novel follows Piya, a marine biologist from Seattle, who has come to study river dolphins in the Sundarbans. Her experiences researching these cetaceans are woven into a larger story of the 'tide country' which has 'no borders here to separate freshwater from salt, river from sea'. At one point in his journal, Nirmal describes seeing dolphins while travelling in a boat with one of the survivors of Marichjhapi, a woman named Kusum, who believes that the shusuk or dolphins are actually Bonbibi's messengers:

> Then there came a moment when one of them broke the surface with its head and looked right at me. Now I saw why Kusum found it so easy to believe that these animals were something other than what they were. For where she had seen a sign of Bon Bibi, I saw instead the gaze of the Poet. It was as if he were saying to me:
>
> 'some mute animal
> raising its calm eyes and seeing through us,
> and through us, this is destiny....'

Though I keep a lookout for dolphins during my voyage, none of them breaks the placid surface of the river. Two species of cetaceans are found in the waters of the delta. Ganges river dolphins are a freshwater species that do not swim out to sea though they can tolerate the mild salinity of intertidal waterways. The Irrawaddy dolphin is a saltwater species found in coastal areas and estuaries of South and Southeast Asia. They often venture upriver and have a bulbous head, attentive eyes and a blunt beak.

Ganges river dolphins were once plentiful in the Sundarbans but their numbers have declined severely, partly because of increased salinity in the estuaries. This is a result of the reduced flow of freshwater from the Ganga, which was dammed in 1975 by the controversial Farakka Barrage, where water is channelled off into irrigation canals. Siltation and riverboat traffic are also factors in the disappearance of *Platanista gangetica* which is more common in the upper reaches of the Ganga and Brahmaputra rivers.

After lunch, the tide begins to rise again and Bapi pilots us through another series of waterways. One of the pleasures of this safari cruise is that most of the time no other boats are around. However, we soon encounter a vessel carrying a dozen or more wildlife photographers. All of them are dressed in camouflage and armed with expensive cameras equipped with enormous telephoto lenses. After cutting in front of us at one of the confluences, they lead us through a narrow creek, while we stay back about 400 metres. At a bend in the channel we notice them stop. All of the cameras are now pointing in the same direction, towards a mudbank on their right. Watching through my binoculars, I can't figure out what they are photographing. Imagining it must be something significant, maybe even a tiger, Bapi speeds up and we soon approach the spot. But as we drift closer, it becomes clear that they are taking pictures of mudskippers sunning themselves just above the tideline.

By now it is almost three in the afternoon and the temperature has risen. The forest seems empty. Even kingfishers are scarce and the incoming tide leaves no room for the shorebirds. Anticipating a couple of slow hours, I begin to doze off on my comfortable divan when, suddenly, with a roar of its engine, the boat full of photographers overtakes us, leaving Maa Ganga rocking in its wake. Before I can figure out what is going on, a second boat appears from another direction and crosses in front of us, spewing a ragged plume of black diesel exhaust. Meanwhile, Nirmal is frantically checking his mobile phone, trying to get a signal. One of the other guides has sent him a cryptic message: 'Come soon!'

Bapi quickly joins the chase and the quiet stillness of the river is shattered by the thunder of marine engines and furrowed waves splashing against the roots of mangroves. Ten minutes later, we follow the other two boats around a corner of the island to our right, into a wide estuary. Facing the opposite shore, I can see a flotilla of at least a dozen other safari boats lined up side by side. By the time we join them, Nirmal has been able to speak to another guide by phone. He tells me that one of the boats spotted a tiger half an hour ago. It was seen walking along the shore, moving in this direction. As we pull into position, I can see a narrow inlet, about 5 metres wide, with steep mudbanks on either side. The guide in the boat next to ours tells us that the tiger is sure to cross this stream. Diesel exhaust fills the air, and everyone's camera is ready. The vessel full of photographers is bristling with lenses like a gun boat. Positioning myself as best I can, at the front of our upper deck, I try to focus my own camera on the trees along one side of the inlet but there are too many boats and people in between. After hours of solitude on the river, we are suddenly in the midst of an agitated crowd, which reminds me of jeep safaris in other national parks, where news of a tiger sighting inevitably results in traffic jams. Lowering my camera, I keep my eyes on the inlet, doubting that the tiger will appear.

Then all at once, a commotion erupts from the boats that have a clearer view. The tiger has stepped out of the mangroves. Seconds later, we see it run down the mudbank and plunge into the water. Its fur is already wet, a dark, ruddy colour. Only the animal's head is visible as it swims across. Without stopping, it emerges on the other side of the inlet and ducks into the trees again. At the same instant, one of the boatmen guns his engine, pushing his way in front of us, hoping to get a better view but the tiger is already gone.

Chaos ensues as the boats now quickly reverse and collide with each other as they head further down the riverbank, hoping for another glimpse of the tiger. While I can now say I have seen a Sundarbans tiger, the sighting lasted no more than ten seconds. The whole experience is depressing and disturbing—a noisy spectacle that undermines the tranquil beauty of these mangrove jungles. Though Bapi and the others are ready to continue pursuing the tiger, I signal that I've had enough, and we can head back to quieter waters.

By now, the tide has turned and more of the shoreline is exposed, where waders are searching for worms and tiny molluscs amongst the mangrove roots. Two whimbrels pick their way through the mud—thin, curved beaks probing the fresh layer of silt, as if searching for something they have lost. An indecisive plover advances and retreats along the margins of the estuary as our boat turns into one of the narrower creeks, heading west. Two chital, a mother and her fawn, are feeding in a stand of dhani grass growing on a sandbar that extends from the trees along a shallow stretch of water. The deer, legs coated in mud, raise their heads as we pass by but do not run, browsing on the thin blades of grass. A mangrove's stilt roots look like a huge birdcage half-buried in the mud. Perched on an overhanging branch is a collared kingfisher, its head and back a greenish-blue, with a bleached band around its neck and white breast feathers.

Parallel tracts of forest extend along either side of the creek. At points, the foliage is so similar that one shoreline could easily be a reflection of the other, as if our boat were passing between two mirrors. The wild, beguiling beauty of the Sundarbans hides a constant struggle for survival. On these islands in the delta nothing is quite what it seems to be: tidal currents flow in opposite directions; a shifting landscape is compressed between river and sky; and contested histories tell of dislocated people and mythical jungles where the goddess and the tiger maintain an uncertain peace.

5

BETWEEN THE HILLS AND THE SEA

When we speak of biodiversity, even in its broadest, most inclusive sense, there is still a prejudice that favours large, conspicuous species while diminutive life forms are often ignored. The majority of people who visit wildlife reserves hope to see imposing predators or colourful birds and they can be easily disappointed. Yet, if we focus on less charismatic creatures, as well as taxa that don't attract much attention, except from specialists in those fields, it gives us an opportunity to discover and appreciate a vast array of species that can be as exciting and rewarding as any tiger or elephant seen in the wild.

'Herping' along the edge of Goa's Netravali Wildlife Sanctuary, we are pursuing amphibians and reptiles, as well as anything else that crosses our path. It is an overcast night and the monsoon jungle is still wet from a thunderstorm in the afternoon. Two young naturalists, Omkar Dhardwadkar and his friend, Dheeraj Halali, lead the way through tunnels of shrubs, trees, and creepers. The understorey is so dense, my headlamp is of little use. Spiderwebs cling to my face and hair as I stumble over fallen branches, rotting humus, and exposed tree roots.

During the past two hours, we have observed dozens of nocturnal creatures from frogs and geckos to bats and moths. These small, reclusive species comprise the marginalia of wild places, often edged out of the picture by more photogenic animals or birds. Wading through dank, dark foliage, it seems as if we are penetrating a hidden realm of living secrets all but invisible within the humid shadows of the night.

As we come to a clearing, Omkar's torch points out a bare tree trunk 2 metres ahead. Switching off our lights, we let our eyes adjust to the darkness. At first there is nothing but a black void. The forest has vanished, and the only evidence of life is the chuckling of frogs somewhere nearby. But gradually, as my pupils dilate, I am aware of a faint aura coming from the direction of the tree. At first, I think it is the afterglow of torchlight on my retinas. Slowly, however, the pale, blue-green aura that emanates from the bark becomes clearer. After several minutes, it is almost as bright as a patch of moonlight shining on the tree, though the clouds and forest canopy blot out the sky.

Bioluminescent fungi that produce this ghostly light are microscopic, covering the surface of the tree trunk like a thin layer of moss. Omkar explains that the chemistry and purpose of this phenomenon remain a mystery. It could be a way of attracting insects for pollination, though this hasn't been proven. Many other fungi glow in the dark under ultraviolet light but this species, which belongs to the genus *Mycena*, generates its own subtle radiance. Most forms of bioluminescence are found in the ocean—in plankton, squid and, famously, in anglerfish that use it to attract their prey. On land, glow-worms and fireflies are the most common examples, both of which occur in Goa, but this fungi's luminosity is different. It seems ancient and almost sidereal, as if it has travelled for centuries through space and settled here like the glimmering dust from distant stars.

In the forested foothills along the Western Ghats of Goa, these glowing apparitions appear throughout most of the monsoon. Many different species of fungi cast their spores during the wet season to ensure that their species will emerge again next year. Bioluminescent fungi colonize tree bark, twigs, dead wood, and other decaying matter on the forest floor. After the monsoon comes to a close, they vanish without a trace.

Fungi are some of the oldest and most mysterious forms of life. We are often unaware of their presence though scientists are beginning to understand the importance of these enigmatic organisms, which include moulds, mildew, yeasts, and mushrooms. Originally, taxonomists classified fungi as botanical species, but they now occupy their own kingdom and mycologists believe that in some ways they are closer to animals than plants. The relationship between fungi and other species is equally intriguing. For example, lichens are a composite organism formed out of fungi and algae. Many plants and animals have a symbiotic relationship with certain species of fungi, sharing nutrients and depending on each other for survival. Fungal networks of thread-like hyphae have been shown to connect trees in a forest and help them 'communicate' through what has been playfully described as the 'wood-wide web'. On the other hand, many fungi are toxic or parasitic. They play a significant role in decomposition, and infect damaged limbs or roots, ultimately causing a tree to rot and die.

Mycologist Merlin Sheldrake's book *Entangled Life: How Fungi Make Our Worlds, Change Our Minds & Shape Our Futures* illuminates the fascinating world of fungi, most of which are invisible to us. Mushrooms, for example, are the fruiting bodies of fungi that appear for a brief period of time, in order to produce spores and procreate. The rest of year, these species lie hidden beneath leaf mulch and soil or within the roots of plants and trees. Though we seldom notice them, fungi are all around us, as Sheldrake explains:

> We all live and breathe fungi, thanks to the prolific abilities of fungal fruiting bodies to disperse spores. Some species discharge spores explosively, which accelerate 10,000 times faster than a Space Shuttle directly after launch, reaching speeds of up to a hundred kilometres per hour—some of the quickest movements achieved by any living organism. Other species of fungi create their own microclimates: spores are carried upwards by a current of wind generated by mushrooms as water evaporates from their gills. Fungi produce around fifty megatonnes of spores each year—equivalent to the weight of 500,000 blue whales—making them the largest source of living particles in the air. Spores are found in clouds and influence the weather by triggering the formation of the water droplets that form rain, and ice crystals that form snow, sleet and hail.

As we explore the periphery of Netravali, we come upon a cluster of bracket mushrooms releasing clouds of spores into the night air. Seen through the beam of a torch, it resembles smoke and in the humid atmosphere the spores turn rainbow hues. Omkar also points out a fungus known as 'dead man's fingers' that looks like the blackened, bloated digits on a human corpse. Another species he calls 'zombie fungus'. With multiple white ganglia, which emerge during its reproductive phase, these delicate fruiting bodies could be mistaken for scraps of white lace clinging to the underside of a clay embankment.

When ants or other insects brush against a zombie fungus, they become infected by the spores, which cause them to behave erratically until it eventually kills them. After the insect dies, the fungus takes possession of its body and feeds off its remains, emerging out of the desiccated corpse like small, white thorns. This zombie fungus in Goa is related to *Ophiocordyceps sinensis*, a Himalayan species that infects and kills the caterpillars of ghost moths. Known as keeda ghaas or caterpillar fungus, it is a valuable ingredient in Chinese medicine, used as a tonic and aphrodisiac.

Earlier, as twilight began to settle over the forested hills, a chorus of frogs, crickets, and cicadas began to call. Amboli bush frogs, no bigger than my thumbnail, were the loudest and most persistent, a ratcheting chirp that echoed from all sides. The sound is amplified by a balloon-like membrane or vocal sac under the frog's throat. Omkar says there are only two species of bush frogs in Goa but further south in Kerala, as many as seventy species can be found. He lifts a finger to point out the call of a Bombay bush frog, also known as a 'typewriter frog'. Its call resembles someone tentatively tapping out words on a keyboard. One of the most distinctive sounds of this wet season, the vocalization of frogs resembles steady, rhythmic incantations. The Rig Veda contains a hymn celebrating frogs, rejuvenated by the monsoon.

> As soon as the season of rains has come, and it rains upon them who are longing, thirsting for it...
> ...the frog leaps about under the falling rain, the speckled mingling his voice with the green...
> Like Brahmins at the over-night sacrifice who speak around the full bowl of Soma, so you frogs around a pool celebrate the day and the year when the rains come.

In folklore, frogs are believed to turn to dust during the dry season when waterbodies dry up, returning spontaneously to life with the arrival of the monsoon. Snakes too become more active during this time of year, largely because many of them feed on frogs. The first one we see is non-venomous, a bronzeback tree snake that has settled down for the night along the branch of a shrub at eye level. Dheeraj catches sight of it when the snake's tail coils around a twig on the bush. He explains it is a diurnal species that sleeps at night. On the ground, in daylight, it would have disappeared quickly into the underbrush, but we are fortunate to find it in a drowsy state. A juvenile, about 30 centimetres long, its large eyes study me cautiously as I raise my camera. The back of the snake is a ruddy brown with dark bands along the upper neck, while its underbelly is a pale green, almost white.

Next to the bush on which the tree snake has sought shelter stands a ruined shed. The jungle has grown in around it. As we enter the semi-darkness and shine our torches above us, Omkar points out a Brook's gecko perfectly camouflaged against a rotting, mildewed beam. Suspended from a crack in the ceiling nearby is a horseshoe bat that observes us warily. The large black ears twitch and its punched-in nose quivers as the tiny mammal hangs by one leg, wings wrapped around its body like dead leaves.

The different patterns in the jungle seem to fit together with an organic symmetry. Giant wood spiders weave their webs in uniform shapes, a wheel of filaments radiating outward like spokes, connected by circles within circles. These eight-legged hunters, with bright yellow stripes on their bodies, have set their snares between the branches of trees and wait patiently, poised to respond to any creature trapped in their nets. A fishing spider crouches on a withered leaf nearby with a white egg sac, waiting for her brood to hatch. In Hindu mythology, spiders are associated with Brahma, the creator. Metaphorically a spider's web represents a chakra, the timeless continuum of life, spun together in a seamless net of transparent threads. These delicate, invisible snares can also be interpreted as maya, the web of illusion in which we are held captive and meet our fate.

Some species disguise and hide themselves against the patterns of leaves and bark. A violin mantis hangs upside down, mimicking the shape and texture of a dry, crumpled leaf. Though I can see it clearly in the torchlight, I cannot believe it is an insect. Only later, after examining a photograph on my camera, am I able to trace the shape of its head, abdomen, and stem-like legs. Other creatures seem to advertise their presence. On a tree trunk are two lantern flies, planthoppers that look like moths with bright yellow spots on their wings and a single prominent purple antenna like a rhinoceros's horn. A blue Mormon butterfly, as big as my palm, opens its wings, which are black above and pale azure below, marked with black veins and bold spots. Even larger and more striking is a luna moth, its delicately tapered wings a greenish white. Dangling from a leafy twig it is like a festive ornament, attracting our attention.

At this time of year, the trees are full of crabs. Several different species live in hollow trunks, filled with rainwater, and feed off insect eggs and larvae. When the dry months of winter arrive, the crabs migrate to wetlands lower down. As they move between these two habitats in a swarm, hundreds of them are crushed by cars on the roads. Crouched in the trees, these crustaceans seem strangely out of place with large purple claws.

Later, as we drive back to our guest house, we come upon a snake crossing the road. Stopping the car but leaving the headlights on, Omkar identifies a hump-nosed pit-viper. This one is about 30 centimetres long, the same size as the one I saw in Agumbe. It slithers slowly across the dirt track and disappears into the grass. Further on, we encounter a Travancore wolf snake, which is half again as long and has a series of pale bands around its grey body. Unlike the pit-viper, the wolf snake isn't venomous, though it does have protruding teeth, from which it gets its name.

Soon afterwards, an Asian palm civet darts across in front of our car. As it scurries into the underbrush, we can see the eyes of a second civet on the other side of the road. Seemingly unafraid, it comes toward us, scuttling low to the ground and sniffing as it follows the scent of its mate. Slightly larger and bulkier than a mongoose it has a dark grey coat and furry tail, with a pinched, weasel-like snout and white facial markings. Palm civets are arboreal and usually appear in the branches of trees overhead. Omkar explains that the small Indian civet is also found in these jungles and it is easy to identify because of its size but also the distinct stripes and spots on its coat.

Civets eat an eclectic diet of fruit, berries, nuts, small rodents, young birds, and reptiles. The Asian palm civet is also known as the 'toddy cat' because it often raids clay pots used to collect the sweet juice from palmyra palms, which is fermented into alcohol. Generally nocturnal, civets often live close to human habitation and sometimes make their homes in the rafters of a house or in rain gutters and drainage pipes. When alarmed or agitated, they expel a pungent fluid from their anal glands that has a foul stench. In the past, this was collected from captive animals and used as an ingredient in perfumes, because it fixes a scent like musk.

The Malabar civet, also known as the Malabar large spotted civet, is a near-mythical creature, endemic to the Western Ghats but probably extinct. Several skins have been identified in the possession of tribal hunters. The last reported sighting was in the 1980s in northern Kerala. A few stuffed specimens exist in museums but it has not been found for more than twenty-five years, even on camera traps. Scientists blame its disappearance on habitat loss.

~

The next morning, dawn brings with it the rain. Tanshikar Spice Farm, where we are staying, lies 5 kilometres outside Netravali Wildlife Sanctuary. A steady downpour filters through variegated umbrellas of leaves. The farm is almost as much of a jungle as the forest we walked through last evening. Pepper and cocoa vines clamber up the tall, straight trunks of areca nut palms. The branches of clove and nutmeg trees lean over the path from my cottage to the dining room while cardamom and turmeric plants cover the ground.

After breakfast, the rain eases and we head towards another section of the sanctuary, parking our vehicle at Juna check point and entering on foot. A badly eroded jeep track leads to a couple of villages inside the sanctuary, as well as a temple near the Karnataka border, though we only walk for a couple of kilometres. Omkar soon recognizes the call of a Malabar trogon and we spot a pair within fifteen minutes of entering the forest. They are shy and hide amidst the foliage but eventually we get a clear view. The male has a scarlet breast with a necklace of white and a distinctive black head, while the female is less colourful, an olive brown. Because of the high canopy and layered foliage, we hear more birds than we can see, including an Asian fairy bluebird and a Malabar whistling thrush that both remain hidden from view. A red spurfowl explodes from hiding, a blur of wings as it rockets out of sight.

Once again, we see a diverse range of smaller species that don't usually attract much attention but represent a complex community of life forms. In the leaf litter at the side of the road, a swarm of red ants are attacking an earthworm like a pack of wild dogs in miniature, hounding their prey. The worm tries to escape but the ants converge relentlessly, biting with their tiny pincers. Further on, a tarantula races across our path, its eight furred legs scrambling over fallen leaves and rocks. Moments later, Omkar points out the reason for its panic. A spider-hunting wasp is in pursuit. Though the tarantula appears larger and would seem capable of defending itself, this spider is taking no chances and quickly hides beneath a piece of bark on the ground. The wasp is bright orange, about 5 centimetres long. Though it has wings, this persistent hunter follows the tarantula on the ground, its long antennae picking up the trail. Omkar explains that spider-hunting wasps sting their prey, which stuns and immobilizes the spider, after which they drag the victim to their burrow. Placing the spider inside, they lay their eggs before sealing the hole with mud. When the eggs hatch, the larvae then feed on the spider's remains until they emerge as adults.

All around us we find evidence of animals hunting for food. Termite castles have been dug up by sloth bears to get at the swarms of white ants inside. Under a fish tail palm lies a pile of debris, part of which is dried flowers but also the husks of fruit. These are the primary diet of the palm civets we saw last night and it's easy to imagine the same pair gorging themselves overhead and dropping the remains of their feast on the ground. Scattered at the foot of another tree are the broken claws of a crab that provided a meal for a bird or mammal. We also find the skull of an Indian giant squirrel that must have been eaten by a raptor or some other forest predator. And I, myself, become prey to leeches, several of which fasten themselves onto my legs and suck my blood.

When we encounter another young bronzeback tree snake, Omkar is quick enough to cover it with both hands until it is calm and lies still for a minute or two. No bigger than a bootlace, it has inflated its body in an attempt to appear larger, revealing a pattern of bright blue interscales underneath the outer layer of bronze. Part of the snake's diet consists of geckos and skinks, which lose their tails as a defensive mechanism. Several of the skinks we see are in the process of growing new tails.

One of the pleasures of walking through the jungles of Goa is that there is no need to keep a lookout for wild elephants. Though herds frequent the other side of the mountains, in Karnataka, Omkar reassures me that they don't cross over. Their absence may be on account of the steepness of the slopes, though most of the ridges rise no more than 1,000 metres above sea level. The other, more likely, explanation is human settlements and activity. Goa's forests are not as extensive as those of its neighbours and for many years these jungles were severely disturbed by iron ore mining, even within the wildlife sanctuaries.

In 2018, after protests and legal challenges by villagers and NGOs, the Supreme Court of India cancelled all mining leases in Goa, effectively imposing a complete ban on extraction of iron ore in the state. This was a significant victory for environmental activists. Not only did it put a stop to large companies like Vedanta, which had secured mineral rights from the state government, but it also closed down a number of smaller, illegal mining operations that were being conducted with the help of corrupt politicians and civil servants.

Several of the roads through the forest that Omkar and I travel on were constructed by mining contractors and the terraced contours of strip mines are visible on the hills, though the jungle has reclaimed much of this land. Unfortunately, instead of replanting indigenous species of trees, a fast-growing Australian wattle has been introduced for reforestation. Nevertheless, Goa's jungles have received a reprieve and it is unlikely that mining will be restarted inside reserve forests and national parks. Any large development projects in Goa now require environmental clearances that involve biodiversity surveys. Naturalists like Omkar have been enlisted to catalogue and document endangered species that could be threatened by these projects. At one point, Omkar gets a call from a journalist who interviews him over the phone about three infrastructure projects awaiting permission, including a new railway line that is supposed to pass through forested areas. After years of being ignored and sidelined, environmentalists now have some leverage when it comes to protecting wild places that would otherwise be destroyed or depleted through wanton exploitation of natural resources. Though many challenges still lie ahead, it is a sign of hope when young naturalists like Omkar, who is just thirty years old, are able to influence policy and inform politicians and the public about the ecology of their region.

When I ask Omkar how he got interested in birds and wildlife, he says it started for him when he was in school in his home town, Ponda. He had joined a nature club with several other students and they were able to persuade the school to purchase a camera so they could take pictures of birds. Eventually, the club put up an exhibition of their photographs, which was well received. One of the people who visited the exhibition was the artist Carl d'Silva who illustrated some of Salim Ali's books. D'Silva encouraged Omkar to continue with his wildlife photography and became a mentor. Though ornithology remains his primary specialty—Omkar is president of the Goa Bird Conservation Network—he has acquired a wide breadth of knowledge about other aspects of natural history, from butterflies and reptiles to trees and fungi. For a couple of years, Omkar worked as a naturalist at a resort, after which he and three other partners formed their own company, Mrugaya Xpeditions, focusing on bird photography and other nature-based tours.

For wildlife conservation to succeed it is not enough to simply create national parks and sanctuaries where animals are protected. It is equally important to encourage, train, and support naturalists who can interpret the ecological heritage of these forests. Good naturalists are good storytellers, and it is their narratives that inspire others to appreciate and understand the biology and behaviour of different species. Leading a successful birdwatching tour is not just a matter of identifying names, as some people might think. Naturalists like Omkar convey a passion for birds and other creatures by explaining the many connections that exist between wild species and by using compelling anecdotes or metaphors to illuminate these forms of life.

∽

On the second evening of my visit to Netravali, we head south towards another gate, where a paved, two-lane highway passes through a section of the sanctuary. Near the forest department checkpoint at Ambeghat, we stop at a sacred grove identified by a signboard as Shree Paik Devasthan. A small, open shrine stands by the side of the road, surrounded by forest. We arrive just before dusk and the overcast sky is a leaden grey, while the trees grow so thick it looks as if their branches are woven together with creepers.

As soon as I get out of the car, I hear a rooster crow and assume there must be someone living nearby, a caretaker for the shrine, perhaps, who keeps some chickens on the side. Seeing no hut, I ask Omkar and he explains that the bird has been released into the sacred grove, as an offering. In earlier days, roosters were sacrificed here, to propitiate the guardian deity. Blood sacrifices are now frowned upon, both on account of changing religious norms and animal rights regulations. As a result, those who make an offering at these sacred groves simply release cocks into the wild (only male birds are sacrificed), allowing nature to take its course. The bird will soon be killed by one or another of the predators that roam these jungles. Omkar then tells me a story about another forest shrine on a road near the Karnataka border, where dozens of roosters are released every day. One year, an opportunistic panther took up residence nearby and contentedly lived off these daily offerings.

We also notice that dozens of laterite bricks are stacked on either side of the shrine at Ambeghat. When people from nearby villages build a new home, they leave one of the bricks here as tribute to the guardian deity, who is depicted as a warrior on a horse with a sword in one hand. The jungle at Ambeghat is so dense I can walk only a few metres up the slope before encountering an impregnable wall of vegetation. In most sacred groves, the forest itself is considered the shrine and there is no man-made structure, only a few stones or terracotta images placed at the roots of trees. Cutting wood or fodder in the grove is forbidden and the jungle is supposed to be maintained in a natural, undisturbed state. Close to a hundred sacred groves have been identified in Goa. Madhav Gadgil, the eminent ecologist who has studied sacred groves in many parts of the country, once told me that he believes one of the reasons Goa has so many of these protected sites is because the Portuguese, unlike the British, did not take away control of forest lands from local communities, allowing them to manage wild spaces according to their traditions and beliefs.

Like many sacred groves in areas that are now accessible to people from outside a tribal or village community, Ambeghat faces inevitable change. Ultimately, over time, this small roadside shrine is likely to become a larger temple and the forest deities will be displaced by the worship of greater gods. The clearest indication of this is a pile of discarded packaging and plastic bags for incense, oil, and other votive ingredients, as well as cigarette boxes and a variety of less sacred trash.

From here we drive on into the wildlife sanctuary, passing through a forest department gate and descending into a deep, forested valley. A pair of great hornbills cross in front of us, wings beating in unison as they fly from one ridge to the next. In the middle of the road, a little further on, Omkar spots the remains of a green vine snake that has been run over, its slender body crushed and mutilated. To my unpractised eye, it could just as easily have been a creeper that had fallen from a tree overhead, though its tapered head is immediately recognizable. Lifting the dead snake by the tail, Omkar tosses it off the side of the road, explaining that some other creature might come to feed on it and get run over as well.

At the bottom of the valley, we come to a large waterfall spilling down a furrowed rockface. Towering trees frame the darkening sky. The roaring cascade dominates the scene, as we wait for night to fall. Though nobody else is around, except for a young couple on a scooter who leave as we arrive, this is clearly a tourist destination with heaps of trash littering the roadside. Goa's waterfalls, the most famous of which is Dudhsagar in Bhagwan Mahavir Wildlife Sanctuary, are popular attractions, especially during the monsoon.

When it is completely dark, we resume our search. Omkar switches on a UV torch and suddenly the hillside in front of us bristles with dozens of neon blue pincers. Scorpions glow in the dark under ultraviolet light, which makes them look even more menacing than they are with sharp claws and barbed tails. Huddled at the entrance to their burrows, inside the crevices of rocks and beneath the cover of leaves, they wait to ambush their prey, mostly insects. The largest of the scorpions we see are about 10 centimetres, slightly longer than my forefinger. A prehistoric family of anthropods, scorpions have lived on earth since the time of the dinosaurs, but new species are still being discovered. Since

2020, scientists have added seven new species found in the Western Ghats. Some live under rocks, while others inhabit tree bark.

Another recently described genus and species is a semi-slug, *Varadia amboliensis*, that looks like a blue and pink snail. It was discovered several years ago by Varad Giri, a renowned taxonomist who has done a lot of his fieldwork in Amboli, Maharashtra, just north of Goa. Being a biodiversity hotspot, the Sahyadri contain many more creatures like these that are only now catching the attention of scientists.

Moments later, over the sound of flowing water, we hear a chirping call. In a stream nearby, Omkar locates a wrinkled frog crouched at the edge of a shallow pool. Twice the size of the bush frog, it has laid a glutinous clutch of eggs on a leaf overhanging the stream. Most of these have hatched, depositing the young directly into the stream. A little further on, we come upon a skittering frog, which is larger still, hidden within dead leaves at the side of the path.

Perhaps the strangest creature we encounter is a tailless whip scorpion, about 12 centimetres long. Flattened against the surface of a rock, its muddy brown colour blends into the moist stone. The whip scorpion's hinged legs and pincers are like folding calipers, giving it an almost mechanical appearance. Seeing many of these night creatures, it is easy to understand how they might inspire stories of the supernatural. Scorpions are often associated with the dark, destructive side of nature and divinity. During the tenth and eleventh centuries, a scorpion deity, Vrishchikadhari—a terrifying manifestation of the goddess Bhadrakali—was worshipped in Hindu and Jain temples. Depicted as a hideous, hag-like woman with withered breasts and an emaciated body, she had a scorpion perched above her navel. The goddess is shown with multiple arms, in some cases with eight limbs, like the arachnid she represents. Some images of Shiva, in his most dangerous and destructive form, show him wearing a garland of scorpions. In addition to being a threatening symbol, these tiny, venomous creatures also evoke erotic motifs. At Khajuraho, where the temples are decorated with mithuna figures engaged in coital pleasures, a few of the seductive female statues have a scorpion carved on the inside of their thighs. In Prakrit poetry, the scorpion's sting has often been used as a metaphor of adultery.

Folklore contains many references to scorpions. In one popular story, a scorpion pleads with a frog to help it cross over to the other side of a river but the frog protests that it is afraid of being stung. Finally, when the arachnid promises not to harm the frog, it is allowed to climb on the amphibian's back and they begin to swim across. Halfway to the other side, however, the scorpion stings the frog. 'Why did you do this?' the frog complains. 'Now both of us will drown!' The scorpion replies, 'I couldn't stop myself. It is my nature to sting other creatures.' A variation on this fatalistic fable is the allegory of a Sufi mystic, seated on the riverbank, who allows himself to be bitten by scorpions. When his followers ask him why he doesn't kill his tormentors, he replies, 'It is the nature of the scorpion to bite, and it is my nature not to do any evil and not to kill.' Because of his wisdom and saintliness, we are told that the Sufi isn't harmed by the scorpion's venom.

Not being a nocturnal species, human beings have an instinctual fear of the dark that leads us to imagine all kinds of paranormal phenomena that haunt the hours between sunset and sunrise. In many cases, night creatures and night sounds are interpreted as evil spirits, ghosts, and witches, not just in India but throughout the world.

After driving back up the winding road, we eventually come to the forest department checkpoint. A guard steps out of a sentry box and raises the metal boom that blocks the road. At the same moment, we hear a screeching sound that I assume is a rusty hinge on the gate. Seconds later, we hear the scream once again. Omkar and I look at each other, confused. The source of the sound is somewhere in the trees above us.

Jumping out of the vehicle we begin to search the foliage overhead with our torches. Again and again, we hear the agonized cry, which sounds like someone calling out in pain or terror. After several minutes, with the help of the forest guards, who also bring their torches to bear on the high canopy of leaves, we finally spot the source of the sound. A large owl is perched above us. At first it is difficult to identify because of intervening branches but when it flies across to another tree, Omkar whispers with excitement, telling me it is a spot-bellied eagle owl, the largest owl in India. It is feeding on a bird it has killed and allows us to watch for fifteen minutes. The owl calls again several times. Though we now know the source of the cry, it still has an eerie, supernatural resonance.

Through the zoom lens on my camera, I can see that the owl's victim has dark feathers, but its head has been torn off, so it is difficult to know what species it is. Omkar and I speculate that it could be a crow or a whistling thrush. Eventually, though, when we get a chance to magnify the photographs on my camera, we realize the owl has killed a male koel. At several points, the huge predator spreads its wings to keep its balance on the branch and we can see how large it is, at least half a metre tall, with a wingspan of more than a metre and a half. Two distinctive tufts on either side of its head are also clearly visible. The pattern of spots on its belly looks like houndstooth tweed.

Omkar is elated by this rare sighting because this is the first time he has seen this species in Goa. When I ask him what its local name is, he smiles and replies, 'Churail.' With a cry like a banshee, the owl shares the same name as a witch.

∽

The next morning, when the sun comes out, it looks as if the entire landscape has changed. Instead of the grey pall of monsoon clouds and the constant dripping of rain, the hills and forests are sparkling shades of green. Even the air seems easier to breathe. This is my last morning at Netravali and we explore a different part of the sanctuary, entering by the main gate and driving through forested foothills to an altitude of 500 metres above sea level. The summit of the ridge above us is just over 830 metres, the third highest peak in Goa. As we circle up a series of hairpin bends, Omkar tells me with satisfaction, 'This road isn't on Google Maps.'

We stop several times to look for birds and are rewarded by the musical call of a white-rumped shama that remains hidden in the undergrowth. Soon afterwards, a crimson-backed sunbird appears, flitting about a flowering shrub, as it feeds on nectar. One of the smallest birds in India, it is just over 6 centimetres from the tip of its curved beak to the end of its stubby tail. As its name implies, the sunbird's back is a deep red colour and above each eye is a shimmering brow of iridescent blue. Sunbirds make up for their miniscule proportions with the flamboyance of their plumage.

A butterfly, its wingspan half again the size of the sunbird, alights on the same shrub. Omkar identifies it as a Paris peacock, one of several swallowtails found in Goa. The dark green forewings reflect the sunshine with a powdery sheen that looks like emerald dust. In flight, the violet patches on the hindwings are more clearly visible than when it is at rest. The sun has coaxed a number of other butterflies out into the open and we also spot another swallowtail known as a Malabar rose.

Keeled skinks, 7 to 8 centimetres long, dart about in the grass at our feet. Unlike geckos, they are active in daylight. The largest member of this family is the brahminy skink, which crosses the road in front of us and looks like a small monitor lizard, about 25 centimetres long. Some of them grow even larger, the length of my forearm. In the trees overhead are flowerpeckers, bulbuls, and mountain imperial pigeons that watch us through a latticework of leaves and branches.

Parts of this ridge used to be iron ore mines. Though the scars are now overgrown, even the monsoon greenery cannot hide the ravaged contours of these hills. Far off in the distance we can see a large reservoir created by the Selaulim Dam, which supplies drinking water to the cities of Panjim and Margao. Before the extraction of ore was stopped, effluents from mining polluted the streams and rivers that fed this reservoir. The Selaulim is a tributary of the Zuari

River that runs out to the sea through tidal marshes.

As human beings reshape the land and redirect the flow of rivers, man-made infrastructure replaces the natural geography of the earth. Meanwhile, the larger forces of climate and seasons, rainfall and sunlight, struggle to redress and balance the changes we have wrought on the earth. Even as we observe the microhabitats of tiny creatures like spiders or frogs it is essential to understand the ecological effects of human activity on a global scale too, from agriculture and mining to industry and transport. In our short-sighted vision of the future, we calculate economic growth as a measure of social and political success while we often forget the other half of the equation: as manufacturing and commerce increases, the natural resources of our planet are diminished and can never be replaced.

Goa's coastline harbours as many wild species as are found in its forested hills. Estuaries of the Mandovi, Zuari, and Chapora rivers are home to numerous aquatic creatures as well as terrestrial and avian species from crocodiles to kingfishers that live at the water's edge. Intertidal channels, where rainfed rivers merge with ocean currents, are a constantly changing environment animated by the cyclical rhythms of earth and sea. Saltwater marshes and shorelines support an assortment aquafauna like mudskippers, prawns, crabs, and other crustaceans, as well as molluscs like mussels and clams that thrive amidst the ebb and flow of tidal backwaters.

Many of the same species of mangroves that grow in the Sundarbans are found in Goa, along estuaries and coastal wetlands as well as on islands offshore. Forming a dense barricade of foliage and tangled roots submerged by the tide, where few other plants can survive, mangroves are the first line of defence against coastal erosion and provide habitats for insects, birds, and other wildlife that live at the ocean's edge.

Two days after my visit to Netravali, I visit Panjim, Goa's capital. With its Portuguese architecture and floating casinos, the city is spread out along the mouth of the Mondavi estuary. Monsoon is a slow season for tourists and under a sagging ceiling of grey clouds, the air is hot and uncomfortably humid. At the WWF-India office in Miramar, I meet programme coordinator, Aditya Kakodkar. Together we go across to Caranzalem Beach, a five-minute scooter ride away. WWF has been working on conservation efforts to protect olive ridley turtles that lay their eggs on Goa's beaches, as well as dolphins and other vulnerable species. Over the past year, Aditya and his colleagues have been running a research project on guitarfish, an endangered family of rays that look very much like their name suggests. The WWF team has been monitoring the catch at Caranzalem, where local fishermen use large drag nets, called rampons. From time to time, several species of guitarfish have turned up in the nets.

By now, the tide is receding, and the day's catch has already been pulled up onto the beach, a laborious process that takes three to four hours. Almost a kilometre long, the rampon is towed out into the bay by a boat that circles around in a broad arc, from one point on the beach to another. The two ends are then drawn in by hand from shore, harvesting whatever comes in its way. It is an indiscriminate but effective method of fishing used by many coastal communities. While boats from Panjim and other ports go far out into the ocean to catch larger species like kingfish and barramundi, the fishermen who dredge the bay at Caranzalem tend to bring in smaller mullets and sardines, averaging 10 to 15 centimetres in length. Aditya estimates that today's catch weighs almost a tonne, a silvery slurry of scales and fins that fills the centre of the net like an overstuffed sausage. In earlier times, everyone from the fishing village participated and shared in the catch but now that many of the young men have gone off to better-paying jobs in Dubai or other parts of the Gulf, the few remaining fishermen, known as ramponkars, have to hire outsiders to help them haul in and sort the catch.

To keep bystanders at a distance and avoid pilferage, one end of the net has been erected as a circular fence, supported by bamboo poles. Inside this enclosure, about thirty boys and men are squatting on the sand, picking through the contents of the net. Each of them has a wicker basket in which he puts the larger fish and those that will fetch a higher price, like pomfrets. Meanwhile, half a dozen women are seated to one side with plastic crates and bins into which the sorted catch is divided. A few of them are already haggling with vendors who have come to purchase the fresh fish. Supervising all of this is the owner of the rampon and two or three older fishermen, who keep urging the others to hurry up, in loud, impatient voices. Flocks of crows and stray dogs have gathered on the beach to try and steal what they can.

Witnessing this wild harvest, I can't help wondering how much longer these fish will survive in the shallow waters off Caranzalem Beach. Very few of them are much longer than my forefinger and the net, with its fine mesh, spares nothing that comes in its way. Most of the smaller species end up being chopped in half or cooked whole, swimming about in oily red curries that are served at every restaurant and beachside shack, from Agonda in the south to Ashvem in the north. Seafood is a staple in most Goan homes and the striped grey mullet, a favourite delicacy, is the state fish.

As we watch the men sorting through the day's catch, a number of species are tossed aside including starfish, seahorses, and jellyfish that lie in the sand.

Some of them are still alive but all of them will be dead, long before the tide comes back in. 'Bycatch' is the fishing industry's equivalent of 'collateral damage'—those species that are unintentionally caught in the nets but have no market value. Commercial fishing, particularly with large trawlers, is a wasteful and unsustainable business that needlessly kills and discards quantities of marine life, on a much larger scale than I observe at Caranzalem. Soon after we arrive, a jeep pulls up on the beach and collects some of the bycatch, which is taken away to be processed into poultry feed.

Though we see no guitarfish, there were several other kinds of rays and small sharks, most of which have been rejected. The other species of bycatch that get tangled in the rampons are sea snakes, which are highly venomous. Whenever a snake is found, the fishermen grab it by the tail and fling it out of the netted enclosure. The first time this happens, I am not paying attention, when a snake comes flying through the air and narrowly misses me, landing on the sand a metre away. Gaurav Patil, a WWF team member, who specializes in snakes, explains that these are beaked or hook-nosed sea snakes, common in the waters off Goa and throughout much of the Indian Ocean. They can grow to a metre in length, though the ones we see are about three-quarters that size. An olive-grey colour, they have a series of dark bands that extend over the length of their bodies. Their tails are paddle-shaped to help them swim.

Sea snakes are at least five times more venomous than cobras and if someone gets bitten it is usually fatal. However, when out of the water, the snakes are sluggish and seemingly docile. They raise their heads occasionally and I can see how their upper lip protrudes like a blunt beak. The men who are sorting through the catch obviously understand the danger but deal with them casually. Gaurav tells me that two deaths caused by sea snakes were recently reported in Karwar, on the Goa–Karnataka border.

By now, the tide has retreated 30 metres down the beach. Though the snakes squirm listlessly in the wet sand, it isn't likely that they will reach the water. Picking one up by the tail, Gaurav carries it down to the sea, carefully holding it away from his body. The snake wriggles slightly but shows no aggression. Once it is released back into the gentle, lapping waves, it swims away slowly out of sight. In this way, Gaurav rescues more than a dozen snakes. Meanwhile, a group of tourists are splashing about in the water, a hundred metres away, blissfully unaware of what is taking place. There are no recorded instances in Goa of swimmers being bitten by sea snakes.

Coastal ecosystems are some of the most precariously balanced environments on earth. They are also the most degraded and abused, on account of pollution from shipping and sewage, as well as waterfront construction and other development projects. Tourism takes its toll too. Beaches in places like Goa attract millions of visitors every year, creating a growing demand for resorts, hotels, and restaurants that cater to their needs. All of this puts relentless pressure on fragile ecotones that knit together the sea and the land. With climate change, which affects both the temperature and level of tidal waters, coastlines are inevitably the first major points of crisis. The many species that live here, from mangroves to mullets, are severely threatened by shifts in global weather patterns that ultimately trigger local catastrophes.

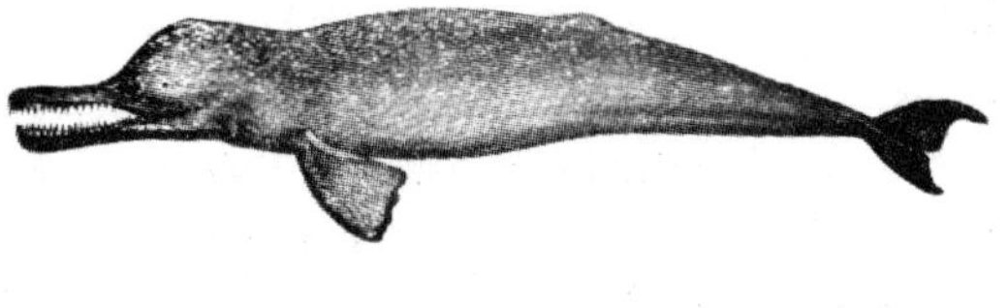

6

ALONG THE CHAMBAL

No other geographical feature delineates a landscape as precisely as does a river. Flowing water shapes the earth into valleys, floodplains, and deltas, carving out a course for itself but also defining the topography on either side. A river is a line but never straight, following the tilt of terrain it passes through, according to the dictates of gravity—the push and pull of its pulsing current. Like all good stories, rivers have beginnings and ends, as well as an extended middle that winds its way through mountains and lowlands on its way to the sea, swelling and shrinking with the seasons. No wonder rivers are employed as metaphors of life and death as well as rebirth. For millennia, poets have dipped their pens in these symbolic streams to describe constancy and change, the paradoxical qualities of fluid states—the persistent force of descending water and its compliance, bending and obeying the contours of the land but always... always finding a way.

The Chambal is a tributary of the Yamuna, which ultimately flows into the Ganga. Each confluence is not just a merging of waters but also the intersection of vital lifelines that harbour India's riverine fauna. The Chambal provides habitat for an array of aquatic species as well as various creatures that live on its banks. For a fish, a turtle, or a crocodile, flowing water is not just its home but also its frame of reference, the enveloping consciousness that an animal occupies and experiences. Each species that inhabits the Chambal knows this river through an inherent awareness of its transient nature, the way the current moves over, under, and around them. They are as much a part of the river as it is a part of them.

Drifting on the still surface of the Chambal, soon after dawn, we glide past a pair of gharial, both more than 4 metres long. These huge reptiles lie basking on the sandy riverbank in the early light. Their narrow snouts are almost a fifth of their length and lined with sharp teeth that protrude on either side of their jaws. Though gharial may look ferocious they feed almost exclusively on fish and pose no threat to human beings. The male has a bulbous nose, like an oversized wart. This round protuberance, consisting mostly of cartilage, is the source of the gharial's name because it looks like a clay waterpot, called a ghara in Hindi. Males use it to make buzzing sounds to attract their mates and to signal their presence to other males. They also produce a loud clapping sound by snapping their jaws shut. Out of the water, gharial appear clumsy and awkward, disproportionately fat in the middle, with relatively small legs. But as soon as they slide into the water, they move swiftly and gracefully, propelled by powerful tails.

In Hindu mythology, the goddess Ganga's vahana or sacred vehicle is the makara, a mythical creature, usually depicted with the head of a lion, the trunk of an elephant, and the tail of a fish. Some have suggested that the makara is a stylized representation of a gharial, while others believe this composite creature is more like a freshwater dolphin which has a similar snout. Both species are found in the Ganga and either could serve as an auspicious symbol of the river they inhabit.

Fossils of gharial, dating back at least 5 million years, have been unearthed in the Shivalik Range at the foot of the Himalaya. These crocodiles evolved in South Asia's ancient waterways and are endemic to this region. Images of them, easily recognizable because of their distinctive snouts, are found on clay seals from the Indus Valley Civilization. They were once common in most North Indian rivers but by the middle of the twentieth century, gharial had been almost wiped out through hunting and destruction of their eggs. Estimates from 1974 placed the total number, at that time, as no more than 250. Protection of habitat and captive breeding programs have rescued gharial from near extinction, though they are still severely threatened. The Chambal River Sanctuary, which extends for roughly 400 kilometres along the state borders of Madhya Pradesh, Rajasthan, and Uttar Pradesh, is one of several places where gharial have been reintroduced and this part of the river now has a relatively stable population that is slowly recovering. A female gharial lays anywhere from 25 to 80 eggs which are buried in the sand and hatch after roughly seventy days. In an unusual reversal of gender roles, the responsibility for protecting offspring is assumed by male gharials, not all of whom may have fathered the newborn hatchlings that take shelter on their backs and heads until they can fend for themselves.

Unlike the Yamuna and the Ganga, into which its waters flow, the Chambal is not considered a sacred river and there are no temples, pilgrimage sites, and bathing ghats on its banks. Few large towns are situated along the Chambal and as a result the river has been spared the worst forms of pollution like industrial effluents and urban sewage. Draining from both the Vindhya Mountains and the southern part of the Aravalli Range, the Chambal flows just over 1,000 kilometres before joining the Yamuna. Several dams have been built along the upper reaches of the river, which affect the flow and restrict the migration of fish and other aquafauna. Sand mining also threatens the habitat of rare species that breed on its shores. The final stretch of the Chambal, roughly 150 kilometres before its confluence with the Yamuna, is fed by numerous ravines that carry seasonal run-off into the river, more than doubling its volume during the monsoon.

The Chambal Ravines are famous for being a lawless maze of wild, eroded terrain where legendary dacoits hid out. Part of the reason this region became a refuge for bandits was because the Chambal serves as the state border between Uttar Pradesh and Madhya Pradesh. Dacoits were able to escape back and forth across the river after committing their crimes. The most famous of the Chambal dacoits was Daku Man Singh, whose village, Rathore, lies near the section of the river I am visiting. Celebrated as a Robin Hood character, who robbed the rich and helped the poor, Man Singh dominated the ravines during the first half of the twentieth century until he was finally killed in 1955. He is still remembered in the Chambal region as a historic figure who blurred the line that separates heroes from villains. More recent legendary dacoits who operated in the Chambal Ravines include Malkhan Singh Daku from Bhind, who had ninety-four police cases filed against him and finally surrendered in 1982. Phoolan Devi, known as the 'bandit queen', was from Jalaun district and surrendered in 1983. After spending eleven years in jail, she was released and joined politics, becoming a member of parliament, before she was assassinated in 2001. Nirbhay Gujjar, a sadistic killer, had more than 200 cases of murder, kidnapping, and rape filed against him by the time the police gunned him down in 2005.

Bachchu Singh, a naturalist and guide accompanying me, recounts legends of these dacoits, along with the mythology and folklore of the river, which is said to be cursed. He tells me the story of an ancient king named Rantideva who performed an epic yagna, or sacrifice, in which thousands of animals were slaughtered. Their blood turned the river red and its banks were littered with rotting carcasses and hides. The Mahabharata contains a reference to this river, which is called Charmanvati, referring to leather drying on its banks. Chambal is believed to be a derivation of that name. Because of the bloodshed and pollution caused by this wanton sacrifice, Bachchu explains that the Chambal is considered unclean. He also mentions that the infamous episode in the Mahabharata, when the Kauravas attempted to strip off Draupadi's sari, also occurred nearby. For this reason, Draupadi cursed the river, saying that anyone who drank its waters would be consumed by an irrepressible urge to seek vengeance. Ironically, the river's tainted mythology has spared the Chambal from excessive human encroachment and made it one of the cleanest and least polluted rivers in India.

Bachchu's home is a village near Bharatpur on the periphery of Keoladeo National Park. He worked there as a naturalist for a number of years before moving to the Chambal Safari Lodge where I am staying. In addition to guiding birdwatchers and tourists, he has assisted with the Bombay Natural History Society's project to protect the nesting sites of Indian skimmers and black-bellied terns. He also took part in a project led by the Madras Crocodile Bank to reintroduce gharial in the Chambal. Bachchu tells me that one of the main threats are feral dogs that raid bird and reptile nests situated on exposed sandbars or along the riverbank. Jackals, mongooses, and civets also feed on the eggs.

'A gharial's eggs are extremely fragile. If you turn them over, the embryos die,' Bachchu says. They are also highly sensitive to temperature. As with many reptiles, the sex of the hatchlings and the length of the incubation period is determined by the temperature at which the eggs incubate. Jeffrey Lang, the lead scientist overseeing the Madras Crocodile Bank's Gharial Ecology Project on the Chambal, has studied temperature dependent sex determination in a variety of crocodilians. In the captive breeding program at the Croc Bank, he notes that eggs incubated at 32 °C produced 89 per cent male gharial. Both below and above this temperature, the majority of hatchlings were females. For this reason, it would seem that gharial and other crocodiles are particularly sensitive to climate change.

As our motorboat continues slowly upriver, we see plenty of red-naped ibises, ruddy shelducks, and bar-headed geese. At this time of year, in early December, the Chambal attracts a variety of migratory birds, including painted storks and lesser whistling-ducks that congregate on islands in the stream. On either side of the river are clay embankments, 50 to 75 metres high. These are cut through by lateral ravines, like miniature canyons, fringed with thorny shrubs. The river has wide, sandy margins, where the water rises during the monsoon. In winter, the Chambal is about 200 metres across at its broadest points. The current is sluggish and barely noticeable. Though the river is much cleaner than the Yamuna and Ganga, its water is a murky grey colour and hardly pristine. Nevertheless, a placid calmness imbues the scene, undisturbed except by the idling sound of our outboard motor. If it wasn't for us, this landscape could be a million years old. There are no buildings or powerlines in sight, no fields or motor roads, simply water and sand, as well as the eroded contours of high banks on either side, which frame this fluid line as it disappears around broad bends both upstream and down.

When I ask what fish are found in the river, Bachchu tells me that the most common species are lanchi, a catfish, and two kinds of carp—rohu and catla. Fishing is illegal inside the Chambal River Sanctuary because gill nets are a threat to gharial and turtles, which become entangled and drown. This ban, if effective, would also ensure that there is plenty of food for the crocodiles and river dolphins that live in these waters, not to mention herons and other fish-eating birds. However, there is rampant disregard for these regulations and many gharial and turtles drown in nets.

Just ahead of us, a pied kingfisher is hovering in the air, its wings beating rapidly to hold its position until it plunges into the water. Moments later, it emerges from the river with a minnow wriggling in its beak. Further on, we spot an osprey perched on a large piece of driftwood. It is feeding on a catfish about the size of my forearm, which it must have dragged out of the water with its powerful talons. Just then, I see my first Indian skimmer, a spectacular black and white bird with long, gull-like wings that slice through the air as it flies just above the surface of the river. Its bright orange beak is unusually shaped, the lower mandible being longer than the upper. As the skimmer swoops down, it scoops up small fish with the lower part of its beak. Also known as a scissorbill, it congregates in noisy flocks on the riverbank, though the one we see is hunting alone.

Bachchu also identifies a group of black-bellied terns on a spit of sand nearby. They are about two-thirds the size of the skimmer but similar in shape with tapered grey wings, a sharply forked tail, sooty underbelly, and black cap. These endangered terns and skimmers are resident species. Their nesting sites on the Chambal face the same risks from predators and habitat loss. As we pass the flock of terns, I can hear their squabbling, high-pitched calls.

In addition to the gharial, plenty of mugger crocodiles live in the Chambal and we see them basking at the water's edge, as well as higher up on grassy mudbanks. Though they feed mostly on fish, muggers also prey on mammals that come down to the water to drink. We often forget that crocodiles are the largest predators in India, half again as long as a tiger and considerably heavier. At one point, we come upon a villager walking along the riverbank. He is searching for one of his goats and I ask him if the crocodiles ever feed on his flocks. With a frustrated shrug, he tells me that he has lost several animals to muggers and that they kill cows and young buffaloes as well as goats.

Later on, we pass a broad sandbar, half a metre above the water. Three gharial and a mugger are sunning themselves. The two species appear to coexist peacefully. All of the gharial have their mouths wide open, which gives them an intimidating appearance, though it is not a sign of aggression. About a metre away from the crocodiles, Bachchu points out two species of turtles. The larger of these is the Indian softshell turtle with a leathery carapace three-quarters of a metre long. It is a greenish, grey colour, similar to the wet mud on the riverbank. The pale, wrinkled neck tapers to a point, with two beady eyes and a pair of tubular nostrils. Its large, webbed flippers, with sharp claws, help it swim through the slow-moving waters. Feeding on fish and amphibians mostly, it also scavenges on carrion, including human remains near cremation ghats. Softshell turtles are revered as the vahana of the goddess Yamuna.

The second turtle is about a third the size of the Indian softshell, roughly 35 centimetres long. It has a much harder carapace, with a ridge down the middle and uneven markings that look like slate tiles. But its neck and head are the most remarkable features with bright red, blue, and yellow stripes that converge on a scarlet chapeau. Known as the red-crowned roof turtle, or painted roof turtle, it is one of the rarest reptiles in the Chambal and critically endangered. From its brilliant colouring we can tell this is a male. Females are about twice as large and do not have the bright stripes on their necks. This turtle's face is different from the softshell's pointed features; it has a blunt snout and upturned nose. The black pupil and pale iris that study me with suspicion are larger than the softshell's eye. As our boat moves closer, both turtles scramble into the water and disappear.

The Chambal is home to eight different species of Testudines. In Hindu mythology, Kurma the turtle is the second of Vishnu's ten avatars, through which he preserves and protects the earth. Kurma is believed to support the world on his shell. He also served as the fulcrum for churning the ocean, when gods and demons sought to extract nectar from the primordial sea. Seeing the turtles basking on the riverbank, it is easy to understand how they might be employed as metaphors of stolid endurance, being species that have survived for many millions of years with their strong, protective shells. At the same time, they live on the edge, both literally and figuratively, emerging from the water to absorb the warmth of the sun but retreating into their fluid world for nourishment and safety.

∽

At Nadgawan Ghat, where we disembark, stands a half-constructed bridge with tall columns of reinforced concrete that might someday connect the two opposite banks of the Chambal, linking Uttar Pradesh and Madhya Pradesh. For the time being, however, the bridge remains unfinished and there seems to be something symbolic in the fact that it is incomplete. The natural boundary formed by the river predates political borders and human history, dividing the land according to geological and hydrological forces, rather than statehood or conquest.

As we drive away from the river on a rough, unpaved road through a section of the Chambal Ravines, I can see how these marginal tracts of wild scrubland would offer the perfect hideout for criminals escaping the law. Overgrown with thorny barricades of ziziphus and babool, as well as tall, dense grasses, the escarpments of yellow clay are riven with deep and devious trenches. Like the famous Chakravyuha labyrinth in the Mahabharata that Abhimanyu enters but cannot escape, it is a place where the most determined policeman could lose all sense of direction and easily fall prey to ambush. Though the threat of dacoits has now diminished considerably, the ravines remain an ideal refuge for wolves, jackals, ratels, and hyenas.

Further on, where we join the two-lane motor road that connects Jarar to Etawah, Bachchu points out a derelict guardhouse and an ancient well. Newer buildings have come up around these two crumbling structures, but I can see that the old walls are made of thin, wafer-like bricks, which means they date back more than a century and a half.

'This used to be one of the old chowkis on the Permit Line,' Bachchu tells me. 'Have you heard of the Great Hedge?'

With a blank expression, I confess complete ignorance.

'In the nineteenth century, the British planted a hedge of thorns to stop people from smuggling salt,' Bachchu explains. 'There's a book about it. We have a copy in the library at Mela Kothi. I'll show you, when we get there.'

Mela Kothi is the ancestral property of Ram Pratap Singh, a descendant of the zamindars of Jarar. A famous cattle fair, or mela, was held here twice a year until the 1980s, after which the spacious residence and surrounding compound fell into disrepair. Ram Pratap and his wife Anu Dhillon have restored the property and turned it into the Chambal Safari Lodge, a haven for birdwatchers and wildlife enthusiasts.

The library is a quiet, comfortable room with framed sepia photographs on the walls. In one of the bookcases, Anu helps me locate Roy Moxham's *The Great Hedge of India*, a remarkable account of one of the most audacious projects the East India Company ever embarked on. Salt was heavily taxed by the British and a primary source of revenue. For the most part, it was acquired either from saline lakes in Rajasthan and Gujarat, where it was extracted by evaporation, or from salt mines in the northern foothills of the Punjab. A limited amount was also transported over the Himalaya from Tibet. Being an essential commodity, the imposition of customs duty on salt was seen by most people in India as an unjust form of commercial exploitation, especially during periods of famine. The smuggling of salt, usually transported in one maund (37 kilograms) jute bags, on a man's head, became a thriving form of illegal trade.

The British began building customs chowkis along most of the main routes entering their territories but these were hardly sufficient to stop the smugglers, who could easily circumvent the outposts. Ultimately, the solution that Company officials came up with was a feat of botanical engineering. Moxham quotes Sir John Strachey:

> To secure the levy of a duty on salt...there grew up gradually a monstrous system, to which it would be almost impossible to find a parallel in any tolerably civilized country. A Customs line was established which stretched across the whole of India, which in 1869 extended from the Indus to the Mahanadi in Madras, a distance of 2,300 miles; and it was guarded by nearly 12,000 men.... It would have stretched from London to Constantinople... (consisting) principally of an immense impenetrable hedge of thorny trees and bushes.

Nothing before or since can match the magnitude of this green barrier which was compared to the Great Wall of China. In many ways, it reflected Britain's imperial arrogance, as well as Victorian attitudes towards nature. Hedgerows are a common feature of the English countryside and replicating these on a much larger scale in India would have seemed a feasible proposition. The forest resources of the subcontinent had already been exploited to build the railways and, by the middle of the nineteenth century, the British had excavated an extensive series of canals that now irrigated large areas of the Gangetic Plain. Simultaneously, the idea of the Indian jungle, as a dense, 'impenetrable' space, was already firmly fixed in the imagination of the Raj. To use wild, thorny flora to block native smugglers appealed to an imperious sense of administrative ingenuity, even if the concept was seriously flawed.

Moxham's book is a lively, well-researched account of his search for surviving evidence of the Great Hedge, which he refers to as a 'quintessentially British folly'. At home in London, he studied maps and documents buried in colonial archives and then made visits to India, during the 1990s, casting about for any living remnants of the hedge. Though first established by the East India Company in the 1820s, the Customs Line was expanded once the British government took control of India following the armed rebellion of 1857, reaching 'its greatest extent and perfection' by 1877. The commercial and historical significance of this botanical boundary, which was shifted at different times during the nineteenth century, as the British added territory, is fascinating in and of itself. But for a naturalist, it offers intriguing insights regarding the ecology of different regions it passed through.

Presiding over the Great Hedge was the Commissioner of Inland Customs, one of whom described it as follows, in his Annual Report:

> In its most perfect form the hedge is a live one, from ten to fourteen feet in height, and six to twelve feet thick, composed of closely clipped thorny trees and shrubs, amongst which the babool (acacia catecha), the Indian plum (ziziphus jujuba), the curounda (carissa curonda), the prickly pear (opuntia, three species), and the thuer (euphorbia, several species) are, according to salt and climate, the most numerous, with which a thorny creeper (guilandina bondue) is constantly intermingled.

Where sections of the Customs Line passed through terrain that made it impossible to plant a hedge because of rocky conditions, stone walls were built or trenches dug to deter smugglers. A 'dry hedge' was also erected at places. This consisted of a barricade of thorny branches cut from bėr or babool trees and staked in place, though these were more susceptible to destruction by fire or termites than a green hedge. In the 1860s, it was estimated that 150,000 tonnes of dry brushwood was cut to maintain the hedge, which required constant upkeep, and was regularly breached by smugglers who simply burned it down and crossed over.

All of this was happening at a time before most invasive species like *Prosopis juliflora* and lantana had arrived in India. Other than the *Opuntia*, or prickly pear listed above, the Great Hedge consisted entirely of native trees and shrubs that were already present in the immediate environment. The idea that indigenous vegetation could physically and symbolically be used to establish a political and economic border, reveals not only how nature was employed and exploited but also how British officials viewed wild species and spaces. As a result of the exorbitant customs duties, many desperate people, especially from landless, migrant communities, whom the British labelled as 'criminal tribes', took up salt smuggling and other illegal activities, which contributed to the lawless reputation of the Chambal Valley.

Roy Moxham faced many obstacles as he struggled to locate living evidence of the hedge, much of which had been built over by roads. He focused on areas of Madhya Pradesh and Uttar Pradesh, between Jhansi and Agra, traversing the path of the Customs Hedge by train, bus, jeep, tonga, and on foot. His book is a compelling account of obsession, of both the colonial crusade to stop salt smugglers and his own compulsive desire to retrace the line of thorny shrubs that marked the edge of British territory.

He also narrates the remarkable career of Allan Octavian Hume, who became Etawah's district magistrate and collector in 1855, at the age of twenty-six. Though he was charged with gathering land taxes in this region, Hume spent much of his time collecting specimens of Indian birds, 63,000 of which were ultimately donated to the Natural History Museum in London, along with 15,500 eggs. Sometimes referred to as the Father of Indian Ornithology, Hume founded and edited the journal *Stray Feathers*. He described well over 150 new species and subspecies of birds and mammals, several of which are named after him, such as Hume's leaf warbler (*Phylloscopus humei*).

In 1857, after rebel forces seized Etawah, Hume raised a local levy of 300 troops loyal to the British and successfully recaptured his district headquarters. Though he fought against the rebels, Hume firmly believed that this uprising, which the British referred to as the mutiny, was fundamentally a result of colonial mismanagement and unjust laws. In the aftermath of the rebellion, Hume showed unusual leniency. He insisted on giving rebel prisoners a fair trial and only seven men were executed in Etawah, as against hundreds elsewhere. Concerned about the cruel methods of hanging, which usually involved a noose thrown over the nearest branch, he designed a more humane gallows that killed a man instantly by breaking his neck rather than through slow strangulation. A contemporary observer, G. O. Trevelyan, reported that Hume treated the rebels with 'fatherly tenderness, for he invented a patent drop for their benefit; so that men prayed—first, that they might be tried by Hume, and next, if found guilty, they might be hanged by him.'

Soon afterwards, he was appointed commissioner of Inland Customs and became directly responsible for overseeing the Great Hedge, which he did effectively and efficiently, reducing corruption along the line and ensuring that the thorny barrier was well maintained. He and his subordinates also collected numerous bird specimens from the hedge, which attracted many different species to its sheltering foliage, as well as the flowers and fruit it produced.

Ultimately, A. O. Hume was elevated to the post of secretary to the Government of India, one of the most senior positions in the Indian Civil Service. Though he shipped his bird skins and egg collection back to England, Hume decided to remain in India after retirement. Interested in Buddhist and Hindu philosophy, he advocated liberal reforms and encouraged Indians to join the freedom struggle. In 1885, Hume helped found the Indian National Congress and served as its first general secretary.

Moxham documents many historical details about the salt trade and describes his own adventures in pursuit of the hedge. But he is curiously circumspect when it comes to his own friendship with a woman he simply refers to as 'Didi', without revealing her name. She and her family host him on his travels and provide him with introductions to various people who help him along the way. Only after I finished reading the book did I learn that Didi was, in fact, Phoolan Devi, the famous bandit queen of the Chambal Ravines. Moxham had written to her in Gwalior Jail, where she was incarcerated, and an unusual friendship developed between this British researcher, who worked as a conservator at London University's library, and the dreaded female dacoit who was ultimately released from jail and went on to a brief career in politics before she was murdered in 2001.

~

Mela Kothi is surrounded by roughly 14 hectares (35 acres) of wooded land, most of which has been allowed to return to the wild. Several enormous tamarind or imli trees dominate the grounds, along with a dense grove of other indigenous species that attract a multitude of birds. For me, there is an immediate personal connection to this landscape because it reminds me of the compound in Etah, where I grew up, 80 kilometres north of here. The smell of the dusty, dry earth is familiar, as is the architecture of the buildings, with their brickwork arches and flat, terraced roofs. As I wander through the gardens and along overgrown pathways, I feel as if I am stepping back into my childhood, though I am carrying binoculars and a camera instead of a catapult.

A shikra is hunting garden lizards in the yard in front of the main house while flying foxes roost in the trees, their furry red bodies and folded black wings suspended upside down like fruit from the branches. A herd of eight or ten nilgai live on the grounds of Mela Kothi and we cross paths several times in my wanderings. They are shy but not skittish. Most of the nilgai are females with a couple of calves, accompanied by one male with short horns and a slate blue hide. In many ways, they remind me of the feral horses in Assam, not entirely wild but certainly not tame.

For an hour or more in the late afternoon, I pursue a grey hornbill that remains just out of sight in the high branches of a gular or cluster fig tree, which also hosts a flock of yellow-footed green pigeons. A female koel, with speckled breast feathers and a long, barred tail, leads me through the underbrush as if we are playing a game of tag. Winter sunlight casts a mosaic of shadows in the dust while overhead, through the canopy of leaves, the sky is an opaque blue. Beyond the edge of the property, yellow mustard fields are flowering and a congregation of cattle egrets skulk near an irrigation ditch. Though I am alone, I can almost hear the clamorous voices of my childhood companions, somewhere nearby, within the thorny margins of a remembered world.

Our nostalgia for wild places we have known in the past is part of the way in which we appreciate nature in the present. Memory is an intrinsic part of observation, triggering associations through sounds, textures, smells, and tastes, as well as visual images. For instance, a rose-ringed parakeet in a neem tree next to the main building at Mela Kothi immediately takes me back to childhood memories of the same two species, recalling and retracing the contrasting shapes and shades of their green feathers and leaves. Similarly, when I pick ripe ber fruit from a ziziphus bush, its sweet, nutty flavour is as distinctive and easily identifiable as the shrub's leaves or thorns. Later, in the evening, when I sit down to a meal at Mela Kothi, I am served tenti or dela and karonda pickles. Their small, sour berries come from plants that would undoubtedly have been part of the Great Hedge.

Natural history is a phrase that isn't used much any more because it suggests an archaic, outdated approach to ecology and biodiversity. However, it invokes elements of environmental study and fieldwork that are now largely ignored because of scientific specialization and advanced technologies. The historical and cultural context in which a species exists is as important as the biome it inhabits or its genetic makeup. While most of the Great Hedge may have disappeared long ago and the Chambal Ravines are no longer 'infested' with dacoits, understanding the legacy of this landscape with its stories of cursed rivers and turtles that carry the world on their backs, helps us absorb and comprehend the complex web of life that exists, here and now, in this particular place.

∽

Returning to the river for a final visit, I am intent on seeing Gangetic dolphins. They are one of the key species that indicate low levels of pollution in the Chambal. Like the gharial and painted roof turtles, river dolphins are endangered, and the silt-clouded waters provide a secure sanctuary where they can hide and hunt with minimal disturbance. *Platanista gangetica* are freshwater cetaceans, somewhat similar in shape to dolphins in the ocean but entirely different in other ways. One of their distinctive features is a long bill, lined with sharp teeth. Though quite a bit shorter than a gharial's snout, it serves the same purpose, to catch the fish on which it feeds. Gangetic dolphins are also unique because they are virtually blind. Their tiny, vestigial eyes register only light and shadow. Living as they do in turgid waters, river dolphins rely on echolocation to navigate and track fish. Sometimes, they also orient themselves by swimming on their sides, one eye sensing the refracted light from above. Being mammals, they must surface to breathe, though they cannot survive out of water.

A fine mist lies upon the river like a haze of smoke and the sun has yet to rise behind the scarred ridgeline to the east. Bachchu Singh is with me again and we are the only boat on this stretch of the Chambal. River lapwings, with neat black crests, strut along the wet sand. Several other waders are also patrolling the waterline—great thick-knees, common redshanks, and little ringed plovers.

The same two gharial we saw yesterday are lying just as they were but a short distance away is a young one, no more than 20 centimetres long, much more animated and alert than its elders. Plenty of predators are nearby that would make a quick meal of this baby gharial. In a tree, on the top of the cliffs, we see a pair of Bonelli's eagles which feed on reptiles as well as mammals and birds. Further upstream, an Egyptian vulture is searching for dead fish and other food where the sand and water meet.

For the first half hour we see no sign of dolphins but then, 50 metres in front of us, the water wells up like a small wave and a humped grey shape appears, barely breaking the surface. Disappearing within a couple of seconds, it leaves a ring of ripples. Two minutes later, another dolphin breaches and we get a glimpse of its snout. The boatman switches off the engine and the silence adds to the suspense. Over the next ten minutes, the two dolphins rise at different places, circling within a radius of 75 metres. Bachchu says they are probably a mother and her calf, for the one looks quite a bit smaller than the other and they are obviously swimming close together.

Watching river dolphins can be a frustrating experience because they remain underwater most of the time. Even when they appear for brief moments, the bulk of their bodies are submerged. Yet, there is something fascinating about not knowing where or when they will rise to the surface and whether a fin or snout will be revealed. Trying to get a photograph is pointless and binoculars are no help. It is better to simply scan the area in which they are rising and spot them with the naked eye. Being blind, there is no chance that they will look at me or acknowledge my presence. Perhaps the only way to appreciate our shared awareness of the river is to close my eyes and imagine their streamlined bodies swimming underwater, guided by sound instead of sight.

As we observe the mother dolphin and her calf in the Chambal, Bachchu explains that most cetaceans are able to sleep without drowning because half of their brain shuts down while the other half remains awake, signalling when they should surface and breathe. While dozing like this, saltwater dolphins often keep one eye open and the other closed, floating close to the surface. By alternating between the two sides of their brains, the dolphins are able to get the rest they require, even as they continue swimming and, sometimes, even feeding in their sleep. Most research has been done on saltwater dolphins rather than freshwater species like *Platanista gangetica* and there is a great deal more to be learned about how these aquatic mammals have adapted to life in a riverine environment. But as I watch the two dolphins surfacing, with a slow, almost languid rhythm, I wonder if they are half awake...or half asleep.

INTERLUDE

WILD LOVESCAPES

Art and literature depict the natural world in a variety of forms, assigning symbolic meaning to a diverse range of flora and fauna. Some of India's earliest written texts and sculptures represent wild plants and animals as key elements of mythology and lore. The imagery that classical sculptors and poets employed suggests not only a fertile creativity inspired by beautiful and wondrous species but also a keen sense of observation that conveys an intimate, first-hand knowledge of these life forms. In many places, beginning with the petroglyphs at Bhimbetka and leading on to Ajanta Caves frescoes, the ruins and rock formations at Hampi, as well as the Mughal gardens surrounding the Taj Mahal, the landscape itself becomes part of an artist's aesthetic imagination.

Nowhere is this more evident than at Mahabalipuram, on the coast of Tamil Nadu. During the sixth and seventh centuries CE, huge rock formations facing the beach and shoreline were transformed by an army of anonymous sculptors into a sprawling temple complex. Most of these monumental structures were not built from the ground up but excavated out of pale granite boulders through a process of elimination. The kings of the Pallava dynasty who commissioned these stone shrines, chose this site for its dramatic location and geological features as well as its proximity to their main port. These rulers and the sculptors they patronized were clearly fascinated by wildlife, representations of which appear throughout Mahabalipuram.

As I walk amidst a cluster of temples, popularly known as the five raths or chariots, each of which is associated with the Pandava brothers and Draupadi, their wife, I can see how these monoliths must have stood here in their natural form long before the artists' chisels began to chip away at the surfaces of the rocks. Sixteen hundred years ago, the stone carvers fashioned elaborate, tiered structures, with supporting pillars and arches as well as images of deities and demigods. What catches my eye, however, more than any of the elaborate shrines, is a life-sized elephant that stands on its own between two of these temples.

The sculptors must have visualized its form in the boulder, after which a perfect likeness of the animal was hewn from stone, down to the folds in its ears and a baleful look in its eyes. Originally, it had two tusks but those have broken off, leaving it a makhna. This lone elephant stands amidst the ornate architecture and statuary of the temples, unadorned with any ceremonial regalia, not even a bell around its neck.

Many other wild creatures appear in the temples and carved friezes throughout Mahabalipuram. Lions proliferate, mostly rampant yali figures that are a common motif in South Indian temples. Heavily stylized versions of the actual beasts, they are not as realistically rendered as the elephant but have flowing manes, sharp claws, and fierce teeth. Some scholars have suggested that the lack of realism in these lion images comes from the fact that this species never inhabited the forests and grasslands of southern India. On the other hand, the deer, peacocks, and monkeys depicted on the rocks have an animated, life-like quality that proves the artists were familiar with their morphology and behaviour. Two stone monkeys, probably bonnet macaques, are seated together on a pedestal, one picking fleas from the other's fur.

The most impressive monument of all is an enormous bas-relief sculpture, roughly 30 metres across and almost 15 metres high, that covers the eastern face of a hill-sized boulder. Carved during the reign of King Narasimhavarman I (630–668 CE), it is often referred to as 'Arjuna's Penance' because it was once thought to depict the great hero of the Mahabharata performing tapasya (ritual austerities), in order to acquire invincible weapons for the battle at Kurukshetra. Contradicting this interpretation, many art historians and archaeologists have concluded that it is more likely that this mythological scene represents the descent of the Ganga.

A mountain range, probably the Himalaya, appears along the top of the carved surface while running vertically down the centre is a channel through which rainwater flows during monsoon storms. Immediately next to this deep groove in the rock stands an ascetic figure performing a yoga asana with both arms lifted over his head while his prominent ribcage shows that he has been fasting. This is very likely the figure of King Bhagiratha, whose extreme penance persuaded the goddess Ganga to descend to earth in her fluid form. Gathered on all sides is a congregation of deities and celestial figures who are witnessing this momentous event. Mingling with the gods and goddesses are dozens of animals including cobras, deer, antelope, lions, tigers, monkeys, and birds, all of whom have gathered to celebrate and pay homage to the sacred river that brings life to the land. Among these is a family of elephants that dominate one portion of the frieze, beautifully and accurately rendered with young calves playing between their mothers' legs. This giant tableau is remarkable for many reasons, not the least of which is the way it affirms a shared mythology that extends across India, from the Himalaya in the north to the southern coastline of Tamil Nadu, a distance of more than 2,000 kilometres

The presence of animals, including a mischievous cat that mimics Bhagiratha's posture, underscores the importance of wildlife in the imagination of artists and their patrons as well as the cultural resilience of India's natural heritage. These living creatures share this cosmic space with omnipotent deities and heavenly beings, occupying the same realm of sacred myths and iconic metaphors. Carved into the channel through which the Ganga descends are three naga figures, identical to those in the Mathura Museum. Two have human heads and torsos, framed beneath a cobra's hood, with the coiled bodies of snakes. The third naga, at the bottom of the channel, is devoid of any anthropomorphic features or symbols—the wild species itself, in its natural form.

∽

The Tamil Sangam poets, of the first and second centuries CE, predated the Pallava dynasty and the sculptures at Mahabalipuram by 400 years. Their verses are considered the epitome of classical Tamil literature for their refinement and subtle imagery. In an essay, 'The Landscape of Love', published in 1954, the naturalist M. Krishnan describes how these ancient poets divided the ecology and terrain of their homeland into five distinct zones, each of which corresponded to different aspects of love. Referred to as 'thinai', these regions correspond to the high, forested slopes of the mountains; pastures and scrub jungles in the foothills; cultivated agricultural land on the plains; coastal areas; and intermediary zones of parched 'wasteland', or forested lands in summer, scorched by the sun and withered by drought. Each of these spaces are clearly defined in Sangam poetry both from an ecological and romantic perspective.

'Love was, in those days and in poetry, mainly an open-air pursuit. The land was less congested then, and lovers could find privacy not too far from the settlement,' Krishnan writes. 'In the first tract, in the hills, love was illicit and triumphant. Here, where there was adequate cover in the rank grasses and undershrubs of the slopes and in the abiding gloom of rainforests, a young man and his lass met and loved, in secret.'

Below these hills lay rolling grasslands and open scrub, with trees of lesser stature and a very different mix of flora that, Krishnan notes, included yellow-blossomed amaltas. Cattle and goats grazed here and for the poets these pastoral landscapes signified solitude, a place where the lover anxiously awaited the arrival of her paramour. Here love was 'chaste and forlorn', Krishnan tells us. Sometimes deer and other animals or birds kept the lonely lover company.

Cultivated lands were associated with marriage, where the forest had been cleared and fields were ploughed. Love was condoned and consummated within the household. At the same time, it was also the setting for infidelities, quarrels, betrayal, and jealousy.

From this domesticated yet fractious domain, the poets moved on to the ocean's edge. 'Love has many moods on the seacoast, but most typically it is sombre and tragic—a man bemoaning his dead love,' Krishnan explains. A wife looks out anxiously at the sea, where her husband has sailed beyond the horizon, perhaps never to return.

Finally, Krishnan directs our gaze to the marginal spaces, where he sounds more like the naturalist he is: 'The barren wastelands had their own tough vegetation—spiky, dwarfed trees and the much-branched, cylindrical cladodes of the kalli (*Euphorbia tirucalli*) and other xerophytes. Here lovers parted, not in anger, but with many promises as the truest lovers must part when their love cannot be publicized.'

Renowned poet and literary scholar, A. K. Ramanujan, translated a selection of Sangam poetry in a book titled *The Interior Landscape*. The first poem of the anthology is about love in the highlands, where the kurinji/kurinci flower blooms once every twelve years. In this wild landscape a young woman is infatuated by her lover.

Bigger than earth, certainly,
Higher than the sky,
More unfathomable than the waters
is this love for this man

of the mountain slopes
where bees make rich honey
from the flowers of the *kurinci*
that has such black stalks.

Ramanujan explains how the poet Tevakulattar does not need to refer directly to lovemaking, relying instead on discrete metaphors embedded in the landscape and its ecology. 'Describing the scene describes his passion.' The bee collecting nectar to produce honey is a familiar symbol of love and by mentioning the kurinji flowers, which grow high up in the mountains, the poet suggests a youthful, furtive tryst.

The imagery from nature, employed by these poets, would have been well known to their audience two millennia ago, just as it is today. 'Each of these landscapes is now a whole repertoire of images—anything in it, bird or drum, tribal name or dance, may be used to symbolize and evoke a specific feeling,' Ramanujan writes. 'A conventional design thus provides a live vocabulary of symbols; the actual objective landscapes of Tamil country become the interior landscape of Tamil poetry.'

While these poems can be appreciated simply for their lyrical beauty and eloquence, as well as subtle hints of love play, they are also early evidence of scientific observation and classification. The botanical knowledge expressed in verse came out of a broader understanding of the rich biodiversity of southern India.

Each of the five ecological zones are associated with a specific flower—kurinji, mullai, marutham, neidal, and palai. Before they were used as metaphors, these flowers had to be identified and named. The kurinji's rare flowering, which occurs once every twelve years, is an important botanical event. By some accounts, the blue colour of this flower is what gives the Nilgiri mountains their name. Fragrant mullai, or jasmine, blooms at lower altitudes. Its flowers are threaded into garlands that adorn a woman's hair, perhaps as she impatiently awaits her lover's arrival. Marutham refers to the flowering arjuna tree with its feathery cream-coloured blossoms. Neidal is the lotus, appropriately an aquatic species that grows at sea level. Palai is the scholar's tree, which has pure white flowers and remains green throughout the year, even in the driest season.

Not only flowers but specific animals and birds are associated with each amorous landscape. The poets use these species, as well as other cultural and religious motifs, to imply either the consummation of love, longing and desire, conjugal relations, and loss. To understand the poems fully requires both an aesthetic and taxonomical appreciation of nature. Carefully observed botanical details are woven into the classical vocabulary of the Sangam poets. The fact that two millennia after these verses were written, a twentieth century naturalist like Krishnan could respond to the romantic metaphors and identify the species too, underscores an awareness of the natural world that is both poetic and precise.

More than likely, the Sangam poets acquired their knowledge of forest plants and wildlife from those who lived closest to nature. Tribal hunters and gatherers would have been the first to classify plants and herbs, both edible and toxic, as well as other species that have aromatic or medicinal properties. Not only did these forest-dwelling communities possess an awareness of biodiversity but, in the imagination of Tamil poets, they also embodied romantic notions of wild places.

Another anthology of Sangam poetry, *Love Stands Alone*, translated by M. L. Thangappa and edited by A. R. Venkatachalapathy, contains a remarkable poem by Kapilar, which begins as a hunting tale and ends up being a love song expressing a woman's anxiety for her husband's safety as he travels alone through the mountains to meet her. With simple yet resonant imagery, the poet describes the hunter's pursuit of a wild boar, which he kills with his arrows. The meat is then distributed by his 'dark-haired wife… among her kinsfolk,' as she voices her fears about the dangers of the forested highlands.

> These are the mountains
> from where you come.
> You may not be afraid
> of the night's treachery,
> or of the jungle and the river bed,
> where an angry tusker waits
> to fight a tiger.
> Only I am afraid
> for your safety.
> For along the narrow mountain path
> there are many termite hills
> where the bears come in crowds
> to dig them up.

∽

In many cultures, the forest is seen as a place of romance and lovemaking, where a couple finds privacy behind curtains of leaves. The wildness of this natural setting also suggests an escape from the constraints and conventions of society. The fecundity of the forest, with its foliated shadows, entangled vines, and fragrant flowers, elicits an erotic allure. The jungle harbours many hidden places—caves, waterfalls, and sheltered glens—where lovers can meet in secret, surrounded by flora and fauna that symbolize emotional and physical aspects of human sensuality and desire.

Folk tales and folk songs often use this imagery in subtle and suggestive ways to tell different stories of love. Verrier Elwin came to India in 1927 as a Christian missionary and then, after briefly becoming a follower of Mahatma Gandhi, gave up on prudish pieties and immersed himself in tribal society. He fell in love with a young Gond woman, Kosi, whom he married. Some years later, after they divorced, he was married again, to Lila, also a Gond. A proponent of indigenous culture, Elwin compiled several volumes of folklore from different regions of the country. One of these is *Folk Songs of the Maikal Hills*, a compendium of lyrics from the Baiga and Gond communities in Central India, translated by Elwin and Shamrao Hivale. The majority of these songs are about love—its lusty passions, physical pleasures, unrequited yearnings, cruel infidelities, and tragic betrayals.

In all of these songs we find simple and frank depictions of sexual relations as well as deeply felt emotional bonds, most of which play out against or within a forested landscape. Here, we find expressions of love in its most innocent, ardent form.

Look at me with the strong eyes of youth
In the cold days the trees are flowering
The wind blows among the hills
Bending the tree-tops
Take my hand, come with me
For you have conquered me
With the strong eyes of youth.

Elwin tells us that most of these songs accompanied folk dances performed during festivals and celebrations. The voices are both male and female, often calling back and forth to each other. They move in rhythm to the ecstatic tempo of drums that animate the dancers and arouse their passions.

Raja, my heart is mad for you
I have gone mad for you
But you have left the warm bed in my house
Where will you find such warmth outside?
You have left me all alone
You would eat roots and fruit outside
Come, my madman, let us go together to the forest.

Green is the green hill
Yellow are the bamboos
Green is the kalindar creeper
Karanda flowers are in my hair
Where in the forest will I find my Raja?
My heart burns for him
Where in the forest will I find my madman?

Some of the folk songs contain explicit references to specific birds, mammals, and insects associated with lovemaking. Impotent husbands are compared to a lamp without a wick that attracts no moths. Hunters with bows and arrows stalk deer just as lovers pursue their sexual partners. Within the jungle, human beings copulate with the same unrestrained instincts and impulses of wild creatures.

Play without fear
Play, dwellers in the jungle
Over you the sun passes like a wave
In the forest the clitoris-bird is feeding
The herdsman drives out his cow
There the deer are grazing
The herdsman's girl drives out her cow
There the deer are grazing
As fresh as new leaves of ganja
Like a wave the sunlight bathes you.

Elwin annotates his translations when the meaning or context is unclear. 'The *ṭiti* or clitoris-bird (probably the red-wattled lapwing),' he explains, 'is the subject of several folk tales generally on the lines of a human girl who, finding herself without adequate sexual equipment, persuades the bird to lend her its clitoris and never returns it.'

While snakes are usually considered symbols of male sexuality in most cultures, within the folklore of Gond and Baiga communities, they are often associated with female beauty and desire.

Lying on their bed the two embrace
The girl is lovely as a cobra...

The girl with cobra eyes
Drew him after her
Do not bite him, girl
I will wait, I will wait
By the river.

While there is something dangerous, perhaps even fatal, in the cobra's gaze, the besotted lover cannot resist. He is entranced and calls to her again and again, anxiously awaiting the serpent's arrival.

You are coming very slowly, why do you delay
O my black cobra?
I have brought you anklets, measured to your feet
Why do you delay, O my black cobra?
I have brought you a sari, measured to your body
Why do you delay, O my black cobra?
I have brought you armlets, measured to your arms
Why do you delay, O my black cobra?

You are coming very slowly, why do you delay
O my black cobra?

These folk songs were recorded more than sixty years ago, when the forests of India were far more extensive and considerably less disturbed than they are today. Adivasi cultures have also undergone drastic changes since the time when Elwin and Hivale collected these songs. And yet, as we read the lyrics and imagine the pulsing rhythms of dancing feet, lithe figures swaying in the firelight, we can appreciate the raw passions that echo in these songs. With the destruction of forests, we have lost more than just wild habitats for threatened species, but also the lovescapes of our primal yearnings.

∽

Modern writers and filmmakers have also explored wild landscapes with a more contemporary eye. Sunil Gangopadhyay's novel, *Aranyer Dinratri* (Days and Nights in the Forest), is the story of four young men from Calcutta who escape the big city, looking for something that they feel is missing in their lives. The group of friends—Shekhar, Robi, Ashim, and Sanjoy—disembark at Dhalbhumgarh, an isolated railway station near the state border between West Bengal and Bihar. Having boarded the train the night before without any clear idea of a destination and travelling ticketless, they choose to get down at this stop on the advice of an anonymous stranger in their compartment. Eager for a cup of tea and something to eat, they discover a dusty market that has little to offer, neither eggs nor butter for their breakfast. After casting about for a place to stay, they come to a forest rest house some distance from the station. It seems the ideal place to spend a few days, surrounded by the jungle and cut off from the rest of the world.

Aranyer Dinratri was first published in 1968 in Bengali and translated into English in 2010. It is a short, unsettling book that captures the disillusionment and discontentment of that period of history, both in India as well as the rest of the world. According to Gangopadhyay's translator, Rani Ray, the author had recently returned from a year at the Iowa Writers' Workshop. He was influenced by the beat poets and Jack Kerouac, whose book, *On the Road*, suggested the footloose plot of *Aranyer Dinratri*. Nevertheless, this novel is much more than just a story of rootless youth and cynical values. The forest dominates the narrative, a constant backdrop and motivation for the men's desire to retreat from the alienation and disquietude they have carried with them from the city.

The forest rest house plays a significant part in their adventure. Though they have no official permission to stay here, they bully and bribe the caretaker into unlocking the rooms, then hire a young man named Lakka to run errands for them. As the novel unfolds, it becomes apparent that the jungle is not as uninhabited or idyllic as they suppose. Dhalbhumgarh is populated mostly by Santals, who are traditional forest dwellers but now face an uncertain, dislocated future in a rapidly changing, modern world. Throughout the book, the sound of axes cutting down trees echoes from somewhere deep within the forest.

A romantic sense of nature being a curative, redemptive force, inspires each of the characters as they seek to connect with the jungle. Ultimately, in a scene that underscores the absurdity and desperation of their quest, the young men strip off their clothes and run naked beneath the trees, as if trying to become wild creatures. Gangopadhyay describes the irony of their surroundings:

> A forest that did not look like one—it would be better to describe this place, with rows of trees...as a...garden. Lakka had told them, when they went for a walk with him one evening, that leopards were a rare sight, and a pair of bears were spotted only once, a couple of years ago. It was usual for people to walk about in the dark carrying just a stick, he said. The young sal trees planted by the government as part of the forestation programme had tender and supple trunks, like the bodies of young men. One could walk unhampered in the forest, which was devoid of wild weeds, brambly bushes and strangling creepers.

Cultivated by the government, this timber plantation is regimented and unnatural. Traditional forest resources and wildlife that sustained the Santals in the past have disappeared. One of the few wild trees that survives is the mahua, from the flowers of which tribal people distill a potent country liquor that helps ease the desperate conditions of their lives. Shekhar and his companions get drunk on the liquor, ogling a group of young Santal women, who represent for them an erotic wildness and promiscuity, outside the bounds of 'civilized' society. For their part, the women eye the men with suspicion but also as an opportunity to earn a few rupees.

While each of the four friends wrestle with their individual demons and desires, we begin to see the forest for what it is—a deceptive fantasy that no longer exists. The idyllic pleasures of this imaginary paradise are interrupted by the arrival of a forest ranger, who warns them that the conservator is expected soon and if he discovers that they have occupied the bungalow without permission, they will be evicted, and the caretaker will lose his job. One of the interesting aspects of the book is the way in which Gangopadhyay presents forest department officials as seemingly congenial yet menacing authority figures with a sinister edge to their indulgent smiles.

The other discovery that the young men make is the presence of an upper middle-class family, living a short distance from the rest house. An elderly timber merchant, Mr Tripathi, owns the property. He has retreated here from the city with his daughter-in-law, Jaya, her young son, and her sister, Aparna. The women play badminton in the yard, obviously bored and craving distraction. Shekhar recognizes Jaya as someone he knew in college, while Ashim and Robi compete for Aparna's attention. Eventually, the family's tragedy is revealed. Tripathi's son and Jaya's husband committed suicide in London, leaving them grieving and confused. The old man has come to the forest to find solace while Jaya, being a widow, has no choice but to accompany her father-in-law to Dhalbhumgarh. Aparna too is dissatisfied with the life she has left behind in Calcutta but unhappy with the isolation and primitive conditions in the forest.

Eventually the story turns violent after the Santals confront the urban interlopers when they cross an invisible line that separates their two cultures. After Robi seduces one of the tribal girls, Lakka and other men attack him and the peaceable sanctuary of the forest becomes a brutal nightmare.

In 1970, Satyajit Ray adapted *Aranyer Dinratri* into a film that bears the same title. His black and white rendition of the story might be described as jungle noir and conveys the same restless mood of discontentment. Minor aspects of the novel have been changed. For example, the four friends arrive in a car and many of the digressions and complexities of Gangopadhyay's plot have been tightened and refocused.

One of the most striking visual elements in Ray's version is the forest itself, which must have been filmed in the dry season and appears stark and virtually leafless. It is a degraded environment, exploited by the forest department for commercial gain. When the four men meet the Tripathi family for the first time, the grandson is wielding a toy gun and demands to be taken to the circus. As the old man explains, it is the only place where they can see wild animals now. Earlier, the jungle was full of creatures but now it is all but empty of life. Tripathi points out a hide at the edge of his property that he had built years ago, to observe wildlife. As Ashim and Aparna explore this abandoned building, speaking of love, the destruction of nature serves as a metaphor that parallels the hollowness of the characters' existence. Only at the end of the film do they catch a brief glimpse of two deer bounding away into the jungle.

In the late 1960s and early 1970s, conservation was still a new and evolving idea in India. The state forest departments governed extensive territories and most forests were considered a source of revenue. Only a few national parks and wildlife sanctuaries had been established. During the first two decades of Independence, the nation's focus was firmly on agricultural self-sufficiency symbolized by the

Green Revolution and industrial development, epitomized by large scale projects like the Bhakra Nangal Dam and the Tata Steel Plant, in Jamshedpur, only a few stops down the railway line from Dalbhumgarh.

The loss of both natural and cultural heritage is one of the underlying themes in both the book and the film, especially as we observe the jungle through the eyes of four city dwellers. At one point, admiring a spectacular sunset against which the bare limbs of trees appear in silhouette, one of the characters in the book exclaims that 'it's just like one of those scenes in Western films starring Burt Lancaster.' Ray captures this moment in his film, obviously struck by the cinematic reference but also by the fact that the characters have a perspective that is directed westward on more than one level. Once again, we are reminded that their notion of wildness is unrealistically romantic. When one of the men imitates Tarzan's yodelling cry, it sounds hollow and contrived.

The forest rest house, where much of the film is shot, is now part of Jharkhand's Palamau Tiger Reserve. Ray obviously chose this location carefully. His camera lingers on the architecture of the bungalow and evocative details like the old punkahs that were pulled by hand. It is a colonial structure, a reminder of the past when British forest officers ruled over the jungle. The deep verandas and high ceilings, flower beds, and lawns evoke a sense of ambivalent nostalgia. For the four young men who have illegally occupied this bungalow, it is a forbidden space in which they are trespassers. The fact that the rest house becomes their refuge for a few brief days and nights in the jungle, suggests a kind of middle ground between an untamed wilderness and the civilized comforts and tensions of Calcutta where they will inevitably return.

Top: Bhimbetka, Madhya Pradesh

Bottom: Prehistoric rock art depicting wildlife at Bhimbetka, Madhya Pradesh

Top: Goral, Jabarkhet Nature Reserve, Mussoorie, Uttarakhand

Bottom: Male blackbuck, Tal Chhapar Wildlife Sanctuary, Rajasthan

Top: Rainforests of the Western Ghats near Agumbe, Karnataka

Bottom: Ajay Giri rescuing a cobra near Agumbe, Karnataka

Top: Votive stones with cobra images near Agumbe, Karnataka

Bottom: Kottigehara dancing frog near Agumbe, Karnataka

Top: One-horned rhinoceros in Dudhwa Tiger Reserve, Uttar Pradesh

Bottom: Terai landscape, Dudhwa Tiger Reserve, Uttar Pradesh

Top: Female sambar, Pench Tiger Reserve, Madhya Pradesh

Bottom: Male tiger in the mist, Bandhavgarh Tiger Reserve, Madhya Pradesh

Top: Chital and langurs in Bandhavgarh Tiger Reserve, Madhya Pradesh

Bottom: Male blackbuck at sunrise in Tal Chhapar Wildlife Sanctuary, Rajasthan

Top: Male nilgai, Tal Chhapar Wildlife Sanctuary, Rajasthan

Bottom: Kishan Bagh Sand Dunes Park, Jaipur, Rajasthan

Bengal monitor, Tal Chhapar Wildlife Sanctuary, Rajasthan

Male elephant, Nagarhole Tiger Reserve, Karnataka

Top: Female hoolock gibbon with infant, Dehing Patkai National Park, Assam

Bottom: Fulvous forest skimmer, Dehing Patkai National Park, Assam

Top: Asian openbill, Maguri Wetlands, Assam

Bottom: Citrine wagtail, Maguri Wetlands, Assam

Top: Feral horses, Dibru Saikhowa National Park, Assam

Bottom: Male leopard, Satpura Tiger Reserve, Madhya Pradesh

Top: Baby sloth bear, Satpura Tiger Reserve, Madhya Pradesh

Bottom: Male sambar, Satpura Tiger Reserve, Madhya Pradesh

Top: Smooth-coated otter in the Kaveri River, Srirangapatna, Karnataka

Bottom: Mangroves, Sundarban Tiger Reserve, West Bengal

Top: Bon Bibi shrine, Sundarban Tiger Reserve, West Bengal

Bottom: Blue mormon butterfly, Netravali Wildlife Sanctuary, Goa

Top: Bronzeback tree snake, Netravali Wildlife Sanctuary, Goa

Bottom: Spot-bellied eagle owl, Netravali Wildlife Sanctuary, Goa

Top: Beaked sea snake, Caranzalem Beach, Goa

Bottom: Gharial, softshell turtle, and painted roof turtle, National Chambal Sanctuary, Uttar Pradesh

Top: Painted roof turtle, National Chambal Sanctuary, Uttar Pradesh

Bottom: Mugger crocodile, National Chambal Sanctuary, Uttar Pradesh

Top: Egyptian vulture, National Chambal Sanctuary, Uttar Pradesh

Bottom: Female lion, Gir National Park, Gujarat

Top: Lesser goldenback, Gir National Park, Gujarat

Bottom: White-breasted kingfisher, Mokarsagar Wetlands near Porbandar, Gujarat

Top: Greylag goose, Mokarsagar Wetlands near Porbandar, Gujarat

Bottom: Golden jackal, Mokarsagar Wetlands near Porbandar, Gujarat

Egrets at sunset in Kuchchadi Wetlands near Porbandar, Gujarat

Top: Young male gaur, Pench Tiger Reserve, Madhya Pradesh

Bottom: Rock formations, Mahadeo Hills, Pachmarhi, Madhya Pradesh

Top: Indian giant squirrel, Nagarhole Tiger Reserve, Karnataka

Bottom: Male urial, Ulley, Ladakh

Top: Ibex, Ulley, Ladakh

Bottom: Snow leopard, Saspochey, Ladakh

Snow leopard, Saspochey, Ladakh

Top: Ayyappa Shrine, Heggala Sacred Grove, Kodagu, Karnataka

Bottom: Rusty-cheeked scimitar babbler, Ramgarh, Kumaon, Uttarakhand

Top: Rock sculpture depicting the Descent of the Ganga, Mahabalipuram, Tamil Nadu

Bottom: Lion-tailed macaque near Agumbe, Karnataka

Top: Two male king cobras in combat, Kanakodu Village, Karnataka

Bottom: Two male king cobras in combat, Kanakodu Village, Karnataka

Top: Oracle possessed by Naga Devatha, Kanakodu Village, Karnataka

Bottom: Oracle possessed by Naga Devatha, Kanakodu Village, Karnataka

Top: Ashy drongo on the great banyan, J. C. Bose Botanic Gardens, Howrah, West Bengal

Bottom: The great banyan, J. C. Bose Botanic Gardens, Howrah, West Bengal

III

ON HIGHER GROUND

Hills–Mountains–Uplands

1

WHEN MOUNTAINS HAD WINGS

Towering 1,069 metres above sea level and dominating the Kathiawar peninsula, Girnar Parvat is the highest mountain in Gujarat. Geologists tell us that it was formed through volcanic eruptions, roughly 65 million years ago. Grey walls of igneous rock rise steeply towards Girnar's three main summits which are considered sacred by Hindus, Jains, and Buddhists. More than a hundred temples, some built over millennia ago, have been constructed on Girnar, many of them perched atop precipitous cliffs. Pilgrims approach these shrines by climbing 10,000 steps hewn out of the rocks or by taking an aerial ropeway. The primary deities worshipped here are the goddesses Amba Devi, Goraknath, and Dattareya. During Mahashivaratri, millions of devotees circumambulate and ascend this holy massif.

One of the intriguing myths associated with Girnar recalls that when the earth was first formed, mountains had wings and flew about in the sky like birds. Eventually, Brahma, the creator, decided to bring order and stability to the world. He dispatched Indra to cut off the mountains' wings, after which they descended to earth and remained fixed in place. Girnar, however, hid in the sea to avoid having his wings clipped but, eventually, he too was lured out onto land and now stands about 100 kilometres from the coast.

Overlooking the town of Junagadh, at the mouth of a valley leading up to Girnar, is a granite boulder more than 3 metres high and approximately the same breadth and width. In 325 BCE, Devanampiya Piyadasi (Beloved of the Gods), the Mauryan emperor better known as Ashoka, had fourteen proclamations inscribed on the surface of this rock, which marked the western frontier of his dominions. Similar rock edicts can be found at four other places in India. All of these assert the key tenets of Buddhist dhamma or dharma, which Ashoka adopted following the horrific battle of Kalinga. Full of remorse because of the brutal slaughter of soldiers and animals, Ashoka was transformed from a fierce conqueror into an advocate of non-violence. The most prominent of the emperor's moral injunctions forbids the killing of any living creature, either as a sacrifice or by hunting. Ashoka made an exception for peacocks and deer, because he enjoyed eating their flesh, though it is noted that 'even these animals shall not be killed in the future'.

In essence, Ashoka's edicts promulgate India's first wildlife protection laws and represent an unambiguous call for conservation etched in stone twenty-five centuries ago. Also carved into the rock at Girnar are instructions for the preservation and planting of medicinal herbs which are to be used for the treatment of human beings and animals. Written in Pali, using the Brahmi script, this ancient text is the earliest concrete evidence of an ethical doctrine that promotes compassion and protection for species other than our own.

The rock is housed inside a masonry building constructed by the nawab of Junagadh in 1900 and later renovated by his successors. The boulder itself is a pale toffee colour with naturally rounded contours. At first, the inscriptions are not visible but as my eyes adjust from the sun's glare outside to a softer light indoors, I begin to see lines of chiselled characters, like the fossilized tracks of small birds. The Brahmi script has simple, neat letters, some geometric like triangles and circles, while others are curved and knotted in more sinuous shapes. Two other inscriptions are also found on the boulder from later rulers, who added their proclamations during the second and fifth centuries CE. Forgotten languages flow across the undulating surface of the boulder, which remains virtually unchanged from the time it was formed out of compressed magma millions of years ago. A piece of the larger mountain, this rock might even be the ossified remains of one of Girnar's mythical wings that fell to earth at the foot of the peak.

Ancient India's most celebrated ruler, who brought most of the subcontinent under his control, Ashoka is an enigmatic figure who was almost erased from history by his opponents and successors. Today, the principles and policies that he espoused are often held up as examples of benign authority, wisdom, and tolerance. Of all the artefacts that Ashoka left behind, perhaps the most iconic is the lion capital, which he had installed atop a pillar at Sarnath. This sculpture, which features three male lions seated together but facing in different directions, with flowing manes and noble features, has become the hallmark of India's modern republic. It appears on everything from government stationery to bank notes. Along with his proclamations regarding the sanctity of all life forms, Ashoka's lions signify our enduring affinity to the natural world.

Until 1973, lions served as India's national animal, but they were deposed by another endangered feline, when Project Tiger was launched. The lion also happened to be Britain's symbol of colonial suzerainty and like many imperial icons, it was perhaps inevitable that it would be replaced sometime after

Independence. Nevertheless, Asiatic lions (*Panthera leo persica*) remain a vital part of India's ecological heritage and the only surviving population is found here in Kathiawar, also known as Saurashtra.

∽

The drive from Junagadh to Gir National Park takes a little over an hour, passing between fields of chickpeas, wheat, and cotton, all of which are ready for harvest at the beginning of February. Our route is bordered by palash trees which are in full bloom. The conflagration of red blossoms justifies their common English name—flame of the forest. In villages along the sides of the road, I see a breed of livestock that is unique to this region. Gir cattle are impressive animals, much larger than most holy bovids, with domed foreheads, bulky horns, and drooping ears. Even the cows have prominent humps and I confuse them for bulls before seeing their swollen udders. In profile, Gir cattle remind me of the ancient images of bulls on seals from the Indus Valley Civilization.

The village of Sasan Gir is located at the entrance to the national park. Once a small outpost on the edge of the forest, it is now a busy tourist hub catering to wildlife enthusiasts that come here to see lions and other animals. Dozens of jungle resorts are located in and around the village, which also has a crowded strip of restaurants, hotels, and souvenir shops. I am booked to stay at Gir Birding Lodge, which lies next to a couple of larger resorts, about a kilometre from the park headquarters. Surrounded by a mango orchard, it is a quiet, unpretentious lodge, happily removed from the clutter and noise along the main road. The mango trees, a hybrid variety known as kesar, are flowering and attract purple sunbirds that sip their nectar as well as white-browed fantails, small minivets, and common tailorbirds that feed on insects drawn to the blossoms.

Gir's forests were once the royal hunting grounds of the nawabs of Junagadh who ruled over this territory until 1947. The name, 'Gir', means mountain and shares a lexical root with Girnar, though the rugged hills in the park are much lower and the topography not as dramatic. Covered in scrub jungles of teak and ziziphus as well as open patches of grassland cut through by several perennial streams, Gir provides the perfect habitat for lions and their prey.

Though closely resembling the African species, India's lions are distinctly different in their distribution as well as their genetic make-up. Field zoologist Ravi Chellam, who has studied the lions of Gir extensively, sums up their biological history.

> The Asiatic lion is a subspecies and has evolved from the African lion, having separated from the base stock about 100,000 years ago. It once

> was found in a vast area stretching from Syria, through Iran, Iraq into most parts of northern and central India. Historical accounts of hunting expeditions and other descriptive accounts enable us to reconstruct the past distribution of this cat. Despite its vast range and, I assume, very high numbers the Asiatic lion very rapidly became endangered. In fact, in the latter half of the 19th century, in barely three decades, the lion was restricted to the Gir forest in the Indian subcontinent. A few stragglers continued to survive outside India, especially in the Euphrates and Tigris valleys but by 1945, Gir became the sole custodian for all the free-ranging Asiatic lions.

Many naturalists have been drawn to this isolated population of large carnivores, whose survival is endangered by habitat loss, the presence of cattle in the forest, poaching, poisoning, and inbreeding. Their precarious existence in a small pocket of Kathiawar raises difficult and complex questions regarding the conservation of lions and their relationship to human beings. 'The Indian lion is one of the rarest and most important of the wild animals of India, and yet it is one of the least known,' wrote E. P. Gee, in 1964. Having visited Gir on three occasions, in 1956, 1960, and 1962, Gee saw the lions when their numbers had dropped below 200. Counting wildlife, especially wary predators, has always been an uncertain business and early efforts were more anecdotal than scientific. Estimates from the 1920s and 1930s ranged from 'about 50' lions to 270, though these numbers are highly unreliable. The first comprehensive census was conducted in 1950 and the estimate was between 219 to 227 lions in Gujarat, of which only 68 were found in Gir, with some animals reported from as far away as Baroda. Eighteen years later, in 1968, another census revealed that most of the lions outside Gir had disappeared and the total population was now believed to be 177.

In the introduction to his book *The Lions of India*, Divyabhanusinh provides an ecological and cultural synopsis of the lion's history in the Middle East and South Asia. Though there is no evidence of them in Harappan culture, which featured tigers, elephants, and other wildlife on its clay seals, 'Lion symbolism gained importance in India from the second half of the first millennium BCE and the concept probably came from Persia.' The association between lions and royalty can be found in their Sanskrit name, Mrigraja—king of the deer. Alexander the Great, following his eastern conquests, issued coins that featured portraits of himself wearing headdresses made from a lion's mane. Subsequently, rulers throughout India co-opted the lion as a symbol of power and nobility, incorporating it into their royal titles, thrones, and crests. The surname Singh or Sinh, used by scions of Saurashtra's numerous principalities, and the royal families of most Hindu and Sikh kingdoms in North India, identifies the maharaja directly with the lion. Muslim rulers, too, including Mughal emperors, associated themselves with lions because they signified prestige and power. At the same time, lions became an important part of religious narratives and iconography. Both Gautama Buddha and Mahavira adopted the lion as their emblem. The Buddha's first sermon is referred to as Simhanada—the roar of a lion. In Hindu tradition, lions are the vahana or sacred mount of the goddess Durga.

Though lions embodied the ideals and aspirations of Great Britain's crown and country, the soldiers, statesmen, and merchants who came to India and established their empire here, were eager to destroy the animal itself. More than anyone, it was British hunters who decimated the lion population in India. Following the Maratha and Sikh wars, in the first decade of the nineteenth century, the East India Company gained control over Delhi and Haryana, which had a sizeable presence of lions.

Raza Kazmi has investigated and documented the story of 'Hurrianah's' lions. He notes that, 'In the immediate aftermath of the initial British encounter with the lions of the Haryana landscape, British military officers and soldiers unleashed a decade of wholesale massacre of these big cats across the region.' William Fraser, political agent and resident in the Mughal court during the first two decades of the nineteenth century, is described as a 'lion-queller par excellence', credited with shooting or spearing eighty-four lions. However, Colonel George Archibald Smith held the record, claiming to have killed a total of 300. By 1824, most of the lions of Delhi and Haryana had been 'extirpated'. An officer, identified only as General Watson, enjoyed the dubious honour of killing the last two lions in Haryana and capturing their cubs. These orphaned survivors were shipped to England, where Watson presented them to George IV, who consigned them to the Tower Menagerie. The male cub grew up to be a handsome, thickly-maned adult, and was named King George, serving as a living emblem of British royalty. He was also, very likely, the sculptor's model for many of the stone lions that proliferated, on buildings and monuments in London.

By the second half of the nineteenth century, when lions had been wiped out in most parts of the subcontinent, Kathiawar's prides attracted the attention of colonial nimrods, who sought them as trophies. The rulers of princely states in other parts of India also felt that killing a lion was their royal prerogative. Being the sole custodian of a dwindling population in Gir, the nawab of Junagadh found himself in a difficult position. Viceroys, governors, and fellow maharajas demanded invitations to conduct lion hunts in his forests. The supply was clearly inadequate for the demand and, in 1879, Nawab Mahbatkhanji II issued a decree banning all forms of shikar in his territories. His successor, Nawab Rasulkhanji, also set in place strict rules that limited the hunting of Junagadh's lions, though this didn't stop neighbouring princes from killing animals that strayed into their domains. The British also used political pressure to extract permission to hunt in Gir, though some senior officials, like William Mansfield, governor of Bombay, realized that the lions were in danger of becoming extinct and encouraged the nawab to protect the few that remained. In 1900, Curzon, as viceroy, was invited to shoot a lion in Gir but when he learned that only sixty to seventy animals were left, he cancelled his hunt.

The precarious existence of these sociable predators continued through the first half of the twentieth century, with many naturalists anticipating their imminent demise. Independence and Partition, in 1947, brought a new challenge. The last nawab of Junagadh, Mahbatkhanji III, on the advice of his wazir, Shah Nawaz Bhutto, decided that his territories should become part of Pakistan, though his kingdom was not contiguous and the majority of his subjects were Hindus. Congress politicians successfully blocked this plan and the nawab went into self-imposed exile. Divyabhanusinh describes his departure: 'As he left for the airport... (bound for Karachi) he looked with tears in his eyes at the majestic Girnar mountains—for the last time as it turned out. In a memorable *sotto voce* to no one in particular he said, "Who will protect my lions now?"'

The nawabs of Junagadh had always treated these regal beasts as their personal mascots and had done their best to save them despite intense pressures. But after Independence, the fate of the lions became even more tenuous as India struggled to formulate and enforce new wildlife regulations. The late 1940s and 1950s were a period of rampant poaching, and the lions were especially vulnerable. Fortunately, after receiving appeals from conservationists, the new prime minister, Jawaharlal Nehru, sent a telegram to local administrators who had assumed control of Junagadh after the nawab's departure. 'I have long been interested in the preservation of lions in India,' Nehru wrote. 'They exist only in Kathiawar now in Gir Forest and it would be a great pity if they were shot or otherwise allowed to suffer extinction.'

Though the lions of Gir had an extensive tract of forest to live in, and roamed where they pleased, by 1947 they were feeding almost entirely on domestic cattle. A pastoral community, known as Maldharis, occupied settlements or nesses in the forest and the lions regularly killed their buffaloes as well as other livestock in villages on the periphery of Gir. Baiting had been practised by hunters for decades and was used by neighbouring princes to lure Junagadh's lions out of their protected jungles. When naturalists like E. P. Gee visited in the 1950s and 1960s, they were escorted by shikaris, who were mostly from the Maldhari community and acted as trackers, locating lions on their kills and often tying up young male buffaloes to facilitate a sighting.

In 1965, after Gir was declared a wildlife sanctuary, the forest department began to encourage tourism. Ten years later, in 1975, the sanctuary was notified as a national park. Through all of this, the practice of baiting continued and inevitably devolved into a routine spectacle in which the lions played along, growing more and more comfortable in the presence of visitors. While they did not live in cages, serious questions arose about whether Gir's lions were actually wild or not. Occasional incidents of villagers being killed or mauled were reported, but man-eating was not part of the lions' regular diet and they tolerated human beings, allowing them to approach on foot within 30 to 40 metres. Some accounts describe shikaris dragging a buffalo carcass into better light for a photographer, while the lions were feeding. And one lioness is reported to have even allowed the trackers to touch her.

'Lion shows', often organized for VIPs, were standard protocol in Gir until 1988, when they were officially banned. However, these continued outside the park where some wildlife resorts used buffalo baits to lure lions into their compounds for the entertainment of their guests. At the lodge where I am staying, a sign posted at reception warns us that lion shows are a serious crime under the Wild Life Protection Act and anyone participating in these will face a fine of ₹25,000 and three to seven years imprisonment.

The encouraging news is that the lions of Gir are now in a healthier position than they have ever been for more than a century and a half. In fact, their population has outgrown the national park and they now wander as far afield as the streets of Junagadh, where they have been seen at night. According to a 2020 census, at least 674 lions now live in Gujarat and their numbers are increasing.

This remarkable turnaround is the result of careful and consistent wildlife management by the forest department as well as other conservation agencies and NGOs. Even more remarkable is the fact that the lions inside the national park are now feeding mostly on wild prey. A study by Paul Joslin, in 1987, showed that 75 per cent of the lion scat he collected contained hair and other remains of domestic animals. Ten years later, in 1997, Ravi Chellam discovered that the situation had been completely reversed and now only 25 per cent of the scat showed evidence of domestic animals, while the rest consisted of the remains of wild prey. A large part of this success story is due to restrictions on cattle grazing from villages outside the park and the relocation of some Maldhari pastoralists and their herds. Reducing overgrazing by domestic cattle has allowed wild ungulates like chital, sambar, and nilgai to multiply and provide the lions with their natural food source.

The successful protection and dramatic increase in the number of Asiatic lions in Saurashtra has led to a political dilemma. Many wildlife scientists have proposed the relocation of some of the lions to national parks in other regions of India but the Gujarat state government and its forest service have resisted this plan. Their reasoning has more to do with regional chauvinism than conservation science. Though Gir's lions have made a remarkable comeback, they remain exceptionally vulnerable to diseases and other threats. Being confined to a single location, they could easily suffer a catastrophic decline because they have very little genetic diversity.

On the other hand, lions are the official mammal of Gujarat and seen as the exclusive property of the state. Mahesh Rangarajan highlights the ironies of this situation: 'Regionalism, once a valued ally, can also be immune to reason.... Curiously, the very regionalism that celebrates the lion is also undermining the ecology of its survival in the long run.' M. K. Ranjitsinh, himself a Gujarati from the royal family of Wankaner in Saurashtra, was the chief architect of the Wild Life Protection Act, 1972, and he has advocated the relocation of lions to national parks in Madhya Pradesh, as well as other sanctuaries in Gujarat. But as Ranjitsinh writes, 'Amongst some Gujaratis the impulse to maintain the monopoly of having the lion in their state alone is of pathological proportions....' He warns that the consequences could be dire and '...Gujarat will have to answer for its "lion in the manger" policy.'

Having read various reports of hunters and naturalists that visited Gir over the past couple of centuries, as well as recent proposals and debates surrounding the current fate of India's lions, I am fully aware that Gir's apex predators have a contested history and an uncertain future. Arriving in this forested corner of Saurashtra, for the first time in my life, I am keen to see its famous lions for myself. And from all accounts, they should be relatively easy to find.

Next morning, a Maruti Gypsy picks me up from my lodge at 6 a.m., long before the sun has risen. Atul, the driver, takes me across to park headquarters where we must check in and have our guide and route assigned. An elaborate gateway marks the entrance. It looks somewhat like a jungle-themed amusement park, with life-sized statues of lions and other wildlife, arranged on an arch of artificial foliage and rocks. Inside, an impatient queue of drivers are waiting in front of a ticket window holding printouts of our safari permits, all of which are now issued online.

Tourists huddle in their vehicles, bundled up against the winter cold. A mood of restless anticipation prevails. Atul tells me that there are 180 Gypsies licensed to enter the park but only fifty are allowed in at any one time. Three safaris are scheduled every day— at 6.30 a.m., 9.30 a.m., and 3 p.m. Thirteen separate routes of about 30 kilometres each have been demarcated to ensure that the Gypsies are spread out and don't all converge on a site where lions are found. The park has a total area of 1,412 square kilometres, of which 258 square kilometres is the core zone. There is also a safari park at Devalia village, 12 kilometres from Sasan Gir, where a bus tour takes tourists through a fenced-in enclosure and lion sightings are guaranteed. The entire experience at Gir is much more organized and controlled than at any other national park I've visited in India.

After fifteen minutes in the queue, Atul emerges with our stamped documents in hand, accompanied by Bharat, the guide assigned to my vehicle. We have been allotted Route 9 and are now fully authorized to enter what the Gujarat Forest Department calls, 'The Majestic Home of the Royal King'. As we pass through another barrier, the Gypsy's headlights reveal the crooked trunks of thorn trees cloaked in mist. The sky is beginning to brighten in the east, though a waning moon is still high above us. In the silent darkness before dawn, I can smell the sweet, musky odour of dust moistened by dew.

After driving for about a kilometre, we come upon a forest guard astride a motorcycle. He is on patrol, monitoring the location of lions. Bharat asks him if there are any nearby and he shakes his head. As we proceed, the landscape gradually reveals itself as a slow dawn breaks over the rolling hills. Many of the trees are teak, though they are gnarled and stunted because of the rocky soil and dry conditions. Most of the leaves, as large as circular thali platters, have fallen with only a few still clinging to twisted branches. Though ziziphus, or ber, is the second most common tree, the park contains a wide range of other arboreal species from banyans and peepul to babool and bael.

As the shadows retreat, we begin to see scattered herds of chital grazing along the sides of the unpaved track as well as a few sambar hinds. Peafowl cross in front of us and wild pigs are rooting in the underbrush. At this hour of the day, the colours are muted and even the flame of the forest flowers look faded. Bharat points out the stark white trunk and branches of a large ghost tree with skeletal branches. All of the leaves have fallen and will only reappear in May. At this time of the year, the bark, which is peeling off in patches, looks as if it has been painted with whitewash. During the monsoon it turns grey-green.

Perched on a branch of the ghost tree is a spotted owlet. A dusty brown and cream colour, its breast feathers are mottled like a sweater knitted out of different shades of undyed wool. About the size of my fist, it watches me with one eye open, as if drifting off to sleep. A crepuscular species, owlets are most active at dawn and dusk, though they also hunt at night. In a hollow of the ghost tree's trunk we spot the female owlet, her head just visible inside the nest, a metre from her mate.

At several places along the forest road multiple pugmarks of lions can be seen, both adults as well as cubs. Though I keep expecting to spot their tawny profiles, in amongst the grass and scrub, there is no sign of the pride. When we reach the broad crest of a hill overlooking a section of the park, Atul stops the jeep and turns off the engine. We listen for alarm calls as the first rays of sunlight wash over the hills. Bharat tells me they often hear lions roaring from here, though today they are silent. Somewhere below us, a peafowl gives a mournful cry. In the distance, to the north-west, I can just make out the blue pyramid of Girnar Parvat rising out of the plains of Saurashtra.

After descending from the hill, we pass other jeeps driving along intersecting routes through the park, but whenever Bharat asks the guides and drivers if they have seen any lions, the answer is always the same—nothing so far. While Gir is similar to other dry deciduous forests in places like Madhya Pradesh and Maharashtra there is something distinctly different about the trees and terrain—a thornier, more ravaged landscape. Mixed in with the stunted teak are terminalias, tamarind, and tendu, all of which seem to have a hardier appearance than elsewhere. Nevertheless, along the streams that crease these rocky hills, we find plenty of green growth including jamuns and some bamboo which offer a verdant contrast to the rest of the dull, dry foliage at this time of year.

As for birds, we come upon a changeable hawk eagle, surveying the forest floor from the high branch of a semal tree, and a brown fish owl huddled in the shadows of a leafy banyan as well as a pair of collared scops owls tucked into the hollow bole of a gnarled teak. Suddenly, over the rumble of the engine, I hear a shrill cry accompanied by an intense flash of yellow and red. A lesser goldenback lands on the trunk of an acacia ahead of us and begins to drill through the bark, searching for insect larvae. This woodpecker is also known as a black-rumped flameback. The feathers from the base of its neck to the root of its tail look as if they've been freshly gilded and its bright scarlet cap would make any socialist proud.

As our route circles through a flat stretch of forest, we pass a small herd of chital including a stag with enormous, six-tined horns. He is pursuing one of the does. Lowering his neck, he emits a mating call, something between a hoarse moan and a wail. Further on, we continue to see chital browsing in amongst low ziziphus and acacia trees. Then, abruptly, one of the deer gives an alarm call which is higher pitched than the stag's cry of desire—a sharp, single note conveying fear. Atul immediately brakes and we scan the jungle for any sign of movement, hoping a lion will appear.

Instead, moments later, we see a tawny, spotted form creeping through the dusty, dappled shadows. It is a leopard and, from the size of the head and slender build, I am almost certain it is a female. She picks her way gingerly through the brittle carpet of dry teak leaves, moving silently away from the chital, who stand alert and watchful. Atul reverses so that we can get a better view. After a few seconds, the leopard steps out into the open, her resplendent coat catching the sunlight. Seemingly untroubled by our presence, she moves slowly along a hedge of lantana, her mouth open and her tail extended in a graceful curve behind her. Despite her full-grown size and predatory demeanour, there is a calm, almost languorous rhythm to her gait, as if she is simply out for an innocent stroll, though the chital are not fooled. Their alarm calls echo back and forth until the leopard finally slips back into cover.

Atul and Bharat are both ecstatic, assuring me that leopard sightings are rare in Gir and I am extremely lucky to have had such a clear and prolonged view. Of course, it is always exciting to see a leopard, especially in daylight, but I have come here looking for lions and when our drive ends, half an hour later, I can't help but feel disappointed. Almost everything I've read about Gir suggests that the chances of seeing a lion are relatively high, even if it is the rarest of India's big cats. The only reassurance is that I have another safari booked at 3 p.m. today and I hope that my luck will change in the afternoon. Returning to the lodge, I learn that some of the other guests were able to see a lioness and her cub this morning on a different route through the park. Realizing that I was being overconfident, I wish I had booked a third safari for tomorrow morning but now I find it is too late. All the available slots online have been reserved.

In the afternoon, I am assigned a different driver, guide, and route—Number 13, which isn't encouraging. We circle through the park again and see a Maldhari settlement in the forest and a large reservoir created by a dam near the headwaters of the Hiran River. An old narrow-gauge railway line runs through one corner of the park and, once a day, a slow passenger train still travels this route, from Junagadh to Delvada near the coast. We see an assortment of birds and plenty of sambar, chital, and a nilgai but no lions make an appearance. The most frustrating part is that we pass an area where lions are known to regularly cross the road, but we fail to see any while other safari vehicles, following after us get a clear view of several lionesses and their cubs. After three hours of driving through the park, we return to the lodge as the sun goes down over Gir.

Though discouraged, I tell myself that I shouldn't be like those wildlife tourists, whom I have often criticized, because they feel their experience is incomplete when they fail to see a large predator. I also try to rationalize the absence of lions by assuming that the reason they are less visible is because they have become more wild. Now that Gir's lions no longer depend on buffalo baits, there isn't any reason for them to exhibit themselves for visitors like me. The fact that they aren't a common sight, despite increasing numbers, should be an encouraging sign because it means the lions have less need to associate with human beings.

In this way, nature adjusts itself, balancing change and restoring order. We often equate wildness with freedom, both of which are human concepts. The big question in Gir is whether the last of Asia's lions are truly wild or free. In both cases, the answer can only reflect the ambiguities attending their existence, hemmed in by human settlements and subject to the laws and predilections of politicians and government officials, who see them less as a wild species and more as metaphors of power.

∽

The following day, I have most of the morning to spare before driving back to Junagadh. Though the lodge manager suggests that I could join a bus tour at Devalia, where I am assured of seeing captive lions in the safari park, I haven't come all the way to Gir just to visit a zoo. Instead, I accept an offer from the resident naturalist, Amit Ram, to go birdwatching with him. At 7.30 a.m., we set off on foot, just after sunrise. The trees are full of red-vented bulbuls and parakeets, both rose-ringed and plum-headed, which are feeding on palash blossoms. We also see several chestnut-shouldered petronias (*Gymnoris xanthocollis*), which used to be called yellow-throated sparrows. To confuse things further, taxonomists have also changed their original Latin name which used to be *Petronia xanthocollis*. Through my binoculars, however, they still look very much like sparrows. We also catch sight of a coppersmith barbet, a plump green bird, slightly larger than my thumb, with a bright crimson bib, yellow throat, and eye patch, and a splash of red above its beak. The smallest of barbets, coppersmiths are often heard but not easily seen, emitting a steady, monotonous call like a delicate hammer tapping a metal bell. All around us, in the sky, green bee-eaters perform aerobatics as they chase flying insects.

Amit is from Nepal, near Chitwan National Park, and he has worked as a naturalist both there and in Kumaon. Four years ago, he moved to Gir. Showing me an oriental white-eye, he says it reminds him of home because it is a common species in the Himalayan foothills. We wander past the gates of several resorts and along the main road, where heavily loaded 'chhakra gaddis' pass us—three-wheeled motorcycle rickshaws, made out of old Royal Enfields equipped with diesel pumps as engines. The birds don't seem to mind the chugging roar of these makeshift vehicles or the other traffic. After a couple hundred metres, we turn off the main road onto a rough footpath. This leads to the banks of the Hiran River, which flows out of the park along one edge of Sasan Gir. Garbage is strewn about—plastic water bottles and disposable plates that picknickers have left behind as well as scraps of discarded clothing and worn-out shoes. It is a depressing sight, though the river itself is beautiful, passing under the motor bridge, along its rocky course, where multiple streams separate into shallow pools and trickling runnels.

A Bengal monitor lizard is basking on a shelf of rock but as soon as we approach, it darts into a dark hole beneath a stone. Waterbirds congregate by the river including black-headed and glossy ibises. We also identify cattle egrets, Indian pond herons, and a pair of woolly-necked storks. Heading downstream, Amit leads me along a cattle track, through thickets of the invasive mesquite, *Prosopis juliflora*. From the quantities of dung along our route, it is obvious that villagers graze their cows and buffaloes here, though this morning there are no animals in sight. For ten minutes, I try to take photographs of a black-winged stilt wading in a marshy pool, but the restless, long-legged bird refuses to stand still, even for a second.

Further on, in the dust, I notice pugmarks and point them out to Amit. He glances at the large impressions of oval pads with round toes. Shrugging, he tells me that lions often prowl through this area at night, regularly entering Sasan Gir village on the other side of the river. He then directs my attention to a purple sunbird on a palash tree nearby. In direct sunlight, its iridescent feathers glisten like stained glass. Moving on, we startle a young peafowl that scurries off into the bushes for safety. Just then, I hear the alarm call of a chital, somewhere on ahead and wonder if it has caught our scent. Amit suggests that a jungle cat or a jackal may have frightened the deer.

A few minutes later, we emerge into a grassy clearing bordered by thorny *Prosopis* bushes. By now, we have been walking for more than an hour and I am about to suggest that we turn back because most of the birds have disappeared. Amit takes a few steps forward and then stops in his tracks. He beckons anxiously. Seconds later, I spot two lions sunning themselves on the other side of a low bush. Both of them are females, stretched out on the grass less than 20 metres ahead of us. They are looking in the opposite direction and don't seem to have sensed our approach. Something in the jungle beyond them has caught their attention, possibly the chital that was calling.

For almost a minute, nothing moves except for the dark tuft at the end of one lioness's tail as she flicks away a fly. Their heads are raised and I can see that the nearer lioness has an injured ear, with crusted blood along the upper edge, probably from a family quarrel. Finally, the lioness with the torn ear, turns her head and looks at us. Her eyes are almost the same colour as her fur but as lustrous as a pair of polished topaz. Even as she studies me with an intense gaze, her expression isn't menacing. The second lioness also turns and stares in our direction. Nothing lies between us but open ground and they could reach us in three or four easy bounds. Lifting my camera slowly, I take several pictures. Neither lioness seems to be disturbed by the soft click of the shutter.

For almost five minutes, we watch each other as our fields of vision converge with a focused stillness that holds us in suspense. After the initial surprise and shock, I begin to feel a growing sense of elation at having finally seen Gir's lions, as well as a twinge of vulnerability, meeting them face to face like this on foot. Eventually, the lioness with the bloodied ear gets up and strides off into the bushes. Her companion stays half a minute longer, peering at us over a thorny branch as if to make sure we pose no threat. Then, she too slips away into the shadows of the trees beyond.

Amit turns and eagerly reaches out to clasp my hand, suggesting in a breathless whisper that we should go on a little further to try and get another glimpse of the lions. I shake my head and gesture for him to follow me, retracing our steps in the other direction. No matter how complacent they are, it would be foolish to take any chances with these predators, who may have cubs hidden in the bushes. The two of them have tolerated our presence and we must respect the distance between us, acknowledging the invisible yet indelible line that separates us from wild creatures.

∽

Following my visit to Gir, I join two friends, Varad Giri and Akshay Shah, for a short excursion to the coastal wetlands near Porbandar, about 100 kilometres west of Junagadh. Varad is the head scientist at the Reliance Foundation, managing an ecological restoration project in Kathiawar. Before this he was in charge of the herpetological collections at the Bombay Natural History Society. An inveterate, irrepressible naturalist, Varad has described more than sixty new species of reptiles and amphibians, mostly in the Western Ghats. Many of these creatures now bear his name. Akshay is director of Woodstock School's Hanifl Centre for Outdoor Education and Environmental Study in Mussoorie, where we are neighbours, though his home town is Ranikhet. Joining us in Porbandar is a local bird expert, Vikrant Singh Jhala. A schoolteacher by profession, he devotes most of his free time to birding. Vikrant has agreed to guide us to several wetlands near the shores of the Arabian Sea where migratory birds gather in winter.

Our first stop is Subhashnagar, a saline backwater near Porbandar's port. Part of this area consists of commercial salt pans. At this time of year, a brackish lagoon attracts large flocks of flamingos that migrate from Kutch, roughly 250 to 300 kilometres north of here. As we drive towards a broad expanse of shallow water, I can see thousands of flamingos like a roseate cloud hovering just above the surface of the lagoon. Vikrant tells us that 10,000 to 15,000 of these birds frequent the Subhashnagar wetlands.

From a vantage point on the shore, we get a clearer view of this congregation of both greater and lesser flamingos. Elegant waders, with tall, straight legs and slender, curved necks, they are feeding in ankle-deep water. Vikrant explains how they use their feet to stir up small aquatic creatures as well as algae. A flamingo's throat is so thin it can only swallow minute crustaceans and invertebrates. Lowering their heads, with their beaks upside down, flamingos scoop up food and filter out the water before raising their necks and swallowing. This unusual feeding process creates a pendulous rhythm within the flock which seems to be perpetually in motion.

The flamingos are almost white with just a blush of pink but when they take to the air, brighter feathers on their wings become visible. During the breeding season, which will begin a few weeks from now, their pink plumage turns much brighter and darker. Varad tells us that flamingos, like many other birds, rub their beaks on a uropygial gland at the base of their tails, which excretes oils that they use for preening, adding a polish to their pink feathers, especially under their wings.

After a few minutes, a group of about 200 flamingos begin moving towards the shore, 150 metres to our left. Vikrant explains that a drainage pipe, from a seafood processing plant nearby, discharges wastewater into the wetlands here. Fetid nutrients from the sewage attract prawns and other small creatures which the flamingos feed on. As we watch, the birds appear to queue up in an orderly procession. Once they have collected a beak full of food, they return to the back of the line. Greater flamingos are about half a metre taller than the lesser species and both are feeding together.

Twenty minutes later, the flock suddenly retreats and we notice three dogs running along the opposite shore. These are the flamingos' primary threat. Near the spot where we are standing, I can see another pack of six dogs asleep in the mud. Vikrant explains that they usually prey on the birds at night. In Kutch, where flamingos breed, feral dogs raid their nests, feeding on eggs and hatchlings. While the flocks of pale pink birds are beautiful, their habitat is squalid. The Subhashnagar wetlands are severely polluted with heaps of garbage strewn on the shore. Behind us, across the road, lies a crowded slum next to the seafood plant and the air stinks of rotting fish.

Fortunately, the Javar and Kuchchadi birding sites, which we visit next, are in a less developed area, some distance from the city. Though the sea is close by, these are freshwater wetlands, recharged each year by monsoon rains. They attract a diverse range of waterfowl from pintails and pelicans to spoonbills and storks. At several places, the forest department has constructed watchtowers, but the road embankments are high enough for us to get a panoramic view of dozens of interconnected ponds and channels covered with flocks of ducks and geese, as well as egrets, herons, and other waders.

Though buffaloes from nearby villages wallow in these marshes and feed on water weeds, most of the area is relatively undisturbed and the birds seem to have enough space and security to safely settle here for the winter. One of the main threats, however, are windmills that have been installed in this region to generate renewable electricity. Though they spin slowly, the giant blades cause many fatal bird hits. Equally dangerous are power lines and Vikrant shows us where he and a group of fellow conservationists have strung up cloth flags to ward off pelicans and other birds.

Many of the migrants fly thousands of kilometres each year from as far away as Siberia and Europe. They have been coming to Saurashtra for centuries, long before Porbandar ever became a port. Among these hardy sky-farers, the most impressive are the Gruidae family. All afternoon, we see scattered flocks of cranes, both common and demoiselle, feeding in fields along the sides of the road. Almost as tall as flamingos, they have streamlined bodies, bustled tails and sharp, slender bills. Common cranes are slightly larger and have black heads with white stripes on either cheek that converge at the nape of their long necks. Demoiselles have grey heads with white tufts behind each eye. The dark feathers on their necks extend like tasselled ruffs below their breasts. As the sun goes down over the wetlands, we can see flights of cranes arriving from all directions to roost at communal sites nearby. Their plaintive, clarinet-like cries pierce the silence as they fly in loose V formations of up to fifty birds. The cranes scrawl across a darkening sky, as if they were lines of animated poetry, each wing a stroke of a calligrapher's pen.

On our way back to Porbandar, Vikrant points out a temple complex on the outskirts of the city, where he tells us a lion killed a cow two years ago. A lone male, he obviously strayed out of the forests at Gir, or was driven out by other lions, and is now living in Barda Wildlife Sanctuary, a low range of forested hills to the north of Porbandar.

The next morning, we are up again before dawn and drive in Varad's jeep to the Mokarsagar wetlands. Spread over 95 square kilometres, this area consists of large lakes and marshy waterways, as well as patches of grass and scrubland. A rough road, built on a dyke that separates the wetlands on either side, bifurcates Mokarsagar. As a crimson sun rises above the marsh grass, we can see two nilgai silhouetted in the distance. Several wild pigs, slathered in mud, also put in an appearance, as does a jungle cat lurking in the reeds by the side of the road. Later in the morning, we come upon four golden jackals that cross in front of us, a lean but healthy-looking pack, much better groomed and more purposeful than the feral dogs that roam the edges of the marsh.

The early light has a special clarity, perhaps because there are no trees to filter the rays or because the sea air is free of dust. Each bird stands out in vivid contrast to the water and swamp grass. A grey heron is poised at the edge of a pond, its long neck and tapered beak stretched out and rigid as a javelin. Purple herons are more skittish and take off when our jeep approaches. The colours in the birds' feathers seem to glow in the morning light from the subtle shades of rust and umber in a bar-tailed godwit's wings to the bright magenta of a purple swamphen. Even an Isabelline wheatear, with drab khaki feathers, seems to gleam in the morning sunlight.

Within the first hour, we count more than fifty species, including western marsh harriers that circle over the wetlands, in pursuit of ducks and other dabblers. Northern pintails, Indian spot-billed ducks, and northern shovelers burst out of the water with a frantic stutter of wings each time a harrier's shadow glides past. A gaggle of greylag geese cruise the edges of the marsh. Their pink beaks look almost artificial, as if made of cheap plastic. We also see several pheasant-tailed jacanas though none of them are in their dramatic breeding plumage.

Birdwatching here is an entirely different experience from what Akshay and I are used to in a Himalayan forest. To begin with, the quantity of birds is much greater and different species mingle together on the water. In a forest, you often hear a bird before you see it, but in these coastal wetlands visibility is better. Though some species hide in the reeds and are well camouflaged, many waterbirds stand out boldly, even at a distance. Using binoculars, it is relatively easy to identify them. As we walk along the embankment, suddenly, the air is full of thousands of insects, miniscule flies that must have just hatched. They swarm around us in a blizzard of tiny, translucent wings. Half a dozen wire-tailed swallows dart through the air, feasting on this sudden bounty.

Varad has parked his jeep next to a sluice gate, where water from one side of the road flows into a man-made canal 2 metres wide. Fishermen have placed a large net, like a funnel, across the mouth of this channel and it is full of small fish no larger than my index finger. Most of them are already dead and it looks as if the net has been left unattended for several days. Vikrant leans over the edge of the sluice gate and pulls up the torn remains of another frayed net, calling out to us.

A snake has got itself entangled in the nylon mesh. At first, it appears to be dead, the limp body wrapped inside twisted layers of snarled fishing net. As Vikrant tries to shake it free, we see the end of its tail coil up and the snake's head protrudes from the other side of the net. Eyeing us with hostility, it puffs out its neck to appear more threatening. Just over a metre long, the snake has a tightly woven pattern of small black and grey diamonds, all along its upper body. Varad immediately identifies it as a checkered keelback and helps Vikrant pull the tattered net loose from an angle iron that supports the metal sluice gate. The snake writhes desperately but it is badly snared.

Checkered keelbacks are also called Asiatic water snakes. Living close to ponds, rivers, and other freshwater wetlands, they feed on fish, as well as amphibians and reptiles. Strong swimmers, they have a well-earned reputation for being extremely aggressive, with a nasty bite. Though checkered keelbacks are not venomous and do not have fangs, both their upper and lower jaws are lined with small, serrated teeth that allow them to catch and hold slippery prey. The last two or three teeth at the back of their mouths are slightly longer and can do the most damage.

Varad kneels beside the agitated snake and quickly pins its neck before grabbing the keelback's head between his thumb and forefinger. The snake snaps its jaws but is unable to bite him. He then takes hold of the tail as the keelback continues to writhe in his grip, flicking its forked tongue. Akshay points out an injury on its body, where a few of the snake's scales have been torn off by the net, but otherwise it seems healthy

Using a razor blade, Vikrant cuts away tangled layers of knotted mesh, a slow process that takes a quarter of an hour, before the snake is finally free. As a defensive mechanism, the keelback excretes a foul-smelling fluid from its cloaca, an anus-like opening under its tail. Varad says that sometimes the stench is so repulsive it makes you vomit but this one doesn't give off too strong an odour. Holding the snake firmly but gently, Varad carries it across to a pile of stones on the far the side of the canal and releases it into a patch of weeds. Within seconds, the keelback slithers away and disappears.

If it hadn't been rescued, the snake would have surely died a slow death, trapped in the synthetic filaments of a man-made web, which had been left in the water through callous indifference and neglect. Like the lions of Gir, and migratory birds, the checkered keelback inhabits a world full of human intrusions and unnatural dangers, even as it struggles for survival in the wild. The only hope for these creatures is that our species might someday heed the call of a Mauryan emperor, who issued edicts of compassion and conservation, two and a half millennia ago.

2

CONFLICT AND KINSHIP IN KUMAON

In 1907, at the age of thirty-three, Jim Corbett killed the man-eating tiger of Champawat, which was responsible for the deaths of 438 human beings in eastern Kumaon. Three years later, he was persuaded to hunt down another man-eating tigress that had claimed twenty-four victims in Mukteshwar. Responding to desperate pleas for help, Corbett arrived there on foot after a two-day trek from Nainital. In those days, Mukteshwar (formerly Muktesar), was an isolated settlement atop a forested ridge, where a Veterinary Research Institute had been established by the colonial government to develop vaccines for treating cattle diseases. A number of villages were scattered over the nearby hills and several fruit orchards had been started in this region. Situated at 2,286 metres above sea level, Mukteshwar offers a panoramic view of snow peaks to the north. As Corbett writes: 'People who have lived at Muktesar claim that it is the most beautiful spot in Kumaon, and that its climate has no equal.'

Though he was well-known in the surrounding hills as a slayer of man-eaters, following his success in Champawat, Corbett had not yet become the famous hunter-naturalist and bestselling author of shikar tales for which he is now remembered. At the time, he was still working as a labour contractor for the railways at Mokameh Ghat in Bihar, handling the trans-shipment of freight across the Ganga. Visiting his home in Nainital for brief periods during the summer, he had to juggle his responsibilities with the railways and his self-declared mission to rid Kumaon of man-eating tigers and leopards. It is important to note that Corbett wrote and published his stories decades after the events he describes and his account of the Mukteshwar tigress does not feature in his first book, *Man-Eaters of Kumaon*, which came out in 1944. It appeared in his final collection of shikar stories, *The Temple Tiger and More Man-Eaters of Kumaon*, which was written after he emigrated to Kenya in 1947, and published in 1954, a year before his death.

Compared to the more famous man-eaters of Champawat, Chowgarh, and

Rudraprayag, Mukteshwar's tigress did not kill nearly as many human beings. Corbett was able to track her down and shoot her relatively easily, within a couple of days, which is probably why he didn't include this story in his first collection. Nevertheless, it is a compelling account of adventure in the jungle, with all of Corbett's raconteurial trademarks, including human pathos, several near-misses, and, finally, a charging tigress that gets put down with a well-placed bullet. Aside from being a classic hunting yarn, this story is interesting on several different levels, particularly in the context of human–animal conflict. Even today, the forest department of Uttarakhand, which includes Kumaon, still commissions hunters to dispatch man-eating predators, though traps and tranquilizers are also employed with mixed results.

Elements of human interest in Corbett's story include an eight-year-old girl he meets along a forest trail, while she is struggling to lead one of her father's bullocks to her uncle's home on the other side of the hill. The man-eater is operating in this area and Corbett accompanies the young girl on her errand, then safely escorts her home, discovering in the process that the tigress has killed one of her uncle's bullocks. At the end of the story, he writes about his sense of fulfilment after successfully stalking and killing his quarry but also the 'greatest satisfaction of all, at having made a small portion of the earth safe for a brave little girl to walk on'. The other interesting relationship in the story is Corbett's friendship with a local landowner, Badri Sah, who owned an apple orchard and vegetable gardens on the outskirts of Mukteshwar. Badri assists Corbett in organizing a beat and tying up a machan, where he spends the night sitting over the dead bullock. He also provides Corbett with tea and meals during the course of the hunt and celebrates the tigress's demise by firing his shotgun ten times in the air. From the story it is clear that Badri and Corbett had a genuine friendship that defied the barriers of colonial society, as well as a shared knowledge and love of the forest where none of rules of race, class, or caste apply.

We are also told that the reason the tigress became a man-eater is that she had a large number of porcupine quills embedded in her right foreleg, which had become infected and caused her to limp. Unable to hunt down wild prey, she had begun to kill cattle and human beings for her survival. In several of Corbett's other stories, man-eating tigers suffered similar injuries after trying to kill a porcupine. One of the repeated refrains in his books is that tigers do not ordinarily attack human beings and it is only when they are disabled by injuries or the infirmities of age that they begin killing people.

Mahesh Rangarajan, in a collection of essays on environmental history titled *Nature and Nation*, describes how Corbett embodied many of the dilemmas and contradictions of human–animal conflict, both then and now. Often praised for being a conservationist, who gave up his rifle in favour of the camera, Corbett advocated the preservation and protection of tigers and other wildlife. Yet, at the age of thirty-five, when he shot the Mukteshwar man-eater, Corbett considered himself primarily a 'sportsman' and an expert on 'jungle lore'. The voice of the conservationist comes from an older Corbett, who recounts these tales towards the end of his life. As Rangarajan observes:

> His sporting ethic...did not measure up to more recent notions of total preservation. It would be anachronistic to associate such ideas with Corbett. Celebration of life in the outdoors was, in his day, centred around the chase and the hunt, the ability to read pug-marks on a jungle trail, the skill of 'calling up' a tiger in order to be able to shoot it. Fish (especially the great mahseer) were taken with rod and line, deer and peacocks killed for meat, and leopards shot for their skins. This was the world Corbett grew up in and never fully transcended. It was the gun, not the camera, that was his chief, though not sole, instrument.

As a hunter, Corbett observes nature with a sharp eye for detail, not just because he is intent on killing the tigress, but on account of a naturalist's discerning awareness of the surrounding environment. As a storyteller, he includes these observations to give his narrative a greater sense of authenticity but also to help his readers imagine the wild space he shares with the tigress. At one point, when the man-eater arrives on its kill after dark, he describes hearing the tigress blowing on the carcass to disperse hornets that are attracted to rotting meat. These are the kind of precise and unusual details that Corbett could only know from first-hand experience.

At another point, while traversing a forest path, seemingly extraneous details catch his attention, even as he remains alert for any sign of the man-eater.

> From this point it was necessary to walk warily for I was now in the man-eater's country. Before zigzagging up the face of a very steep hill the road runs for some distance over flat ground on which grow the orange-coloured lily, the round hard seeds of which can be used as shot in a muzzle-loading gun. This was the first time I had climbed that hill and I was very interested to see the caves, hollowed out by the wind, in the sandstone cliffs overhanging the road. In a gale I imagine these caves must produce some very weird sounds, for they are of different sizes and while some are shallow, others appear to penetrate deep into the sandstone.

Corbett's awareness of the landscape he traverses is not limited to the dangerous animal he pursues (which may well be pursuing him). Instead, he is attentive to each and every aspect of terrain and ecology that he encounters. This is his umwelt, an intimate, personal knowledge of the natural world that he experiences through all his five senses, as well as the sixth sense of premonition that Corbett most certainly believed in. While tracking man-eaters through the jungle, he is always intensely aware of the connections between himself and other life forms or natural phenomena. At numerous points in his shikar stories, Corbett experiences almost mystical moments of heightened consciousness that could be described as a hunter's or naturalist's trance.

One of the most intriguing digressions in the story of the Mukteshwar man-eater occurs immediately after Corbett sees the tigress for the first time. Walking across a fallow field about 400 metres away, she is coming towards him. But, instead of describing his reaction to her sudden appearance or leading us on the chase that ensues, he flashes back to a memory of an incident, several years in the past, when he was sitting up for a tiger in another part of Kumaon near a sacred grove and forest shrine called Baram ka Than.

'Baram is a jungle God who protects human beings and does not permit the shooting of animals in the area he watches over,' Corbett explains. 'The forest in the heart of which this shrine is situated is well stocked with game and is a favourite hunting ground of poachers for miles round, and of sportsmen from all parts of India. Yet, in my lifetime's acquaintance with that forest, I do not know of a single instance of an animal having been shot in the vicinity of the shrine.'

He then goes on to relate how the tiger he was pursuing, a cattle-lifter that villagers had begged him to shoot, appeared at the edge of the sacred grove and advanced towards him. When the tiger was about a hundred metres away, and just as Corbett was preparing to take aim and fire his rifle, a small jamun tree that stood between them toppled over on its own and knocked down two other trees, blocking the path. As if on cue, the tiger quickly turned around and disappeared back into the jungle. Corbett then tells us, 'that the trees were young and vigorous; that no rain had fallen recently to loosen their roots; that not a breath of air was stirring in the forest; and, finally, that the trees had fallen across the track leading to the shrine when the tiger had only another seventy yards to cover to give me the shot I was waiting for.'

Interjecting this seemingly random memory into the story, at the climax of his hunt for the man-eater, is an unusual narrative device that risks having readers doubt Corbett's credibility at the very least. And yet, he devotes two full pages to the digression, before returning to the present in Mukteshwar and wrapping up his tale. This intriguing interlude about the sacred grove of Baram ka Than suggests that Corbett either genuinely believed in the powers of forest deities or felt, somehow, that the jungle lore of Kumaon contains both natural and supernatural enigmas that defy explanation. It also hints at his awareness of an indigenous conservation ethic that contests his role as a colonial sportsman or shikari.

∽

Before a network of motor roads penetrated Kumaon, most people travelled through these hills by foot or on horseback. Ramgarh, a scattered settlement between 1,400 and 1,900 metres above sea level, was one of the first halts along the main bridle trail heading north-east from Nainital. This arduous route was used by government officials on tour, as well as mule trains bearing fresh produce and other supplies, shepherds migrating with their flocks, and pilgrims proceeding to remote Himalayan shrines. The original dak bungalow at Ramgarh, built in 1830, still stands on a wooded knoll that overlooks a broad valley and a steep range of hills, beyond which lies the historic town of Almora, two days' march to the north. Off to the east, the forested slopes above Ramgarh extend in precipitous contours for more than 12 kilometres. Mukteshwar is situated at the furthest point on this ridge, where the sun appears at dawn.

Surrounded by terraced orchards, Ramgarh is sometimes referred to as the 'fruit basket' of Kumaon. The old dak bungalow and several cottages nearby have been restored and converted into a heritage resort by the Neemrana chain of hotels. In 1910, Jim Corbett stayed here overnight. 'The dak bungalow *khansama* (cook, bottle-washer, and general factotum) was a friend of mine,' he writes, 'and when he learnt that I was on my way to Muktesar to try and shoot the man-eater, he warned me to be very careful while negotiating the last two miles into Muktesar for, he said, several people had recently been killed on that stretch of road.'

Following in Corbett's footsteps, I spend two nights at Ramgarh, where my accommodation is considerably more luxurious than it would have been in his day. The old stables next to the dak bungalow have been converted into a dining room and instead of the lone caretaker, an attentive retinue of cooks and other hotel employees cater to guests, who come here to enjoy the colonial ambience and cool mountain air. A venerable grove of banj oaks, some of which probably date back over two centuries, surround the dak bungalow, along with a stand of horse chestnuts, locally known as pangar. More recent plantings include a weeping willow and two cinnamon trees as well as apples, apricots, peaches, lemons, and pomegranates.

My first morning in Ramgarh, when I wake up before sunrise, a pair of rusty-cheeked scimitar babblers are calling somewhere in the underbrush near the orchard outside my room. Though their repeated cries sound like the voice of a single bird, it is actually a synchronized duet. The male begins with a sharp '*cue-pee*' to which the female immediately responds with a shrill '*quip*'. Together, they persistently call out, '*cue-pee-quip… cue-pee-quip!*' Though scimitar babblers are noisy birds, they are often difficult to see, hiding within the understorey and reluctantly emerging from cover. If alarmed, each of them emits a panicked, high-pitched cry, transliterated as a rapid, '*Wheat… jig, jig, jig, jig*'. Corbett credits rusty-cheeked scimitar babblers for being one of the common birds of Kumaon that reliably alerted him to the presence of tigers or leopards.

This morning there are no predators nearby and the babblers express no alarm. Seated under the eaves of a low-roofed veranda, enjoying my first cup of tea, I can identify a dozen different species of birds. A pair of streaked laughingthrushes are building a nest in an ornamental shrub next to my room, industriously going back and forth with sprigs of grass in their beaks. Unbothered by my presence, one of them lands on the side table next to my chair and looks up at me with a seemingly insistent expression, as if demanding that I help them construct their nest. Two spotted doves are perched together on a bare branch overlooking the valley. Off to my right, and up the hill a bit, a couple of black drongos are squabbling with a trio of Himalayan bulbuls and a black-headed jay, all of whom are trying to lay claim to the uppermost branches of the willow. A great barbet appears briefly, as does a blue whistling thrush and a rose-ringed parakeet, while an oriental white-eye and a green-backed tit fidget about in the lower branches of an apricot tree. They are joined by a grey bushchat and his mate. The male's streaked feathers look as if they've been sketched with chalk and charcoal while the female is buff and brown.

Eventually, one of the scimitar babblers surprises me by coming out into the open, next to the drooping white blossoms of a datura (belladonna) bush. A slender, scruffy bird with a longish tail, it is about the size of a jungle babbler. Its curved beak resembles the crescent-like blade of a sultan's sword. While its cheeks and both sides of its neck are a rich, rusty-brown, as if dyed with henna, the most distinctive feature are its fierce-looking eyes that watch me intently for a minute or more before the bird darts back into hiding.

One of the Neemrana cottages in Ramgarh is called the Writer's Bungalow. At different points during the twentieth century, this quiet settlement, surrounded by orchards, was home to poets like Mahadevi Verma (1907–87), Ramdhari Singh, 'Dinkar' (1908–74), and Sachchidananda Hirananda Vatsyayan, 'Agyeya' (1911–87). Preceding all of them, in 1903, Rabindranath Tagore spent a summer in Ramgarh. One of his daughters, Renuka Devi, was suffering from tuberculosis and doctors had recommended that he take her up to the hills. Despite Tagore's efforts to nurse Renuka back to health, she died here a few months later at the age of thirteen. Though it isn't clear where Tagore stayed on that first, tragic visit, he later moved into a cottage near the crest of the ridge that is known as Tagore Top. On several subsequent occasions, the Nobel Laureate came back to Kumaon, living and writing both in Ramgarh and Almora.

A plaque at the Writer's Bungalow commemorates Tagore's historic presence and recounts how he reprimanded the gardeners for making noise to scare away birds that were raiding the fruit trees. 'Let the birds eat the fruits that also belong to them. Besides, your shouting disturbs my thoughts!' There is also a suggestion that Ramgarh was where he wrote some of the poems in his famous collection of verse, *Gitanjali,* published in 1910. Later on, in 1916, he also published a collection of short poems and aphorisms titled *Stray Birds*, some of which may have been inspired by the winged creatures of Kumaon. The opening stanzas suggest the passing seasons in the hills, tinged with a hint of sadness.

> Stray birds of summer come to
> my window to sing and fly away.
> And yellow leaves of autumn,
> which have no songs,
> flutter and fall there with a sigh.

Another line in this slim book evokes a further sense of nostalgia and solitude, which must have drawn the poet back to these hills.

> In the dusk of the evening the bird of some early dawn
> comes to the nest of my silence.

~

After breakfast, I set off for Mukteshwar with Rafik Ahmad, who has driven me to and from many out-of-the-way places. Most of our route today follows an alignment well above the old walking path that Corbett would have taken, though it passes through sections of forest on the north slope of the ridge that are probably much the same as they were more than a century ago. Banj and moru oaks are the two dominant species, small acorns forming amongst their tough, serrated leaves. Plenty of other trees hold their own in these dense jungles, including kaphal (box myrtle), burans (rhododendron), bhamora (dogwood), and anyar (lyonia). Sections of the hills have been planted with chir pines, most of which have blackened trunks, evidence of recent wildfires. For too many years, the forest department has propagated these tall, relatively fast-growing conifers as a source of timber and resin. Monoculture plantations of chir pines choke out indigenous shrubs, plants and grasses with a thick carpet of fallen needles which the slightest spark will ignite during the dry season.

Skirting the reserve forests, on patches of private land, extensive orchards have been planted across slopes cleared of native trees and shrubs. A farmer is selling apples at a roadside stall and when we stop to buy a kilo, I ask if monkeys raid his crops. The young man shakes his head in frustration and produces a catapult from his pocket. He also says they use fireworks to scare away monkeys. When I enquire about bears, he tells me they sometimes raid the fruit but mostly they destroy vegetable plots and fields of maize. At different points along our drive, we come upon troops of rhesus macaques and langurs loitering near the edge of an orchard.

One of the puzzles surrounding Corbett's stories about man-eaters in Kumaon is that the forests of this region are not ideal habitat for tigers, which prefer lowland jungles, preying primarily on sambar and chital. This range of Himalayan foothills, rising above 2,000 metres, contains very few sambar and no chital at all. On the other hand, the vast forests of the Terai, which hadn't yet been cleared for agriculture, were prime habitat for sambar and chital as well as tigers. Judging from Corbett's books, an unusual number of tigers seem to have ascended from the Terai into the highlands of Kumaon soon after 1900. Corbett notes that no man-eaters were reported here before 1905. Of course, plenty of leopards lived in the Himalaya, preying on barking deer, goral, wild pigs, porcupines, langurs, and other small mammals, but these species were not an ideal food source for tigers.

In hindsight, we can only speculate about the reasons behind the unusual proliferation of tigers in the foothills of Kumaon during the time that Corbett was hunting. However, wildlife scientists have recently discovered that the pressures of habitat loss and human disturbance are forcing some tigers to wander even higher into the Himalaya, up to altitudes above 3,000 metres where they have been recorded on camera traps in the upper reaches of Garhwal and Bhutan. Once again, reading between the lines of Corbett's accounts, it is obvious that the Terai forests were severely disturbed at the end of the nineteenth and early twentieth centuries, mostly because of the extraction of sal timber for use by the railways. During this period the government issued firearms licences to farmers, ostensibly to protect their crops. Corbett bemoans the widespread and unregulated killing of deer and other wildlife that ensued. This suggests that many tigers retreated into Kumaon at the turn of the twentieth century because their habitat and prey base was being diminished and disturbed. Struggling to survive on smaller mammals like porcupines and wild pigs, the displaced tigers inevitably turned to killing cattle and human beings out of desperation, particularly if they were injured.

Today, no man-eaters prowl the forests surrounding Mukteshwar, though the human population has proliferated. As we cross over to the southern face of the ridge, I can see hundreds of individual cottages and small settlements scattered across the slopes and valleys. Hotels, resorts, and restaurants crowd the roadside. More than horticulture, tourism now drives the economy of this region. As visitors from the plains escape to the hills, many of the farms and orchards have been converted into holiday homes.

About 4 kilometres short of Mukteshwar, the motor road enters an oak forest and the clutter of houses and hotels disappear. This section of the route, running on a level about a hundred metres below the crest of the ridge, probably follows the same alignment as the old bridle path that Corbett followed. Asking Rafik to stop the car, I decide to get down and walk the last stretch. It is a clear morning, though it rained last night, and the ground beneath the oaks is thick with ferns and other monsoon plants including peacock orchids and wild ginger. Very little traffic disturbs the silence of the trees that grow in twisted, moss-laden shapes with a thick canopy of leaves overhead. This is the section that Corbett had been warned about by the caretaker of the dak bungalow in Ramgarh, where the tiger had killed several people, though this morning there is no suggestion of danger. The only wildlife I encounter is a troop of langurs in the oaks, feeding on acorns. They grunt and climb higher into the branches as I pass by but mostly they ignore me.

After half an hour, I reach a small market on the left side of the road. To the right are several old cottages which seem to be abandoned. Signs indicate that this land belongs to the Indian Veterinary Research Institute (IVRI) the main buildings of which occupy the ridge above me. In addition to the oaks, tall stands of mature deodars and Himalayan fir trees line the sides of the road. Two hundred metres further on lies the main entrance to IVRI, with an imposing gate attended by a uniformed guard who brusquely waves me away, when I ask if I may enter.

Surprisingly, other than a couple of tea shops, there are no hotels or restaurants and hardly any tourists here. The old IVRI bungalows with brownstone walls and red sheet-metal roofs are scattered over the undulating contours of the ridge sheltered beneath the deodars. Unlike every other hill station I know, Mukteshwar seems to have changed very little in the last hundred years, as if lost in time. All the recent development has occurred on the outskirts of the town, five or more kilometres away, while the centre of Mukteshwar remains untouched. The main reason for this is that virtually all the land belongs to the veterinary institute, which has protected the forests as well as the old buildings, some of which are being carefully restored without changing the original architecture or design.

IVRI has branches in other parts of the country, particularly in Pune, where it began in 1889 as the Imperial Bacteriological Laboratory. The main campus was moved to Mukteshwar in 1893, primarily because this was a secluded location, and there was less likelihood of the virulent pathogens that are studied here infecting the local population of animals and human beings. Most of IVRI's research focuses on producing vaccines for viruses and other microbes that cause livestock diseases like hoof and mouth, rinderpest, anthrax, and sheep pox. These days, in the uncertain aftermath of the recent pandemic, with increasingly plausible reports that the Covid-19 virus 'escaped' from a lab in Wuhan, China, it is strangely ironic and almost surreal to find this nineteenth century institution of virology still functioning in bucolic isolation on a hilltop in Kumaon.

Just beyond the IVRI gate stands the original post office, from where Corbett sent a telegram to his mother in Nainital informing her that he had arrived safely at Mukteshwar. Though the small, single-storey building has been renovated, a simple plaque on the wall announces that it was built in 1905, five years before the man-eater was shot. When I peer through the service window at the main counter, I can see a line of wooden pigeonholes for sorting mail though all of them are empty.

Wandering about Mukteshwar, as the monsoon mist filters through fern-laden branches of ancient trees, I feel as if I have stepped back in history, not just to the colonial period when these bungalows were built but to an older, indeterminate age. A hundred metres ahead of the post office, a winding staircase leads up to a temple complex where five or six shrines are located on the summit of the ridge overlooking the snow peaks of Nanda Devi, Trishul, and Panchachuli. This morning the high Himalaya are hidden by clouds but there is an impressive view of the broad valley and layered ridges on all sides, with villages and terraced fields spreading below the forested hills. The Mukteshwar Mahadev Mandir is virtually deserted, with only one pandit seated inside the main sanctum sanctorum, reciting Sanskrit verses in a hushed voice. A newlywed couple that arrived before me, whisper to each other and fold their hands in front of the temple which is overshadowed by a sacred grove of deodars and oaks.

Retreating slowly down the steps, I can hear the priest blowing on a conch shell, its resonant moaning sound echoing through the trees and out across the valley. At the same time, the young couple reach up to ring brass bells that hang like tangled chains above the threshold of the shrine. The clamorous chiming of the bells and the single, prolonged note of the conch seem to amplify the solitude and sanctity of this site. As the mist closes in, I wonder how many prayers for protection have been offered here, pleading for immunity from man-eating tigers, mutating viruses, and marauding monkeys or bears.

Exactly a century after Corbett came to Mukteshwar in pursuit of the man-eating tigress, anthropologist Radhika Govindrajan conducted her PhD fieldwork in nearby villages during 2010–11. Her book, *Animal Intimacies: Beastly Love in the Himalaya*, tells a very different story, though much of it focuses on human–animal conflict, as well as the close and often intimate relationships between people and other mammals, both domestic and wild. As a post-modern scholar who documents the lives of villagers in Kumaon, and the animals they associate with, Govindrajan presents an insightful and provocative perspective on varying definitions of wildness, conflicting gender narratives, and the socio-cultural nuances of inter-species affinity.

Instead of focusing on tigers, which are no longer found in the forests near Mukteshwar, Govindrajan tells the stories of goats, cows, rhesus macaques, wild pigs, and Himalayan black bears. She also includes an epilogue about village dogs and the leopards that prey on them. Though Govindrajan approaches her subjects from an academic point of view, her writing is often as lively and compelling as Corbett's storytelling, though it obviously has none of the suspense of a shikar tale, nor a naturalist's detailed depictions of forest ecology. Nevertheless, Govindrajan does present us with unique aspects of jungle lore, as recounted by women and men, in and around Mukteshwar.

Conflict between human beings and rhesus macaques in Kumaon is a serious, ongoing problem, with both economic and political consequences. Often referred to as 'the monkey menace' it is a complex and contentious wildlife issue that affects cities as well as small towns and rural communities. The exploding population of rhesus macaques, most of whom scavenge on household waste in urban areas, or raid fields and orchards near villages, is the most obvious example of a wild species adapting its behaviour because of an increasing dependence on human beings. In some parts of Uttarakhand, troops of monkeys have become so prevalent and destructive that farmers have abandoned agriculture altogether. In hill stations like Nainital and my home town of Mussoorie, macaques have lost their fear of human beings and become aggressive, snatching food from tourists, stealing fruit and vegetables from street vendors, or attacking and biting schoolchildren.

Govindrajan explores the fraught relationship between villagers and macaques, recounting how many of her informants differentiated between two kinds of monkeys. Those that originally lived in the nearby forests were seen as less destructive and hostile, while others that had been trapped in towns or developed areas and then released in the vicinity of Mukteshwar were considered more aggressive and caused greater damage to fields and orchards. This analysis of 'outsider/insider' monkeys has considerable validity, because many municipalities in Uttarakhand hire professional monkey catchers to trap macaques and relocate them 'back into the wild' though they are usually released into someone else's backyard. After experiencing the trauma of being caught and transported to an unfamiliar place, often multiple times, it is only natural that these outsider monkeys would approach human beings with greater distrust and hostility.

One of the fascinating aspects of Govindrajan's book is that she explores different levels of anthropomorphism and the blurred lines that separate species. Recounting the many ways in which villagers assign human traits and emotions to the animals they interact with, she speaks of 'inter-species mutuality'. Not only do human beings recognize elements of themselves in other animals but those same creatures sometimes respond to us in a manner that suggests they share a corresponding awareness and empathy. The macaques, for example, are seen as outsiders, invaders, and enemies, while cows and goats are often treated like family members, with love and affection. As Govindranjan writes: 'When people in Kumaon said that they were related to animals, the metaphors of kinship were grounded in what they saw as truth...the animals whose lives were imbricated with those of humans would often convey their sense of relatedness to particular individuals, both human and animal.'

Monkeys, in particular, pose a difficult challenge when it comes to wildlife management. Because of religious and cultural associations, it is not possible to cull this rapidly growing population. Until the 1970s, rhesus macaques were captured and used for scientific research, including vivisection, but wildlife protection laws have correctly put an end to that. The only feasible solution to the monkey menace would be for the government to launch a widespread birth control campaign aimed at sterilizing large numbers of rhesus macaques to stop them from overbreeding.

Another species that causes a great deal of damage to crops in Kumaon are wild pigs. Sounders of ten to fifteen animals can root up and destroy entire fields of potatoes or maize in a single night. Wild boar are also known to be aggressive and will attack human beings with little provocation, using their sharp tushes to inflict serious injuries. Though wild pigs are listed under Schedule III of the Wild Life Protection Act, the state government of Uttarakhand recently declared them to be vermin. This means that farmers can shoot wild pigs that threaten their crops, though the time-consuming process of complying with regulations about reporting these deaths, and the limited availability of firearms and ammunition, deters most agriculturalists from resorting to these extreme measures.

In her conversations with villagers near Mukteshwar, Govindrajan discovered an unusual story that attempts to explain why wild pigs in this region are particularly aggressive and destructive. The Indian Veterinary Research Institute maintains a research farm for livestock, including domestic pigs, on which vaccines and other medications are tested. Evidently, at some point, one of the sows escaped from the farm and wandered off into the forest. Though the IVRI staff searched for her, she was never found and the villagers claimed that this feral sow bred with wild boars and produced several litters of ravenous and highly aggressive offspring.

This story illustrates the way in which an agrarian community's struggle for survival, and their anxieties over crops being ruined by wildlife, invokes the image of a semi-mythological sow who produces cross-bred piglets of demonic proportions. It also raises interesting questions about different degrees of wildness and what it means when a tame creature escapes into the forest. Because of the injections she received, and other scientific experiments, 'the runaway sow's' offspring are seen as wilder, more savage creatures than ordinary pigs of the forest.

As she records and interprets these stories, Govindrajan is attentive to the social hierarchies and divisions that exist amongst people in Kumaon. She is also keenly interested in gender relations, both inside and outside a family. Living in the village for extended periods of time, she was able to establish a considerable level of trust with several of the women, who confided in her about their relationships with their husbands and in-laws. In this context, she discovered another remarkable story of inter-species relatedness, what the women referred to as 'bhalu ki baat', or the talk of bears.

Himalayan black bears are another wild creature that damages crops, particularly fields of millet and corn, as well as fruit orchards. Though not as common as monkeys or pigs, they are a nocturnal presence in the forested hills of Kumaon. Bears are also extremely dangerous and maul human beings with their claws and teeth, often killing their victims. As in many cultures, Himalayan bears are thought to have insatiable appetites, not only for food but also when it comes to sex. Folk tales in other parts of the Himalaya, especially in Arunachal Pradesh, recount the lustful behaviour of male bears who take female humans as sexual partners, sometimes by force but also through seduction. The women Govindrajan spoke to believed that if they came upon a bear in the forest, there was a strong possibility they might be raped. In some of the stories she recorded, intercourse was said to be violent but in other accounts the bears were described as gentle, tenderly licking a woman's feet, for example.

As an anthropologist, Govindrajan is not suggesting that these tales of bestiality are true; her focus is on what they might represent. She interprets the bhalu ki baat as a subversive genre of folklore told by village women for whom the bears offer an alternative narrative to their own life stories of violent or unresponsive husbands. 'As I listened to multiple tellings,' she writes, 'I recognized that they shared something more in common than just the fact that they deliberately gestured toward the flourishing of women's sexuality in the face of sustained efforts to repress it. These were stories that stoked desire and longing....'

Govindrajan suggests that imagining these wild and dangerous liaisons provides an emotional and psychological release from the constant pressure of social constraints and abusive family relationships. In one story, a woman runs away from her husband and lives with a bear for several years, becoming a wild creature herself with matted hair and walking on all fours, until she is rescued and brought back to the village, against her will.

Coincidentally, Jim Corbett also recorded the story of a teenaged girl whom he speculated may have been abducted by a bear. In 1914, she was found in the forest near Ratighat, not far from Mukteshwar and Ramgarh. Completely naked and with long, matted hair, she was terrified of human beings, biting and scratching anyone who approached her. Brought to the Crosthwaite Hospital in Nainital, she was named Goongi, because she was mute. The doctors estimated that she was fourteen years old and they found that she was physically healthy except for scratches on her upper back. Journalists, at the time, dubbed her 'The Nainital Wolf-Child'.

Corbett didn't see the girl himself, though he investigated the case and interviewed the doctors. By this time, Goongi had died of heat stroke after being sent to a 'lunatic asylum' in Bareilly. Based on information he gathered, Corbett writes that if, in fact, the girl was raised and nurtured by a wild animal, it is more likely to have been a Himalayan black bear than a wolf. He based this assumption on Goongi's behaviour, including the manner in which she ate, and her preference for raw food, as well as a rumour that she was seen in the company of a bear that was shot by a forest official. Corbett then explains:

> Bears throughout the Himalayas have the reputation of molesting women, and so strong is this belief that when certain fruits are in season women refrain from going into the forests adjoining the villages. The scratches on Goongi's shoulders and on the upper portion of her body need explanation. If she had acquired these scratches in her passage through thorns she would also have had scratches on the lower portion of her body, and on her arms and legs.

Though he wrote the story of Goongi and shared the manuscript with R. E. Hawkins, his editor at Oxford University Press, Corbett obviously had doubts about its authenticity for he chose not to include it in any of his books. Hawkins eventually published the piece in an anthology of Corbett's work, which came out in 1978. A bizarre, unsettling, and ultimately tragic tale, it shares many similarities with the narratives that Radhika Govidrajan compiled from the same region of Kumaon, a hundred years later.

Whether it is tigers, rhesus macaques, wild pigs, or Himalayan black bears, the stories we tell of these species are intimately entwined with our own, as we seek to recognize something of ourselves in forest creatures and recover elements of what has been lost through the process of civilization. The adversarial yet strangely complicit relationship between wild animals and villagers in Kumaon reflects widespread antagonisms and affinities that connect human beings to wildlife throughout the Himalaya and in many other parts of India too.

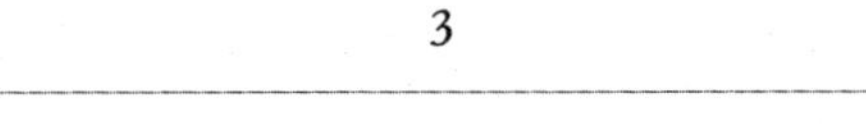

3

THE CENTRAL HIGHLANDS

At first light, a shrill crowing erupts from a line of trees and underbrush on the far side of a shallow pond. Still water, dark as smoked glass, reflects a brightening sky. A grey junglefowl is calling, its cry similar to that of a village rooster but higher pitched and more strident. Both grey and red junglefowl coexist in the forests surrounding Pachmarhi, a hill station located 1,000 metres above sea level, atop the Satpura Range in Madhya Pradesh. Red junglefowl are distributed eastward from here into Assam and throughout the foothills of the Himalaya. Grey junglefowl are found exclusively to the south. These two living ancestors of domesticated chickens share a narrow band of common territory along this line of mountains, which extends laterally, east to west, across the midriff of India.

The Satpura Range serves as an ecological divide between the Gangetic Plains and the Deccan Plateau. Swift, spring-fed streams that spill down the northern slopes of these mountains join the Narmada River, which flows slowly westward, impeded by giant dams, until it eventually drains into the Arabian Sea. Immediately south of the Satpura is the Tapti River, which follows a parallel course, also flowing towards the west through a rift valley. Most other rivers in India flow from west to east because the subcontinent is tilted in that direction. Central India's highlands represent a watershed in more ways than one—hydrological, of course, but also geographical, environmental, historical, and cultural. At the same time, this natural boundary is not an impermeable barrier but more like a porous seam, through which different life forms have passed from one part of the subcontinent to the other.

In 1937, an ichthyologist, Sunder Lal Hora, began to suspect that the Satpura Range once served as a land bridge for species that entered India from Southeast Asia millions of years ago. Hora served as director of the Zoological Survey of India and in 1953 he published a seminal paper titled, 'The Satpura Hypothesis'. Essentially, he proposed that a westward migration of species occurred soon after primordial India collided with Eurasia (roughly 45 million years ago, by his reckoning). In particular, fish from the Malaysian peninsula dispersed along ancient rivers, as India's physical contours changed and shifted during the Eocene and Miocene epochs. While geological forces were reshaping the surface of the subcontinent, extreme climatic events, particularly a series of ice ages, led to dramatic shifts in temperature and humidity that would have encouraged migration across this region.

Hora based his suppositions on the distribution of several fish species found in torrential streams that flood during the monsoon. Bottom feeders like loach and certain catfish have mouths like suction cups, allowing them to hold onto rocks, so as not to be swept away in a deluge. After conducting extensive field research, Hora proposed that these fish entered India from the north-east and established themselves in various tributaries of the Ganga and Brahmaputra that flowed out of the Himalaya. Simultaneously, the fish found their way into torrential streams in the Satpura and from there they moved on to the Western Ghats. In 2001, R. J. Ranjit Daniels published an article, 'Endemic Fish of the Western Ghats and the Satpura Hypothesis', which summarizes the methods and data that Hora used and then goes on to explain how subsequent research and discoveries by geologists and ichthyologists have rendered Hora's conclusions 'untenable'. Considerable revisions have occurred in fish taxonomy since Hora conducted his studies, and most of the species that he believed had migrated are now thought to be the result of '*in situ* evolution'. Meanwhile, more recent geological dating of the Western Ghats and Satpura uplifts doesn't match his timeline.

Though scientists have now dismissed Hora's hypothesis, he succeeded in focusing attention on one of the key questions regarding the diversity and distribution of flora and fauna in India. Extending his ideas well beyond rivers and streams, other naturalists like Salim Ali picked up on Hora's writings and raised similar biogeographical questions. Many writers have noted that closely related species of plants and animals are found both in the Himalaya as well as the mountains of western and southern India, but seldom in between. These populations are separated by hundreds of kilometres. Anyone who looks at a topographical map of India can understand the logic behind Hora's argument that the Satpura formed an elevated causeway connecting the north-eastern parts of the subcontinent to the Western Ghats, and from there further south.

In late February, accompanied by naturalist Ram Kumar, I explore the undulating plateau surrounding Pachmarhi. We search mostly for birds near wetlands and along peripheral tracts of jungle that lie at the edge of town. Many of the species we encounter are either the same or very similar to those

I know from my home in the foothills of the Himalaya. A Malabar whistling thrush skulks in the shadowy undergrowth. When it finally emerges, I recognize the bird instantly, though it is several shades brighter than the blue whistling thrush of the Himalaya and its beak is black instead of yellow. The calls of these two species, though somewhat similar, are distinctly different. Further on, we spot a restless pair of grey-headed canary flycatchers and a black-lored tit, with bright yellow and green plumage. My well-thumbed copy of *Birds of the Indian Subcontinent* contains maps showing the distribution of these two birds, which illustrate the unique location and biogeographical significance of the Satpura Range. The flycatcher is a common resident in the Himalaya as well as the mountains of southern India, while an isolated, disjunctive population is found in and around Pachmarhi. The tit's range extends southward into the Sahyadri and Nilgiri mountains, while a completely separate distribution occurs along the lower reaches of the Himalaya. Recently, this species was split and the birds found in Pachmarhi and further south are now known as the Indian yellow tit, though in appearance they are virtually identical to the Himalayan black-lored tit.

In 1861, a twenty-two-year-old forest officer employed by the East India Company, Captain James Forsyth, arrived in Pachmarhi to assess the timber resources of this region. He immediately noticed the diversity of species and wrote: 'Few parts of India present so great a range of interesting natural objects for investigation as this. Situated in the very centre of the peninsula, the ethnical, zoological, botanical and even geological features of north and south, and of east and west, here meet and contrast themselves.' Forsyth's book, *The Highlands of Central India: Notes on their Forests and Wild Tribes, Natural History, and Sports,* contains a detailed and colourful record of the ecology and terrain of the Satpura Range around the time it was brought under British rule.

Forsyth's views on the human population of these hills, particularly the Gond and Korku tribes, are full of racial prejudices, but he provides significant and valuable information regarding the forests and wildlife. Though his primary mission was to find sal trees that could be extracted and used as sleepers for the railways, this didn't deter him from pursuing his favourite pastime of shikar. His book is a classic of the colonial genre of jungle memoir, written by a hunter-explorer. Forsyth was delighted by the many opportunities for shooting game in the Pachmarhi hills and describes, in great detail, stalking gaur, which he referred to as 'bison', as well as tigers and bears. Soon after he set up camp in Pachmarhi, an elderly leopard attacked the herd of goats and sheep he'd brought with him to provide mutton. The panther also tried to kill one of his prized spaniels, though another hunting hound drove the aged predator away.

Clearly enchanted by the forest cover and topography of Pachmarhi, Forsyth noted that its rolling meadows and small lakes gave these highlands a 'park-like' appearance. He had been charged to build a permanent lodge at a suitable location, which would serve as a rest house for other officers who might follow. Masons and carpenters were brought up from the plains and a team of Gonds and Korkus cut wooden beams and helped make bricks. The project took longer than expected but Forsyth used every opportunity to explore the encompassing hills and canyons. He was an observant naturalist and gave detailed descriptions of everything from the variety of forest cover at different altitudes to the relative size and shape of the horns on the gaur he shot. His book provides evidence that barasingha or swamp deer were found in the Denwa Valley, at the foot of the Satpura Range, though this species has not been seen there since.

Forsyth is often credited with 'discovering' Pachmarhi, though the area was already inhabited by tribal people and under the control of a Gond thakur, who reluctantly assisted in constructing the lodge. Several Europeans had visited Pachmarhi preceding Forsyth's arrival, including a contingent of East India Company troops that arrived here in 1818. They had been sent to arrest Appa Saheb Bhonsle, the deposed ruler of Nagpur, who had taken refuge in the Mahadeo Hills. The British soon realized the commercial and strategic importance of what they referred to as 'The Gondwana Highlands'. In 1832, the assistant agent at Hoshangabad, Captain Ouseley, trekked up to Pachmarhi, conducting a botanical and geological survey. Others followed including a second detachment of troops pursuing Tatya Tope in 1859, who had also retreated into the mountains, following the rebellion of 1857. Though Forsyth was certainly not the first Englishman to reach Pachmarhi, he was the most astute observer and his book brought attention to the Satpura region. Soon enough, Pachmarhi became a popular summer resort for British colonials and a sanatorium for troops stationed in nearby cantonments like Jabalpur. The picturesque terrain of the Central Highlands caught the imagination of visitors and Forsyth's descriptions often read like a persuasive travel brochure:

> To the south, as far as the eye can see, lie range upon range of forest-covered hills, tumbled in wild confusion. To the east a long line of rampart-like cliffs marks the southern face of the Mahadeo range, the deep red of their sandstone formation contrasting finely with the intense green of the bamboo vegetation, out of which they rise. Here and there they shoot into peaks of bare red rock, many of which have a peculiar and almost fantastic appearance, owing to the irregular weathering of their material – beds of coarse sandstone horizontally streaked by darker bands of hard vitrified ferruginous earth. Looking across this wall of rock, to the north-east, a

> long perspective of forest covered hills is seen, the nearer ones seeming to be part of the Puchmurree plateau, though really separated from it by an enormous rift in the rock, the further ranges sinking gradually in elevation, till, faint and blue in the far distance, gleams the level plain of the Narbada valley.

Forsyth also makes note of the religious significance of the Mahadeo Hills, which are considered the sacred abode of Shiva and visited by Hindu pilgrims from the plains. He recounts how lowland people were fearful of the wild animals that live in the mountainous jungles, not to mention evil spirits and ghosts that haunt these hills. The eroded sandstone ridges, falling away into deep gorges, and the rugged peaks rising like ruined castles out of a verdant sea of foliage give the landscape a wild and forbidding appearance. Waterfalls that stream down cleft rocks add to a romantic sense of nature's sublime and tumultuous beauty.

A number of caves and ancient rock shelters are located in the Pachmarhi region. Five of these, near the centre of the town, give the hill station its name. According to local mythology, these caves provided refuge for the five Pandava brothers in the Mahabharata, who were exiled in the forest for thirteen years. Though archaeologists have suggested that the caves are more likely the monastic retreats of Buddhist bhikkhus, or monks, from later times, most of the shrines in Pachmarhi reflect Hindu lore and traditions. At the same time, I saw several caves that were obviously occupied by Muslim fakirs while the tribal people have their own religious sites that are part of an older, animistic tradition. A spreading mango tree near one of the crossroads in town is surrounded by memorial tablets carved out of wood. These are left here by members of the Korku community to commemorate recent deaths. Funeral ceremonies are conducted beneath the tree, including feasts and dancing to honour the dead. Christ Church, the main protestant sanctuary in Pachmarhi, built in 1875 by the British, is an imposing structure made entirely out of rocks from the nearby hills. It is the same rusty grey colour as the Pandava caves nearby, while its rough stone walls and arched windows are similar to the stratified cliffs of the Mahadeo Hills.

The main market in Pachmarhi is a clutter of shops and restaurants but the rest of the town still preserves its spacious, colonial ambience. Being a military cantonment, it has been spared much of the unregulated development of other hill stations in India. Though it attracts a number of tourists from Bhopal and other nearby towns, the final approach is a narrow 'jalebi road', as my taxi driver complained, with winding switchbacks and blind curves, barely wide enough for a single vehicle. The town also lies within the Pachmarhi Biosphere Reserve, which imposes a variety of environmental restrictions. Most of the military bungalows and barracks are spread over the plateau, at the centre of which is a sprawling golf course with broad fairways that provide stray cattle with pasture. A number of large banyan trees grow on the plateau like natural pavilions with domed canopies of foliage supported by columns of aerial roots.

While most of Pachmarhi is relatively clean and well-maintained, many of the forested areas are littered with trash, including the site of a stone cenotaph, erected in memory of two British residents killed during the Afghan campaign. The view from here at sunset is spectacular, as the shadowy ridges darken against a saffron sky, but the scattered remains of broken beer bottles and snack wrappers are a reminder of the careless indifference of tourists who come to the hills for their natural beauty yet despoil the same landscape they profess to admire. The other depressing sight is garbage dumped in the jungle by caterers for marriage parties. Heaps of plastic glasses and plates, as well as aluminium containers and food waste have been tossed into the bushes, where wild pigs, monkeys, peacocks, and sloth bears scavenge on the rotting remains of wedding buffets.

Ram Kumar, my guide to the natural history of Pachmarhi, grew up in this town. He is thirty-eight and works as a schoolteacher at a village nearby but in his free time he leads birdwatching tours and treks. Ram's father and uncle, both retired, used to work for the army as civilian employees. Having grown up in these mountains, Ram has first-hand knowledge of the forests and he has taught himself common names for many species of birds, mammals, and plants. On my second morning in Pachmarhi, he takes me to see vultures nesting on cliffs across the valley. Ram's brother-in-law and nephew accompany us. After scrambling up a low hill above the town, we skirt around the ridge to avoid the army's firing range, before descending the other side to a grassy lookout point. An amaltas tree is blooming close by with showers of yellow blossoms. The sun has just risen, burnishing a broad band of red sandstone cliffs on the other side of the valley. This forested gorge, which lies in shadow, drops several hundred metres into a thick jungle below. Ram explains that the valley is called Jambudvip, a name that puzzles me. In Hindu cosmology, Jambudvip is a mythical island or continent surrounded by ocean. According to stories in the Puranas, Mount Meru rises out of the centre of this island, which is covered with fruit trees. When I ask Ram why this valley has the same name, he says it comes from the wild jamun or jambu trees that grow along the stream at the bottom of the gorge.

Across from us, several slender-billed vultures have built their nests on precarious aeries. Through my binoculars I can see them huddled in pairs and count twelve adults altogether. Two of the nests, built mostly of sticks and dry grass, house young chicks, a reassuring sight. The past three decades have been a dismal time for vultures in India, as their numbers plummeted to the point where extinction seemed imminent. These aerial scavengers used to be common throughout India and critical for the disposal of carrion. By the beginning of the twenty-first century, however, they had all but disappeared. For several years it remained a mystery until researchers pieced together an answer: the vultures had been feeding on carcasses of cattle that contained residual traces of a veterinary drug, diclofenac, which is toxic for the birds and causes kidney failure. The symptoms are weakness and lassitude. Before they die, many of the birds sit with 'slumped posture and drooping necks'. As Rishad Naoroji, the raptor expert, wrote in 2005, 'The population crashes in South Asia of the Indian white-backed, Indian long-billed and slender-billed vultures are unprecedented in magnitude and impact.' Conservationists campaigned for a ban on diclofenac and urgent efforts were made to save the birds, including captive breeding programs. Though relict populations, like these near Pachmarhi, provide hope, the possibility that these huge scavengers may disappear is still very real.

In 1861, Forsyth described seeing vultures and other raptors in Pachmarhi, nesting on the same cliffs. Ram tells me that he remembers hundreds of vultures circling overhead when he was a boy. They would feed on dead cattle and other carrion at a boneyard beyond the edge of town. Hunched on the precipitous rockface, the birds look like the last survivors of a fatal catastrophe. At this hour of the day, the adults are hardly moving, as the morning sun shines against grey-brown feathers, which range from shades of pale ash to almost black. Their naked heads and necks turn occasionally from side to side. One of the birds responds to its chick which is clamouring for attention. Seen from a distance, the slender-billed vultures are almost identical to the long-billed, being roughly the same size and appearance.

As we watch through binoculars, Ram tells his nephew the story of Jatayu, the noble vulture king in the Ramayana. When the demon Ravana abducted Sita, carrying her off through the air to his stronghold in Lanka, Jatayu attacked him and attempted to rescue Rama's wife. However, the demon was much stronger than the elderly vulture and their battle ended tragically when Ravana cut off Jatayu's wings and he fell to earth. Shortly afterwards, Rama and Lakshmana came upon the mortally wounded bird who told them, before he died, that Ravana had kidnapped Sita. Sacrificing his life for a righteous cause, Jatayu became a martyr and a symbol of selfless loyalty.

Listening to this story, while watching the great birds at their nests, the desperate fate of India's vultures seems to signify an environmental dilemma of epic proportions that tests our moral principles. Protecting birds that feed on the dead and rescuing them from extinction is an ecological imperative. It is not just compassion or a protective impulse that we feel for this endangered species but also a sense of righting a wrong for which human beings must hold themselves accountable.

After an hour, the sun floods the valley and the void between us is filled with light, warming the air. The giant birds have become more active, shifting positions and ruffling their feathers. Finally, as a breeze begins to blow through the gorge, two of the vultures take flight. At first, they circle beneath us on outspread wings, which they flap occasionally to gain height. Soon enough, they catch a thermal and quickly rise above us, wheeling close enough overhead so that I can hear their feathers whispering in the morning air before they soar away out of sight.

∽

The following day, Ram takes me on a short trek into the Jambudvip Valley. After driving to a roadhead, 3 kilometres south of the main town, we descend on foot, following a rough track where a side valley funnels into the gorge. The forest contains a large number of *Terminalia elliptica*, or saaj, also known as the crocodile-bark tree. Their trunks are covered with rough, segmented patterns that have a scaly, reptilian appearance. We also pass beneath several enormous wild mango trees which are just beginning to flower. I am told that the fruit they bear is small but very sweet.

Because we are entering the Satpura Tiger Reserve, a forest guard accompanies us. Shankar Singh Thakur, in his fifties, tells me that he has spent most of his career patrolling these jungles. He wears a dark green uniform with the reserve's logo, an image of a giant squirrel, on his shirt pocket. As we descend through the forest, both he and Ram keep pointing out medicinal and aromatic herbs. One creeper, a wild clematis, is santai, also known as old man's beard, which is used to cure rheumatism and gout. Another plant, anantmool, or Indian sarsaparilla, has roots that are boiled into a herbal tea that cures stomach aches and promotes digestion. Growing close to the ground is a delicate clover-like plant known as brahmi, which Ram assures me is good for the brain. I am also shown a silver fern with white powder on the back of its fronds that leaves a clear impression, like a stencil, on the sleeve of my shirt. Another shrub with round, alternate leaves is called panchdhara because its flowers have five petals. In Sanskrit it is known as panduphali, presumably because its small white berries are edible and may have been eaten by the Pandavas during their exile in the forest. Both Shankar and Ram explain that snakes and scorpions avoid this species, which is planted near village homes as a form of protection. Another belief, amongst tribal people, is that if a judgement is about to be passed, either by village elders or in government courts, the plaintiff will clutch a twig of panchdhara in his fist to ensure that the case is decided in his favour.

Listening to this litany of plant lore, I can't help but feel as if the entire jungle is an organic text in which each species represents a separate chapter. As my companions recite the names and attributes of different plants and trees, I become increasingly aware of a richly layered oral taxonomy based on Ayurvedic tradition and the indigenous knowledge of forest dwellers who have an intimate association with these plants. All of this runs parallel to and corresponds with modern scientific names and classification. Though some of it may seem arcane or even contradictory, ultimately these various strands of botanical knowledge reinforce each other.

About a third of the way down the hill we come to a clearing, where a large concrete tank is fed by a trickling stream. Ram tells me that this is a swimming pool built years ago by the British. Though it appears to be in disrepair, almost empty and coated with green algae, Shankar says that the forest department will clean it up in a few weeks and open it to the public during summer. Pachmarhi has a cooler climate than the plains of Madhya Pradesh but it still gets hot in May and June before the monsoon.

Our path continues steeply downhill through dense forest until we come to a meandering brook at the bottom. No more than 2 metres across and less than a metre deep, this stream is clear but sluggish as it flows between grass-covered banks. Hundreds of small water-skimmer insects are swarming on the surface, and I see a few minnows that may be one of the species that Hora studied, though this is anything but a torrential stream. A short distance ahead, we come to a mud-walled shack with a temporary roof made of blue plastic tarpaulins spread over rough wooden rafters and bamboo. Ram introduces me to the owner, whose name I will change to Deepak, a congenial, talkative man in his forties who is seated by an open hearth outside the front door of his hut.

As he makes tea for us, Deepak explains that his family has lived here for several generations and they originally came to Pachmarhi as washermen. The stream we just crossed used to be the old dhobi ghat, where linen from the military sanatorium and other establishments like the Pachmarhi Club was sent to be washed. Loads of laundry were carried up and down the hill on men's backs as well as on ponies and mules. When the dhobi ghat was finally shut down in 1941, Deepak's grandfather was offered a pension but he asked instead to be given an acre of land by the stream. This shack is all that remains of the family farm where they grew vegetables and raised cattle over the years. All this area is now part of the Satpura Tiger Reserve.

Judging from the fact that the hut has lost its original roof, as well as its doors and windows, I guess that efforts have been made to evict Deepak from his homestead and it's difficult to know what the whole story may be. Nevertheless, he insists that he still lives here, while he has a house in Pachmarhi too, where he keeps a few cows and goats. Deepak complains about being harassed by government officials and the forest department, though he and Shankar seem to be on good terms. While he agrees that protecting the environment and wildlife is important, Deepak keeps emphasizing that the forest needs to be used, particularly for tourism and camping. He is planning to set up a campsite on his land, where trekkers can spend the night and explore the Jambudvip Valley. Though I find him a pleasant, engaging raconteur, I can't help thinking that there is an element of opportunism to his claims.

Painted on the walls of the hut is a slogan in Devanagri: 'Astik Muni ki Duhai Hai'. These words invoke the blessing and protection of an ancient, mythological sage, whose mother was Manasa, a serpent goddess. The Mahabharata contains an episode in which Astik Muni saves the life of Takshaka, the serpent king. This event is celebrated during the Naga Panchami festival, which is marked by an annual pilgrimage in Pachmarhi. Deepak explains that he has painted the slogan to give him protection from cobras and scorpions, as well as tigers and other predators like leopards and bears. He says that when he spends the night in his hut none of these wild creatures disturb him, though there are no doors or windows.

'Tigers often come by at night and I can hear them roaring but they never attack me or my animals,' he insists.

After serving us tea, Deepak prepares a lunch of Maggi noodles, boiling them in a soot-blackened pan over the wood fire. For plates, Shankar collects large, circular leaves from a *Bauhinia* vine and sews these together, using stems of grass. As we sit in the shade, Deepak points out a stand of jamun trees nearby, which will bear fruit in a couple of months. He boasts that everything he needs is available here in the forest and that Jambudvip is an idyllic Eden where a person can live off the land. Nevertheless, it is packets of instant noodles and a box of biscuits that provide us with sustenance.

Shortly after lunch, two other visitors arrive. Ram introduces us, explaining that they are field workers employed by the Wildlife Conservation Trust based in Mumbai. Their team is monitoring otters in the Pachmari Biosphere Reserve. As we speak, I learn that they have set traps along the stream, hoping to catch an otter and tag it, though until now they have been unsuccessful. Surprisingly, the species they are studying is the Eurasian otter instead of the more common smooth-coated otter. Though widely distributed throughout Europe and Asia, this palearctic mammal is rarely found in India, except in Ladakh, though in recent years it has been identified in the Western Ghats and a few other parts of the country. With embarrassed smiles, the two fieldworkers admit that they haven't actually seen a Eurasian otter since their project began two years ago.

After I express some scepticism about the presence of otters in the shallow brook, one of the men shows me a video on his mobile phone. The footage is from a camera trap that clearly recorded a pair of otters gambolling at the water's edge. The fieldworkers have also located several spraints, or communal latrines, where they collect the otters' scat for analysis. A large part of the otters' diet is freshwater crabs, which are plentiful in the streams around Pachmarhi.

Just as the Satpura Range provides refuge for a unique array of species, it also contains numerous rock shelters with prehistoric paintings of animals and birds. One of the objectives of our trek is to visit a shelter located in Jambudvip. Deepak leads the way, an axe slung over one shoulder. Though there doesn't seem to be any path, he confidently wades through the underbrush, telling me that he knows every inch of this forest, having spent his childhood here grazing his family's cattle. As before, I am treated to a running commentary on each plant and its therapeutic properties. Ram insists that I taste the leaf of one shrub, which is extremely bitter, and I spit it out. He says it is used to treat diabetes and after chewing this leaf nothing tastes sweet for several hours, not even sugar. Another plant is used to stop bleeding and the bark of one tree cures coughs, if mixed with wild honey. Shankar also points out a small insectivorous plant growing flush with the ground. When a fly lands on its sticky, pink petals they close like a trap.

The rock shelter lies about a kilometre from Deepak's hut, at the foot of a high cliff. Roughly 30 metres in length and between 2 to 3 metres deep, it is like an extended veranda beneath an overhanging rock. A decade ago, this shelter was fenced in by the Archaeological Survey of India, though it doesn't look as if anyone has visited this site for the past few years. Images of animals cover the walls—elephants and gaur, as well as a fierce-looking sloth bear with shaggy fur and a sambar stag that appears startled by our arrival. The paintings are almost identical to those I saw at Bhimbetka. Clusters of human figures appear on the rocks, though most of the paintings are of wildlife and it is easy to imagine this valley teeming with deer and other herbivores that provided meat for hunter-gatherers who lived here long ago.

Deepak obviously considers himself the self-appointed custodian of this site. Like an experienced tour guide, he identifies the different creatures depicted in the rock art, as well as scenes of hunters carrying bows and arrows, and swordsmen on horseback.

'These images date back to the time of the Mahabharata,' he tells me. 'They were painted by survivors of the great war, who retreated into the jungle.'

Deepak also claims that those epic heroes buried treasure nearby, though nobody has been able to find it. Most of what he recounts seems to be the product of a fertile imagination. Listening to his tall tales, I can picture him coming here as a boy, herding cows, and lying in the shade of the rock shelter, daydreaming of ancient myths.

~

The next day, I visit Bison Lodge, a natural history museum and interpretation centre, situated on the site where James Forsyth built Pachmarhi's first bungalow. In a strange way, the museum's exhibits are very similar to the cave paintings, displaying images of wildlife and indigenous culture. In one of the dioramas, a life-sized tiger feeds on a chital stag. Though I was expecting to see a collection of old hunting trophies the animals are not zoological specimens preserved through taxidermy, but three-dimensional models made of brightly coloured synthetic materials. An imposing pair of gaur stand amidst artificial bamboo and a jungle of plastic foliage. Staring at me through a pane of glass in which I can see my own reflection, their eyes are alert and wary. Nearby are models of bats and birds, each of which have been carefully labelled. Just like the rock art of prehistoric hunter-gatherers, the museum's displays replicate each animals' appearance, while suggesting something of its behaviour. These scenes are meant to inform a viewer but also to tell a story, combining science with jungle lore.

One of the galleries contains an assortment of snakes, including models of a rock python, Indian cobra, and a green vine snake. Lizards and other reptiles are represented too, basking in the artificial glow of electric bulbs. A young family of tourists, with two wide-eyed children, stand staring at these creatures, as if hypnotized by their gaze.

Another room of the museum houses a display of tribal culture with photographs, paintings and artifacts. This too reminds me of the scenes of human activity painted on the walls of the rock shelters—lines of barefoot dancers, arms linked, celebrating a festival, or simple tools and implements fashioned out of wood and stone. The signage in this exhibit is culturally sensitive and presents a positive image of the Gond and Korku communities who inhabited the Satpura Range long before others settled here. Unlike Forsyth's book, there are no references to 'wild tribes', 'primitive' beliefs and practices, or an indifference to 'modern civilization'. Yet, in the same way that the rock art juxtaposes images of early human society with pictures of animal herds, the enduring story, handed down through generations, is a struggle for survival in wild places and the many ways in which our species has always been connected, both historically and biologically, to other forms of life.

~

My visit to Pachmarhi coincides with the Mahashivaratri festival, an annual celebration of Shiva's omnipotent powers. Also known as Mahadeo, the supreme deity, Shiva assumes the form of a divine ascetic and retreats into the mountains where he sits in meditation, dressed in the skins of animals, with matted dreadlocks and a cobra coiled around his neck. A natural cave below the summit of one of the highest peaks of the Satpura Range, roughly 10 kilometres outside Pachmari, is the site of the main Mahadeo temple. The surrounding hills are full of smaller shrines, often located in caves or under the shade of tilted rocks, where Hindu mendicants take shelter.

During Mahashivaratri, Pachmarhi is flooded with pilgrims. This festival extends over nine days and nights, before the new moon appears in the month of Phalguna which marks the end of winter. One of the most popular temples in Pachmarhi is Jatashankar. This natural shrine, inside a precipitous gorge, is a short distance from the main bazaar where buses unload thousands of devotees during Mahashivaratri. The open plateau becomes a colourful fairground full of food stalls, tea shops, and vendors selling everything from vermilion powder and sacred brooms to bamboo flutes. Lines of temporary shops extend along either side of the road leading to the Jatashankar shrine.

As I walk this route, on the third day of the festival, I can feel the energy and excitement building. The majority of shops are selling an assortment of herbal remedies and natural cures. Most of these stalls advertise themselves as Ayurvedic dispensaries and their banners display photographs of saintly-looking herbalists dressed in ascetic robes. Knowledge of the medicinal properties of wild plants is often associated with mendicants who retreat into the mountains and forests. Living in the jungle they have access to the pharmacopeia of nature—roots, leaves, flowers, seeds, resins, and bark. The connection between medicinal plants and Shiva—sometimes called Vaidyanath, the divine pharmacist—is one of the underlying themes of the festival in Pachmarhi.

Ayurvedic medicine has been practised in India for millennia. This ancient healing tradition prescribes an array of botanical therapies. Ayurveda has proven its effectiveness with many ailments and is a popular alternative to allopathic medicine though Western science has not always endorsed its efficacy. While a few well-regulated Ayurvedic drug manufacturers maintain high standards of pharmacology, many herbal medicines in the market are neither tested nor approved by recognized authorities. In some cases, particularly when it comes to sidewalk vendors and amateur healers who set up stalls at festivals like this one, the drugs they sell are often spurious and possibly even toxic.

Having already been briefed on my trek, regarding the medicinal plants of the Pachmarhi Hills, I am now able to see how these curative flora are processed, packaged, and marketed. Each vendor has an elaborate display of pills and potions, balms and powders, as well as raw materials that are sold to pilgrims suffering from various maladies. At one shop, I overhear a conversation in which the herbalist is explaining to a group of young men how one bottle of medicine will make them gain weight, while another can help them lose a few kilos. Further on, a bearded pharmacist dressed in saffron is prescribing a decoction of wild honey to improve his patient's eyesight. Across the way sits an elderly woman, whose hair is matted into dreadlocks. She is selling an assortment of plastic bags full of dried herbs alongside bottles of a dark, viscous tonic that looks like used motor oil.

The proprietor of another stall nearby is a middle-aged man with thick glasses and a yellow tilak on his forehead. The banner in front of his shop identifies it as an 'Adivasi Jadi Booti Bhandar'—a tribal herbalist. Just as mendicants who live in the forest are credited with an understanding of wild remedies, so are communities of forest dwellers, who possess a rich store of indigenous knowledge about plants and trees. Among other things, this man promises cures for high blood pressure, diabetes, and sexual impotence, as well as skin problems and flatulence. He shows me bottles of tablets and capsules, of different potencies, to treat each of these complaints. His display includes several large bulbs labelled as 'wild onions', though they look suspiciously like a garden variety of spider lilies.

Originally, the Jatashankar shrine was only accessible from the valley below because the steep cavern is choked with boulders. The spring that emerges from beneath these huge rocks is the source of the Jambudvip stream we visited earlier. Several small grottoes with sacred pools lie within the cave complex. Steep staircases have been built into the rocks, allowing pilgrims to enter this gorge from above.

Removing my shoes at the upper threshold of the shrine, I make my way down a series of slippery concrete steps, descending about a hundred metres until I come to a small platform decorated with tridents. From here the steps branch off in several directions. Two of the caves contain stalagmites that are worshipped as lingams. Women in saris are standing knee-deep in a murky pool at the mouth of the cave, preparing to submerge themselves in the water. As with most pilgrimage sites, a variety of natural phenomena have been assigned mythical significance. The name Jatashankar refers to the tangled locks of Shiva's hair, which are knotted and braided like patterns in the eroded rocks. Some of the overhanging ledges remind pilgrims of Vasuki, the many-headed cobra that spreads its hood to provide shade for the meditating Mahadeo.

Lower down, where the forest is just visible beyond the mouth of the gorge, lies a narrow cave that runs laterally along the base of a cliff. It is dark and full of shadows, well beyond the reach of any daylight. Inside the low cleft, I can see a man seated by a dim electric bulb connected to a wire that snakes its way back up to the top of the staircase. Stooping, I am able to make out a line of small stalagmites where water has dripped from the ceiling. It looks like a crenellated spine with a protruding snout and a long, ridged tail. Incense is burning and fragrant smoke spirals up through the electric aura. Near the entrance to the cave is a steel donation box, painted green. After two devotees crawl out from this claustrophobic space, I ask the man what the stalagmites represent.

'A muggermuch,' he replies, as if it's obvious, and in the faint glimmer of the low wattage bulb I am able to see that the shapes in the rocks look vaguely like a crocodile.

Climbing back up the staircase, I retrieve my shoes and sit down under a grove of trees that grow along the rim of the gorge. While I am knotting my laces, the shell of a seedpod drops from above and lands on the rock beside me. Looking up, I see a movement amidst the foliage. Silhouetted against the sky, it is difficult to make out what animal it is, but I soon recognize an Indian giant squirrel, almost a metre long, including its bushy tail. This arboreal rodent, the largest squirrel on earth, is feeding on a vine that grows in amongst the branches of the tree. After I get up and move to one side, I can see its red and black features peering down at me as the squirrel gnaws a seedpod held in both forepaws. Its dark, attentive eyes study the queue of pilgrims descending the stairs, apparently undisturbed by their presence and purpose in this gorge.

The squirrel's awareness of the world it inhabits is focused mostly on the food it eats—the nuts, fruit, flowers, and bark of the trees in which it lives and where it builds its nest and breeds. It does not know the common or Latin names of botanical species on which it feeds, their curative properties, or the myths and stories related to these plants. Instead, it forages in the leafy canopy with a basic, instinctual understanding of the differences and similarities that exist in nature—the smells, tastes, and textures that signal what is edible and what is not. However, despite its ignorance of pharmacology, the squirrel knows many things that you and I will never comprehend.

4

ABOVE THE SNOW LINE

For the past three hours we have been scanning the high cliffs with our binoculars and spotting scopes, searching for any hint of life amidst a seemingly barren expanse of rock and ice. The stark landscape, scarified by erosion, reminds me of those 'magic eye' puzzles, an optical illusion of repeated shapes and patterns containing a hidden image. Every few minutes, I lower my binoculars and let my eyes adjust to the contours of the mountains without magnification. Staring through lenses brings everything closer but also leaves me strangely disoriented. From time to time, I catch sight of an unusual shadow or a lifelike blur amongst the stones but when I try to locate the object again, with my naked eye, it is lost. Meanwhile, my imagination keeps conjuring up snow leopards crouched in the lee of boulders, or watching me from remote vantage points, only the tops of their heads and ears protruding from behind a scab of snow.

At roughly 4,000 metres above sea level, the small village of Ulley, in Ladakh, is surrounded by prime snow-leopard habitat. Situated north of the Indus, in the trans-Himalayan region, Ulley is one of the best places to see the highest-roaming predator on earth, *Panthera uncia*, known as shaan in Ladakhi. The Snow Leopard Lodge at Ulley, where I am staying, caters to wildlife enthusiasts who come here in winter to try and get a glimpse of this rare cat.

During a week's visit, at the beginning of March, the temperature never climbs above freezing, even in bright sunlight. This high-altitude desert seems bereft of life and the thin air leaves me short of breath. The inaccessibility and harshness of the snow leopard's domain is part of its allure. Peter Matthiessen contributed to this mystique through his book, *The Snow Leopard*, which chronicles a trek he took in Nepal with the field zoologist George Schaller, who was studying bharal, one of the cat's primary prey. The fact that they never saw a snow leopard during the weeks spent in Dolpo is part of the moral of Matthiessen's story. As a student of Zen Buddhism, he teases our minds with the invisible presence of this elusive creature, suggesting that not seeing something can be as meaningful as a sighting.

However, after several days go by without any sign of 'the grey ghost of the Himalaya', I find little consolation in that message. Though I try to be philosophical about this search, I cannot help but feel a certain disappointment, especially since this trip to Ladakh began on an optimistic note. The day I flew in, we got news that a pair of snow leopards had been located near Mangyu, a village to the south of the Indus, about an hour's drive from Ulley. Spotters had heard the mating call of the shaan the night before, and had seen them consorting on the cliffs directly above Mangyu. My hosts assured me that when a pair settles down to mate, they usually remain in the vicinity for four or five days, copulating every few hours, and allowing themselves to be observed. The chances were good that we might get a clear view of their breeding behaviour.

After a compulsory forty-eight hours of acclimatization in Leh, I had set off for Mangyu and arrived at the village by ten in the morning. Two spotters with Zeiss scopes were already positioned on a ridge above the village, keeping an eye on the crags where the snow leopards had been seen. A young Russian photographer, equipped with a very long telephoto lens, was also there. He showed us video clips on his camera of the two leopards engaged in some foreplay before the male mounted the female.

But the cliffs were now deserted and the pair had vanished. Like eager voyeurs we peered through the eyepieces of the spotting scopes, keyholes of light that picked out the rocky ledges on which the leopards had appeared the day before. While the pair had been about 200 metres away when observed, close enough for the camera lens to fill the frame with their lithe and agile forms, the spotters were now scanning the farther slopes that funnelled out of the valley at distances of 800 metres to a kilometre. The scale of the landscape was overwhelming and even through my binoculars the distant ridges seemed too far away for me to see anything at all.

Half an hour after our arrival, a bearded vulture, or lammergeier, swept the sky with its two-metre wingspan. The bird's profile was silhouetted against a snowfield while its shadow followed on the moraine a hundred metres below. Only a flying creature can move through this rugged topography with ease and the raptor's sharp eyes could probably pick out the snow leopards, wherever they were hiding. Thirty minutes later, a male ibex appeared atop a crag to the west, a miniscule shape but easily recognizable with his two long horns punctuating the sky like a pair of inverted commas. Over the next hour, we watched him move down into the valley.

To the right of the ibex, about half a kilometre across the cliffs, was a narrow cleft in the rockface with a zigzag path leading up to its mouth. When I asked the spotters the purpose of the path, they explained that a cave lay inside the gorge where monks retreat for meditation. A small gompa at Mangyu is linked to Alchi, one of the oldest monasteries in Ladakh, which is about 20 kilometres away, along the Indus. The austere terrain seems to inspire acts of self-abnegation.

Buddhist mythology from Tibet contains a story about the great poet and saint, Milarepa, who retires alone into the high snow-bound mountains and survives for months by turning himself into a snow leopard. Eventually, when his devotees assume that he has died, Milarepa reveals himself in feline form, perched atop a high rock. Thinking the leopard has eaten their spiritual master, the devotees follow him to a cave, where they find that the predator has turned back into the poet, singing his songs in blissful solitude.

Above Mangyu, the higher summits have a dusting of snow but the lower slopes are brown, marked by the mangled shapes of stratified rocks that bear witness to the tectonic collisions that formed the Himalaya. Millions of years of geological history lie exposed, and I imagine that this is what the earth must have looked like before the simplest forms of life evolved. Yet, these mountains were once the floor of the Tethys Sea, teeming with aquatic creatures like molluscs that now lie fossilized in the rocks.

The scarcity of life is unnerving and when something does appear, it startles me. One day, after searching for animals all morning, suddenly a flock of red-billed choughs took to the air like a cloud of flying cinders. Their black wings swarmed across the sky, a brief, transient reminder that this high country harbours living things whether they are seen or unseen. At another point, while squinting into my binoculars, scanning a broad slope of scree littered with boulders, I spotted the distinct outline of an ibex. But instead of a live creature, it was a petroglyph etched on the coppery surface of a rock centuries ago. Stone age hunters left behind thousands of these images throughout the Indus and Nubra valleys, testimony to the wildlife that thrived here after the last ice age ended.

Ladakh has a way of playing tricks on your eyes and mind. During earlier visits, I have been struck by the hidden colours in the soil and rocks. At first, the mountains seem monochromatic, bald ridges creased with shadows and daubed white where the harsh sun fails to melt the snow. Everything seems two-toned, from the black and white Eurasian magpies that scavenge near a village, to the ice-rimmed streams that trickle between margins of frost-bitten grass. But as my vision becomes accustomed to a nuanced palette, mineral hues begin to appear on the slopes. What seemed a uniform brown is now a range of pigments that change with the arc of the sun. Rocks turn from drab, shapeless features into richly textured earthen tints, shot through with reds and purples. The magpie's dark feathers are no longer black but an iridescent, midnight blue and green. A large boulder, shaped like a two-humped Bactrian camel, is suddenly full of complex patterns of lichens that have turned bright orange and yellow, as psychedelic as coral under the sea.

A sharply angled peak casts its shadow on the opposite slope like a giant sundial. Though wild goats and sheep know nothing of hours and minutes, their instincts tell them when to migrate and when to seek shelter and sleep. They understand the seasons but unlike human beings they do not calibrate time. Instead, they recognize the changes through shifts in light or temperature and other signals in the atmosphere, a scent on the breeze as well as the secretions of glands in their bodies. As the morning sun warms the air, lammergeiers sense the thermals rising beneath their wings, riffling their feathers. And in early spring, the snow leopards feel an urge to find a mate, abandoning their solitude and emitting plaintive cries of desire, between a yowl and a roar.

One of the lessons that Ladakh teaches us is patience. Just as we acclimatize to the elevation and reduced levels of oxygen in the air, we must adjust to the rhythm and pace of this high region. Time becomes stratified like the rocks. It also flows slowly through the frozen veins of glaciers and melts in streams and rivulets that seep and trickle into the Indus, which slides westward between the high ranges, an inexorable current, older than the mountains themselves. At this time of year, the river is a bright turquoise, unlike the muddy torrent of meltwater that flows here in summer. Scanning the ice-covered margins, we search without success for Eurasian otters that live in the Indus.

Another unusual myth from Ladakh and neighbouring Baltistan suggests that snow leopards and otters mate with each other. Leopards are said to be the female of the species while the otter is the male. When a snow leopard is ready to breed, she comes down to the riverbank on a full moon night and calls to her mate. The otter emerges from the water and copulates with her. The leopard then goes back up into the high mountains during gestation but returns to the river to give birth. Those of her offspring that are male enter the flowing water and remain there while the female cubs accompany their mother back to the upper regions of snow and ice.

This is one of several folk tales compiled by the Snow Leopard Conservancy, a non-profit organization founded in 2000 by zoologist Rodney Jackson and based out of California, with branches in several different countries. Preserving these stories is part of a larger effort to protect the snow leopard and create public awareness about its endangered status. The Snow Leopard Conservancy's India chapter was founded in 2003 by Rinchen Wangchuk, a Ladakhi mountaineer and naturalist. They work with remote communities in Ladakh and Spiti to encourage wildlife tourism as a means of promoting conservation.

Folklore and mythology in Ladakh contain many stories of fantastic beasts like dragons and wind horses. The Drukpa sect of Buddhism, from which the Rinpoche of Hemis monastery traces his lineage, goes back to its founding teacher, Tsangpa Gyare, who went on a mission to establish a monastery in Western Tibet. He and his disciples were blessed with a vision of nine dragons emerging from the earth. As these auspicious creatures ascended into the sky a blizzard of flower petals rained down from heaven. Druk means dragon and the sect is prevalent in both Ladakh and Bhutan, which is known as Drukyul—land of the thunder dragons.

Our quest for the snow leopard is secular rather than spiritual but it also reveals mysterious and marvellous creatures, though nothing as grand or grotesque as a dragon. We come upon golden eagles and Himalayan vultures, ibex and urial, a wild sheep. There are wolves too and red foxes, as well as timid mouse hares or pika that hide within the scree. Though the Western Himalaya contain much less biodiversity than the mountains to the east, an assortment of birds are found here—white wagtails, black redstarts, and Alpine accentors. Large coveys of chukar partridges forage about the lodge in Ulley. From my window, I watch the plump grey birds, with their red beaks and barred wings, try to negotiate a frozen stream, waddling up to the slick surface before losing their footing and sliding on the ice in a comical, slapstick routine. The smarter ones simply fly across.

In folklore and mythology, chukar are associated with Chandra, the lunar deity and by some accounts they feed on moonbeams. These birds are said to pine away with longing and sadness on nights when the moon isn't visible. Chukar also happen to be the national bird of Pakistan, which lies no more than 40 kilometres downstream from Leh, along the Indus. On several occasions, when we came in sight of the river, I was jokingly told, 'If you want to get to Pakistan, just jump in the Indus.' Tensions between India and its neighbours have led to a military build-up in the Western Himalaya and Eastern Karakoram. Tens of thousands of soldiers are stationed at altitudes above 5,000 metres. Border roads, bunkers, trenches, artillery, and all of the attendant hardware encroach on one of the wildest regions of the globe, causing severe environmental destruction.

Ironically, many of the military units facing off against each other along disputed borders have adopted mountain mammals as part of their insignia. India's Ladakh Scouts have an ibex as their emblem, while the snow leopard has been appropriated by Chinese high-altitude commandos. The markhor, a large species of wild goat found in the Himalaya and Hindu Kush, is the national animal of Pakistan, while wolves figure in a variety of military iconography. Of course, the animals themselves have no respect for political boundaries, crossing back and forth with impunity.

~

On my second day at Ulley, a pack of four wolves show up, appearing on the cliffs to the west of the village, half a kilometre away. Even from a distance, it is apparent that they are healthy predators, perfectly adapted to the cold climate with shaggy winter coats. As they prowl the skyline, their long-legged shapes have a restless, vigilant demeanour.

In no hurry to disappear and far enough from the village to feel no fear, they linger on the rocks, peering down at us with canine curiosity. Their fur is pale shades of grey and brown, with white patches on their chests and between their legs. The colouring provides camouflage but also gives them a spectral quality, as if they were ghostly apparitions from the past. Wolves have a way of eliciting ancient, ancestral fears in us, mythical predators that haunt our dreams with wonder and dread. Migrant, pastoral cultures have always demonized wolves. The Rig Veda contains a hymn to Pusan, a solar deity who rides in a chariot drawn by goats and 'presides over roads and journeys'. In one of the verses, a traveller cries out for protection from 'the evil, vicious wolf that threatens us, Pusan, chase him away from our path'. Elsewhere, the wolf is depicted as having an insatiable appetite, capable of devouring a hundred rams.

Yesterday, the wolves killed a young yak near Ulley, part of a small herd that belongs to Tsewang Norboo, owner of the lodge where I am staying. His wife had let the animals out to graze in the morning and when they returned in the afternoon, the calf was missing. The pack had chased it down the hill and across the valley. What's left of the kill can be seen, scraps of black hide and a few bones gnawed white, on which three magpies have settled, picking over the remains. The wolves have finished feeding and are moving off to another valley in search of their next meal.

Angchuk, my driver, tells me that the Ladakhi name for wolves is shanku. Though they prey on yaks, as well as sheep and goats, shanku do not threaten human beings. 'More dangerous than the wolves are the khipshank,' Angchuk explains, 'a cross between a wolf and feral dogs.' These hybrids are said to be responsible for the deaths of women and children, though it is hard to separate facts from hearsay. Nevertheless, the problem of dogs mating with wolves and producing mixed-breed pups has been documented by Salvador Lyngdoh of the Wildlife Institute of India. Aside from the genetic consequences of crossbreeding, feral dogs have become a significant problem in Ladakh, where they feed off food waste from military bases. Mostly thick-coated sheepdogs related to Tibetan mastiffs, they are large animals and can be aggressive. Several instances of dog packs attacking human beings have also been recorded. They chase down wildlife too, including urial and ibex, and there are videos of feral dogs hounding Himalayan brown bears, which also feed at military garbage dumps.

An intriguing parallel to contemporary accounts of interbreeding between dogs and wolves can be found in genetic studies conducted on Tibetan mastiffs. Researchers in China have shown that these Himalayan dogs are especially suited to surviving at high altitudes because their ancestors crossbred with high-ranging wolves approximately 20,000 years ago. Similar studies on human populations have also revealed genetic traits amongst people in Tibet that allow their bodies to function with less oxygen. Ancestral liaisons between *Homo sapiens* and a now-extinct species of early hominids known as Denisovans appear to be the source of this adaptation.

Salvador Lyngdoh has been studying wolves in the Himalaya for the past decade, using radio collars to track them. He has discovered that they roam over a territory as large as 2,000 square kilometres, covering an average of 20 kilometres per day. Wolves that inhabit the Himalaya and trans-Himalayan region are often called Tibetan wolves and classified as *Canis lupus chanco*, a subspecies of the grey wolf, native to Europe and the Arctic. However, their taxonomy is the subject of an ongoing debate. Some zoologists, including Lyngdoh, believe that Himalayan wolves are a separate species, *Canis himalayensis.* Genetic testing suggests that they have an older lineage and split from a canid progenitor more than 100,000 years before grey wolves. Whatever their ancestry, Himalayan shanku are noticeably different from Indian wolves (*Canis lupus pallipes*) found on the plains, which are smaller and have shorter coats. Seriously endangered because of the pressures of human settlement and poaching, Indian wolves number less than 3,000. Himalayan wolves also face some of the same threats though they have considerable space to roam in the high mountains and are found across Tibet and parts of Central Asia. Lyngdoh estimates that there are only 350 wolves in the Indian Himalaya.

Traditionally, shepherds in Ladakh have treated wolves as a threat and caught them in traps known as shangdong. I was shown one of these that is no longer used, essentially a deep pit encircled by a waist-high wall of rocks. The carcass of a dead goat or sheep is lowered into the pit as bait. The wolves jump in but can't climb out and are stoned to death. Conservationists have made efforts to discourage the use of shangdongs by constructing chortens next to the pits as a symbol of compassion. They have also introduced insurance schemes that reimburse shepherds for livestock killed by wolves.

When I ask Norboo how he feels about the loss of his yak, he responds:

'Of course, one feels sadness and regret, but the wolves and snow leopards must eat to survive.'

In recent years, Norboo has adjusted to a livelihood that depends upon wildlife tourism rather than animal husbandry. His grandfather and father were shepherds and he grew up herding flocks of goats and sheep in this valley, taking them up to high pastures in summer. Now fifty-two years old, he makes a reasonably good living leasing out his property to the Snow Leopard Lodge, promoted and managed by Hashim Tyabji and his partners. In addition to the lease, Norboo is paid to serve as chief spotter and tracker in Ulley. Several villagers are employed as staff at the lodge or as drivers. Norboo and the others still plant their fields with barley in the spring and collect milk from their animals, but the winter months are now a busier, more productive time of year.

Sitting on floor cushions in Norboo's home, I can see that he and his family live a relatively comfortable life. They have electricity for light and heating as well as a metal bukhari fuelled by yak dung that warms the room. A television attached to a dish-antennae provides entertainment, mostly the Ladakhi channel of Doordarshan broadcasting from Leh. Norboo's wife serves me a glass of chang, barley beer, which has a fresh, sour flavour. She adds a couple spoons of tsampa, parched barley flour, as Norboo recalls his childhood.

'I saw my first snow leopard when I was eight or nine years old,' he tells me. 'I didn't know what it was but it attacked the flock of goats I was tending and made off with one of them. In those days people considered shaan a menace to be killed or poisoned but now we understand their value both as a rare animal and a source of income.'

He explains how the Snow Leopard Conservancy holds seminars and meetings with villagers to encourage conservation and income generation activities related to wildlife.

'My grandfather lived until the age of eighty-seven. He used to hunt animals with a muzzle loader, particularly in winter when the ibex and urial moved down to lower altitudes because of the snow. With that kind of gun, you only got one chance because it took fifteen minutes to reload and by then all the animals had run away.'

Hunting is now banned in Ladakh and Norboo says there is hardly any poaching. Altogether, he estimates that fifteen different snow leopards pass through the valley around Ulley, covering a huge territory that intersects with other predators.

'My grandfather used to tell me that in the old days the raja in Leh would send hunters to Pangu (a narrow valley 3 kilometres below Ulley). They were the best marksmen, armed with muskets. The hunters positioned themselves on either side of the valley, then drummers and musicians would start playing and drive the ibex ahead of them. When the hunters fired, the animals ran back and forth, from one side of the valley to the other. In this way, fifteen or more ibex were killed for the Losar feast.'

Earlier in the day, Norboo had pointed out a ruined watchtower on the spur of a ridge above Ulley, where the rajas of the Namgyal dynasty used to maintain an observation post to keep watch on the villagers and make sure the feudal rulers got their share of the crops and other revenue.

The current government provides roads and schools, as well as assistance in planting apricot orchards and stands of willow trees that are used as wattle for constructing the roofs of houses. Ulley appears to be reasonably prosperous with good-sized houses surrounded by a terraced patchwork of fields. A line of prayer wheels and chortens occupies the centre of the settlement next to a frozen stream and a single juniper tree. Stacks of yak dung are piled up as fuel, along with some wood and kindling. Skulls and horns of ibex and urial decorate the stone walls and mudbrick dwellings. These desiccated relics are the remains of animals that died of natural causes or were killed by predators. They are a reminder that mortality is an inevitable part of the cycle of life, especially here in the mountains.

Several yaks with thick, long hair and lethal-looking horns, wander about the courtyard between Norboo's house and the lodge. He also owns a couple of dzos, which are a cross between yaks and cows. Most of them are black but the largest is a steel grey colour, with a white muzzle. He is docile except with the younger animals, driving them away from the feeding trough. A couple of house cats patrol the premises and a friendly dog—left here by a foreigner who was forced to abandon her because of the Covid pandemic, Norboo explains. These tame creatures add to a feeling of rustic domesticity.

About 500 metres above Norboo's house lies the highest home in Ulley, where an elderly couple live with their sheep and goats. The corral in which their animals are kept has a sturdy wire-mesh cover so that snow leopards cannot break in and attack the animals. Earlier, if a leopard entered the corral, it would often kill all of the sheep and goats inside. The Snow Leopard Conservancy promotes these caged corrals to guard against this threat. To one side of the house is a small shrine that has an unprepossessing exterior and looks like a storehouse but inside the walls are covered with murals. Bright colours in the paintings offer a vivid contrast to the stark winter landscape outside.

A couple of wildlife films made in Ulley have featured Norboo and his family, one for BBC Planet Earth, *On Snow Leopard Mountain*, directed by Justin Anderson, and another titled, *Gyamo: Queen of the Mountains,* made by Mike and

Gautam Pandey. During evenings at the lodge, Kiran, who is the tour leader for a group of seven wildlife enthusiasts, shows these and other films projected from a laptop onto the wall of the common room. Seeing Norboo on the screen and the familiar landscape around Ulley, the village seems less isolated and more a part of the contemporary, technological world.

The tour group consists of five clients from Mumbai and two from Chennai, a congenial mix of individuals. All of them are regular travellers and over dinner they compare notes on excursions to places like Antarctica, the Galapagos, Papua New Guinea, and Kenya. Wildlife tourism has become a popular pastime, particularly for wealthy travellers, and the lodge at Ulley is expensive and exclusive. But searching for snow leopards is not a luxurious holiday. Though our accommodation provides a remarkable level of comfort, and the food is excellent, the weather is cold and changeable. It snows lightly several times during my visit and outside temperatures remain below zero. While the rooms have electric heaters there is no running water in the bathrooms because the pipes freeze. Hot water for bathing and cold water for flushing toilets is delivered in buckets. The altitude at Ulley takes some getting used to and visitors experience insomnia, headaches, and a loss of appetite. Nevertheless, the possibility of seeing a snow leopard makes up for these discomforts.

Locating snow leopards requires technology and manpower. The lodge employs several spotters in addition to Norboo. Phuntsok is a tough, laconic man in his fifties whose eyes never seem to stop searching the ridges around us. Marup is a few years younger, with a calm, more easy-going manner. Both men speak only Ladakhi and a few words of Hindi, so we communicate mostly through gestures. Every morning, these spotters are up at daybreak, outfitted with heavy winter gear to protect them against the cold. When clients are visiting the lodge, they work throughout the day, putting away their spotting scopes only after sundown. In addition to this, camera traps have been positioned at different points around us to monitor the movement of snow leopards. Phuntsok treks up to the pass above Ulley and checks the trap before descending the other side of the ridge to try and locate pugmarks. When we meet up with him, he reports that a mother and cub have crossed over and he has found fresh scat and pugmarks in the valley. Later, after another sortie on foot, he arrives with a pair of urial horns, retrieved from an old kill.

Each day, after an hour or two of glassing the surrounding ridges at Ulley, we drive to neighbouring valleys hoping to cross paths with snow leopards and other wildlife. One of the largest villages nearby is Hemis-shukpachan, situated about 15 kilometres west of Ulley. The name of this settlement refers to a stand of juniper trees, called shukpa in Ladakhi, that grows on a low hill overlooking the valley. Junipers are the only evergreens that survive at this altitude. They grow as tall as 4 or 5 metres but are weather-beaten, haggard trees with contorted limbs and dusty foliage. Several chortens have been built in this sacred grove and a small gompa stands nearby. Juniper branches are burnt as incense—a rite of purification performed every morning in homes and monasteries.

Trees are rare in Ladakh though several species of willows and poplars grow here, usually on the banks of streams and rivers. Hardier and more plentiful are the sea buckthorn bushes with prickly dry branches and wild musk roses that bloom in late spring but are now like coils of barbed wire, with a few dry hips clinging to brittle stems. It's hard to imagine how the ibex and urial find anything to eat at this time of year for the grass is sparse and the only other foliage is piles of dead leaves on the ground beneath the bare branches of willows.

At Hemis-shukpachan, a large Buddha statue sits on a hill at the centre of the village. The idol's skin is painted gold while the garments and jewellery are bright enamel colours that contrast with the tawny landscape. About 5 metres tall, it has been built on the remains of an old monastery that has crumbled into dust, only one or two walls remaining. We climb to the foot of the statue and set up our scopes to scan the opposite ridges, where a scattered herd of urial are foraging. The Buddha's unblinking eyes seem to project his gaze in the same direction, as if he too is searching for wildlife.

The next morning, when we set out soon after dawn, two urial rams cross the road in front of our vehicle and clamber up the slope, pausing about 20 metres above us. One of them tries to hide behind a boulder but his headgear protrudes above the rock, two thick horns curling back and tapering to points. His one eye watches me with nervous intensity before the two animals race out of sight up the vertical terrain.

Later, near an apricot orchard that has shed its leaves, we come upon a herd of more than forty urial, or shapo, as they are locally known, at the outskirts of a village. As I get out of the car to take a photograph, they panic and scatter. Most of them cross a frozen stream and disperse on the slope across from us about a hundred metres away. Many are ewes, with a few younger animals in tow, escorted by four large rams. During earlier visits to Ladakh, in summer, I have often seen urial but this is the first time I have been able to observe large males, most of whom retreat to the higher ranges as soon as the snow melts. Impressive animals, they stand over a metre at the shoulder. Their tan pelage is accented with dark brown patches on the chest and hind legs. Some of their faces are darker than others. In the confusion of their flight, one of the lambs has been separated from its mother and lets out a helpless, bleating cry that is answered by a maternal 'baa…baah' similar to the call of domesticated sheep.

Ibex, known as skin in Ladakhi, remain aloof and stand sentinel atop distant ridgelines, keeping watch on either side. My last morning in Ulley, however, we encounter a herd of six males ambling up the side of the hill, 50 metres away, seemingly indifferent to our presence. Most of them are 'saddlebacks' with light brown patches extending from their shoulders to their rumps, as if someone has spread a blanket on their backs. Their tails are dark brown, almost black and the rest of the thick fur is a rich chestnut brown. All of them have dark beards protruding beneath their chins. Somewhat larger and heavier than the urial, they are equally agile on the rocks, with hooves that seem to find purchase on the smoothest, most precipitous surfaces. All the males have massive horns that sweep back from their foreheads like blunt scimitars with knobbed segments that mark their age. The oldest ibex has horns almost a metre long. While these serve as weapons against rival males and predators, the horns are heavy and can slow an ibex down when pursued by a snow leopard or wolves, especially after the mating season when their strength has been sapped.

Comparing the ibex to the urial, it is obvious that one is a goat and the other a sheep, two separate families of Caprinae that split from a common ancestor roughly 4 million years ago, adapting to this harsh landscape and climate in their own distinctive manner. Later on, we come upon two female ibex feeding on fallen willow leaves at the edge of a field. They are much smaller than the males and have stubby, peg-like horns. Both females look well fed, despite the scarcity of forage on these wintry slopes.

Norboo has a small flock of sheep and goats, ten or twelve animals altogether. These are the remnants of the herds that his father and grandfather once owned. The domesticated sheep are much smaller and look quite different from the urial, half the size of the wild animals and covered in a matted fleece of dirty white wool. Their horns are hardly 15 centimetres around the curve. The tame goats too are unlike the ibex in most respects, except for their hooves and the general shape of their heads. Through selective breeding, over hundreds of years, human beings have changed the size and appearance of goats and sheep, though they still carry traces of wild Caprinae in their genes.

Leaving Ulley after six days of searching for snow leopards, I feel a sense of regret that we saw no big cats, though the trip has been a success in other ways. I do not pretend to have Peter Matthiessen's Zen perspective or George Schaller's patience. It would have been nice to have caught a glimpse of this rare predator, but that was not to be and I console myself with the memory of wolves patrolling the skyline and the red fox that haunts the edges of the village like a furtive shadow. He is seldom still, seeking out pikas amongst the rocks or an unwary chukar but more often finding kitchen scraps.

As we reach the junction of the main road to Leh, which follows the Indus, we come within range of a mobile signal and Angchuk's phone rings. One of the team that has organized my visit reports that a snow leopard was spotted earlier this morning above Mangyu. Suddenly, our plans change and instead of heading directly to Leh we cross the Indus and follow the rough track back to the village where my search began six days ago.

Spotters have set up scopes on a patch of level ground near the gompa. When we arrive, they point out a herd of ibex about 800 metres away, bunched together on a rockface as if defending themselves from an invisible threat. We are told that earlier a snow leopard had been stalking the herd and one of the spotters shows us a photograph taken on his phone through the eyepiece of the scope, a blurred but recognizable image of a furred creature with a long tail.

Straining our eyes for another two hours we wait for the snow leopard to reappear. But after a while the ibex leave the rocks and begin to disperse, lowering our hopes. The danger they had sensed seems to have departed though none of us has seen the leopard retreat. Our disappointment is tempered by the arrival of a herd of bharal, also called blue sheep, on the shoulder of a ridge 400 metres above us. Though they could be mistaken for urial at this distance, their slate grey colour and the sweptback shape of the male bharal's horns is distinctive.

After watching this herd for a quarter of an hour, we spot a lone wolf eyeing us from a ledge above Mangyu. At first, there is some debate whether it might be a dog, because only his face is visible, resting on his forepaws and surveying the scene below. But when the wolf rises we can see his long forelegs and the lanky shape of his body. A couple of dogs in the village see him too and begin to bark. He slowly moves away and disappears into the rocks. Reconciled to the fact that we aren't going to see a snow leopard, I depart for Leh.

∽

One year later, on the first of March, I am back in Ladakh again. After the required forty-eight hours acclimatization, a vehicle picks me up at my hotel and we set out by 9.30 a.m. Dorje, the driver, says that the lodge in Ulley has been packed with visitors this winter and there have been regular snow leopard sightings. In fact, earlier this morning, a mating pair were spotted near

Saspochey, about 12 kilometres short of Ulley. We are going directly there. Though Dorje sounds confident, I can't help but remember that last year I was given the same news but by the time we reached the site, the pair had vanished.

Mountains on both sides of the Indus are covered with snow, though the lower slopes are bare and brown. The temperature this morning is just below freezing. Military camps and installations line both sides of the highway. Signs warn us that this is a 'No Drone Zone' and 'Trespassers Will be Shot'. The gateway above the entrance to a Ladakh Scouts camp displays their emblem, an ibex with arching horns. Further on, a Naga Regiment proudly proclaims itself 'The Head Hunters'. Since my last visit, skirmishes between Indian and Chinese troops have occurred along the disputed frontier while border tensions with Pakistan continue to fester.

The Indus is a deep blue colour, edged with white crusts of ice. Poplars and willows growing near the river have lost their leaves; it will be another two months before they turn green again. The arid landscape unfolds in front of us like the creased and rumpled contours of a canvas tarpaulin. Though the air is frigid, the sun scorches the earth with its harsh light. As we leave the outskirts of Leh behind, I feel a familiar sense of release, escaping into the wild expanse of high mountains.

An hour and a half later, Dorje turns off the paved road onto a dirt track that leads to Saspochey. Last winter I visited this village several times but all I remember seeing here was a flock of choughs and a few scattered urial. A shallow, twisting stream, mostly frozen, flows down the eastern side of the valley, where rough slopes of rock and scree rise almost vertically to the snow-laden ridges above. The western side of the valley is broader and less steep. Terraced fields surround a settlement of roughly forty flat-roofed homes. Eroded chortens punctuate the contours of this high valley, hemmed in by scarred cliffs on either side. We are 3,712 metres above sea level.

At the upper end of the village is a line of parked vehicles. When Dorje pulls up next to these, I can see about thirty people congregated on an apron of level land nearby. An arsenal of spotting scopes and cameras with telephoto lenses are poised on tripods facing the opposite ridge. Hurrying across, I can see that everyone's attention is fixed on a rocky outcropping about 400 metres away. Sections of the slope are still in shadow but this pile of boulders is well lit by the sun. Focusing my binoculars, I try to find what everyone else is looking at, but all I can see are rocks and rubble as well as a few thorny shrubs.

After several minutes of searching unsuccessfully, I feel someone tap my shoulder. A young Ladakhi woman in a green parka suggests that I try using a spotting scope positioned nearby. Removing my glasses, I squint into the eyepiece.

Instantly, two snow leopards appear, their thick, mottled coats slightly paler than the tan rocks. As I watch, the male mounts the female who is crouched on the ground. When she turns her head aside and tries to squirm out from under him, he gently grabs her neck in his jaws and then copulates for about a minute. After she is released, the female rolls on her back as if to shake off her mate before sitting up. Watching them, I hold my breath. Remembering my disappointment last year, it seems absurdly easy now to observe this mating pair, less than five minutes after my arrival.

Unwilling to accept what I've just seen through the spotting scope, I try once again to locate the snow leopards with my binoculars. It takes a while, but eventually I find them lying together in the sun. The magnification is much less but I can see the sooty, smudged patterns on their fur and the plush girth of their luxuriant tails. From time to time, they glance in our direction, conscious that they are being watched, though safely separated by the deep valley between us. The snow leopards are obviously aware of the distant crowd of observers but they seem unbothered by our presence. Eventually, when I lower my binoculars and stare across the valley, the cats disappear, blending into the landscape. I know exactly where they are and recognize the rock formation beneath which they are resting, but I cannot see them with my naked eyes.

For the rest of the day—a full six hours—the mating pair remain in view. Every time I check, I can see them through the scope or binoculars, as well as my camera, which produces blurred images of the leopards. Most of the time they sleep, curled up in the sun. At intervals of forty-five minutes to an hour, they mate repeatedly, a total of seven times. The male initiates coitus, circling around and licking the female's head. For the most part, she is receptive, though at one point she irritably turns on him, snarling and striking the male with her forepaw. After mating, the pair arch their backs and lick their genitals before lying down to sleep again.

Amongst the crowd, I recognize Norboo and we greet each other. He tells me that yesterday, one of the spotters from Saspochey caught sight of the female on this side of the valley, above the village. During the night, they heard the pair calling back and forth. Norboo imitates the mating cry, an ardent yowl. He explains that this morning the spotters located the pair on the opposite slope.

'They will mate as often as fifteen times a day,' he says, 'until the job is finished. Three months from now, in June, the female will give birth. Usually, she has a litter of two cubs, sometimes as many as four, but not all of them survive. The weaker ones die off.'

Norboo has brought ten guests from Ulley to Saspochey. Another group has come from the lodge at Mangyu. Several independent guides and their clients have turned up too. As word spreads, more and more people arrive during the afternoon, including a brigadier and his staff from an army camp nearby. By the end of the day more than a hundred spectators have gathered on the flat. Seizing the opportunity, a couple of women from the village set up a stall selling tea, bottles of sea buckthorn juice, and apricot oil, as well as snow leopard dolls made of felt.

The woman who spoke to me earlier is named Dolkar and I learn that she works as a guide at the lodge in Ulley. After helping me take a video and photographs of the snow leopards using my iPhone, through the eyepiece of the scope, she explains that Saspochey is her village. Dolkar is one of six siblings and she studied in the local school until class eight. Now in her mid-twenties, she is a confident, articulate young person, able to speak both Hindi and some English, as well as her mother tongue, Ladakhi.

'This is my first season working at the lodge in Ulley,' she tells me. 'Before that, I went to Delhi to try and find work but I wasn't happy there and came back.'

When I ask if she used to see snow leopards as a child, Dolkar shakes her head and smiles. 'No, we would hear them calling sometimes, but only after I started working at Ulley did I actually see one. Now I am learning more about the wildlife near my home.'

Though the gawking crowd with its expensive scopes, binoculars, and cameras is disconcerting, I am as much a part of it as anyone else. Each time I look across at the pair on the opposite slope, the leopards seem remote and disconnected from our human world, as if they exist in another dimension. The calm, yet attentive expressions on their feline faces and the fluid grace of their movements sets them apart from the babble of voices and the jostling figures that surround me. Ultimately, the distance between us is reassuring, as is the fact that so many people from this region are now earning a living because of their presence, which can only help ensure the snow leopard's survival. After the sun drops behind the ridge at 5 p.m., we pack up and leave for Ulley. As darkness descends around them, the pair of snow leopards remain where they are. Norboo and others reassure me that the mating pair will stay here for several days.

However, the next morning, when we return, only one leopard can be seen. The female has disappeared during the night and the male is sleeping alone on a rocky ledge, about 50 metres below the spot where we saw him yesterday. For the first two hours, he doesn't move but eventually, he sits up and stretches, peering across at us with indifference. Though abandoned by his mate, he seems in no hurry to leave and as the crowd gathers again, the snow leopard dozes in the sun, occasionally glancing about.

Later, in the afternoon, he suddenly gets to his feet and starts climbing the hill. Yesterday, Norboo had pointed out an old ibex kill about 200 metres up the slope and the leopard heads in that direction. A magpie harasses him as he approaches the kill. Through my binoculars, I see him suddenly pick up speed and lunge forward. Until then, I hadn't noticed that a dog was feeding on the kill, gnawing on bones and frozen scraps of flesh. The snow leopard springs on the dog, which frantically scrambles out of reach and then tumbles down the steep slope, a pinwheel of brown fur. Though I expect the leopard to sit down and feed on the kill, he is not interested in the desiccated carcass, which has been lying here for more than a week, picked clean by lammergeiers and other scavengers.

Moving off, the leopard crosses a rocky snowfield, his slender, long-tailed profile silhouetted against the white background. Moments later, he disappears over the crest of the ridge. Though I expect this is the last we will see of him, Norboo and the other spotters race down the valley to another viewpoint and locate him once again. Our eager pack of photographers and tourists follow and for the rest of the afternoon, we watch the snow leopard lounging at this spot. However, his apparent indolence has a purpose. About 150 metres below him is a herd of a dozen urial, grazing in a dry ravine. The leopard has seen them but they are unaware of his presence. All afternoon, he waits for the wild sheep to come within range.

Eventually, when the herd remains where it is, he climbs above and around the ravine to a point directly across from them. For half an hour, we watch him stalk the urial but by now the sun has gone down and the temperature has dropped. The snow leopard waits as darkness falls and we are finally forced to depart. Later, the spotters tell us that his hunt was unsuccessful. Altogether, I calculate that we have watched the snow leopard for a total of fourteen hours, yesterday and today. Yet, time seems irrelevant to these patient predators that we are privileged to observe. They live and move at their own pace, animated by the ancient rhythms of their mountain habitat.

5

WHERE THE HAND OF MAN HAS NEVER SET FOOT

Sacred groves, as their name suggests, represent a localized religious tradition in which forest spirits and deities are revered and worshipped amidst their natural habitat. Trees, plants, and animals that occupy this sanctified domain are protected because they are part of a spiritual and biological ecosystem. In essence, the grove itself is a living temple, not made of bricks and marble, but of trees, herbaceous plants, ferns, and lianas. Symbolically, there is something reassuring about these scattered refugia, which harbour the possibility, if not the promise, of environmental regeneration.

The link between animism and conservation exists in many parts of the world, particularly amongst people who live close to the land. Those who depend upon nature for sustenance, shelter, and survival, obviously assign special significance to wild species and wild places. India has a large and eclectic population of indigenous communities, some of whom are still forest dwellers while the majority were resettled one or more generations ago. An ongoing connection persists between natural habitats and tribal livelihood, lore, and ethics. Most of this ecological legacy lies outside the grasp of India's cultural mainstream and is part of an oral or performative tradition. Essentially, it is an organic heritage in which human beings recognize that their bodies, emotions, and beliefs, as well as their social interactions, are closely tied to a much larger, syncretic web of life.

Both the Mahabharata and the Ramayana, as well as Brahmanical and Buddhist mythology, portray forests as inherently sacred spaces full of magical and mysterious beasts as well as therapeutic herbs, intoxicating perfumes, and luminous substances. Ayurvedic texts like the *Sushruta Samhita*, advocate an understanding of the sacred and mystical attributes of botanical species, not just their pharmacological properties. The *Arthashastra* contains references to protected forests in which animals like elephants were permitted to roam wild. Many other examples from ancient literature and art, including the Kalpavriksha, or tree of life, underscore a fundamental reverence for forests enshrined in India's collective imagination.

From the perspective of environmental activists who want to promote conservation today, this ancient eco-spiritual heritage is an attractive and persuasive argument that can be used to influence popular opinion. The ongoing existence of sacred groves throughout India offers a compelling example of human beings nurturing nature's resilience by invoking the presence of divinity. Essentially, sacred groves provide a compelling model for conservation at a local level because they are easy to explain, condoned by tradition, and offer a hopeful message for the future.

Nevertheless, it is important to recognize that superficial, romantic depictions of sacred groves can be misleading. To begin with, it is a mistake to assume that all of these sanctuaries are the same and that they contain some kind of universal, ecological truth. Each grove is unique to its specific location, biome, and cultural context. A hectare of rainforest in Kerala contains completely different species from a hectare of conifers in Himachal Pradesh. Similarly, local gods and goddesses, by definition, are endemic to their immediate environment. And the devotees who demarcate each grove, and who venerate that territory, have differing motives. One grove might be protected because medicinal herbs grow there. Another could be the site of a legendary event while a third may be considered sacred, simply because a cobra was seen here. Rituals and practices in each grove also differ and are subject to change.

Madhav Gadgil has emphasized the importance of sacred groves as repositories of biodiversity and an effective model for forest management. Both as an ecologist and as a social activist, Gadgil is an outspoken proponent of handing over responsibility for protecting and utilizing forest resources to tribal people, because of their indigenous knowledge as well as their cultural and spiritual connections to wild places. He argues that the colonial model of forest management, which persists in India today, has done more damage than good. Gadgil also believes that people who are traditional stewards of nature should be given the responsibility of protecting not just sacred groves but much larger tracts of forest land. In a recent article, he writes:

> I have witnessed sacred groves being destroyed but also being preserved, revived or even newly established in the face of the active hostility of the developmental state. An ecological crisis in the Indian subcontinent, brought about by the relentless commercial exploitation of natural resources is prompting a vibrant revival of these sacred spaces. This assertion of ancient values of reverence for nature, too often derided as

> primitive superstition, represents the most hopeful news about Indian ecology to emerge in decades.

India's forest policies, though still enshrouded by the cobwebs of colonial practice and prejudice, have gradually been amended and changed, largely through the influence of experts like Gadgil who have made concerted efforts to encourage state forest departments to empower local people. In this hard-fought campaign, sacred groves have served as an enduring example of the effectiveness of grassroots management. On occasion, they have even caught the jaded imaginations of bureaucrats and politicians.

At the same time, many of our preconceptions about the religious and historical heritage of the groves have been challenged. Eliza Kent, in her book, *Sacred Groves and Local Gods,* approaches the question from the perspective of a religious historian. Her fieldwork in Tamil Nadu reveals that some groves in that region are not sylvan relicts from the age of hunter-gatherers but instead a phenomenon that dates back only to the eighteenth century. The forest gods aren't animistic spirits but deified images of moustachioed Poligar chieftains on horseback, brandishing swords. These guardian figures emerged out of a feudal system in which villagers offered tribute to the Poligars in exchange for their protection. Kent also suggests that the groves themselves, far from being unspoiled pockets of primal wilderness, have been consistently 'disturbed'.

> In a context in which policies are being designed and implemented about how best to preserve these ecologically significant patches of forest, some of which are guided by incorrect or unconsciously normative assumptions about religion, it seems especially important to listen carefully to what the people who have protected the flora and fauna surrounding sacred groves over time have to say about them. Confounding simplistic representations of the religious beliefs and rituals surrounding sacred groves, close study demonstrates that local practices regarding sacred groves are at once more imaginative and pragmatic than previously thought.

Aside from academic debates, a growing awareness about sacred groves has led to concerns regarding their future and the many ways in which they are being subsumed within mainstream culture. Dr Erach Barucha, an eminent conservationist based in Pune, has written about his personal experiences with sacred groves, describing how they are threatened by dams, motor roads, and other infrastructure projects. He laments how the natural lore and ecological narratives associated with these sanctuaries are being lost. Sacred groves are not just a safe haven for plants and animals but also a refuge for folk tales and myths.

As he writes, 'These stories illustrate the mythical bridges that can be revitalized to save these groves—by reviving the local socio-cultural-religious sentiments that have saved the groves through many generations in the past and bring about a new appreciation.'

Barucha describes the depressing fate of several groves he has visited over a period of more than twenty-five years. One example he cites is the Adarwadi grove in the Western Ghats of Maharashtra. At one time, it had a dense evergreen canopy and was filled with hornbills and flycatchers as well as giant squirrels and flying lizards. A large strangler fig grew above a modest shrine dedicated to Kalkai Mata, a mother goddess who protected the grove. For many years, this site was accessible only on foot. Being a remote location, it was visited primarily by local people. Eventually, however, a highway was built along the ridge where the grove is situated. As traffic increased on this route, the site became a popular halt for travellers and picknickers. Inevitably, a paved access road was built, leading into the heart of the grove where a large temple was constructed. While villagers profited from the crowds that visited Adarwadi, these outsiders 'left behind wasted food, plastic bags, bottles and plates. Mounds of garbage now despoiled the sacredness of the grove'. The birds and squirrels soon left and all that remained was a conventional religious shrine, polluted by transient visitors. Though the goddess, Kalkai Mata, was reputed to become 'vengeful and dangerous if her grove was disturbed', she seemed helpless in the face of these destructive developments.

To gain a better appreciation and understanding of the various kinds of sacred groves that exist in India, as well as some of the beliefs and traditions associated with these forest shrines, I set out to visit a few of the different regions where they are found. In particular, I chose Meghalaya in the Northeast, Haryana on the outskirts of Delhi, and Kodagu in western Karnataka, hoping to see the contrasts between them but also the similarities. Of course, there are many other places where sacred groves are maintained by village communities and each are unique, though they represent a widespread and consistent spiritual and ecological tradition throughout South Asia, of preserving wild spaces and wild species from destructive practices that have denuded other forest lands.

MAWPHLANG

Twelve years ago, friends took me to see the sacred grove at Mawphlang but it was a hurried visit and I didn't fully comprehend the significance of this protected wood in the highlands of Meghalaya. Yet, it is a place that has remained fixed in my mind, ever since, and I was determined to go back and experience it again. After spending the night in a homestay nearby, I set off on a brisk January morning with my host and guide, Marchborn Lyngdoh. He and his family live in the village of Mawphlang, and are members of the dominant clan of this region in the East Khasi Hills. Thirty-eight years old, with a thoughtful, sincere manner, Marchborn is a member of the Pentecostal Church of God. He explains that roughly 70 per cent of the villagers are Christians, both Protestants and Catholics. The rest of the community are Seng Khasis who follow an ancient animistic faith.

Marchborn leads me first to a hill at the edge of the village overlooking the sacred grove. Grass-covered slopes fall away gently to the dense line of trees half a kilometre away. On the crest of the hill is a circle of rough, oblong stones standing upright, half-buried in the earth. This serves as an altar, Marchborn explains. Villagers gather here during festivals and other special occasions for prayers and sacrifice.

From the hilltop we can see a panorama of ridgelines and valleys, stretching in all directions. Patches of forest and open grassland cover the undulating contours of the landscape like an embroidered shawl. Mawphlang's sacred grove lies 1,700 metres above sea level and extends over 76.8 hectares (190 acres) with a forest canopy that appears as thick as moss. Beyond the grove lies a fertile valley where rice is cultivated. Potatoes are the other main crop in these hills. All of this territory is part of the Mawphlang Hima, or kingdom, containing twenty-three villages.

Descending towards a gate that marks the upper entrance to the grove, we meet an elderly man, accompanied by his two granddaughters, five or six years old. The old man wears a wool cap and has a red and black striped shawl draped over his shoulders. His creased features bristle with a sparse white moustache and beard. Marchborn introduces him as E. Khonghat, explaining that he is one of the Seng Khasi elders in the village. After a few awkward questions and answers, translated by Marchborn, the old man switches from Khasi to Hindi and our conversation becomes more animated and relaxed.

He tells me that he is eighty-nine years old. Most of his life has been spent here, though he once travelled to Delhi as part of a tribal delegation. This morning, he and his granddaughters have been out for a morning walk to the spring at the edge of the grove.

'The water from the spring is pure. First class! Not like the supply from these pipes,' he tells me, pointing to a galvanized iron pipeline running along the roadside. 'This water can be used for cooking and washing, but for drinking... only from the forest spring.'

Gesturing towards Marchborn with a chiding smile, he complains, 'These Christians bury their dead and pollute the earth and water. We burn our dead, completely, until there is nothing left but ash.' He gestures with his fingers to suggest a fine powder. Despite his critical remark, it is clear there is no real conflict between animists and Christians, many of whom participate in the Seng Khasi rituals.

When I ask about the sacrifices that take place on the hill above, he says: 'We believe that the rooster is the messenger of God. After killing a cock, we take out its entrails and they reveal if God is angry or not. It is very difficult to interpret the omens, which requires special knowledge. We also offer eggs as a sacrifice at the altar and read signs in their yolks.'

After taking our leave of the old man, we continue downhill. A number of uncarved monoliths, similar to those in the altar, have been positioned along the route to the sacred grove. Marchborn explains that the ritual stones that stand upright are considered male and those that lie flat are female. Scattered across the undulating fields of grass, they add a mystical dimension to the landscape.

'This sacred grove is eight hundred years old,' Marchborn tells me. 'There is a story that long ago the villagers planned to fell trees here, but a wise man lay down in front of the forest and said, "Why would you kill my mother?"' From that time onwards, the villagers have protected this wild space and follow a strict set of rules: cutting wood, collecting leaves, and killing animals in the grove is forbidden. Wild fruit, nuts, and medicinal herbs can be consumed in the forest but not taken outside. Within the precincts of the sanctuary, people must behave in a respectful, reverent manner.

Tambor Lyngdoh, a resident of Mawphlang, and author of the book, *A Collection of Knowledge on Khasi Herbal Plants, Stories & Poems,* describes the consequences of not following these rules. If anyone removes something from the forest, his or her neck gets twisted around, so that they are forced to constantly look back over one shoulder in the direction of the grove. Some of the other lore includes the story of a government official who picked up a rudraksha seed and carried it away in his pocket. Soon, the man grew sick and faced a variety of misfortunes until he finally came back to Mawphlang and replaced the seed where he'd found it. In another story, a woman went to visit her brother who had suddenly taken ill. When a snake crossed her path, she realized that it must be an omen and prayed to the serpent, until it disappeared, allowing her to proceed. Arriving at her brother's house, she questioned him, and he confessed to having cut firewood in the sacred grove. The sister then took her brother to the village elders who conducted rituals to propitiate the deities and he was eventually cured. In each of these tales, the message is clear: the grove is a wild and holy space that must be kept intact and unspoiled. All forms of life found here are protected and preserved in a natural state.

We enter the forest through a tunnel of foliage. The flagstone path is a recent addition because a large number of visitors come here and the dirt trail was being damaged. Less than 25 kilometres from Shillong, Mawphlang has been widely publicized and it is a popular tourist attraction. A village committee manages the grove, charging entry fees and providing guides, who explain the ecological and cultural significance of this site while ensuring that no disturbance or desecration occurs.

At this time of year, in mid-winter, the forest is still green, though it is much drier and not nearly as overgrown as it becomes during the monsoon. Thirty-five kilometres away lies Mawsynram, the wettest place on earth, receiving more than 11 metres of annual rainfall. In another month or so, the monsoon will begin and then continue until November. As soon as the rains start, the grove bursts forth with ferns, orchids, and fungi, while the moss turns vibrant shades of green. Heavy mist transforms the wooded hills into cloud forests, full of leeches, snakes, and frogs. In winter, however, the grove is imbued with a peaceable, dormant stillness. Only a few birdcalls break the silence and instead of the monsoon mist, soft morning sunlight seeps through the strata of leaves, creating an ethereal aura.

'In Mawphlang, we are blessed with nature's presence,' Marchborn declares.

He then draws my attention to a variety of indigenous trees. *Rhododendron arboreum* grow here, known in the Khasi language as dieng tiewsaw. Common throughout most of the Himalaya, they have blood red blossoms that bloom in early spring. One of the tallest trees is a rudraksha, its buttressed trunk rising like a massive column through the lower canopy of leaves and spreading a broad crown high overhead. On the ground we find its seeds, which are ornately grooved and often used as prayer beads. Another tall tree that Marchborn identifies is a Khasi pine. Needles of sunlight pass through its branches, casting intricate patterns on the dry leaf-litter at our feet. Marchborn tells me that his grandmother used to prescribe the resinous buds of this conifer, which she made him chew, whenever he had a cough or sore throat. Next to the pine is a cinnamon tree, its distinctive leaves marked by parallel veins. Crushing a dry leaf, I can smell the sweet, spicy fragrance. Meanwhile, Marchborn collects a few hulled kernels from the ground beneath another tree and tells me these are hazelnuts. Growing nearby is a Himalayan yew, the bark of which is processed into drugs that are used to treat cancer. Further on, we come to a fallen giant that blocks the path. *Myrica esculenta*, called sohphie in Khasi, is a species of box myrtle or bay berry. In late spring, it produces a red and purple stone fruit that has a tart sweetness.

Just beyond the fallen tree, we come upon another altar of stones covered in moss. The sides of the path are bordered by more monoliths. This is a site where sacrifices used to be performed. Only male members of the Lyngdoh clan were allowed to participate.

'A red bull was brought here,' Marchborn tells me, pointing to a cluster of stones about 15 metres from the main altar. 'This is where preparations were made for the sacrifice. Beyond this point, there was no turning back.'

The elders of Mawphlang studied the bull's entrails for auspicious signs, after which the tripe was washed and cooked without salt. The rest of the bull's flesh was distributed amongst the participants in these rituals. When I ask if these sacrifices are still performed, Marchborn shakes his head. 'Not any more. It stopped in the 1970s, maybe earlier.'

The main path through the grove takes us further on to the traditional coronation site of the Lyngdoh kings, where a royal turban was tied on their heads. Three stone benches are arranged on a natural terrace under the trees. Upholstered with dry moss, these rustic thrones look as if they haven't been used for decades. Marchborn tells me that the coronations are now held at other locations like the Durbar Hall in the village. The current king, who is in his mid-thirties, was elected in 2019.

Even as traditions change, the sanctity of this sacred grove endures. My first visit to Mawphlang left me with a powerful memory, not because of any dramatic encounters with wild species but on account of the spiritual resonance of a secluded forest where the only evidence of human activity was the placement of natural stones in irregular rings and clusters. My second visit confirms that here in this quiet yet flourishing woodland, we can discover some of the simple truths that nature teaches—the entwined roots of knowledge, the healing essence of herbs, the ethics of instinct versus intellect, shared stories and songs—those things that remind us that we as a species are an integral part of the multiplicity of life that surrounds us.

MANGAR BANI

The steel, concrete and glass skyline of Gurugram, formerly known as Gurgaon, glistens in the morning sunlight as slow streams of vehicles flow along the highway, ferrying commuters from home to work. A Metro train shoots by overhead on an elevated line, which connects a network of stations throughout the National Capital Region (NCR). In less than fifty years, what was once a dusty district town, surrounded by sugar cane fields and *Prosopis* jungles, on the outskirts of Delhi, has been transformed into a futuristic constellation of multi-storey office buildings and residential complexes. Gurugram represents the aspirations and priorities of twenty-first century India, a symbol of progress, technology, wealth, and human enterprise. The original landscape, which included vestiges of the ancient Aravalli Range, has disappeared beneath slick architecture and an abstract gridwork of urban planning.

Driving east along the highway towards Faridabad, I can see evidence of further expansion—satellite settlements under construction, marble and granite suppliers, half-hidden slums full of migrant labourers, glossy hoardings advertising new development projects, and everywhere...everywhere, the glitzy offices of property dealers that look like pop-up casinos. Nineteen kilometres beyond Gurugram, next to the village of Bandhwari, we pass a mountainous landfill of refuse that rises 37 metres above ground level, much higher than any of the eroded Aravalli summits nearby. More than 1,800 tonnes of solid waste from Gurugram and Faridabad are dumped here every day, attracting swarms of black kites. These aerial scavengers wheel above the fetid, smouldering massif-like harbingers of an environmental apocalypse.

Fifteen minutes later, we turn off the highway onto a narrow, two-lane road that passes through a scrub jungle of *Prosopis* trees. The GPS system on my mobile phone leads us to Mangar village, which lies in a shallow valley, where the road winds its way down a steep slope before passing through a prosperous settlement. Most of the residents of Mangar are Gujjar cattle herders by tradition but with skyrocketing property values and employment opportunities nearby, the village feels more like a suburb of Delhi than a rural hamlet, though most of the homes have buffaloes tethered outside. After several wrong turns, we reach the far side of Mangar where Sunil Harsana is waiting.

A conservationist and voluntary custodian of the Mangar Bani sacred grove, Sunil grew up in this village and has first-hand knowledge of its ecology and lore. Leaving my taxi parked in the shade of a neem tree, we set off on foot along an unpaved track that leads to the cave shrine of Gudariya Das Baba, patron saint of the grove. Almost immediately, Sunil points out a pair of collared scops owls peering down at us from a hollow in a tree trunk. On the other side of the track is a mixed flock of great tits and Hume's warblers, skittering through the branches of a dhak or palash tree that is just beginning to flower.

Two young men on a motorcycle pass by, going in the direction of the shrine, which lies at the head of the valley. A short distance further on, we turn off the main track and follow a dusty trail through a dry deciduous forest with very little undergrowth. Though we are still on the valley floor, I can see where the ground slopes up ahead of us.

'I prefer this walk instead of going to the temple,' Sunil tells me, 'because you see the forest as it is and there aren't any vehicles or people.'

He explains that Gudariya Das Baba was an ascetic who renounced the world, 'more than a thousand years ago', and lived in a cave, where the shrine is now situated.

Though I assume that the saint's name is derived from Gadariya, a shepherd caste, Sunil corrects me and explains that gudar is a reference to clothes. At the end of his life, the baba suddenly disappeared and all that remained were the garments he'd worn. His followers believe that he simply dissolved into nature and became one with the trees and other living things in the grove.

'Gudariya Das Baba was attuned to the forest. When a camel browsed the leaves on a tree, he complained that it was pulling at his hair,' Sunil says. 'And if someone cut a branch, he would feel the pain in his own limbs. He instructed our ancestors to protect the trees and not to remove anything from the grove.'

The Gujjar community has maintained that trust for generations, preserving roughly 274 hectares (677 acres) that extends along both sides of the valley up to the ridgeline and plateau. They do not graze their cattle in the forest or cut firewood and timber. Mangar Bani is common land, under the jurisdiction of the village panchayat. However, Sunil suggests there are ambiguities regarding its status.

'Originally, when this was part of the Punjab, before Independence, British gazetteers listed this area as uncultivatable hill tracts (gair mumkin pahar),' he says.

The valley and rocky hills surrounding Mangar were considered wasteland, though most of it has always been covered with trees. Much later, when Haryana was created in 1966, the new state forest department added to these ambiguities. Large areas of forest adjoining Delhi were 'regularized', a bureaucratic euphemism for switching their status so that they could be cleared and developed. Both legal and illegal quarries were located in the vicinity of Mangar, providing quartzite stone and gravel for the construction industry. Fortunately, in 2002, the Supreme Court of India stopped all mining in the region. At one point, as Gurugram and Faridabad began to expand, the village panchayat evidently sold part of their common land to private real estate companies, though these transactions were contested and remain mired in legal disputes. Beginning in the 1980s, the Asola Bhatti Wildlife Sanctuary was established next to Mangar Bani and what little remains of the Aravalli Range on the periphery of Delhi was deemed an 'eco-sensitive zone'.

By the time Sunil has recounted the convoluted history of these jungles, our path has begun to climb an uneven slope littered with stones. The predominant tree in the grove is dhau or dhok, the same species that grows in the forests of Kuno Palpur, where it is called kardhai. As Pradip Krishen writes, 'Dhau is the "habitat specialist" of the Aravalli hills, thriving on hot, dry slopes and rocky soil where most other trees would not survive. Parts of the Ridge in Delhi (where the Aravallis peter out) were once forested with dhau, but it has been heavily grazed. Dhau responds to lopping and grazing by growing shrubby and low, covering the ground in horizontally spreading mats. It has a hair-trigger response to rain in the dry season.'

'Ninety per cent of the trees in Mangarbani are dhau,' Sunil explains. 'They spread as clonal communities with interconnected roots.' This may explain why the invasive *Prosopis* remains largely excluded from the grove, though it has taken over most of the surrounding ridges. Sunil points out some of the other trees that are found here, including ronjh, a native acacia that is common in and around Delhi, ber and bistendu, both of which have round orange fruit, the former sweet and edible, and the latter bitter.

After a few minutes' climb, we come upon an old road paved with rough cobblestones that ascends in crumbling switchbacks up the ridge. It is obviously not used any more for the trees have closed in around it. At several places we have to duck down and scramble under their branches.

'This route probably dates back to Mughal times and must have been used by Banjaras, who carried salt and other produce to Delhi,' Sunil suggests. Banjaras are nomadic gypsy traders—their name means 'forest graziers'—whose caravans of camel carts and pack animals were once a common sight in North India. Ethnically and culturally, they share close ties with the Romany people of Europe. Mangar Bani has obviously been visited by migrant communities for centuries. Recently, Sunil has been documenting petroglyphs that he discovered in several ancient rock shelters within the valley. Though the provenance of the petroglyphs is uncertain, archaeologists have identified Mangar Bani as a significant Palaeolithic site where many stone tools have been found near cave dwellings. All of this helps underscore the significance of this sacred grove and the need to protect these forests from the degradation that has occurred in other parts of the Aravalli.

When I ask about wildlife in Mangar Bani, Sunil says that leopards, nilgai, and wild pigs are common here, along with small mammals like golden jackals, striped hyenas, Indian crested porcupines, and ratels or honey badgers. A few years ago, he participated in a wildlife survey conducted by the Wildlife Institute of India. Though hunting is taboo, some poaching occurs, mostly using snares and traps. Aside from itinerant tribal hunters that pass through the forest, some pastoralists will catch animals for meat or medicinal purposes. He tells me how certain shepherds kill jackals and boil their meat to make a broth that is fed to goats and sheep in the belief that it protects them from disease.

A large part of Sunil's conservation efforts are now directed towards young people. In 2015, he started the Mangar Eco-Club for students from the village school. They study the natural history of Mangar Bani and learn to identify birds, animals, trees, and plants. The club also engages in voluntary activities like maintaining paths and collecting litter. All of this helps sustain awareness within the Gujjar community about the importance of protecting their surrounding environment and maintaining the legacy of this sacred grove.

From the top of the ridge, we have a clear view of the valley and the nearby ridges. Looking eastward, beyond the village, Sunil points out where there used to be two or three year-round ponds formed by rainwater that drained off these hills during the monsoon. These are now dry, and villagers depend mostly on borewells. On the other side of the ridge, Gudariya Das Baba's shrine can be seen, its semi-circular, whitewashed structure and domed minaret protruding above the dry forest canopy. Unlike most domes on monuments in and around Delhi, this one is elongated like a tulip bud. Standing here, one can almost forget the urban sprawl that has consumed most of this landscape and, perhaps, imagine the baba's spirit stirring a breeze that rustles the branches of dhau trees.

KODAGU

Kodagu is a 4,000 square kilometre district in southwestern Karnataka, bordering Kerala. Earlier it was known as Coorg, a sovereign kingdom on the eastern flank of the Sahyadari Range. Though Coorg was annexed by the British East India Company in 1834, the people of this region have always retained an independent identity with a unique culture and language. While Kodavas are agriculturalists by tradition, they have a proud martial history and hunting was also a central part of their lives. Because of a special dispensation, granted by British authorities in the nineteenth century, this is the only place in India where people are allowed to own firearms without a licence. Nevertheless, India's wildlife protection laws apply to Kodagu's forests and hunting is now illegal. This region is also famous for its many sacred groves, which are called devarakadu.

Nanaya Konerira, a forest biologist, has agreed to show me some of these sites. He is a member of the faculty at the College of Forestry in Ponnampet, which is under Keladi Shivappa Nayaka University of Agricultural and Horticultural Sciences, Shivamogga. Our tour begins near Heggala village, about an hour's drive south of Madikeri, the district headquarters and former capital of Coorg. We remove our shoes at the entrance to the grove, where a broad, masonry staircase ascends the forested slope. The shallow steps curve gradually to the left, so that our destination remains hidden behind a screen of foliage until we reach the top. A faint, floral fragrance lingers in the air. It could be from the giant champak or magnolia tree that stands at the head of the staircase, but I can't see any of its pale yellow blossoms on the high branches overhead.

Just beyond this point lies a large courtyard, paved with flat stones and marked out in squares and rectangles by freshly whitewashed parapet walls. At the centre of this open space stands a venerable jackfruit tree next to which is a shrine without a roof. A relatively recent structure, made of polished grey granite, its pillars are carved with stylized patterns of smoke rising from round censers. This shrine is dedicated to a forest deity known as Ayyappa Bhagvati.

'The god of hunters,' Nanaya tells me, then adds, 'he is different from the famous Ayyappa worshipped at Sabarimala in Kerala. Here in Kodagu, we have many Ayyappa shrines. You can easily recognize them because they have no roof and Ayyappa Bhagvati is always accompanied by his hunting dogs.'

At the base of the jackfruit tree, amongst its gnarled roots, are dozens of small terracotta images of dogs that have been left here by devotees. Some appear new while others are weathered and broken. No idol occupies the main shrine, though there are five black stones, similar to Shivalingams. Each of them is adorned with red hibiscus flowers, which have been placed here by a priest who must have visited the grove earlier this morning. He has also left a handful of boiled rice as an offering next to a natural boulder that protrudes from the earth on one side of the courtyard. Nanaya explains that this forest shrine has been rebuilt and modified in recent years.

'Traditionally, we Kodavas were animists and ancestor worshippers,' he says, 'but everything changes. Some devarakadu now include Hindu deities. This is part of a process of Sanskritization. With each generation there are new priorities and practices.'

As we circle the shrine, Nanaya identifies several of the prominent trees in this grove, including *Dysoxylum malabaricum*. Sometimes called white cedar, it is also known as devdar, the tree of the gods. Unlike the deodar of the Himalaya, *Dysoxylum* isn't a conifer and has broad compound leaves. An endemic species of moist evergreen forests in the Western Ghats, its tall, straight trunk is covered with grey, corky bark that flakes off in patches. Many of the trees in this devarakadu are considered sacred, including another arboreal giant, commonly known as black damar. This tree exudes a dark-coloured sap that is used as incense. The buttressed roots are often scored with deep gashes from which the fragrant essence oozes and then hardens into brittle, translucent lumps. Nanaya says that black damar are often burned to extract the sap and large trees like this are seldom found today except in devarakadus.

After leaving the main shrine and descending the staircase, we walk across to a water source at the edge of the forest. Several shallow pools are hemmed in by bamboo. Nanaya points out a different species of jackfruit, which has a similar but smaller fruit. He then picks a leaf from another tree and asks me to taste it. The leaf is so sour, I can't help but grimace. *Garcinia gummi-gutta* is sometimes called Malabar tamarind and shares the same genus as kokum (*G. indica*). Its fruit is processed into a syrup, which is used as a souring agent that gives Kodagu pork curry its distinctive flavour. In recent years, herbalists have touted *Garcinia* as a natural weight-loss medicine, though its efficacy hasn't been proven.

The devarakadu at Heggala is roughly 40 hectares (100 acres) thought it abuts a much larger reserved forest and we can see that the hill behind us is covered in trees. According to Dr Cheppudira Kushalappa, dean of the College of Forestry and an expert on sacred groves, there are 1,214 devarakadu in Kodagu. Though each of them is unique, collectively these sites represent a 'living tradition' of forest management and wildlife conservation, providing safe refuge for rare flora and fauna. Most devarakadu also contain springs or small ponds which supply villagers with drinking water.

In consultation with Dr Kushalappa, Nanaya has made plans for me to visit four devarakadu in Virajpet and Ponnampet talukas. After showing me the grove at Heggala, he takes me to another Ayyappa shrine about 10 kilometres away, near the village of Kolthodu. As we drive along the winding hill roads, coffee bushes with their dark, glossy leaves seem to be everywhere. These are the main cash crop in Coorg and the landscape has been transformed by coffee plantations, which have replaced much of the original forest cover. Earlier, the existing forests were thinned out and coffee bushes, which require shade, were planted in amongst the native trees. Today, however, silver oaks, an exotic species from Australia, which is easier to maintain, have replaced most of the indigenous trees on plantations. Near the entrance to the Kolthodu devarakadu, several coffee bushes are flowering with white tassel-like blossoms that emit a strong perfume.

'Sometimes, after it rains and all of the bushes are blooming, the fragrance is so strong it can give you a headache,' Nanaya tells me.

Along the edge of the grove, we can see where coffee plants have self-propagated, invading the wild vegetation. Nanaya is surprised to find that since his last visit a year ago, the path to the devarakadu has become a paved road. When we reach the threshold of the shrine, I can see that it has been decorated with strings of saffron pennants that hang from tree branches. Two enormous black damar stand side by side, like twin pylons supporting the sky. A majestic wild mango, almost as tall, also towers above us. Each of these trees must be more than a hundred years old.

The clearing in the middle of the grove contains another square courtyard, with low masonry walls. At the centre is a rough granite monolith, about 2 metres tall. This stone represents Ayyappa, who is never depicted in human form. A second monolith, slightly smaller, is positioned on the other side of the mango. The heavy stones were probably brought here from a hill about 3 kilometres away, where similar rocks are found. Their simple, natural shapes represent a concept of divinity that takes its iconography from nature rather than anthropomorphic images. At the base of each of the monoliths, someone has placed small, silver masks with prominent eyes. Nanaya says that a devotee whose vision was failing must have prayed here and left these emblems in the hope of having his or her eyesight restored.

One of the other trees near the shrine is *Hydnocarpus pentandrus*, popularly known as jangli almond. Common in the rainforests of this region, it has a variety of medicinal properties. The oil extracted from its nuts is prescribed as a treatment for leprosy and skin ailments. It is also used as fuel for oil lamps. Buried in the pale bark of this tree are several iron arrowheads, as if someone has used the *Hydnocarpus* for target practice. Nanaya says that in the past he has seen bows and arrows placed at the foot of this tree to propitiate Ayyappa, and invite his blessings for the hunt.

The third devarakadu we visit, near the village of Hathur, is the most accessible. It lies next to a motor road and is dedicated to the goddess Bhadrakali. An impressive concrete gateway marks the entrance, with a fearsome image of the goddess holding the severed head of a demon in one hand and a blood-stained cleaver in the other. Nanaya tells me that drivers often stop here and make an offering to assure protection for their vehicles, as this is known as a 'vahan rakshak' shrine. A paved walkway leads under the overhanging trees to a concrete enclosure, with a substantial temple at the centre, its sloping roof covered with terracotta tiles. Though nobody is in sight and the main door of the shrine is locked, it obviously attracts plenty of devotees. Offerings of flowers, fruit, and coconuts are piled on the front plinth and in one corner of the enclosure is a stack of more than fifty metal tridents, many of which have lemons stuck on their sharp tines.

Until now we haven't seen many birds and no wildlife in any of the devarakadu but as we circle the temple, a troop of bonnet macaques clamber down to investigate our presence. Nanaya explains that these macaques were trapped in a nearby town by professional monkey catchers who then released them in Bhadrakali's devarakadu. Smaller than rhesus macaques, they have longer tails, and are a pale tan colour. Their most distinctive feature is a prominent tuft of hair on their heads, which appears to be carefully combed with a neat middle part. As we watch, one of the young males leaps down and picks up a piece of coconut to eat.

While leaving the shrine, Nanaya shows me a burrow in the clay bank near the roots of a tree. It looks like a rathole but the earth next to the round opening has been daubed with vermilion and turmeric as a sign of veneration.

'Someone must have seen a cobra going into that hole,' Nanaya surmises. 'Soon enough there will be a permanent shrine here to Subramania (the cobra deity).'

As we get into our taxi, he tells me that the fourth devarakadu we are going to visit is the 'least developed'. Another 15 kilometres from here, it is on the way to Ponnampet, next to Echur village. This is also one of the smallest groves, less than 3 hectares (7 acres). Like the first two, it is dedicated to Ayyappa. When we arrive at the site, it doesn't look promising. A discoloured signboard with peeling paint is covered with creepers and a line of ragged toddy palms stand guard.

Nanaya leads me along an overgrown path that hasn't been used in months. A thicket of lantana blocks our way, forcing us to scramble into a trench about 2 metres deep and full of dead leaves. This marks the outer boundary of the grove. Climbing up the other side, we make our way through a jungle of thorny vines and wild shrubs. Brushing aside spider webs and dangling lianas, we finally enter a sheltered glen. The trees form a thatch-like canopy overhead, admitting no direct sunlight.

Once again, a black damar dominates this grove. Growing beneath its high branches is a smaller tree, *Madhuca neriifolia*, which is related to mahua. On one of the laterite walls, a palm civet has left its droppings, which contain half a dozen black, undigested seeds from the toddy palms. Civets also feed on coffee beans and connoisseurs believe that the best brew is made from beans that have passed through a civet's digestive tract.

In the shadows, I can see a square enclosure, about 4 metres on each side, made of rusty red laterite bricks that rise to the height of my chest. This sacred structure lies within a larger courtyard, surrounded by a low retaining wall, also made of laterite. Being an Ayyappa shrine there is no roof and the entire space is open to the leaves and twigs that fall from above. Four simple stones, each about the size of my hand, are framed inside the open doorway of the inner sanctum. Standing upright, they have traces of vermilion on their flat surfaces. A single rusted trident is stuck in the ground behind them.

The villagers of Echur worship here only once a year. The rest of the time, this devarakadu lies undisturbed by human activity. Ayyappa's shrine appears empty and abandoned, as if the divine huntsman and his faithful hounds have gone off in pursuit of distant prey. At first, I feel nothing, aside from a mild sense of claustrophobia because of the enveloping foliage. We have removed our shoes at the edge of the clearing and the ground beneath my bare feet is littered with layers of decaying leaves and twigs. Treading cautiously, I keep a lookout for snakes and scorpions. Though the forest feels deserted, I remind myself that the silent stillness of the grove is filled with a myriad forms of life. In addition to the trees that Nanaya has identified, the grove contains thousands of other species, whose names I will never know and most of which I cannot see. Microscopic organisms pass through the air and inhabit the soil. Miniscule insects live and breed in the tree bark and humus. Many of these tiny creatures are unknown to science and may never be discovered. Some will become extinct before we have recognized their existence.

Though less than a hundred metres wide, this small patch of forest suddenly feels as if it extends forever, beyond the limits of my imagination—an intimate, yet infinite universe of which I am only vaguely aware. Every form of life in this sanctuary, from the larvae that tunnel through tree bark, to the seeds in a palm civet's excreta, and the ants crawling up my ankles, possess a biological purpose that nature bequeaths. Each of the sacred groves I have visited contains its own unique ecology, stories, and symbols, yet standing here I can feel a connection between them, as if they share something intangible and mysterious—linked together by a wild sense of origins and enigmas.

6

OPHIOPHAGUS HANNAH

Nine months after my first visit, I return to Agumbe during the second week of April. Ajay Giri has informed me that the breeding season for king cobras has commenced, and this is the best time of year to see them. Flying into Mangaluru (formerly Mangalore), I hire a taxi to drive me up from the coast to the crestline of the Western Ghats. The weather is hot and dry, unlike the constant rain and humidity of the monsoon which I experienced last June. As we begin the final climb from the foot of the hill to Agumbe, negotiating more than a dozen tight hairpin bends, I spot a lion-tailed macaque on a parapet wall at the side of the road. A full-grown male, he stands about 40 centimetres at the shoulder with a glossy black coat and silver mane.

When we stop, the macaque rises up on his hind legs and peers expectantly into the side window of the car. As soon as I roll down the glass to take a photograph, he leans forward and extends a slim black hand, begging for food. Though he is a handsome monkey with dignified black features and attentive eyes, his behaviour is troubling for this macaque has become dependent on tourists for handouts. In the trees behind him, I can see four others of his kind. Lion-tailed macaques are an endangered species, endemic to the Western Ghats, and rarely seen because they live deep inside the mountainous rainforests of south-western Karnataka, Kerala, and Tamil Nadu.

Another unique primate from this region that has similar pelage is the Nilgiri langur. Roughly the same size, but with a leaner build and much longer tail, the langur's fur is also black and it has a pale ruff around its face, though its facial hair is far less dramatic than a lion-tailed macaque's hirsute features. This monkey's prominent mane gives it more of a lion-like appearance than does its tufted tail. The local Kannada name is singalika. They are a sociable species living together in troops of as many as thirty to forty individuals. While the male by the roadside remains silent during our encounter, lion-tailed macaques are known for their complex vocalization. Dominant males communicate with their extended families through hoots and murmurs, along with a loud cooee that sounds very much like a human being lost in the forest, trying to attract the attention of his or her companions.

Ordinarily, these omnivorous creatures feed on wild fruit and plants, as well as insects, but along the roadside near Agumbe they are lured out of hiding through the misguided charity of *Homo sapiens*. Feeding monkeys is considered, by some, to be an act of piety as well as a form of entertainment, though it can seriously harm wild creatures. Tourists tend to give monkeys the kind of food they eat themselves such as packaged snacks, which are unhealthy and can even be toxic. Bananas and other fruit may be closer to a monkey's natural diet, but the dependency these offerings create alters the animal's behaviour and makes it less able to survive in the wild. Added to this, there is the risk of the rare macaques being run over by vehicles on the road.

The Karnataka Forest Department has put up signs along the route to Agumbe warning people not to feed monkeys. Guards are stationed at a lookout point, where lion-tailed and bonnet macaques used to congregate, but the opportunistic primates now lurk at different points along the hill road, collecting biscuits, potato chips, and sweets from passers-by. Though I do not give the macaque what he wants, he continues sitting on the parapet for ten minutes or more, watching me with his dark, close-set eyes. The rest of his family remain in the shadows of the nearby trees. Later in the morning, they will retreat into the forest, as the day grows warmer. On my last visit to Agumbe, I tried to see lion-tailed macaques several times but without any luck. Researchers estimate that only about 4,000 survive in the wild and much of their habitat has disappeared. They are also hunted by poachers who kill them and Nilgiri langurs for their meat, which is considered an aphrodisiac.

More than any other mammals, primates remind us of ourselves. The lion-tailed macaque's face bears an uncanny resemblance to an elderly man with a full grey beard and long hair teased out in a shaggy coiffure. I notice that his hands appear almost human, with long, dexterous fingers and nails that look as if they've been carefully manicured. As he sits with his arms resting casually on his knees, and his head turned to one side, his pose suggests an entitled attitude of idle insouciance. While taking a photograph, I catch him looking in my direction, out of the corner of his eye, and I have to wonder whether this monkey recognizes something of himself in me.

∽

When we arrive at the Agumbe Rainforest Research Station, Ajay is out in the field but a volunteer, Gautam Bhupathiraju, is there to greet me. A naturalist from Bangalore, Gautam has come to stay at ARRS for a month, helping to manage the facility, assist in research, and coordinate with visitors. Two other guests are staying here, an American reptile conservationist from Florida and a lawyer from Mumbai, both of whom have been at ARRS for several days and are leaving this afternoon.

Gautam and the others tell me that yesterday they witnessed a male king cobra attacking a female in an act of cannibalism. Around midday, Ajay had received a rescue call from a village nearby where the snakes had been spotted. At first, when they arrived on the scene, the pair appeared to be mating but it soon became clear that the male was pursuing the female to eat her not to breed with her. Gautam shows me a series of videos and photographs in which the king cobras are coiled together and biting each other. At one point the female tried to escape by diving into a well but the male followed her and for over an hour they fought with each other in the water. One photograph shows them knotted together in a death grip and Gautam says they were sure the female had been killed, though she broke free after a while. Even though the pair had bitten each other numerous times, most venomous snakes, including king cobras, are immune to their own toxins.

Finally, when the owner of the property urged him to save the king cobras, not wanting them to die in his well, Ajay decided to rescue the snakes using a ladder. It was a risky operation, but he knew that even if the female was killed, he would have to get the male out of the water because the well was too deep for the king cobra to escape on its own. After successfully rescuing both snakes, he released them at different locations.

Ophiophagus, the generic Latin name for king cobras means 'snake eater'. Its diet consists mostly of rat snakes and checkered keelbacks but it also feeds on cobras, vipers, and kraits, as well as members of its own family. In this way, king cobras help control the population of venomous snakes, reducing the risk of human beings getting bitten. Nevertheless, king cobras are a frightening sight, growing as long as 4 metres or more. Though they have a reputation for attacking people, Romulus Whitaker disputes this prejudice in his field guide, *Common Indian Snakes*.

> Much has been written about the aggressive nature of this magnificent snake, but these accounts are more imaginative than factual. We have encountered King Cobras in South India and the Andamans, and in our experience they are timid snakes, unwilling to attack and always seeking escape when possible... In the field, King Cobras are awesome-looking indeed and both man and snake beat a hasty retreat. If restrained or injured,

> the snake may charge with open mouth at the aggressor, emitting a deep growl. King Cobras behave with an intelligence and awareness unusual in snakes... The venom is slightly less toxic than the cobra's but the massive venom glands can contain up to 6 cc of venom, enough to kill an elephant.

Whitaker, who first visited Agumbe in 1971, on the recommendation of Kenneth Anderson, the famous hunter and author of shikar books, has a special relationship with king cobras. He set up the Rainforest Research Station with the primary objective of studying these imposing reptiles, the largest venomous snake on earth. When I met him, after my first visit to Agumbe, he told me that as far as he is aware, in the past twenty years, only three people in India have died after being bitten by king cobras.

'All three of them were snake catchers and they were either drunk or careless,' he said. 'One guy was holding a king cobra with one hand and reached into his shirt pocket to get his phone to take a selfie when the snake bit him.' Rom reminded me that in India there is no anti-venom for the neurotoxins a king cobra injects with its fangs.

When I asked about the king cobra's eyesight and how much they can see, he explained that unlike most snakes, including other cobras, it's possible that they may have binocular vision, which would mean they are better at observing their prey.

'Though they have excellent eyesight, we still don't know exactly what they can see when they're looking at us,' Rom told me. 'With king cobras, if you stand still, they don't seem to be able to spot you, though they are aware of any movement. A few years ago, I was watching two males engaged in breeding combat. When one came towards me, I froze and let it go right between my legs. Once it was behind me though, it swung around and bit me on the butt. Fortunately, I was wearing jeans and the fangs got caught in the fabric.'

He explained that snakes have no ears or eardrums and are virtually deaf, but they can feel vibrations on the ground and respond to certain loud, low frequency sounds. Smell is a snake's strongest sense and they use their tongues to collect pheromones and other scent particles from the air, transmitting these to the paired Jacobson's organs on the roof of their mouth. Herpetologists used to think all snakes, including king cobras, were colour-blind but researchers have discovered cone cells in their retinas, which are sensitive to colour.

Rom himself is partially colour-blind, which may help explain his affinity for reptiles. Even before he came to India as a boy in 1951, he was fascinated by snakes. His mother, Doris Norden, moved here from the United States with her children and married Rama Chattopadhyaya, who set up one of India's first colour motion picture processing labs. Growing up in Bombay and attending an international boarding school in Kodaikanal, in the Western Ghats, Rom continued pursuing snakes, which became his passion and profession. After spending several years at the Miami serpentarium in Florida, working with his mentor, Bill Haast, he was drafted into the US Army for two years during the Vietnam War, serving as a medical lab technician at Camp Zama in Japan.

Returning to India, Rom became a naturalized Indian citizen. He has made a number of wildlife films, including *King Cobra*, an Emmy award-winning documentary for National Geographic. In recognition of his conservation efforts, he has received many honours including the Whitley Prize, two Rolex Awards, and a Padma Shri from the president of India. In 1972, he founded the Snake Park in Chennai, where visitors can observe and learn about India's many different species of snakes. In 1976, with his former wife, Zai Futehally, Rom founded the Madras Crocodile Bank at Mahabalipuram, which runs a captive breeding programme for endangered reptiles like gharials. One of his many projects involves the Irula tribal community, who are snake catchers by tradition. After the Wild Life Protection Act made killing snakes illegal in 1972, Rom helped them transition from selling snakeskins to collecting venom. The Irula Snake Catcher's Cooperative has become India's primary source of snake venom, which is used to produce millions of vials of lifesaving antivenom, vital in a country where over 50,000 rural people die from snakebite every year.

At the age of eighty, Rom is no longer actively chasing snakes and he claims to have 'switched off' but when he speaks about Agumbe's king cobras, his eyes light up and I can tell that the adrenaline from his first encounter with *Ophiophagus hannah* is still coursing through his veins. His wife, nature writer Janaki Lenin, is the author of *My Husband and Other Animals,* a two-volume collection of her popular column, which appears in *The Hindu* newspaper. In one of these pieces, Janaki describes Rom's first visit to Agumbe, when he was out in the forest and caught sight of a snake's tail disappearing into the bushes. Thinking it was a rat snake, he ran forward to grab it.

> Without a moment's hesitation, he dove, bruising elbows and knees, but he had the tail. An instant later, he heard a deep growl. Rom looked up to see a king cobra, with an expanded hood, towering over him.
>
> The snake's golden hood was iridescent in the evening light, and its eyes were pinned on Rom. Lying flat on his belly, Rom was incapable of defending himself. The king cobra's glossy tail fell from his fingers, and the snake slid away like mercury through the undergrowth.
>
> Coming to his senses and feet, Rom raced after it. He seized a stick

and halted the snake in its track. When he grabbed it by the tail a second time, the king cobra swung around and charged open-mouthed. Somehow, holding the snake at a safe distance with the stick, Rom managed, one-handed, to pull a sleeping bag out of his rucksack, and prop it open with sticks. The frightened snake saw the dark opening of the bag as an escape and slid inside. That first knee-quaking encounter with a wild king cobra was not only a career milestone for Rom, but he felt he came of age then.

~

Soon after lunch, we get word from Ajay that he has received a rescue call for a king cobra that has entered a farmhouse. He shares the GPS location, on the edge of Kudremukh National Park, towards the town of Sringeri. Piling into my taxi, Gautam and I set off immediately. Half an hour later, we catch up with Ajay in the ARRS jeep. His wife, Meghna, along with her mother and sisters are with him, visiting from Bangalore. All of us are eager to see our first king cobra. The farm is surrounded by forest and there is a partially constructed house in which the snake has taken shelter behind several sacks of building materials. The farmer and his family are standing anxiously outside.

Near the entrance to the half-built house, Ajay sets up a green canvas bag, with a short PVC pipe positioned at its mouth and held in place with two bricks. Having watched him rescue a spectacled cobra last year, I am familiar with the routine, though this time the snake is likely to be three times as large. With his snake hook in hand, Ajay enters the house to investigate. After a few minutes, he calls us in one by one. Shining a headlamp from above, into the space between the sacks and the wall, we can see the slate-grey coils of the king cobra lying on the concrete floor. Its girth is as thick as my wrist and I can just make out the pale bands on its body. After each of us has had a quick look and retreated outdoors, Ajay drags one of the sacks aside. The king cobra, an adult male, remains where he is but lifts his head and extends his hood. Through an open window, I can see him clearly, about 4 metres away.

The huge serpent, most of his body coiled under him, watches us intently with a steady, unwavering gaze. Snakes don't blink because they have no eyelids. Instead, a transparent, protective lens covers their eyes, which is shed along with their skin several times a year. The king cobra's eyes are round, his black pupils ringed with pale irises. He flicks his tongue repeatedly, gathering chemicals from the air that his brain will interpret, providing him with a scent-based awareness of his surroundings. His focused demeanour conveys an obvious intelligence, perhaps not as complex as the lion-tailed macaque's but honed to his specific needs as a predator that hunts on the ground, in water, and trees.

The ventral scales covering the king cobra's throat and on the underside of his hood are a rich cream colour, while most of the upper body is a metallic grey. The colouration of king cobras can vary from almost black to much lighter shades, as with this snake. Scales on its head are of different sizes and shapes. Herpetologists have names for each of these, from the rostral scale at the tip of a snake's nose to preoculars, supraoculars, and postoculars surrounding its eyes. All of them fit together in a symmetrical pattern like an intricate mosaic. The scales on the back of its hood and the rest of its body are smaller, no bigger than kernels of corn. Their lustrous grey colour gives them the appearance of chain mail, while the pale bands that encircle the king cobra's body at regular intervals look like inlaid gold melded with steel.

After all of us have retreated to a safe distance, Ajay moves in with the hook and gently slides it under the snake's body before catching hold of its tail as the king cobra uncoils itself. It is just over 3.5 metres long, almost twice Ajay's height. Struggling to escape, it writhes in the air as he guides it out the front door of the half-built house. We all move back several steps, as the king cobra swings its hood back and forth like a whip that has a life of its own. Holding it above the ground, at waist level, Ajay keeps the snake from gaining the traction it needs to escape. He tries to direct it towards the pipe and bag, but this big male has other ideas and turns aside with a swift, looping movement. For a moment, the tail slips free, but Ajay deftly raises the hook and catches hold of it again. I feel as if I am watching a juggler performing a balancing act. Again, he tries to manoeuvre the snake towards the bag, but the king cobra slings its body in the other direction and briefly touches the ground, trying to slide away. While all of us have been told that we should stand still if the snake gets loose, everyone hurriedly retreats another metre or two.

Though the king cobra isn't being aggressive and is only trying to flee, its flared hood and swift, agitated movements appear threatening. After a third unsuccessful attempt to bag the snake, Ajay takes several steps backwards, keeping his eyes fixed on the venomous creature he holds in his grasp. I'm worried that he's going to trip over the rocks and construction materials strewn about the yard but pivoting to his right, Ajay is able to approach the pipe from a different angle this time. Finally, the king cobra sees the dark opening and glides safely inside, like oil pouring into a funnel. Pressing the hook down, across the upper end of the canvas bag, to keep the snake from escaping, Ajay removes the pipe and ties a secure knot. The whole operation has taken no more than two or three minutes, but it feels as if I've been holding my breath for half an hour.

Once the king cobra is in the bag, Ajay weighs it—6.4 kilograms. He also checks to see if it is an individual that he's caught before but the handheld monitor with which he scans the bag shows that no microchip has been implanted in the snake's tail. After this, the farmer's name and address are noted down. A GPS reading of the location has been recorded and photographs taken, all of which will be added to ARRS's database.

Until now, I haven't really had a chance to speak to Ajay beyond a hurried greeting when we arrived. After introducing me to his wife and family, he admits that the king cobra gave him more trouble than he would have liked. Though he has been handling these big snakes for years, each one is a challenge. While we're talking, his phone rings. Answering it, he speaks in Kannada for several minutes before signing off.

'We've been monitoring a mating pair for the last two days,' he tells me, with a satisfied smile. 'Both the male and female are inside a burrow near a village, 20 kilometres beyond Agumbe. Now the villagers are saying two other males have showed up and they've started their combat.'

All of us rush to get into the vehicles and retrace our route to the main road. Along the way, at a forested spot, out of sight of any homes, Ajay releases the captive snake, which slips out of the bag and vanishes into the undergrowth without looking back.

Driving as fast as the narrow, twisting roads will allow, it takes us about forty-five minutes to reach the village of Kanakodu. A small settlement of five or six homes, it lies at the end of an unpaved track that passes through stretches of fragmented jungle, broken up by fields and areca nut plantations. As soon as we pull up near the front gate of the first house, I can see the two king cobras about 30 metres away in a patch of forest bordering the village. Their long, lithe bodies are wrapped around each other like the braided lianas that hang from the trees. Each of them is about the size of the snake that Ajay just rescued and released, more than 3.5 metres long.

By now, it is four o'clock in the afternoon and the combat started an hour ago. Getting down from our vehicles, we approach the two snakes on foot. A dozen villagers, both adults and children, are watching from only a few steps away. We join them, everyone taking photographs or recording videos on their phones or with cameras. The king cobras ignore us and are focused entirely on each other. They seem to be in a trance, consumed by their instincts and absorbed in an impulsive battle to breed. During this annual performance the snakes abandon their fear of human beings and other predators, exposing themselves to dangers they would ordinarily avoid.

The two combatants appear to be dancing rather than fighting and I can immediately see how this behaviour would inspire images of entwined cobras that appear in so many sculptures, on temples, and other monuments throughout India, as well as countless votive stones placed at the base of peepul trees. Their sinuous bodies have a fluid grace even as they struggle to dominate each other. Raising his head, one of the males tries to press down on his opponent's neck but before he succeeds, the other male lifts himself slightly higher and tries to do the same. In this way, they move in rhythm with one another, coiling and uncoiling, thrusting and twisting. Though the pair of males look as if they are mating, this biological ritual is simply a prelude to the act of procreation, which can only occur after one of the males is defeated.

Unlike the vicious fight between the male and female that took place yesterday, there is very little violence to this combat. Neither of the males bites the other and they keep their hoods closed as they wrestle. At no point during the combat do I see either snake flick its tongue, as if they have no need to comprehend anything beyond the knotted friction of their supple bodies.

Ajay warns us to stay alert because at any point during the combat, one of the snakes may break loose and try to escape. Only then will the victor try to bite his opponent and there is the danger of getting caught in between.

'When the loser gives up and runs away, he moves very fast for more than a hundred metres, racing for cover,' Ajay says. After that, the winner searches for the female.

More than likely, the two combatants don't realize that their prospective mate is already in the company of another male who got here before them. All three of the suitors have followed her scent trail, which signals that she is ready to breed. While the latecomers engage in a contest to determine who will inseminate the female, neither of them may get that opportunity.

As we continue to watch, the two males keep moving slowly forward, advancing through the patch of forest and reaching a dirt path running along a fence of bamboo and sticks that marks the edge of one villager's yard. Neither of the snakes seems ready to submit as we follow closely, a couple of metres behind them. At one point, Ajay creeps forward with the handheld monitor and checks to see if they have been tagged. He discovers that both king cobras have microchips implanted in their tails. One was captured and released in 2021, the other last year.

Except for the occasional slap of their tails on dry leaves, as they lash about on the forest floor, the snakes make no sound at all, presenting a silent but relentless spectacle. Meanwhile, their audience is noisy—villagers call out to each other, children laugh and play as they watch. After our initial awed response, when our group spoke in whispers, we have become talkative too, sharing stories and information. I am reminded of watching the pair of mating snow leopards in

Ladakh, when the crowd of human spectators kept up a running commentary as we observed the breeding behaviour of the two rare cats. In Kanakodu there are far fewer people than the crowd at Saspochey and instead of being 400 metres away, with a valley in between, the snakes are right here in front of us. But even if the king cobras were attentive to our presence, they wouldn't be able to hear our voices, being deaf. At one point, Ajay asks one of the village boys if he understands what is taking place. With a mischievous smile the child responds: 'WWF!' Obviously, he doesn't mean the Worldwide Fund for Nature but instead the Worldwide Wrestling Federation, which broadcasts bouts on TV.

Even at close range, it is impossible to tell the two snakes apart because their size and colouration are virtually identical. They could be twins. As they cling together, they look like a single creature with two separate heads. The breeding behaviour of these snakes has been widely documented and studied but there are many questions that remain unanswered. In the Western Ghats near Agumbe, female king cobras become ready to breed once a year for a period of a month or more, usually during March and April, but sometimes earlier. Mating can be a slow process, taking place over several days or weeks. The male, who is much larger, will actively rub his body against the female and even butt her until she is ready to copulate. Their sexual organs are located in the cloaca on the underside of their tails, beneath anal plates. Once a female is receptive, king cobras will mate several times a day. After that they often stay together until the female builds a large nest of leaves and twigs, gathering them up with her coils. This process can take over a week or two.

Of the more than 3,000 species of snakes in the world, king cobras alone build nests. The female then lays her eggs deep in the centre, where the decomposing leaves provide heat for incubation, while keeping them sheltered from the torrential monsoon rain, which arrives soon after the eggs are laid. Here in Agumbe, female king cobras abandon their nests almost immediately, leaving the eggs vulnerable to being eaten by predators like mongooses. In other parts of India and Southeast Asia, the mother remains on or in her nest, guarding it until the eggs are ready to hatch. Then, just before the babies slice their way out of their leathery shells, using a protruding 'egg tooth' on the tip of their snouts, the female leaves abruptly, possibly because if she stayed, her instincts would force her to feed on her brood. The unique breeding behaviour of females in and around Agumbe suggests that they may be a separate species. Geneticists studying the DNA of king cobras from different regions are close to splitting them into three or four different species.

One of the mysteries that hasn't been fully understood is the cannibalistic behaviour that occurs during the breeding season. By some accounts, male king cobras stop feeding at this time of year, their appetites suppressed to keep them from devouring their mates. In 2008, the team at ARRS observed a breeding pair over a period of four weeks, during which the male and female remained together, sharing a burrow without any conflict. By this time, the female was gravid and preparing to lay her eggs. Suddenly, a third king cobra appeared on the scene and engaged in combat with the resident male. Because of their similar size and appearance, the field assistants who observed this encounter couldn't be sure which of the combatants was the outsider and which was the original consort. Eventually, one of them was defeated and escaped, after which the victor approached the female. Though he initially seemed ready to mate, the male suddenly attacked and killed the female. He then began to swallow his victim, consuming two-thirds of her body before he reached a point where the eggs had formed inside her. Balking at the increased girth, he regurgitated the female's remains and quickly departed.

This gruesome incident, which was filmed, has led to unproven speculation that male king cobras will kill gravid females to ensure that a competitor's offspring do not survive. At the same time, it's possible that the aggressor was actually the original mate and something occurred, a hormonal change perhaps, to turn him against her. Recalling this cannibalistic behaviour, Ajay is concerned for the female who is still in her burrow, a hundred metres away.

By this time, several others have joined us, including two young men in their twenties, Abhi and Venu. They come from another village close by and have worked with ARRS on a radio telemetry project, tracking king cobras. The project, which was started in 2008, was stopped during the Covid-19 pandemic but Ajay is hoping to restart it soon and he is in the process of renewing permissions with the forest department. As the two male snakes continue their struggle, Abhi and Venu speak about one of the king cobras they monitored and followed. Dubbed M5, he was an enormous male well over 4 metres long and weighing 9.4 kilograms.

The two trackers followed him every day for months, using a handheld-antennae that picked up signals from a thumb-sized transmitter surgically implanted in the coelomic cavity under his skin. On several occasions they witnessed M5 engaging in combat with other males.

'He never lost any of his matches,' says Abhi with a note of pride in his voice.

'M5 was an amazing king cobra,' Ajay agrees. 'We got so much data from him.'

Though this dominant male is probably still roaming the forests near Agumbe, the team has lost track of him and by now the batteries in his transmitter will be dead.

'There's still so much we don't understand about king cobras,' Ajay says. 'For example, we know that they follow scent trails. But how do they know which direction the other snake is going? Something tells them to turn right or left.'

For the past two days, Abhi and Venu have been keeping watch on the female in her burrow, which is an old rathole under a pile of rocks overgrown with a hedge of thorns and weeds. It lies between two of the village homes, about 20 metres from each. Taking a break from observing the brawling males, I let the trackers show me the burrow. Creeping forward and trying to keep my movements to a minimum, as instructed, I can just see the female's dark head protruding from the hole and her tongue licking the air. I'm told that females grow darker when they breed, turning almost black, while males become lighter in the breeding season. According to Venu, who has seen her basking in the sun, she is a metre shorter than the males and quite a bit thinner. Nobody is sure if the other male is still with her or if he may have left during the night.

Returning to the duelling pair, I find they have circled around and are now heading back towards our vehicles. Raising their heads in tandem, they continue to tangle with each other. By now, the combat has gone on for more than two hours and the snakes must be exhausted. The light is also beginning to fade as the sun sinks towards the treetops. Most of the children have grown bored with the combat and only a few villagers keep watching the snakes, the rest going about their chores or tending to their cattle.

Tomorrow, there is going to be a local festival, we're told, at a cobra shrine next to Kanakodu, and we've been invited. Meanwhile, a young PhD scholar named Vikram has joined us. He is researching earthworms in the forests near Agumbe but hearing about the king cobra combat, he's come on his motorcycle to witness this rare event.

Suddenly, there is a commotion on the other side of the farmhouse, near the burrow where the female is hiding. All of us run across to see what is happening and we learn that the male, who was with her, has left the burrow and was seen moving away, towards the fields, west of the house. Abhi and Venu track him down and show us where the king cobra has disappeared into a thicket of bamboo. Moments later, the snake emerges and climbs into a mango tree, slithering effortlessly onto a branch 3 metres above the ground. We can see him looking down at us, his broad head protruding through the leaves and his forked tongue licking the air anxiously.

Whether the male is leaving the burrow for good or if he intends to return isn't clear. Rather than disturbing him any more than we have already, Ajay and the rest of us retreat, leaving Abhi to keep an eye on him. By the time we get back to the two combatants, it is past 6.30 and the sun has set. For another half hour, I wait with the others but once it is dark there isn't much point in hanging around. The two king cobras have moved into a patch of undergrowth and through the leaves only the occasional writhing of their bodies is visible in the shadows. After a long day, I am ready to head back to ARRS, while Ajay and his team remain in Kanakodu to keep monitoring the snakes using headlamps.

Serpents have always been a part of our spiritual consciousness, for they embody nature in one of its most mysterious and beautiful forms. At the same time, some snakes are dangerous and evoke conflicting emotions of awe, fear, and revulsion. As the tribal folk songs from the Maikal Hills, in Central India, tell us, cobras also elicit an erotic response in human beings that infuses our dreams and desires. All of this merges into a primal sense of the sacred and the sublime that lies at the core of any mystical experience.

When faced with a cobra, most people are overcome by an irrepressible feeling of vulnerability and terror, though this is often combined with fascination. A snake's ability to move swiftly and gracefully without any limbs gives it a magical, mesmerizing appearance. The colours and patterns on its scales have a jewelled brilliance even as they arouse our deepest anxieties. Somewhere in our instinctual memory, perhaps encoded in primate genes, is a warning that we should step back. And yet, there is also something that draws us forward, urging us to follow what we fear. Human encounters with nature are replete with these paradoxical moments. Fierce thunderstorms or high waves crashing against a rocky coast, frighten and enchant us at the same time. Poisonous herbs with beautiful flowers captivate us just like a tiger's menacing presence and striking coat can evoke both loathing and wonder. Animistic traditions often draw upon these conflicting responses to nature that simultaneously attract and repel us.

While observing the king cobras, I am aware of a powerful sense of ambivalence that these creatures conjure up in the human psyche. Expressions of this unsettling yet enduring relationship, between us and venomous species, can be found in religious iconography, scripture, mythology, and folklore. It is also an integral part of the enduring legacy of sacred groves.

Next morning, when we return to Kanakodu, the combat has ended. Ironically, the loser, who finally gave up the struggle and fled, took shelter in the same burrow where the female is hiding, while the victor was left on his own. All this happened in the dark, after my departure last evening. Altogether, the combat lasted more than four hours, the longest Ajay and the others have ever witnessed. Its conclusion was something of an anti-climax, with both the original mate and the successful challenger unexpectedly leaving the scene.

Nobody is sure if the third male is still in the burrow with the female or whether he too has slipped away during the night. Meanwhile, the villagers of Kanakodu are preparing for their festival at the nearby Nagavana, or cobra's grove, about 200 metres from the site where the combat occurred. Recorded music is playing over a loudspeaker, dominated by the resonant notes of a nadaswaram—the double-reed instrument played at most festivals and weddings in South India. Twice the size of a North Indian shehnai, it sounds a bit like a snake-charmer's pungi or been.

We spend a couple of hours waiting outside the burrow to see if any king cobras reappear but there is no sign of the males and only the female's head is visible at the mouth of the rathole. At least we know she is alive and hasn't been attacked by her suitors. With all of the activity around her, she isn't likely to emerge. Throughout the morning, there is a lot of coming and going from the Nagavana and excitement is building. The villagers are dressed in festive attire, women in bright saris, men and boys in crisp shirts and trousers, and some of the young girls in party frocks.

Around 11 a.m., we are told that the puja is about to begin, and our hosts insist that we must attend. Walking across to the forest shrine, I can see an open, metal-roofed shed, its supporting steel pillars decorated with fresh banana stalks and a bamboo gateway festooned with mango leaves. On all four sides of the shrine is a dense, undisturbed stand of wild trees, including a small banyan, with knitted roots and serpentine tendrils that have strangled and killed another tree. Removing our shoes at the entrance to the Nagavana, we join a crowd of about fifty people. Relatives and other guests from neighbouring villages have been invited. Some are seated on plastic chairs, while others are standing around, chatting with each other.

At the centre of the shed is a brick hearth, where a sacred fire is burning, giving off more smoke than flames. Several priests, one in a yellow dhoti and another in pink, are attending to their rituals. Open to the sky, the shrine stands at the far end of the shed, just beyond the edge of the roof. About 3 metres high, it consists of an arched masonry wall at the centre of which is a prominent image of a cobra with its hood extended and the body coiled in a figure eight. Like the wall, the cobra is painted yellow and outlined in white with black spots to indicate scales. This image has been garlanded with strings of jasmine and other blossoms while the concrete platform beneath is covered in a large heap of fruit and flowers, especially the fresh inflorescence of areca nut palms. The broom-like clusters of bright yellow stems are covered with tiny petals of the same colour. A large bunch of bananas has also been placed in front of the shrine. As music continues to play over the sound system, priests light incense and oil lamps, while preparing trays with coconuts, rice, and other offerings.

This puja, sponsored by the main landowner in Kanakodu, has no direct connection to the breeding behaviour of king cobras, but all of the villagers witnessed their combat yesterday, which heightens the relevance of the rituals. Strictly speaking, the cobra deity, or Naga Devatha honoured here, is a representation of *Naja naja,* the smaller Indian or spectacled cobra, not *Ophiophagus hannah*, but the distinctions between species get blurred. Gautam and Vikram help explain the rituals and translate for me. The male members of the landowner's family are dressed in purple and ochre lungis, all of them bare-chested. After the music is abruptly switched off and before the ceremonies begin, one of the men makes a speech welcoming everyone and announcing that he hopes the festival will bring prosperity and blessings to the village.

The shrine contains no images of deities other than the Naga Devatha. On the packed mud floor, to one side of the shed, is a stylized depiction of three cobras drawn in rice flour. Next to this is an oil lamp made from half a green papaya, as well as hibiscus flowers, and offerings of puffed rice and coconuts. While the puja proceeds, some of the crowd are attentive, particularly the older generation, though the younger men and children seem bored and restless.

Everyone is waiting for the oracle to arrive. Gautam explains that he is known as the Ghanna Maga or the person who gets possessed. In this case he is referred to as a Naga Ghanna because it is a cobra deity. The oracle is not from the village but has been summoned from elsewhere for the ceremony. As the puja proceeds, both Gautam and Vikram tell me about a recent Kannada film, *Kantara*, which revolves around the story of a forest deity that embodies the spirit of a wild boar. The oracle is vividly portrayed with dramatic special effects. A box office success, *Kantara* conveys a message of conservation along with lots of action and suspense.

After half an hour, the priests finish their prayers and conclude the puja, offering everyone prasad—a sip of buttermilk and a stem of flowers from an areca nut palm. The crowd pushes forward eagerly, and I can sense their anticipation. People keep looking over their shoulders towards the entrance, expecting the oracle to appear.

Five minutes later, a man arrives at the edge of the Nagavana and approaches the shrine. He is about thirty years old, bare-chested and dressed only in an ochre dhoti. Clean-shaven, with a slender build, his long hair is brushed back from his forehead and falls to his shoulders. He doesn't look at anyone as he steps through the crowd with a passive expression on his face. The priests welcome him as he folds his hands in front of the cobra's image. The Naga Ghanna then splashes some water on his face and rinses his hands.

Earlier, I had noticed two musicians seated at the back of the shed. One is holding a saxophone and the other has a pair of drums suspended in front of him on a shoulder strap. Without warning, they begin to play a raucous, discordant tune. With its loud, reedy notes, the saxophone sounds somewhat like the nadaswaram. The percussionist beats on both drums with short sticks, setting an uneven but urgent tempo. Meanwhile, several men begin ringing bells and striking gongs which adds to the dissonant cacophony. After several minutes of this, the oracle begins to tremble.

Stretching out his arms, he gestures for the priests to give him a bunch of areca nut flowers, which he clutches to his face and chest with both arms. Swaying back and forth, he buries his head in the yellow blossoms. A minute later, when he looks up, his face is covered with tiny round petals like gold sequins. His eyes are now bulging, rolling back in their sockets and he is breathing heavily, demanding more flowers from the priests, who hand him several fresh bunches. After the oracle rubs his face in the yellow inflorescence, his skin looks as if it is covered with scales.

Many of the people in the crowd have folded their hands, watching the Naga Ghanna with concentrated devotion, believing that the cobra deity has entered his body. Gesturing for more flowers, the oracle clutches the yellow plumes to his face and chest then drops to the ground. Stretching out his legs, with his ankles crossed, he begins to squirm about like a snake, dragging himself forward with writhing movements. Slowly, he advances towards the hearth, then turns back suddenly and circles the rice flour image of cobras decorating the floor. The priests and others hurriedly move the oil lamps, afraid he will tip them over. All this time, the music continues, the saxophone blaring over the incessant rattle of drums.

While the oracle's possession is unsettling, his performance holds me and the rest of the crowd enthralled, just as we were transfixed by the combat of king cobras yesterday. For at least fifteen minutes, the Naga Ghanna makes his way around the outside of the shrine. When he reaches the banyan, it looks as if he wants to escape into its twisted roots but then he returns to the centre of the shed. Here the oracle finally rises to his feet again, swaying from side to side while still holding the bunches of flowers with both arms. Then, as suddenly as the music began, the saxophone and drums fall silent, followed by an expectant hush.

When the Naga Ghanna begins to speak, his voice has a high-pitched, hectoring tone. The oracle's breathing is laboured and the yellow petals still cover his face, while his hair is in disarray and his eyes remain wild. Again, Gautam translates for me, whispering that the Naga Ghanna is saying that the puja is inadequate. He demands that the landowner perform two pujas every month. The old man, who has sponsored this event, stands with his hands folded but shakes his head, a worried look on his face. In a respectful voice, he tells the oracle it is impossible, he can't afford to pay for so many pujas but the deity is adamant. For a few minutes, they seem to be negotiating, though nothing is resolved.

At this point, one of the women, a daughter-in-law from the landowner's family, becomes possessed, gasping and holding both hands over her head. I recognize her from yesterday as one of the people who was watching the king cobras. When she collapses on the ground, her husband catches her by the shoulders. The Naga Ghanna is annoyed by this interruption. He waves one hand dismissively, instructing her family to take her away. Now, another villager steps forward, a stocky, unshaven man in his fifties. With folded hands, he tells the oracle that he has suffered many misfortunes in his life, especially during the last few years.

'Of course, you have!' the Naga Ghanna interrupts him. 'Two years ago, you burned my home. Now you must ask for my forgiveness.'

The man nods, acknowledging that he may have lit a fire at the edge of his fields where a cobra lived. Gautam provides a rough translation but he has difficulty following the oracle's words as others in the crowd come forward and ask for guidance and advice. One woman mentions a land dispute and the oracle reassures her.

'Be patient. Everything will get resolved,' he says.

The questions and answers continue for half an hour. Looking around the shed, I can see that many of the villagers are listening to every word that is spoken, with complete conviction. However, a few of the younger men, standing at the edge of the crowd, appear more sceptical. They are checking messages on their phones and gossiping quietly with each other, ignoring most of what is going on.

Eventually, the oracle indicates that he is finished by handing out sprigs of palm flowers as prasad. Each of the villagers steps forward and accepts this token of blessing. Until now, the ARRS team has been standing to one side, watching silently but the landowner waves Ajay forward and begins to introduce him to the oracle, explaining that he rescues and releases snakes.

Again, the Naga Ghanna interrupts the man impatiently and declares, 'I know who he is. He helps me and I help him!'

With that, the oracle instructs the priests to give Ajay the entire bunch of bananas lying in front of the shrine. Through this spontaneous gesture, the Naga Ghanna recognizes and validates Ajay's efforts to protect cobras and other snakes in the rainforests surrounding Agumbe.

Whatever I may feel about these ceremonies and the authenticity of spirit possession, for the villagers of Kanakodu this oracle represents their forest deity and speaks on the Naga Devatha's behalf. My comprehension of what has taken place is as limited as my understanding of the breeding rituals of *Ophiophagus hannah*, an ignorance that disqualifies me from passing any kind of judgement. Nevertheless, there is no doubt in my mind: both events I have witnessed represent profound enigmas that lie at the core of our relationship with the natural world. Yesterday, the two king cobras performed an epic battle, driven by biological impulses that tested and determined which of them was the fittest to pass on his genes. Today, we have observed a form of religious theatre in which a human being assumed the role of a snake. The worship of the cobra in this forest shrine is a living tradition that harks back to the naga deities in the Mathura Museum and images carved into the rocks at Mahabalipuram. By channelling the Naga Devatha, the oracle gives voice to our innermost fears and fascination for wild creatures and wild places, leading us beyond the reach of intellect or rationality, into the realm of metaphors and myths.

When we speak of India's wild heritage it is not restricted to biological narratives or stories of geology and climate, but also includes our cultural and spiritual responses to the ecological world we inhabit. The idea of 'wildness' does not necessarily suggest a clear line of separation but rather a paradox through which we human beings recognize elements of ourselves in other species while imagining those same life forms existing in an environment undisturbed by man. Anthropomorphism is a far more complex set of projected attributes than just the talking animals in fables and folklore or the human names we assign to individual tigers or cheetahs. It is, in a much broader sense, a way of perceiving other species based on an empathetic desire to merge our consciousness with theirs.

Beyond this mystical connection lies an enduring conservation ethic rooted in indigenous traditions, which emphasize that we have a moral responsibility to preserve and protect the natural world in all its abundance and diversity. Much of this animistic ethos has been lost in our headlong rush to cultivate, develop, and industrialize the earth, especially during the modern era. As we are now discovering that wildlife and wild places are becoming more and more of an abstraction than a reality, it is critical for us to understand that our survival is tied to the tenuous existence of endangered plants and animals. While scientists continue to decode and interpret the secrets of biology, we must not lose sight of the parallel mysteries embedded in stories, songs, and rituals that remind us of our ancestral understanding and appreciation of life in all its multiple manifestations. The protective presence of cobra deities, river goddesses, and holy mountains symbolize our ancient ties to primal landscapes that are fast disappearing.

When naturalists seek out and observe both rare and familiar species, they try to see the living world for what it is, but also for what it represents. Watching an insect, bird, mammal, or reptile, we contemplate the marvellous order and chaos of life as it has evolved over millions of years. And yet, what often inspires us more than anything else are those fleeting, intimate moments in which we see a wild creature looking back at us with a shared awareness of our mutual presence. As our eyes meet the other's gaze, it reaffirms the simple fact that we, as a species, are not alone on this earth.

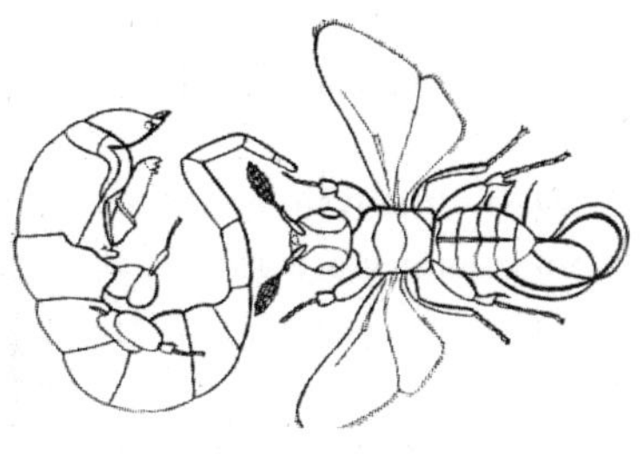

EPILOGUE

THE GREAT BANYAN

A white-throated kingfisher is perched on a culm of bamboo overlooking a large pond, green with algae. The bird's turquoise wings and tail feathers have a mineral brilliance like polished gems. A line of tall palms on the far side of the water rustle in the morning breeze, as does the grass along the shoreline near my feet. It is mid-November, but the air is warm and the sun slants through the leafy branches of a kachnar. In full bloom, its purple blossoms attract butterflies of different colours, shapes, and sizes. As I observe this idyllic scene, appreciating the beauty and solitude as well as the diversity of life it contains, there seems to be nothing unnatural about it, except that I am in the middle of one of the busiest, most populous cities on earth.

The Calcutta Botanical Garden in Howrah was founded in 1787 by Colonel Robert Kyd, an officer of the East India Company's army. It is now known as the Acharya Jagadish Chandra Bose Indian Botanic Garden, in honour of one of India's greatest scientists. Often described as a polymath, J. C. Bose (1858–1937) is best known for his contributions to physics, particularly his research on radio microwaves. He also conducted experiments on plant neurobiology, studying the response of species like touch-me-nots to various stimuli including microwaves.

Located on the north bank of the Hooghly River, the botanic garden occupies 109 hectares (270 acres) of prime urban real estate. Several other botanical gardens were established by the East India Company in other parts of the subcontinent, including Saharanpur (1816), Poona (1827), and Madras (1836). The primary objective of these horticultural estates was to evaluate and exploit the economic potential of botanical species found within this part of the British empire. Among many other contributions, the botanical garden in Howrah can claim to have introduced India to tea, which was first grown here from plants smuggled out of China.

Several pioneering botanists served as superintendents of the Calcutta Botanical Garden, beginning with William Roxburgh and Nathaniel Wallich, who helped describe and classify many Indian plants using the Linnean system of taxonomy. As a result, their names are attached to a wide variety of species, including the chir pine (*Pinus roxburghii)* and the kail or blue pine (*Pinus wallichiana*).

Over the years the purpose of the garden has changed, from its colonial origins as a living laboratory for researching the commercial value of plants, to being an herbarium and arboretum that preserves and protects rare and unusual species. In addition to Indian trees, the garden contains an assortment of exotic or foreign species like a bayleaf palm from Central America and a foxtail palm from Australia. There is also an indigenous tali palm, known as talier in Bengali (*Corypha taliera*), which is now extinct in the wild. A sturdy-looking tree about 10 metres tall, it has huge, shaggy fronds that form a matted crown. This talier is only twenty-seven years old and hasn't reached its full height, which can exceed 30 metres. The lower portion of its trunk is covered with overlapping stubs of dead leaf stalks, known as boots, that form a loose, woven pattern encasing the trunk.

A sign next to this tree tells the story of *Corypha taliera*, which flowers only once in its lifetime, after growing for 60 to 100 years. The inflorescence produces millions of seeds, following which the tree dies. Talier was once common in Bengal and proliferated throughout Birbhum and other districts. In 1935, a widespread flowering coincided with a famine in Bengal. Villagers interpreted this inflorescence, which gives the palm a ghostly, supernatural appearance, as an inauspicious sign. As a result, hundreds of trees were cut down before they could produce seeds. Over the years, many others have met the same fate, leaving only a few tali palms surviving in protected gardens. The tree in Howrah was cultivated from seeds in 1996 and won't flower for another half a century at least.

In this way, botanical gardens serve as refugia for endangered species, in much the same way as do sacred groves, though they can hardly be considered wild spaces. The gardens are carefully cultivated, monitored, and maintained by professional botanists and an army of gardeners. The Calcutta Botanical Garden contains a rosarium full of hybrid blooms, as well as a Hibiscus Section featuring varieties with names like 'Hot Shot Hollywood'. Another section is dedicated to ornamental species of ginger while an Aquatic Plants Section has ponds full of waterlilies and lotuses. The garden also serves as a city park and is used by morning walkers, day dreamers, and furtive couples in search of privacy. Stern signs warn visitors about the rules and regulations: 'Do Not Make Noise', 'No Fire', 'No Alcohol', 'Don't Pluck Flowers', and 'Obscene Photography Prohibited'.

A popular place for birdwatching, this cultivated landscape may not be wild itself, but attracts a diversity of avifauna both resident and migratory, as well as reptiles and small mammals. Aside from kingfishers, I spot a greater coucal lurking in a jungle of overgrown creepers. A rufous treepie (*Dendrocitta vagabunda*), remains true to its scientific name, loitering in the lower branches of a bougainvillea, recently pruned. The invisible line that separates wild species from those that have been propagated by human beings is not always easy to determine and, inevitably, ambiguities creep in. Along its untended margins, the botanic garden is full of wild plants, whether they are invasive weeds or floral specimens that have escaped from their assigned beds and now grow according to their natural inclinations.

Wildness can be a state of mind. Over the past two years, I have travelled thousands of kilometres to see hoolock gibbons in their natural habitat, snow leopards traversing remote, precipitous slopes, and Malabar trogons perched amidst a disorienting profusion of tropical foliage. Undisturbed, unsettled places have a raw and lonely beauty that evokes a sense of sanctity and leaves us entranced. Every naturalist is a pilgrim in search of ecological truths. To experience a wild environment and observe the species it sustains gives me a greater reverence for the mysteries of life, wherever or whatever they may be. Wandering through this garden, with its colonial history as well as its profusion of indigenous flora, I am conscious of a hidden wilderness within the shadow of a dying leaf and an irrepressible, creative force that pushes open the petals of a rose.

Wild creatures like the treepie don't think of themselves as wild. We do. Our understanding of nature is entirely subjective and organized according to categories that human beings have invented. Whether we express it through Sanskrit verse or Latin binomials, taxonomy is nothing but a series of metaphors that make other species comprehensible to us. They, on the other hand, have no need to give us a name.

The centrepiece of the Acharya Jagadish Chandra Bose Indian Botanic Garden, is an enormous banyan tree (*Ficus benghalensis*), popularly known as the Great Banyan. According to a sign in the garden, this tree, with its 4,033 prop roots, covers an area of 1.89 hectares (4.67 acres). Roughly 250 years old, it predates the garden itself. K. C. Sahni, in his *Book of Indian Trees,* confidently asserts this banyan's origin: 'It was ascertained to have grown from seeds dropped by birds in the crown of a date palm in 1782.' Like most banyans, this noble tree took root as an epiphytic strangler fig, five years before Colonel Kyd established the garden.

As I approach the tree, its sprawling branches, supported by colonnades of aerial roots, extend in all directions. Today, the Great Banyan is protected by a walled enclosure and visitors are no longer permitted to wander through its labyrinthine galleries or sit beneath its capacious shade. The leathery, oblong leaves are a bright, fresh green and clusters of red figs, no bigger than prayer beads, grow at the ends of most of the branches. The interior of the tree is so dense, I cannot see through to the other side. Towards the centre is a clearing where the banyan must have originated, though the mother tree appears to have died and rotted away, along with the date palm that once supported it.

As I begin to circumambulate the Great Banyan, a number of birds are moving through the branches overhead, mostly ashy drongos feeding on insects attracted to the ripening figs. Yellow-footed green pigeons and lineated barbets are feasting on the figs themselves. The outer branches of the tree also contain a collection of tissue paper kites that must have been flown from rooftops nearby and got snagged in the foliage. Their bright colours give the tree a festive look. After I have completed half a circuit of the banyan, my path is blocked by the perimeter wall and I resist the temptation to jump over this barrier. Remembering the banyan tree from my boyhood in Fatehgarh, I want to swing on its aerial roots and scramble into its branches to hide.

Banyans are the largest trees on earth. They are also living anthologies of stories—historical, mythological, and ecological—all of which converge and are plaited together like the tree's multiple limbs and roots. In Sanskrit and Hindi, the banyan is known as vata vriksh and is sometimes considered the male consort of the peepul (*Ficus religiosa*), both sharing the same genus. The common English name is connected to the Bania community of traders, who used to set up shop under the branches of large banyans. Fig trees of different species have long been associated with cobras and stone images of nagas are placed at their roots. The banyan is also linked to Yama the god of death, and this tree is often found growing near cremation ghats. As a result, it also features in ghost stories about vetal or vampires and other evil spirits that haunt its shadowy branches. Sadhus or mendicants take shelter under spreading banyans because the tree provides shade and protection from rain, as well as being associated with Shiva the divine ascetic. Ultimately, because of its longevity, the banyan is also considered an emblem of immortality.

Science too has stories to tell and botanists recount how banyans, like most *Ficus* species, have a unique and complex process of reproduction. Though the figs that form on its branches may look like fruit, they are actually receptacles for dozens of minute flowers, which bloom inside the fig rather than opening their petals outward. Male and female blossoms, as well as gall flowers that are sterile, form inside the soft, fleshy casing of a fig. The only way in which they can be pollinated and produce seeds is through the assistance of tiny insects called fig-wasps, which burrow into the fig and lay their eggs in the gall flowers.

After hatching and passing through the larval stage, male and female wasps mate inside the fig. The wingless male soon dies where he was born while the female wasp emerges, covered in pollen from the male flowers. She then flies off to another tree where the process begins all over again. In this way, the enormous banyan and the miniscule wasp are entirely dependent upon each other for the reproduction of their separate species.

Metaphorically, poets, philosophers, and politicians have extolled the banyan as a symbol of unity, integrity, and diversity, its many branches and supporting roots suggesting the idea of collective strength and wisdom. For this reason, *Ficus benghalensis*—the vata vriksh—was chosen to be India's national tree.

As I retrace my steps and circle back to the point where I began, admiring the monumental architecture of the banyan's limbs, the scaffolding of aerial roots and the breadth of its canopy, I think of those tiny seeds that formed inside the pollinated figs, two and a half centuries ago. They were then dispersed by hungry birds and squirrels, leading to a fateful moment when that speck of life germinated high above the ground, in the moist, accommodating crown of a wild date palm. Sprouting from a single seed, the delicate epiphyte began to grow while clinging to its host, until it eventually descended to earth and then slowly, inexorably spread its roots in all directions. No metaphors or myths can match the profound life story of the Great Banyan, which will, undoubtedly, live on for another century at least, outlasting us all.

ACKNOWLEDGEMENTS

My sincere thanks to everyone who assisted with this book. Undoubtedly, the list of names below is incomplete and my apologies to anyone I may have inadvertently forgotten. Without the help of each of these individuals, listed alphabetically, I would not have been able to complete my travels, research, and writing:

Rafik Ahmad, Joseph Alter, Angchuk, Gautam Bhupathiraju, Shaminder Boparai, Devika Cariapa, Somil Daga, Omkar Dharwadkar, Anu Dhillon, Arpita Dutta, Madhav Gadgil, Ajay Giri, Varad Giri, Runap Gogoi, Bikram Grewal, Dheeraj Halali, Sunil Harsana, Pallul Hazarika, Vithoba Hegde, A. J. T. Johnsingh, Aditya Kakodkar, Raza Kazmi, Nanaya Konerira, Vidisha Kulkarni, Ram Kumar, Cheppudira Kushalappa, Marchborn Lyngdoh, Ajay Mark, Gerry Martin, Prasun Majumdar, Arvind Krishna Mehrotra, Nirmal Mondal, Sanjay Narang, Vishal Negi, Tsewang Norboo, Renu Oberoi, Meera Anna Oomen, Bivash Pandav, Bijay Panika, Sudarshan Pathak, Manash Pratim, M. K. Ranjitsinh, Dinkar Samore, Vivek Sarkar, Kartik Shanker, K. S. Sheshadri, Bachchu Singh, Meenakshi Singh, Ram Pratap Singh, Shiv Singh, David Sonam, Satyendra Tiwari, Kay Hassall Tiwari, P. K. Varma, Sejal Worah.

I am deeply indebted to Pradip Krishen, Janaki Lenin, Akshay Shah, Hashim Tyabji, and Rom Whitaker for their support and encouragement, and for reading and commenting on portions of the manuscript. Their extensive knowledge and sharp eyes have helped me avoid numerous blunders, though whatever errors the text contains are mine alone. As always, I am most grateful to David Davidar and Aienla Ozukum at Aleph Book Company. And, finally, my love and thanks to Ameeta, Jayant, and Shibani.

Arvind Krishna Mehrotra's poem, 'Ramapithecus and I', which appears as an epigraph, is reprinted with permission of the author, for which I am extremely grateful.

LIST OF SPECIES MENTIONED IN THIS BOOK

MAMMALS

Asian elephant *Elephas maximus*
African cheetah *Acinonyx jubatus jubatus*
Asiatic cheetah *Acinonyx jubatus venaticus*
Asiatic lion *Panthera leo persica*
Bandicoot rat *Bandicota indica*
Barasingha (swamp deer) *Rucervus duvaucelii*
Barking Deer (muntjac, kakar) *Muntiacus muntjak*
Bengal slow loris *Nycticebus bengalensis*
Bharal (blue sheep) *Pseudois nayaur*
Blackbuck (hiran, ena) *Antilope cervicapra*
Black-naped hare *Lepus nigricollis*
Bonnet macaque *Macaca radiata*
Capped langur *Trachypithecus pileatus*
Caracal *Caracal caracal*
Chital (spotted deer) *Axis axis*
Chinkara (Indian gazelle) *Gazella bennettii*
Chousingha (Four-horned antelope, kurunga) *Tetracerus quadricornis*
Clouded leopard *Neofelis nebulosa*
Common palm civet (toddy cat) *Paradoxurus hermaphroditus*
Desert fox *Vulpes vulpes pusilla*
Eurasian otter *Lutra lutra*
Feral horse *Equus caballus*
Fishing cat *Prionailurus viverrinus*
Five-striped palm squirrel *Funambulus pennantii*
Ganges river dolphin *Platanista gangetica*
Gaur *Bos gaurus*
Golden jackal *Canis aureus*
Golden langur *Trachypithecus geei*

Goral *Nemorhaedus goral*
Great bandicoot rat *Bandicota indica*
Greater one-horned rhinoceros *Rhinoceros unicornis*
Grey mongoose *Herpestes edwardsii*
Grey slender loris *Loris lydekkerianus*
Grey wolf (shanku) *Canis lupus*
Himalayan black bear *Ursus thibetanus*
Himalayan brown bear *Ursus arctos isabellinus*
Hoolock gibbon *Hoolock hoolock*
Human being *Homo sapiens*
Ibex (skin) *Capra sibirica*
Indian crested porcupine *Hystrix indica*
Indian flying fox *Pteropus giganteus*
Indian fox *Vulpes bengalensis*
Indian giant squirrel *Ratufa indica*
Indian pangolin *Manis crassicaudata*
Indus river dolphin *Platanista gangetica minor*
Irrawaddy dolphin *Orcaella brevirostris*
Jungle cat *Felis chaus*
Kashmir red deer (Kashmir stag, hangul) *Cervus elaphus*
Ladakh pika (mouse hare) *Ochotona ladacensis*
Leopard *Panthera pardus*
Leopard cat *Prionailurus bengalensis*
Lion-tailed macaque *Macaca silenus*
Malabar civet *Viverra civettina*
Markhor *Capra falconeri*
Mouse deer *Moschiola indica*
Nilgai *Boselaphus tragocamelus*
Northern pig-tailed macaque *Macaca leonina*
Pallas's squirrel (red-bellied squirrel) *Callosciurus erythraeus*
Ratel (honey badger, bejoo) *Mellivora capensis*
Red fox *Vulpes vulpes*
Red panda *Ailurus fulgens*
Rhesus macaque (bandar, vanara) *Macaca mulatta*
Rufous horseshoe bat *Rhinolophus rouxii*
Sambar *Rusa unicolor*
Schomburgk's deer *Rucervus schomburgki*
Sloth bear *Melursus ursinus*
Small Indian civet *Viverricula indica*

Smooth-coated otter *Lutrogale perspicillata*
Snow leopard (shaan) *Panthera uncia*
Striped hyena (lakarbagga) *Hyaena hyaena*
Three-striped palm squirrel *Funambulus palmarum*
Tiger *Panthera tigris*
Urial (shapu) *Ovis orientalis*
Wild buffalo *Bubalus arnee*
Wild dog (dhole) *Cuon alpinus*
Wild pig *Sus scrofa*
Wild yak *Bos mutus*

BIRDS

Alpine accentor *Prunella collaris*
Ashy bulbul *Hemixos flavala*
Ashy drongo *Dicrurus leucophaeus*
Asian fairy bluebird *Irena puella*
Asian openbill *Anastomus oscitans*
Asian paradise flycatcher *Terpsiphone paradisi*
Bank mynah *Acridotheres ginginianus*
Barn swallow *Hirundo rustica*
Bar-headed goose *Anser indicus*
Bar-tailed godwit *Limosa lapponica*
Baya weaver *Ploceus philippinus*
Bay-backed shrike *Lanius vittatus*
Black drongo *Dicrurus macrocercus*
Black francolin *Francolinus francolinus*
Black kite (pariah kite) *Milvus migrans*
Black redstart *Phoenicurus ochruros*
Black-backed forktail *Enicurus immaculatus*
Black-bellied tern *Sterna acuticauda*
Black-capped kingfisher *Halcyon pileata*
Black-headed bulbul *Pycnonotus atriceps*
Black-headed ibis *Threskiornis melanocephalus*
Black-headed jay *Garrulus lanceolatus*
Black-lored tit *Parus xanthogenys*
Black-winged kite (black-shouldered kite) *Elanus caeruleus*
Black-winged stilt *Himantopus himantopus*
Blood pheasant *Ithaginis cruentus*
Blue-bearded bee-eater *Nyctyornis athertoni*

Blue-tailed bee-eater *Merops philippinus*
Blue whistling thrush *Myophonus caeruleus*
Bonelli's eagle *Aquila fasciata*
Brahminy kite *Haliastur indus*
Brown-cheeked rail *Rallus indicus*
Brown-winged kingfisher *Pelargopsis amauroptera*
Cattle egret *Bubulcus ibis*
Chukar *Alectoris chukar*
Changeable hawk eagle *Nisaetus cirrhatus*
Chestnut-shouldered petronia (yellow-throated sparrow) *Gymnoris xanthocollis*
Chestnut-bellied nuthatch *Sitta cinnamoventris*
Citrine wagtail *Motacilla citreola*
Collared kingfisher *Todiramphus chloris*
Collared scops owl *Otus (bakkamoena) lettia*
Common crane *Grus grus*
Common greenshank *Tringa nebularia*
Common kestral *Falco tinnunculus*
Common kingfisher *Alcedo atthis*
Common mynah *Acridotheres tristis*
Common reed bunting *Emberiza schoeniclus*
Common redshank *Tringa totanus*
Common sandpiper *Actitis hypoleucos*
Common tailorbird *Orthotomus sutorius*
Common woodshrike *Tephrodornis pondicerianus*
Coppersmith barbet *Megalaima haemacephala*
Crested serpent eagle *Spilornis cheela*
Crimson-backed sunbird *Leptocoma minima*
Darter *Anhinga melanogaster*
Demoiselle crane *Grus virgo*
Dusky crag martin *Ptyonoprogne concolor*
Egyptian vulture *Neophron percnopterus*
Eurasian collared dove *Streptopelia decaocto*
Eurasian coot *Fulica atra*
Eurasian curlew *Numenius arquata*
Eurasian magpie *Pica pica*
Eurasian roller *Coracias garrulus*
Eurasian spoonbill *Platalea leucorodia*
Fire-breasted flowerpecker *Dicaeum ignipectus*
Gadwall *Anas strepera*

Glossy ibis *Plegadis falcinellus*
Golden eagle *Aquila chrysaetos*
Golden oriole *Oriolus kundoo*
Golden-headed cisticola *Cisticola exilis*
Great barbet *Megalaima virens*
Great crested grebe *Podiceps cristatus*
Great egret *Casmerodius albus*
Great hornbill *Buceros bicornis*
Great Indian bustard *Ardeotis nigriceps*
Great thick-knee *Esacus recurvirostris*
Great white pelican *Pelecanus onocrotalus*
Greater coucal *Centropus sinensis*
Greater goldenback (greater flameback) *Chrysocolaptes lucidus*
Greater necklaced laughingthrush *Garrulax pectoralis*
Greater painted snipe *Rostratula benghalensis*
Greater flamingo *Phoenicopterus roseus*
Greater racket-tailed drongo *Dicrurus paradiseus*
Green-backed tit *Parus monticolus*
Green bee-eater *Merops orientalis*
Green imperial pigeon *Ducula aenea*
Green-billed malkoha *Rhopodytes tristis*
Grey bushchat *Saxicola ferreus*
Grey heron *Ardea cinerea*
Grey francolin *Francolinus pondicerianus*
Grey junglefowl *Gallus sonneratii*
Grey peacock-pheasant *Polyplectron bicalcaratum*
Greylag goose *Anser anser*
Grey-headed canary flycatcher *Culicicapa ceylonensis*
Grey-headed fish eagle *Icthyophaga ichthyaetus*
Grey-headed woodpecker *Picus canus*
Himalayan bulbul *Pycnonotus leucogenys*
Himalayan monal *Lophophorus impejanus*
Himalayan vulture *Gyps himalayensis*
Hume's leaf warbler *Phylloscopus humei*
Indian eagle owl *Bubo bengalensis*
Indian grey hornbill *Ocyceros birostris*
Indian pond heron *Ardeola grayii*
Indian roller *Coracias benghalensis*
Indian skimmer *Rynchops albicollis*

Indian spot-billed duck *Anas poecilorhyncha*
Indian vulture (Indian long-billed vulture) *Gyps indicus*
Indian yellow tit *Parus aplonotus*
Isabelline wheatear *Oenanthe isabellina*
Jerdon's babbler *Chrysomma altirostre*
Jerdon's courser *Rhinoptilus bitorquatus*
Jungle babbler *Turdoides striata*
Kalij pheasant *Lophura leucomelanos*
Koel *Eudynamys scolopaceus*
Laggar falcon *Falco jugger*
Lammergeier (bearded vulture) *Gypaetus barbatus*
Lesser adjutant stork *Leptoptilos javanicus*
Lesser flamingo *Phoeniconaias minor*
Lesser goldenback (lesser flameback) *Dinopium benghalense*
Lesser sand plover *Charadrius mongolus*
Lesser whistling duck *Dendrocygna javanica*
Lineated barbet *Megalaima lineata*
Little ringed plover *Charadrius dubius*
Malabar trogon *Harpactes fasciatus*
Malabar whistling thrush *Myophonus horsfieldii*
Montagu's harrier *Circus pygargus*
Mountain imperial pigeon *Ducula badia*
Nicobar pigeon *Caloenas nicobarica*
Northern pintail *Anas acuta*
Northern shoveler *Anas clypeata*
Orange-headed thrush *Zoothera citrina*
Oriental white-eye *Zosterops palpebrosus*
Osprey *Pandion haliaetus*
Pacific golden plover *Pluvialis fulva*
Painted stork *Mycteria leucocephala*
Peafowl *Pavo cristatus*
Pheasant-tailed jacana *Hydrophasianus chirurgus*
Pied falconet *Microhierax melanoleucos*
Pied kingfisher *Ceryle rudis*
Pink-headed duck *Rhodonessa caryophyllacea*
Plain martin *Riparia paludicola*
Plain prinia *Prinia inornata*
Plum-headed parakeet *Psittacula cyanocephala*
Purple heron *Ardea purpurea*

Purple sunbird *Cinnyris asiaticus*
Purple swamphen *Porphyrio porphyrio*
Pygmy blue flycatcher *Muscicapella hodgsoni*
Red junglefowl *Gallus gallus*
Red spurfowl *Galloperdix spadicea*
Red-billed chough *Pyrrhocorax pyrrhocorax*
Red-breasted parakeet *Psittacula alexandri*
Red-crested pochard *Netta rufina*
Red-headed trogon *Harpactes erythrocephalus*
Red-naped ibis (Indian black ibis) *Pseudibis papillosa*
Red-rumped swallow *Cecropis daurica*
Red-vented bulbul *Pycnonotus cafer*
Red-wattled lapwing *Vanellus indicus*
River lapwing *Vanellus duvaucelii*
River tern *Sterna aurantia*
Rose-ringed parakeet *Psittacula krameri*
Rosy pipit *Anthus roseatus*
Ruddy-breasted crake *Porzana fusca*
Ruddy shelducks *Tadorna ferruginea*
Rufous treepie *Dendrocitta vagabunda*
Rufous woodpecker *Micropternus brachyurus*
Rusty-cheeked scimitar babbler *Pomatorhinus erythrogenys*
Sarus crane *Grus antigone*
Scaly-breasted munia *Lonchura punctulata*
Scarlet minivet *Pericrocotus speciosus*
Sclater's monal *Lophophorus sclateri*
Shikra *Accipiter badius*
Siberian stonechat *Saxicola maurus*
Slender-billed vulture *Gyps tenuirostris*
Small minivet *Pericrocotus cinnamomeus*
Small niltava *Niltava macgrigoriae*
Spotted dove *Stigmatopelia chinensis*
Spotted owlet *Athene brama*
Spot-bellied eagle owl *Bubo nipalensis*
Streaked laughingthrush *Garrulax lineatus*
Streaked wren babbler *Napothera brevicaudata*
Sultan tit *Melanochlora sultanea*
Swamp francolin *Francolinus gularis*
Swamp prinia (swamp grass babbler) *Prinia cinerascens*

Tawny eagle *Aquila rapax*
Terek sandpiper *Xenus cinereus*
Western marsh harrier (Eurasian marsh harrier) *Circus aeruginosus*
Western tragopan *Tragopan melanocephalus*
Whimbrel *Numenius phaeopus*
White wagtail *Motacilla alba*
White-breasted waterhen *Amaurornis phoenicurus*
White-browed fantail *Rhipidura aureola*
White-browed wagtail *Motacilla maderaspatensis*
White-crowned forktail *Enicurus leschenaulti*
White-eyed buzzard *Butastur teesa*
White-rumped shama *Copsychus malabaricus*
White-rumped vulture *Gyps bengalensis*
White-tailed stonechat *Saxicola leucurus*
White-throated kingfisher *Halcyon smyrnensis*
White-winged duck *Asarcornis scutulata*
Wire-tailed swallow *Hirundo smithii*
Woolly-necked stork *Ciconia episcopus*
Yellow-footed green pigeon *Treron phoenicopterus*

REPTILES

Asian water monitor *Varanus salvator*
Brahminy skink (keeled skink) *Eutropis carinata*
Bengal monitor *Varanus bengalensis*
Bronzeback tree snake *Dendrelaphis tristis*
Brook's gecko *Hemidactylus brookii*
Brown vine snake (brown-speckled whipsnake) *Ahaetulla pulverulenta*
Checkered keelback *Fowlea piscator*
Common dotted garden skink *Riopa punctata*
Common house gecko (chipkali) *Hemidactylus frenatus*
Common krait *Bungarus caeruleus*
Desert monitor *Varanus griseus*
Gharial *Gavialis gangeticus*
Giri's bronzeback *Dendrelaphis girii*
Green keelback *Rhabdophis plumbicolor*
Green vine snake *Ahaetulla nasuta*
Hegde's gecko *Hemidactylus hegdei*
Hook-nosed sea snake *Hydrophis schistosus*
Hump-nosed pit viper *Hypnale hypnale*

Indian cobra (spectacled cobra) *Naja naja*
Indian flapshell turtle *Lissemys punctata*
Indian fringe-fingered lizard *Acanthodactylus cantoris*
Indian softshell turtle *Nilssonia gangetica*
King cobra *Ophiophagus hannah*
Malabar pit viper *Craspedocephalus malabaricus*
Mugger crocodile *Crocodylus palustris*
Oriental garden lizard *Calotes versicolor*
Rat snake *Ptyas mucosa*
Red-crowned roof turtle (painted roof turtle) *Batagur kachuga*
Russell's viper *Daboia russelii*
Saltwater crocodile (estuarine crocodile) *Crocodylus prorosus*
Saw-scaled viper *Echis carinatus*
Southern flying lizard *Draco dussumieri*
Spiny-tailed lizard *Saara hardwickii*
Travancore wolf snake *Lycodon travancoricus*
Trinket snake *Coelognathus helena*

AMPHIBIANS

Amboli bush frog *Pseudophilautus amboli*
Asian common toad *Duttaphrynus melanostictus*
Bombay bush frog *Raorchestes bombayensis*
Himalayan toad *Duttaphrynus himalayanus*
Kottigehara dancing frog *Micrixalus kottigeharensis*
Malabar gliding frog *Rhacophorus malabaricus*
Skittering frog *Euphlyctis cyanophlyctis*
Wrinkled frog (castle rock night frog) *Nyctibatrachus pertraeus*

FISH

Barramundi (chonak, Asian sea bass) *Lates calcarifer*
Boroli *Barilius barila*
Catla *Labeo catla*
Goroi *Channa punctata*
Grey mullet *Mugil cephalus*
Guitarfish Rhinobatidae
Hump-backed Mahseer *Tor ramadevii*
Kingfish (king mackerel, Surmai, Seer) *Scomberomorus guttatus*
Kokila (Asian needlefish) *Xenentodon cancila*
Kuchia (eel) *Ophichthys cuchia*

Lanchi *Wallago attu*
Loach *Balitoridae*
Magur (Asian catfish / walking catfish) *Clarius magur*
Mudskipper *Oxudercidae*
Pomfret *Pampus argenteusa*
Puthi *Puntius saphore*
Rohu *Labeo rohita*
Sardine *Sardinella longiceps*
Singhi (xingi, fossil cat) *Heteropneustes fossilis*

INSECTS

Ant lion (larva of lacewings) *Neuroptera*
Luna moth *Actias selene*
Bagworm *Eumeta variegata*
Baronet butterfly *Symphaedra nais*
Blue mormon butterfly *Papilio polymnester*
Blue tiger butterfly *Tirumala limniace*
Common tiger butterfly *Danaus genutia*
Fig wasp *Eupristina masoni*
Fulvous forest skimmer *Neurothemis fulvia*
One-spot grass yellow butterfly *Eurema andersoni*
Paris peacock butterfly *Papilio paris*
Malabar rose butterfly *Pachliopta pandiyana*
Mosquito (most common species in Terai) *Anopheles culicifacies*
Spider-hunting wasp *Pompilidae*

ARACHNIDS

Asian forest scorpion *Heterometrus*
Long-horned spiny orb weaver *Macracantha arcuate*
Fishing spider *Dolomedes*
Funnel web spider *Agelenidae*
Giant wood spider *Nephila pilipes*
Tailless whipscorpion *Amblypygi*
Tarantula *Annandaliella travancorica*

CRUSTACEANS

Fiddler crabs *Ocypodidae*
Tree crabs *Ghatiana atropururea*

INVERTEBRATES

Earthworm *Drawida nilamburensis*
Leech (most common near Agumbe) *Haemadipsa dussumieri*
Semi-slug *Varadia amboliensis*

TREES

Amaltas *Cassia fistula*
Amla *Phyllanthus emblica*
Anyar (lyonia) *Lyonia ovalifolia*
Areca nut palm *Areca catechu*
Arjuna *Terminalia arjuna*
Ashoka (sita-ashok) *Saraca asoca*
Australian wattle *Acacia auriculiformis*
Babool *Acacia nilotica*
Bain (Indian mangrove) *Avicennia officinalis*
Bandar dima *Dysoxylum gotadhora*
Bael *Aegle marmelos*
Banj oak *Quercus leucotrichophora*
Banyan (strangler fig) *Ficus benghalensis*
Bayleaf palm *Sabal mauritiiformis*
Ber (jujube, reni) *Ziziphus mauritiana*
Bhamora (Himalayan dogwood) *Cornus capitata*
Bistendu *Diospyros cordifolia*
Black damar *Canarium strictum*
Champak *Michelia champaca*
Chandan (sandalwood) *Santalum album*
Chir pine *Pinus roxburghii*
Churail papadi (bandar ki roti, Indian elm) *Holoptelea integrifolia*
Cinnamon *Cinnamomum cassia*
Deodar *Cedrus deodara*
Dhok (dhau, kardhai) *Anogeissus pendula*
Eucalyptus (forest red gum) *Eucalyptus tereticornis*
Fishtail palm *Caryota urens*
Foxtail palm *Wodyetia bifurcata*
Gadasi *Ficus macrocarpa*
Genwa *Excoecaria agallocha*
Ghiriya (bhirra, satinwood) *Chloroxylon swietenia*
Ghost tree (kulu, gum karaiya) *Sterculia urens*
Gorjon *Rhizophora apiculata*

Gular (cluster fig) *Ficus racemosa*
Gulmohur *Delonix regia*
Haldu *Haldina cordifolia*
Hazelnut *Corylus ferox*
Himalayan yew *Taxus wallichiana*
Hollong *Dipterocarpus retusus*
Horse chestnut (pangad) *Aesculus indica*
Jackfruit *Artocarpus heterophyllus*
Jamun (jambu) *Syzygium cumini*
Jangli almond *Hydnocarpus pentandrus*
Jhinjheri *Bauhinia recemosa*
Juniper *Juniperus tibetica*
Kachnar (camel foot tree) *Bauhinia variegata*
Kadamba *Neolamarckia cadamba*
Kaim (Krishna kadamb) *Mitragyna parvifolia*
Kankra *Bruguiera gymnorhiza*
Kaphal (box myrtle, bayberry) *Myrica esculenta*
Karonda *Carissa congesta*
Keora *Sonneratia apetalia*
Khasi pine *Pinus kesiya*
Khair *Acacia catechu*
Khejdi (jhand) *Prosopis cineraria*
Kokam *Garcinia indica*
Kumatiyo *Acacia senegal*
Madhuca neriifolia
Mahua *Madhuca longifolia*
Malabar tamarind *Garcinia gummi-gutta*
Mango *Mangifera indica*
Moru oak *Quercus floribunda*
Mulberry (shahtoot) *Morus alba*
Neem *Azadirachta indica*
Otenga (elephant apple) *Dillenia indica*
Palash (flame of the forest, dhak) *Butea monosperma*
Peepul *Ficus religiosa*
Rhododendron (dieng tiewsaw, burans) *Rhododendron arboreum*
Rohido (Marwar teak) *Tecomella undulata*
Ronjh (reonjha) *Acacia leucophloea*
Rudraksha *Elaeocarpus ganitras*
Saaj (crocodile bark tree) *Terminalia elliptica*

Sal *Shorea robusta*
Sargooro (soajna) *Moringa concanensis*
Scholar's tree (devil's tree, blackboard tree) *Alstonia scholaris*
Semal (silk cotton) *Bombax ceiba*
Shisham *Dalbergia sissoo*
Silver oak *Grevillea robusta*
Sonjna (drumstick tree) *Moringa oleifera*
Sundari *Heretiera fomes*
Talier (tali palm) *Corypha taliera*
Tamarind (imli) *Tamarindus indica*
Teak (sagun) *Tectona grandis*
Tendu *Diospyros melanoxylon*
Tenti (kareel, kair, dela) *Capparis decidua*
Vilayati babool (baavlia) *Prosopis juliflora*
Weeping willow *Salix babylonica*
White cedar (deodar) *Dysoxylum malabaricum*
Wild banana *Musa acuminata*
Wild date palm (khajoor) *Phoenix sylvestris*
Wild jackfruit *Autocarpus hirsutus*

PLANTS

Anantmool (Indian sarsaparilla) *Hemidesmus indicus*
Baru (jangli-jowar, Johnson grass) *Sorghum halepense*
Bhabar grass (sabai) *Eulaliopsis binata*
Black pepper *Piper nigrum*
Brahmi *Bacopa monnieri*
Bui (desert cotton) *Aerva javanica*
Calcutta bamboo (male bamboo) *Dendrocalamus strictus*
Cane (rattan, baint) *Calamus rotang*
Dabh *Desmostachya bipinnata*
Dhani grass *Porteresia coarctata*
Ekora grass *Saccharum ravennae*
Gangeti *Grewia tenax*
Geedar tambaku *Verbascum chinense*
Gendali-bon *Ageratum houstonianum*
Gulhari *Spatholobus parviflorus*
Jangli haldi (wild turmeric) *Curcuma aromatica*
Jargu *Dichanthium annulatum*
Kalli *Euphorbia tirucalli*

Kans (kas, khagori) *Saccharum spontaneum*
Kheemp *Leptadenia pyrotechnica*
Kunai *Imperata cylindrica*
Kurinji/kurinci *Strobilanthes kunthiana*
Lantana *Lantana camara*
Marijuana (bhang) *Cannabis sativa*
Missi (cowpea witchweed) *Striga gesnerioides*
Munj *Saccharum bengalense*
Musk rose *Rosa macrophylla*
Oont kaintalo *Echinops echinatus*
Paan *Piper betle*
Panchdhara (panduphali) *Flueggea leucopyrus*
Pippali (long pepper) *Piper longum*
Poolongi *Sporobolus marginatus*
Rattlepod plant *Crotalaria juncea*
Santai *Clematis vitalba*
Sea buckthorn *Hippophae rhamnoides*
Sensitive Plant (touch-me-not, shame plant) *Mimosa pudica*
Sevan (lilon) *Lasiurus scindicus*
Sugar cane (ganna, ikshu) *Saccharum officinarum*
Sundew *Drosera peltata*
Tachula (Mauritian grass) *Apluda mutica*
Thhor *Euphorbia caducifolia*
Tulsi (holy basil) *Ocimum tenuiflorum*
Vajradanti *Barleria prionitis*
Water hyacinth *Eichornia crassipes*

FUNGI

Bioluminescent fungi *Mycena*
Bracket mushrooms *Ganoderma*
Dead man's fingers *Xyleria polymorpha*
Keeda ghaas *Ophiocordyceps sinensis*
Zombie fungus *Ophiocordyceps unilateralis*

NOTES

PREFACE: BHIMBETKA

1 **'Tools, bones and artefacts found at an excavation':** Devika Cariapa, *India Through Archaeology: Excavating History*, Chenna: Tulika Books, 2017, p. 26.

5 **Pathak and Clottes suggest these are 'spirit riders':** Meenakshi Dubey-Pathak and Jean Clottes, *Madhya Pradesh Rock Art and Tribal Art*, New Delhi: Aryan Books, 2021, pp. 230–232.

7 **'The forest has tigers and it should never be cut':** Mahabharata (5.29.47–48) quoted in Romila Thapar, 'The Lion: From Pride to Metaphor', in Valmik Thapar, Romila Thapar, and Yusuf Ansari (eds.), *Exotic Aliens: The Lion & Cheetah in India*, New Delhi: Aleph Book Company, 2013, p. 39.

PROLOGUE: A NATURALIST'S TRANCE

10 **'The hunter's trance' is a phrase that I first came upon in a book:** Carl Von Essen, *The Hunter's Trance: Nature, Spirit and Ecology*, Great Barrington: Lindisfarne Books, 2007.

11 **'In a twist my mind came free and I was aware':** Edward O. Wilson, *Biophilia: The Human Bond with Other Species*, Cambridge: Harvard University Press, 1986, p. 7.

12 **'Wild animals, like wild places, are invaluable to us':** Robert Macfarlane, *The Wild Places*, London: Penguin Random House, 2008, p. 307.

12 **'Even when animals share the same senses with us':** Ed Yong, *An Immense World: How Animal Senses Reveal the Hidden Realms Around Us*, New York: Random House Trade Paperbacks, 2022, pp. 6–7.

15 **'Jab se dekha unki aankhon ko/Halka halka sa suroor rehta hai':** Shemaroo Musical Maestros, 'Yeh Jo Halka Halka Original Song by Nusrat Fateh Ali Khan', YouTube, 13 December 2016, available at www.youtube.com/watch?v=3R1eUfVxOGI.

17 **'Between the space of wood and leather':** Reshma Aquil, *Sleeping Wind*, Singapore: Ethos Books, 2001, p. 2.

19 **Born Camilla Koffler in Vienna, in 1911:** Pryor Dodge, 'Ylla 1911–1955', Pryordodge.com, 2019, available at pryordodge.com/ylla.html.

20 **'I do not understand that need in man to affirm himself heroically by killing':** Camilla Koffler (Ylla), *Animals in India*, London: Hamish Hamilton, 1958, p. 18.

22 **The other book that made an indelible impression.:** Astrid Bergman Sucksdorff, *Chendru: The Boy and the Tiger*, tr. by William Sansom, London: Collins, 1960.

23 **For a brief period, Chendru became a star.:** John Joseph, 'Bastar's Tiger Boy Passes Away', *Times of India*, 30 September 2013.

23 **Tambu's fate is unrecorded:** Bharat Desai, 'Growing Hero of a "A Jungle Tale" still tries to fit into tribal life 20 years later', *India Today*, 30 April 1996.

PART I: LIVING LANDSCAPES

CHAPTER 1: AT AGUMBE

28 **Lal points out that, '...the eastern coastline of Madagascar fits'.:** Pranay Lal, *Indica: A Deep Natural History of the Indian Subcontinent*, New Delhi: Penguin (India Allen Lane), 2016, p. 189.

30 ***Rhacophorus* is a large family of tree frogs, consisting of more than 300 species:** Heather Heying, 'Rhacophoridae: Old World Tree Frogs', Animaldiversity.org, 2003, available at animaldiversity.org/accounts/Rhacophoridae.

30 **While Madagascar has many snakes:** 'Snakes of Madagascar', WildMadagascar.org, available at www.wildmadagascar.org/wildlife/snakes.html.

31 **'...an apocryphal anecdote of a rather famous racket-tailed drongo.':** Manoj Nair, 'Seasons in the Sun: An Avian Rhapsody', in Prerna Singh Bindra, Sonali Ghosh, and Anurajan Roy (eds.), *Wild Treasures: Reflections on Natural World Heritage Sites in Asia*, New Delhi: Aryan Books, p. 86.

36 **Aristotle believed that a snake's forked tongue:** J. A. Smith and W. D. Ross (eds.), *The Works of Aristotle*, Oxford: Clarendon Press, 1912, p. 94.

41 **The frog's so-called 'dancing' is actually a breeding display:** Morgan Erickson-Davis, 'Researchers Unearth the Surprising Secret of India's Dancing Frogs', India.mongabay.com, 31 March 2016, available at news.mongabay.com/2016/03/researchers-unearth-the-surprising-secret-of-indias-dancing-frogs.

CHAPTER 2: LOST JUNGLES

43 **'The Naga was the patron deity, perhaps aboriginal cult-object.':** D. D. Kosambi, *Myth and Reality*, New Delhi: Sage, 2020, p. 9.

43 **In classical dance traditions, like Bharatanatyam and Kuchipudi:** 'Dancing Krishna', carlos.emory.edu, available at carlos.emory.edu/htdocs/ODYSSEY/SOUTHASIA/krishna.html.

44 **This is a case of mistaken identity:** Pradip Krishen, *Trees of Delhi: A Field Guide*, New Delhi: Dorling Kindersley, 2006, p. 149.

51 **In his book, *Trees of Delhi*, Pradip Krishen lists four 'ecotones':** Ibid., pp. 19–21.

52 **'The native word means in strictness only waste, uncultivated ground':** Henry Yule and A. C. Burnell, *Hobson–Jobson: A Glossary of Colloquial Anglo-Indian Words and Phrases, and of Kindred Terms, Etymological, Historical, Geographical, and Discursive*, William Crooke (ed.), New Delhi: Munshiram Manoharlal, 2016, p. 470.

52 **Francis Zimmermann, a French anthropologist, has published a provocative book:** Francis Zimmermann, *The Jungle and the Aroma of Meats: An Ecological Theme in Hindu Medicine*, New Delhi: Motilal Banarasidass Publishers, 2011, p. 2.

53 **'All medicinal herbs and substances should be used as fresh as possible':** Kaviraj Kunja Lal Bishagratna (ed.), *An English Translation of the Sushruta Samhita Based on the Original Sanskrit Text*, Kolkata: S. L. Bhaduri, 1907, p. 339.

53 **The name pippali hasn't changed for at least two millennia**: 'Pippali', 1mg.com, available at www.1mg.com/ayurveda/pippali-169.

54 **'Now I shall describe the properties of the different species of edible meats':** Bishagratna, *An English Translation of the Sushruta Samhita Based on the Original Sanskrit Text*, p. 480.

54 **'The flesh of the Elephant tends to produce a state of extreme parchedness':** Ibid., p. 488.

55 **'In the party were Krishna, Arjuna, their wives and servants.':** Irawati Karve, *Yuganta: The End of an Epoch*, Hyderabad: Black Swan, 2021, pp. 108–109.

CHAPTER 3: TERAI ELEGY

57 **Most varieties of sugar cane planted today are hybrids of *Saccharum officinarum*:** Lallanji Gopal, 'Sugar-Making in Ancient India', *Journal of the Economic and Social History of the Orient*,

Vol. 7, No. 1, 1964, pp. 57–72, available at doi.org/10.2307/3596080.

61 **'I asked him once just what it was about tigers that so gripped his imagination.':** Geoffrey C. Ward and Diane Raines Ward, *Tiger-wallahs: Encounters with the Men Who Tried to Save the Greatest of the Great Cats*, New York: HarperCollins Publishers, 1993, p. 81.

61 **In Ward's biographical account of Billy's upbringing:** Ibid., pp. 67–75.

61 **'I walked along the edge of the forest for a little way, exploring the area':** Arjan Singh, *Tiger Haven*, London: Macmillan, 1973, p. 17.

63 **'Billy was devastated: Juliette had been the gentlest':** Ward and Ward, *Tigerwallahs*, p. 87.

64 **'The air we breathe and the water we drink stem from the biodiversity':** Bittu Sahgal, 'Meet Billy Arjan Singh,' *Sanctuary Asia*, Vol. 20, No. 9, 2000, available at www.sanctuarynaturefoundation.org/article/meet-billy-arjan-singh.

64 **One of the signs at Tiger Haven read: THE ANIMALS HAVE FIRST PRECEDENCE HERE:** Ward and Ward, *Tiger-wallahs*, p. 87.

66 **The World Wide Fund for Nature (WWF) and the Wildlife Trust of India (WTI):** 'Successful translocations grow rhino population in India's Terai region', Worldwildlife.org, available at www.worldwildlife.org/stories/successful-translocations-grow-rhino-population-in-india-s-terai-region.

67 **Three elephants were killed in 2003:** Kr Raghavendra Singh, 'Dudhwa National Park on wrong tracks', *Times of India*, 18 June 2003.

67 **And in 2006, a young tigress was fatally struck by a train:** 'Tiger killed by train in Dudhwa national park', *Hindustan Times*, 26 April 2006.

68 **'This was also the period when IUCN's Cat Specialist Group':** Shaminder Boparai, *Billy Arjan Singh: Tiger of Dudhwa*, New Delhi: HarperCollins Publishers, 2011, p. 158.

68 **Billy was naturally sceptical of the claim:** Ibid., p. 160.

70 **'With a wave from Billy Arjan Singh, we moved slowly forward':** George Schaller, 'Foreword', in Boparai, *Billy Arjan Singh*, p. 10.

70 **Swamp deer numbers have diminished steadily because of the loss of wetlands:** 'Barasingha', Iucnredlist.org, available at www.iucnredlist.org/species/4257/22167675.

73 **'I would argue that tiger tourism should be reinvented':** Ullas K. Karanth, *Among Tigers: Fighting to Bring Back Asia's Big Cats*, Chicago: Chicago Review Press, 2023, p. 216.

CHAPTER 4: RETURN OF THE CHEETAH

74 **Cheetahs became extinct in India roughly three-quarters of a century ago.:** Divyabhanusinh, *The Story of India's Cheetahs*, Mumbai: The Marg Foundation, 2023, pp. 199–218.

75 **'Cheetahs are back; economy and ecology not in conflict':** Esha Roy, 'Cheetahs are back; economy and ecology not in conflict: PM', *Indian Express*, 17 September 2022.

75 **'The flourishing of these mega fauna preservation efforts':** Divyabhanusinh, *The Story of India's Cheetahs*, p. 220.

78 **'The cheetah is a survivor; its challenging evolutionary history':** Laurie Marker, Jack Grisham, and Bruce Brewer, 'A Brief History of Cheetah Conversation', in Philip J. Nyhus, Laurie Marker, Lorraine K. Boast, and Anne Schmidt-Kuntzel (eds.), *Cheetahs: Biology and Conservation*, USA: Elsevier Academic Press, 2018, pp. 3–16.

79 **'I believe there was never an "Asiatic cheetah".':** Valmik Thapar, Romila Thapar, and Yusuf Ansari (eds.), *Exotic Aliens*, New Delhi: Aleph Book Company, 2013, p. 20.

80 **Romila Thapar, Valmik's aunt and one of India's most respected historians:** Ibid., pp. 25–61.

80 **He presents carefully researched and convincing evidence:** Divyabhanusinh, *The Story of India's Cheetahs*, p. 211.

80 **Divyabhanusinh and wildlife scholar Raza Kazmi, have also published:** Divyabhanusinh and Raza Kazmi, 'Asiatic Cheetah Acinonyx jubatus venaticus in India: A Chronology of

Extinction and Related Reports', *Journal of the Bombay Natural History Society*, Vol. 116, 2019.

81 **Kazmi has also meticulously researched various accounts**: Raza Kazmi, 'The Last Hurrah of "Hurrianah" Lion *Panthera leo persica*—Part I: A Chronological Record of Hitherto Unknown References to Lion Hunting in Present-day Haryana and Related Reports', *The Journal of Bombay Natural History Society*, Vol. 118, 2021, p. 177.

81 **Extensive surveys of the flora and fauna were conducted**: A. J. T. Johnsingh, 'Kuno is Ready to Receive Lions from Gujarat', unpublished manuscript, 2017.

82 **This is not the first time that wild predators have been translocated:** Raza Kazmi, 'The Story of Translocated African Lions of Kuno', Roundglasssustain.com, 10 March 2023, available at roundglasssustain.com/wild-vault/african-lions-kuno.

83 **At the beginning of November 2022, six weeks after their arrival:** Iram Siddique, 'Freddie and Elton Kill Again: Why India's cheetah pair is being tracked so closely', *Indian Express*, 12 November 2022.

83 **on 27 March, there was bad news:** Esha Roy, 'Namibian cheetah Siyaya gives birth to four cubs, first cheetahs to be born on Indian soil in over 70 years', *Indian Express*, 29 March 2023.

83 **One of the South African males, named Uday, died suddenly on 23 April.:** Esha Roy, 'Preliminary autopsy suggests cheetah of cardiopulmonary failure; samples sent for forensic test', *Indian Express*, 25 April 2023.

84 **each tree can produce 300 kilograms of flowers in a single season.:** Pradip Krishen, *Jungle Trees of Central India*, New Delhi: Penguin India, 2014, pp. 118–119.

86 **The park also contains large herds of feral cattle.:** A. J. T. Singh, unpublished manuscript, 2017.

87 **Palpur Garhi was built in the eighteenth century.:** P. Naveen, 'Madhya Pradesh: Royal family demands fort and land back in soon-to-be cheetah land, moves court', *Times of India*, 3 September 2022.

CHAPTER 5: RESILIENCE AND RECOVERY

91 **In 1877, a fast-growing species of mesquite from Central America:** Krishen, *Trees of Delhi: A Field Guide*, pp. 278–279.

92 **Though the maharaja's hunting expeditions ended in 1966:** Asad Rahmani, 'Tal Chhapar: The Golden Grasslands of Churu', Roundglasssustain.com, 6 August 2021, available at roundglasssustain.com/habitats/tal-chhapar.

93 **A recent botanical survey, conducted between 2015 and 2017:** Mandeep Kaur, Pankaj Joshi, Kiranmay Sarma, et al, 'Assessment of Plant Community Structure in Tal Chhapar Sanctuary, Rajasthan, India', *Species*, Vol. 21, No. 67, 2020, pp. 126–139.

93 **Permanent residents at Tal Chhapar, laggar falcons feed on reptiles:** Rishad Naoroji, *Birds of Prey of the Indian Subcontinent*, London: Christopher Helm, pp. 597–604.

93 ***Hobson-Jobson* spells it as Neelgye or Nilghau:** Yule and Burnell, *Hobson-Jobson*, William Crooke (ed.), pp. 621–622.

95 **Four species of monitors exist in India and the desert monitor:** Gerry Martin, 'Of Forked Tongues and Scaling Fort Walls: Story of the Bengal Monitor Lizard', Roundglasssustain.com, 25 May 2022, available at roundglasssustain.com/species/bengal-monitor-lizard.

95 **Growing mostly in dry, sandy soil, its roots can extend 10 metres beneath the surface.:** Krishen, *Trees of Delhi: A Field Guide*, pp. 276–277.

95 **The Bishnoi community, who live along the margins of the Thar Desert:** Namit Hans, 'Khejri, the tree that inspired Chipko movement, is dying a slow death', *Indian Express*, 4 December 2016.

96 **Bishnois espouse a philosophy of non-violence and respect:** Ashutosh Bishnoi, 'The 29 Rules of Bishnoi Religion', *Speakingtree.in*, 24 June 2011, available at www.speakingtree.in/blog/29-principles-of-bishnoi-religion.

96 **'It is only around Bishnoi settlements':** M. Krishnan, *Nature's Spokesman: M. Krishnan and*

Indian Wildlife, Ramachandra Guha (ed.), New Delhi: Penguin India, 2007, pp. 240–241.

97 **More than fifteen different species of spiny-tailed lizards:** Karin Tamar, Margarita Metallinou, Thomas Wilms, et al., 'Evolutionary History of Spiny-tailed Lizards (Agamidae: *Uromastylxi*) from the Saharo-Arabian Region', *Zoologica Scripta*, Vol. 47, No. 2, 2017, pp. 159–173.

97 **Having survived catastrophic events and dramatic changes in climate:** 'Spiny-tailed Lizard's in India's wildlife trade', Traffic.org, 7 July 2022, available at www.traffic.org/publications/reports/factsheet-on-indian-spiny-tailed-lizard-in-illegal-wildlife-trade.

97 **Two centuries later, his descendant, Maharaja Umaid Singh, decided to grow *Prosopis*:** Yash Mishra, 'Umaid Singh: Jodhpur's "Flying Maharaja"', 22 July 2021, Livehistoryindia.com, available at www.livehistoryindia.com/story/people/umaid-singh.

100 **To help visitors identify species in the park:** Pradip Krishen, *The Small Plant Guide to Rao Jodha Desert Rock Park*, Jodhpur: Mehrangarh Museum Trust, 2011.

CHAPTER 6: THE WHITE BABBLER OF BANDHAVGARH

106 **The German–American magicians and entertainers, Siegfried and Roy:** See www.republicworld.com/entertainment-news/others/what-happened-to-montecore-find-out-where-the-white-tiger-is-now.html.

112 **Archaeologists estimate that the idol is more than 1,000 years old:** Deshdeep Saxena, 'Madhya Pradesh: 1000-year-old Vishnu sculpture restored,' *Times of India*, 24 January 2022.

113 **Now that the mist has evaporated:** Hashim Tyabji, *Bandhavgarh National Park*, Tala: Churhat Kothi, 2004, p. vi.

114 **A sacred tree, these terminalias are mentioned in the Rig Veda.:** Pitchandikulam Forest, 'From our Herbarium: The Sacred Arjuna Tree', *PitchandikulamBlog*, 12 September 2016, available at pitchandikulamblog.wordpress.com/2016/09/12/from-our-herbarium-the-sacred-arjuna-tree.

115 **In his book, *The Wild Life of India*:** E. P. Gee, *The Wild Life of India*, London: Fontana Books, 1969, pp. 82–90.

116 **The Wildlife Trust of India has initiated a National Elephant Corridors Project:** 'National Elephant Corridors Project', Wti.org.in., available at www.wti.org.in/projects/right-of-passage-national-elephant-corridors-project.

CHAPTER 7: CARBON FOOTPRINTS

122 **Recently, the forest minister of Assam:** 'Assam: Over 70 people, 80 elephants die every year due to human-animal conflict, says minister', *Mid-day*, 16 March 2023.

124 **Brachiation is the scientific term for this form of arboreal ambulation:** 'Hoolock Gibbons', Wwfindia.org., available at www.wwfindia.org/about_wwf/priority_species/lesser_known_species/hoolock_gibbons_.

129 **About 40 per cent of male elephants in India do not have tusks:** Stephen Alter, *Elephas Maximus: A Portrait of the Indian Elephant*, New York: Harcourt, 2004, pp. 48–49.

INTERLUDE: THE SPARROW AND THE HORNBILL

133 **'exchanging notes, exhibiting interesting specimens':** Salim Ali, 'Bombay Natural History Society: The Founders, the Builders, and the Guardians Part I', *Journal of the Bombay Natural History Society*, Vol. 75, No. 3, 1978, p. 559.

133 **Their first official meeting took place at the Victoria and Albert Museum:** Ibid., p. 562.

134 **'I remember the feeling of nervousness—almost of fear and trembling':** Salim Ali, *The Fall of a Sparrow*, New Delhi: Oxford University Press, 1985, p. 7.

134 **Another famous bird is the great hornbill:** H. M. Phipson, 'The Great of Indian Hornbill in Captivity', *Journal of the Bombay Natural History Society*, Vol. X, 1897, pp. 307–308.

136 **'I do not enjoy the killing':** Ali, *The Fall of a Sparrow*, p. 195.

138 **'Known in Hindi as ghulab-sir':** Salim Ali, *Words of Birds: The Collected Radio Broadcasts*, Tara Gandhi (ed.), Ranikhet: Black Kite, 2021, p. 191.

138 **'Some of the last pink-headed ducks':** Ibid., pp. 204–205.

138 **Then, suddenly, in 1986, an ornithologist named Bharat Bhushan:** Sharad Vats, 'Jerdon and Tickells', Indiabirdwatching.com, 14 April 2020, available at www.indiabirdwatching.com/jerdon-and-tickells.

139 **Another sighting of Jerdon's courser, in 1996, was reported by Aasheesh Pittie:** Aasheesh Pittie, *The Living Air: The Pleasures of Birds and Birdwatching*, New Delhi: Juggernaut Books, pp. 9–12.

139 ***Coelognathus helena nigriangularis*:** Harikrishnan S., '*Coelognathus helena nigriangularis*', Indiabiodiversity.org, available at indiabiodiversity.org/species/show/281137.

141 **'There is the black rat, the brown rat, the field-rat':** E. H. Aitken, *Tribes on my Frontier: An Indian Naturalist's Foreign Policy*, New Delhi: Penguin India, 2007, p. 12.

142 **'(He) was born in 1851 at Satara':** Ruskin Bond, 'Introduction', in E. H. Aitken, *Tribes on my Frontier: An Indian Naturalist's Foreign Policy*, p. xi.

142 **'I wander into the jungle':** E. H. Aitken, *A Naturalist on a Prowl*, New Delhi: Penguin India, 2007, pp. 1–2.

143 **'Without a collection, a man's knowledge of natural history becomes nebulous':** Ibid., p. 2.

143 **of most of the great naturalists in the West, from Aristotle to Darwin:** Robert Huxley, *The Great Naturalists*, London: Thames & Hudson, pp. 22–26.

143 **'Has a butterfly ears':** Aitken, *A Naturalist on the Prowl*, p. 5.

144 **(Gee is) a fairly heavily built man, balding:** Salim Ali, *The Fall of a Sparrow*, p. 189.

145 **'Imagine the year 2000':** Gee, *The Wild Life of India*, p. 204–205.

145 **'At times a profound truth is embodied in a jocular saying':** M. Krishnan, 'Ecological Patriotism', in Krishnan, *Nature's Spokesman*, Ramachandra Guha (ed.), p. 272.

146 **'Would we have seemed upside down to the bear?':** M. Krishnan, 'Five Encounters', in Krishnan, *Nature's Spokesman*, Ramachandra Guha (ed.), p. 83.

147 **'One of the best naturalists of present-day India':** Gee, *The Wild Life of India*, p. 28.

147 **'His character is, I think, nicely revealed':** Ramachandra Guha, 'Introduction', in Krishnan, *Nature's Spokesman*, Ramachandra Guha (ed.), p. 12.

147 **'Krishnan represents the voice of the unrelenting preservationist.':** Mahesh Rangarajan, *Nature and Nation*, Ranikhet: Permanent Black, 2017, p. 231.

148 **'The Great Indian Bustard is a bird of the open country.':** M. Krishnan, 'The Great Indian Bustard' in Krishnan, *Nature's Spokesman*, Ramachandra Guha (ed.), p. 49.

148 **'I know a lake in such a place where I have seen kites fishing.':** M. Krishnan, 'Freebooters of the Air', in Krishnan, *Nature's Spokesman*, Ramachandra Guha (ed.), p. 136.

148 **'Such is the bandicoot.':** M. Krishnan, 'Bashing a Bandicoot', in Krishnan, *Nature's Spokesman*, Ramachandra Guha (ed.), p. 126.

PART II: TRACING THE EDGE

CHAPTER 1: AFTER THE FLOOD

154 **shifting sandscapes which are known as a char or chapori in Assamese.:** Chandrani Sinha, 'Brahmaputra's River Islands Threatened by Burning and Clearing of Grasslands', Roundglasssustain.com, 6 May 2022, available at roundglasssustain.com/conservations/brahmaputras-river-islands.

155 **On 15 August 1950, one of the most severe earthquakes:** Ajanta Sharma and Fara Zama, 'The Great Assam Earthquake of 1950: A Historical Review', *Senhri Journal of*

Multidisciplinary Studies, Vol. 4. No. 1, 2019, pp. 1–10, available at senhrijournal.ac.in/wp-content/uploads/2020/12/The-Great-Assam-Earthquake-of-1950-A-Historical-Review.pdf.

155 **'Dibru-Saikhowa was once a rainforest':** Anwaruddin Chowdhury, 'The Dibru and Dihing Landscapes', Sanctuarynaturefoundation.org, available at www.sanctuarynaturefoundation.org/article/the-dibru-and-dihing-landscapes.

157 **Sometimes referred to as a walking catfish (or Asian catfish):** Bibha Chetia Borah, 'Asian Catfish *Clarius Magur* (HAM), A Wonder Fish for Health and Nutrition', *ACTA Scientific Nutritional Health*, Vol. 4, No. 2.

158 **They feed on fish and snails**: Sanna Quasmieh, '*Anastomus oscitans* Asian Openbill', Animaldiversity.org, available at animaldiversity.org/accounts/Anastomus_oscitans.

159 **About half a kilometre away from Maguri:** Roopak Goswami and Sahana Ghosh, 'Baghjan oil blowout: report indicated a long road to recovery and ecological restoration', India.mongabay.com, 5 July 2021, available at india.mongabay.com/2021/07/baghjan-oil-blowout-report-indicates-a-long-road-to-recovery-and-ecological-restoration.

161 **These are called singhi or xingi.:** '*Heteropneustes fossilis*', Fishbase.se, available at fishbase.se/summary/4885.

163 **One story recounts how a bird pecked out the snake's eyes:** Verrier Elwin, *Myths of the North-East Frontier of India*, New Delhi: Munshiram Manoharlal, 1999, pp. 74–75.

163 **The Kaman Mishmi tribe, in the Lohit Valley:** Ibid., p. 76.

163 **In another story told by the Wancho tribe:** Ibid., pp. 135–136.

165 **Ganges river dolphins are called sisu or hisu in Assamese:** 'Facts', Worldwildlife.org, available at www.worldwildlife.org/species/ganges-river-dolphin.

165 **One of the oldest mammals on earth:** 'Facts', Worldwildlife.org, available at www.worldwildlife.org/species/indus-river-dolphin.

167 **Feral animals can cause a lot of damage to fragile ecosystems:** Australian Government Department of Sustainability, Environment, Water, Population and Communities, 'Feral Horse (Equus Caballus) and Feral Donkey (Equus Asinus)', available at www.agriculture.gov.au/sites/default/files/documents/feral-horse.pdf.

167 **In 2020, six of them were confiscated:** Mohsin Khaiyam, 'Six Feral Horses Released in Dibru–Saikhowa Islands', *The Telegraph*, 8 March 2020.

CHAPTER 2: DENWA BACKWATERS

174 **One of the trees that catches my eye is ghiriya, also called bhirra.:** Krishen, *Jungles Trees of Central India*, pp. 310–311.

175 **The uniform dark colouring of their hides:** Vivek Menon, *Indian Mammals: A Field Guide*, New Delhi: Hachette, 2014, pp. 168–169.

178 **'The change came fast':** Hugh Allen, *The Lonely Tiger*, New Delhi: Rupa Publications, 2014, p. 128.

179 **'The urge to go hunting was still as strong':** Ibid., p. xv.

179 **'...my old idea that a writer's life was one of idleness and ease':** Ibid., p. 212.

179 **'stretched out on the concrete floor of a garage'.:** Ibid., pp. 133–134.

179 **'...as he lay by the water's edge':** Ibid., p. 137.

182 **The Satpura Hills are full of sacred sites:** Chandra Prakash Kala, 'Traditional Ecological Knowledge, Sacred Groves and Conservation of Biodiversity in the Pachmarhi Biosphere Reserve of India', *Journal of Environment Protection*, Vol. 2, No. 7, 2011, pp. 967–973.

CHAPTER 3: WATER DOGS AND FOREST BABIES

186 **In the 1890s, a Dutch expatriate named Eugene Van Ingen:** Navin J. Anthony and Prathima Nandakumar, 'Wild wild stuff: How the British loot of India's jungles fuelled the world's largest taxidermy firm', *The Week*, 19 March 2023.

188 **S. H. Prater's *The Book of Indian Animals*:** S. H. Prater, *The Book of Indian Animals*, Bombay: Bombay Natural History Society, 1971, p. 153.

188 **While otters may appear to be gentle:** Remal Sudhindran, et al., '"Otter Attack!"', *Hornbill*, April–June 2020, p. 25.

190 **The institute recently accepted large donations:** Garima Prasher, 'The Green Mile', *Bangalore Mirror*, 21 February 2022.

193 **'Historical records suggest':** Smitha D. Gnanaolivu, Marco Campera, K. Anne-Isola Nekaris, et al., 'Medicine, black magic and supernatural beings: cultural rituals as a significant threat to slender lorises in India', *People and Nature*, Vol. 4, No,. 4, 2022, p. 1016, available at besjournals.onlinelibrary.wiley.com/doi/epdf/10.1002/pan3.10336.

194 **'For 30 of the 58 reported cases':** Ibid., pp. 1012–1013.

194 **'As primates with large forward-facing eyes':** Ibid., pp. 1015–1016.

194 **'The number of cases related to black magic':** Ibid., p. 1015.

CHAPTER 4: THE GODDESS AND THE TIGER

195 **The total area of the Sundarbans:** Annu Jailas, *Forest of Tigers: People, Politics, & Environment in the Sundarbans*, London: Routledge, 2010, p. 2.

195 **The World Wild Life Fund for Nature estimates**: 'Facts', Worldwildlife.org, available at www.worldwildlife.org/species/tiger.

195 **In 2021, West Bengal's Forest Department:** Shiv Sahay Singh, 'Sunderbans Home to 96 Tigers, Bengal Forest Dept. estimates', *The Hindu*, 30 July 2021.

196 **'If in the literature of the region a rather crude opposition':** Jailas, *Forest of Tigers: People, Politics, & Environment in the Sundarbans*, p. 7.

197 **'If the harsh environment of the Sundarbans':** Ibid., p. 10.

201 **Because of illegal timber extraction:** Ananda Banerjee, 'Sundari Trees in Sundarban Delta Are Dying a Slow Death. Is Anyone Listening?', *Outlook*, 4 June 2020.

202 **Asian water monitors are the second largest lizards in the world:** Jerry Martin, 'Living Dragons: Weapons, Defences, and the Water Monitor Lizard', Roundglasssustain.com, 27 July 2022, available at roundglasssustain.com/species/water-monitor-lizard.

204 **'The idea that the forest is a sacred place':** Jailas, *Forest of Tigers: People, Politics, & Environment in the Sundarbans*, p. 135.

205 **While the mythology of Bonbibi and Dokkhin Rai:** Ibid., pp. 191–192.

206 **'tide country':** Amitav Ghosh, *The Hungry Tide*, New Delhi: HarperCollins Publishers, 2004, p. 7.

206 **'Then there came a moment':** Ibid., p. 235.

207 **Ganges river dolphins were once plentiful in the Sundarbans:** Sahana Ghosh, 'Gangetic river dolphins in the Indian Sundarbans struggle with swelling salinity', India.mongabay.com, 17 January 2019, available at india.mongabay.com/2019/01/gangetic-dolphins-in-the-indian-sundarbans-struggle-with-swelling-salinity.

CHAPTER 5: BETWEEN THE HILLS AND THE SEA

212 **'We all live and breathe fungi':** Merlin Sheldrake, *Entangled Life: How Fungi Make our World, Change Our Minds and Shape our Futures*, London: Vintage, 2020, p. 6.

212 **When ants or other insects brush against a zombie fungus:** Jennifer Lu, 'How a parasitic fungus turns ants into zombies', *National Geographic*, 18 April 2019, available at www.nationalgeographic.com/animals/article/cordyceps-zombie-fungus-takes-over-ants?fbclid=IwAR0Uk5wz6pygvw8GzyR99V5X0tEe0IekrZNG_8QEiCD4osPTN9hpAZ6Tx4.

213 **'As soon as the season of rains has come':** Wendy Doniger O' Flaherty (trans.), *Rig Veda: An Anthology*, London: Penguin Random House, 1981, p. 233.

214 **Civets eat an eclectic diet:** Prater, *The Book of Indian Animals*, pp. 92–94.

220 **Since 2020, scientists have added seven new species:** Vinaya Kurtoki, 'Newly described

species of scorpions from the Western Ghats highlight need for more research and conservation', India.mongabay.com, 18 May 2021, available at india.mongabay.com/2021/05/newly-described-scorpion-species-from-western-ghats-highlight-need-for-more-research-and-conservation.

220 **During the tenth and eleventh centuries:** Phyllis Granoff, 'Vrscikodari: A Study of the Relationship between Myth and Image in Indian Art', *East and West*, Vol. 30, No. 1, 1980, pp. 77–96.

220 **In Prakrit poetry:** Aravind Krishna (trans.), *The Absent Traveller: Prakrit Love Poetry from the Gathasaptasati of Satavahana Hala*. New Delhi: Penguin Random House India, 2008. p. 20

221 **A variation on this fatalistic fable:** Jurgen Wasim Fremgen, 'The Scorpion in Muslim Folklore', *Asian Folklore Studies*. Vol. 63, No. 1, 2004, pp. 93–125.

CHAPTER 6: ALONG THE CHAMBAL

228 **Fossils of gharial, dating back at least 5 million years:** Laurie J. Vitt and Janalee P. Caldwell, *Herpetology: An Introduction Biology of Amphibians and Reptiles*, 4th edn, USA: Elsevier Academic Press, 2014, pp. 545–552.

228 **In an unusual reversal of gender roles:** Janaki Lenin, 'Croc Creche: Why Crocodilians Make Great Babysitters', Roundglasssustain.com, 5 August 2021, available at roundglasssustain.com/columns/crocodilian-males.

230 **Jeffrey Lang, the lead scientist:** W. Jeffrey Lang and Harry V. Andrews, 'Temperature-dependent Sex Determination in Crocodilians', *The Journal of Experimental Zoology*, Vol. 270, No. 1, 1994, pp. 28–44, available at doi.org/10.1002/jez.1402700105.

234 **'To secure the levy of a duty on salt':** Roy Moxham, *The Great Hedge of India*, London: Constable, 2002, p. 3.

234 **'its greatest extent and perfection':** Ibid., p. 107.

235 **'In its most perfect form':** Ibid., p. 7.

235 **Where sections of the Customs Line:** Ibid., p. 99.

235 **Hume spent much of his time:** Ibid., p. 201.

236 **'fatherly tenderness, for he invented a patent drop':** Ibid., 200.

236 **Ultimately, A. O. Hume was elevated:** Ibid., 202.

239 **While dozing like this:** Hussain Kanchwala, ScienceABC.com, 8 July 2022, available at www.scienceabc.com/nature/animals/dont-dolphins-drown-theyre-sleeping.html.

INTERLUDE: WILD LOVESCAPES

241 **The most impressive monument of all:** C. Sivaramurti, *Mahabalipuram*, New Delhi: Archaeological Survey of India, 1978.

242 **'Love was, in those days and in poetry, mainly an open-air pursuit.':** M. Krishnan, 'The Landscape of Love, in Krishnan, *Nature's Spokesman*, Ramachandra Guha (ed.), p. 24.

243 **'Bigger than earth, certainly':** A. K. Ramanujan, *The Interior Landscape*, New York: NYRB/Poets, 1967, p. 1.

243 **'Describing the scene describes his passion.':** Ibid., 94.

244 **'Each of these landscapes is now a whole repertoire of images':** Ibid., p. 91.

245 **'These are the mountains':** M. L. Thangappa (trans.), *Love Stands Alone: Selections from Tamil Sangam Poetry*, A. R. Venkatachalapathy (ed.), New Delhi: Penguin India, 2010, p. 81.

246 **'Look at me with the strong eyes of youth':** Verrier Elwin, *Folksongs of the Maikal Hills*, Bombay: Oxford University Press, 1944, p. 135.

246 **'Raja, my heart is mad for you'**: Ibid., p. 124.

247 **'Play without fear':** Ibid., p. 138.

247 **The *titi* or clitoris-bird:** Ibid., p. 138.

247 **'Lying on their bed the two embrace':** Ibid., p. 152.

247 **'You are coming very slowly, why do you delay':** Ibid., p. 153.

249 **'A forest that did not look like one':** Sunil Gangopadhyay, *Nights in the Forest*, Rani Ray (tr.), New Delhi: Penguin India, 2010, p. 9.

PART III: ON HIGHER GROUND

CHAPTER 1: WHEN MOUNTAINS HAD WINGS

255 **More than a hundred temples:** Diana Eck, *India: A Sacred Geography,* New York: Three Rivers Press, 2012, pp. 34–39.

257 **'The Asiatic lion is a subspecies':** Ravi Chellam, 'The Lions of Gir', in Divyabhanusinh (ed.), *The Lions of India*, Ranikhet: Permanent Black, 2008, pp. 229–230.

258 **'The Indian lion is one of the rarest':** Gee, *The Wild Life of India*, p. 97.

258 **Counting wildlife, especially wary predators:** Divyabhanusinh, 'Introduction', in Divyabhanusinh (ed.), *The Lions of India*, p. 21.

258 **The first comprehensive census:** M. A. Wynter-Blyth and K. S. Dharmakumarsinhji, 'The Gir Forest and Lions Part I', in Divyabhanusinh (ed.), *The Lions of India*, p. 137.

258 **Eighteen years later, in 1968:** M. K. Dalvi, 'Gir Lion Census', in Divyabhanusinh (ed.), *The Lions of India*, p. 159.

258 **'Lion symbolism gained importance in India':** Divyabhanusinh, 'Introduction', in Divyabhanusinh (ed.), *The Lions of India*, p. 8.

259 **Both Gautama Buddha and Mahavira:** Ibid., pp. 7–16.

259 **'In the immediate aftermath':** Kazmi, 'The Last Hurrah of "Hurrianah" Lion *Panthera leo persica*—Part I: A Chronological Record of Hitherto Unknown References to Lion Hunting in Present-day Haryana and Related Reports', p. 177.

259 **William Fraser, political agent and resident:** Divyabhanusinh, 'Introduction', in Divyabhanusinh (ed.), *The Lions of India*, p. 14.

259 **By 1824, most of the lions of Delhi and Haryana had been 'extirpated'.:** Kazmi, 'The Last Hurrah of "Hurrianah" Lion *Panthera leo persica*—Part I: A Chronological Record of Hitherto Unknown References to Lion Hunting in Present-day Haryana and Related Reports', p. 181.

260 **"Who will protect my lions now?":** Divyabhanusinh, 'Introduction', in Divyabhanusinh (ed.), *The Lions of India*, p. 21.

260 **Fortunately, after receiving appeals from conservationists:** Mahesh Rangarajan, 'Region's Honour, Nation's Pride', in Divyabhanusinh (ed.), *The Lions of India*, p. 254.

261 **And one lioness is reported:** M. K. Ranjitsinh, 'Lion' in Divyabhanusinh (ed.), *The Lions of India*, p. 183.

261 **A study by Paul Joslin, in 1987:** Paul Joslin, 'The Environmental Limitations and Future of the Asiatic Lion,' in in Divyabhanusinh (ed.), *The Lions of India*, p. 209.

261 **Ten years later, in 1997:** Chellam, 'The Lions of Gir', in Divyabhanusinh (ed.), *The Lions of India*, p. 236.

262 **'Regionalism, once a valued ally, can also be immune to reason':** Rangarajan, 'Region's Honour, Nation's Pride', in Divyabhanusinh (ed.), *The Lions of India*, pp. 258–259.

262 **'Amongst some Gujaratis':** M. K. Ranjitsinh, *A Life with Wildlife*, New Delhi: HarperCollins Publishers, 2017, pp. 324–326.

272 **Checkered keelbacks are also called Asiatic water snakes.:** Jerry Martin, 'I Want it All: the Checkered Keelback's Gameplan', Roundglasssustain.com, 12 May 2022, available at roundglasssustain.com/species/checkered-keelback.

CHAPTER 2: CONFLICT AND KINSHIP IN KUMAON

274 **'People who have lived at Muktesar':** Jim Corbett, 'The Muktesar Man-eater', in Jim Corbett, *The Temple Tiger and More Man-eaters of Kumaon*, New York: Oxford University Press, 1955, p. 43.

275 **'greatest satisfaction of all'.:** Ibid., p. 68.
276 **'His sporting ethic...did not measure up':** Mahesh Rangarajan, *Nature and Nation: Essays on Environmental History*, Ranikhet: Permanent Black, 2015, p. 213.
276 **'From this point it was necessary to walk warily':** Corbett, 'The Muktesar Man-eater', in Jim Corbett, *The Temple Tiger and More Man-eaters of Kumaon*, p. 45–46.
277 **'Baram is a jungle God':** Ibid., pp. 62–63.
277 **'that the trees were young and vigorous':** Ibid., 63–64.
279 **The male begins with a sharp '*cue-pee*':** Salim Ali, *Indian Hill Birds*, Bombay: Oxford University Press, 1949, p. 36.
279 **If alarmed, each of them emits a panicked, high-pitched cry:** Robert L. Fleming Sr. and Jr. and Lain Singh Bangdel, *Birds of Nepal*, Kathmandu: Flemings, 1976, p. 186.
280 **'Stray birds of summer':** Rabindranath Tagore, *Stray Birds*, New Delhi: Niyogi Books, 2018, p. 7.
280 **'In the dusk of the evening':** Ibid., p. 47.
285 **'When people in Kumaon':** Radhika Govindranjan, *Animal Intimacies: Beastly Love in the Himalayas*, New Delhi: Viking, 2019, pp. 8–9.
287 **'As I listened to multiple tellings':** Ibid., p. 232.
287 **'Bears throughout the Himalayas':** Jim Corbett, 'Goongi', in R. E. Hawkins (ed.), *Jim Corbett's India*, Bombay: Oxford University Press, 1978, pp. 117–122.

CHAPTER 3: THE CENTRAL HIGHLANDS

290 **In 2001, R. J. Ranjit Daniels published an article**: R. J. Ranjit Daniels, 'Endemic Fishes of the Western Ghats and the Satpura Hypothesis', *Current Science*, Vol. 81, No. 3, 2001, pp. 240–244.
291 **My well-thumbed copy of *Birds of the Indian Subcontinent*:** Richard Grimmett, Carol Inskipp, and Tim Inskipp, *Pocket Guide to the Birds of the Indian Subcontinent (Helm Field Guides)*, New Delhi: Oxford University Press, 2009.
291 **'Few parts of India':** J. Forsyth, *The Highlands of Central India: Notes on their Forests and Wild Tribes, Natural History, and Sports*, London: Chapman and Hall, 1998, p. 22.
292 **Several Europeans had visited Pachmarhi:** Pradip Krishen, *Unpublished report about Satpura National Park*.
292 **'To the south, as far as the eye can see':** Forsyth, *The Highlands of Central India: Notes on their Forests and Wild Tribes, Natural History, and Sports*, p. 93.
295 **'slumped posture and drooping necks':** Rishad Naoroji, *Birds of Prey of the Indian Subcontinent*, London: Christopher Helm, 2006, pp. 59–60.
296 **In Sanskrit it is known as panduphali:** Hemanth Tripathi, 'Bushweed', FlowersofIndia.net, available at www.flowersofindia.net/catalog/slides/Bushweed.html.

CHAPTER 4: ABOVE THE SNOW LINE

306 **Buddhist mythology from Tibet:** Garma Chang (trans.), *The Hundred Thousand Songs of Milarepa*, New York: Harper and Row, 1962, p. 12.
307 **Another unusual myth from Ladakh:** See snowleopardconservancy.org.
308 **Folklore and mythology in Ladakh:** 'Tsngpa Gyare Founder of the Drukpa Lineage', available at drukpa.ch/en/information/history/tsangpa-gyare-founder-of-the-drukpa-lineage.
309 **The Rig Veda contains a hymn to Pusan:** O' Flaherty (trans.), *Rig Veda: An Anthology*, p. 194.
310 **An intriguing parallel to contemporary accounts:** Virginia Morell, 'Tibetan Dogs Can Survive at High Altitudes Thanks to Ancient Breeding with Wolves', Science.org, 6 November 2016, available at www.science.org/content/article/tibetan-dogs-can-survive-high-altitudes-thanks-ancient-breeding-wolves.
310 **Salvador Lyngdoh has been studying wolves:** Salvador Lyndoh, 'Woolly Wolf: An Ancient Lineage in the Himalaya', Roundglasssustain.com, 9 August 2021, available at roundglasssustain.com/species/woolly-wolf-ancient-lineage-himalayas.

310 **Traditionally, shepherds in Ladakh:** Esha Roy, 'Ladakh's Plan to Save its Wolves: Stupas and Insurance', *Indian Express*, 22 August 2022.

315 **Comparing the ibex to the urial**: University of Edinburgh, 'Gene study shows how sheep first separated from goats', ScienceDaily.com, available at www.sciencedaily.com/releases/2014/06/140605141851.htm.

CHAPTER 5: WHERE THE HAND OF MAN HAS NEVER SET FOOT

322 **'I have witnessed sacred groves':** Madhav Gadgil, 'Sacred Groves: An Ancient Tradition of Nature Conservation', *Scientific American*, 1 December 2018, available at www.scientificamerican.com/article/sacred-groves-an-ancient-tradition-of-nature-conservation.

323 **'In a context in which policies are being designed':** Eliza F. Kent, *Sacred Groves and Local Gods*, New York: Oxford University Press, 2013, p. 8.

324 **'These stories illustrate the mythical bridges':** Barucha Erach, 'Sacred Groves: Memories of What Had Been' in Prerna Bindra, Sonali Ghosh, and Anurajan Bose (eds.), *Wild Treasures*, p. 250.

324 **'left behind wasted food':** Ibid., p. 254.

326 **Tambor Lyngdoh, a resident of Mawphlang:** Tambor Lyngdoh, *A Collection of Knowledge on Khasi Herbal Plants, Stories, and Poem*, self-published, 2022.

329 **Nineteen kilometres beyond Gurugram:** Vishakha Chaman, 'Bhandwari landfill site is 37m tall now & 1,800 tonnes being added daily', *Time of India*, 17 March 2021.

330 **'Dhau is the "habitat specialist"':** Krishen, *Trees of Delhi: A Field Guide*, p. 91.

331 **archaeologists have identified Mangar Bani:** Manon Verchot and Sanshay Biswas, 'Mangar, on the outskirts of Delhi, looks to the past to protect its future', India.mongabay.com, 7 September 2021, available at india.India.mongabay.com/2021/09/mangar-on-the-outskirts-of-new-delhi-looks-to-its-past-to-protect-its-future.

CHAPTER 6: OPHIOPHAGUS HANNAH

338 **Lion-tailed macaques are an endangered species:** Vivek Menon, *Indian Mammals: A Field Guide*, New Delhi: Hachette, 2014, p. 80.

340 **'Much has been written about the aggressive nature of this magnificent snake':** Romulus Whitaker, *Common Indian Snakes: A Field Guide*, Chennai: Macmillan, 2008, pp. 61–62.

342 **'Without a moment's hesitation, he dove':** Janaki Lenin, *My Husband and Other Animals 2*, New Delhi: Westland Books, 2018, pp. 211–212.

344 **The colouration of king cobras:** Whitaker, *Common Indian Snakes: A Field Guide*, p. 75.

347 **The unique breeding behaviour:** P. Gauri Shankar, Priyanka Swamy, Rhiannon C. Williams, et al., 'King or royal family? Testing for species boundaries in the King Cobra, Ophiophagus hannah (Cantor, 1836), using morphology and multilocus DNA analyses', *Molecular Phylogenetics and Evolution*, Volume 165, 107300, 2021, available at doi.org/10.1016/j.ympev.2021.107300.

347 **One of the mysteries that hasn't been fully understood:** Janaki Lenin, 'Evolutionary Anomolies and Eating your Kind', Roundglasssustain.com, 4 January 2023, available at roundglasssustain.com/columns/king-cobras-mates-cannibalism.

EPILOGUE: THE GREAT BANYAN

357 **He also conducted experiments on plant neurobiology:** Prakash Narain Tandon, 'Jagdish Chandra Bose and Plant Technology', *Indian Journal of Medical Research*, Vol. 149, No. 5, 2019, pp. 593–599.

357 **The Calcutta Botanical Garden was founded in 1787:** D. Chatterjee, 'Early History of the Royal Botanic Garden', *Nature*, Vol. 161, 1948, pp. 362–364.

359 **'It was ascertained to have grown from seeds':** K. C. Sahni, *The Book of Indian Trees*, Bombay: Bombay Natural History Society/Oxford, 1998, p. 154.

360 **the banyan is also considered an emblem of immortality:** Devdutt Pattanaik, 'Under the Banyan Tree', Devdutt.com, 26 October 2008, available at devdutt.com/articles/under-the-banyan-tree.

360 **Science too has stories to tell:** Krishen, *Trees of Delhi: A Field Guide*, pp. 321–332.

SELECT BIBLIOGRAPHY

Aitken, E. H., *A Naturalist on the Prowl*, New Delhi: Penguin India, 2007. First edition published in 1905.

———*Tribes on my Frontier: An Indian Naturalist's Foreign Policy*, New Delhi: Penguin. First edition published in 1883.

Ali, Salim, 'Bombay Natural History Society: The Founders, the Builders, and the Guardians Part I', *Journal of Bombay Natural History*, Vol. 75, No. 3, 1978, p. 559.

———*The Book of Indian Birds*, Bombay: Oxford University Press, 1979. First edition published in 1941.

———*The Fall of a Sparrow*, New Delhi: Oxford University Press, 1979. First edition published in 1941.

———*Words for Birds: The Collected Radio Broadcasts*, Tara Gandhi (ed.), Ranikhet: Black Kite, 2021.

Allen, Hugh, *The Lonely Tiger*, New Delhi: Rupa Publications, 2014. First edition published in 1960.

Alter, Stephen, *Elephas Maximus: A Portrait of the Indian Elephant*, New York: Harcourt, 2014.

Anwaruddin Chowdhury, 'The Dibru and Dihing Landscapes', *Sanctuarynaturefoundation.org*. First published in *Sanctuary* Asia, Vol. 40, No. 10, 2020.

Aquil, Reshma, *Sleeping Wind*, Singapore: Ethos Books, 2001.

Banerjee, Ananda, 'Sundari Trees in Sundarban Delta are Dying a Slow Death. Is Anyone Listening?', *Outlook*, 4 June 2020.

Barucha, Erach, 'Sacred Groves: Memories of What Had Been', in Bindra, Prerna, Ghosh, Sonali, and Bose, Anuranjan (eds.), *Wild Treasures: Reflections on Natural World Heritage Sites*, New Delhi: Aryan Books, 2019.

Bhutia, Lhendup G., 'India's Most Hated Tree,' *Open*, 12 July 2018.

Bisagratna, Kaviraj Kunja Lal, *An English Translation of the Sushruta Samhita Based on the Original Sanskrit Text*, Kolkata: S. L. Bhaduri, 1907.

Bond, Ruskin, 'Introduction', in Aitken, E. H., *Tribes on my Frontier: An Indian Naturalist's Foreign Policy*, New Delhi: Penguin, 2007.

Boparai, Shamdinder, *Billy Arjan Singh: Tiger of Dudhwa*, New Delhi: HarperCollins Publishers, 2011.

Borah, Bibha Chetia, 'Asian Catfish, *Clarius Magur* (HAM), a Wonder Fish for Health and Nutrition', *ACTA Scientific Nutritional Health*, Vol. 4 Issue 2, 2020.

Cariapa, Devika, *India through Archaeology: Excavating History*, Chennai: Tulika Books, 2017.

Chaman, Vishakha, 'Bhandwari landfill site is 37m tall now & 1,800 tonnes being added daily', *Times of India*, 17 March 2021.

Chatterjee, D., 'Early History of the Royal Botanic Garden, Calcutta,' *Nature*, Vol. 161, 1948, pp. 362–364.

Chellam, Ravi, 'The Lions of Gir', in Divyabhanusinh (ed.), *The Lions of India,* Ranikhet: Permanent Black, 2008.

Dalvi, M. K., 'Gir Lion Census, 1968', in Divyabhanusinh (ed.), *The Lions of India,* Ranikhet: Permanent Black, 2008.

Daniels, R. J. Ranjit, 'Endemic Fishes of the Western Ghats and the Satpura Hypothesis', *Current Science*, Vol. 81, No. 3, 2001, pp. 240–244.

Desai, Bharat, 'Growing Hero of "A Jungle Tale" still tries to fit into tribal life 40 years later', *India Today,* 30 April 1996.

Divabhanusinh and Kazmi, Raza, 'Asiatic Cheetah *Acionyx jubatus venaticus* in India: A Chronology of Extinction and Related Reports', *Journal of the Bombay Natural History Society*, Vol. 116, 2019.

Divyabhanusinh (ed.), *The Lions of India*, Ranikhet: Permanent Black, 2008.

Divyabhanusinh, *The Story of India's Cheetahs*, Mumbai: The Marg Foundation, 2023.

Dubey-Pathak, Meenakshi and Clottes, Jean, *Madhya Pradesh Rock Art and Tribal Art,* New Delhi: Aryan Books, 2021.

Eck, Diana, *India: A Sacred Geography,* New York: Three Rivers Press, 2012.

Elwin, Verrier, *Folksongs of the Maikal Hills*, Bombay: Oxford University Press, 1944.

———*Myths of the North-East Frontier of India*, New Delhi: Munshiram Manoharlal, 1999. First edition published in 1958.

Erickson-Davis, Morgan, 'Researchers unearth the surprising secret of India's dancing frogs', *India.mongabay.com*, 31 March 2016.

Forsyth, J., *The Highlands of Central India: Notes on their Forests and Wild Tribes, Natural History, and Sports*, London: Chapman and Hall, 1889. Reprinted by Alpha in 2019.

Fremgen, Jurgen Wasim, 'The Scorpion in Muslim Folkore', *Asian Folkore Studies*, Vol. 1, No. 1, 2004, pp. 93–125.

Gadgil, Madhav, 'Sacred Groves: An Ancient Tradition of Nature Conservation', *Scientific American*, 1 December 2018.

Gangopadhyay, Sunil, *Days and Nights in the Forest (Aranyer Dinratri)*, Rani Ray (tr.), New Delhi: Penguin India, 2010.

Gee, E. P., *The Wild Life of India,* London: Collins/Fontana, 1969.

Ghosh, Amitav, *The Hungry Tide*, New Delhi: HarperCollins Publishers, 2016.

Ghosh, Sahana, 'Gangetic river dolphins in the Indian Sundarbans struggle with swelling salinity', *India.mongabay.com*, 17 January 2019.

Gnanaolivu, Smitha, Campera, Marco, Nekaris, K. Anne-Isola, et al., 'Medicine, black magic and supernatural beings: cultural rituals as a significant threat to slender lorises in India', *People and Nature*, Vol. 4, No. 4, 2022, p. 1016.

Gopal, Lallanji, 'Sugar-making in Ancient India', *Journal of the Economic and Social History of the Orient*, Vol. 7, No. 1, 1964, pp. 57–72.

Goswami, Roopak, and Ghosh, Sahana, 'Baghjan oil blowout: report indicates a long road to recovery and ecological restoration', *India.mongabay.com,* 5 July 2021.

Granoff, Phyllis, 'Vrscikodari: A Study of the Relationship between Myth and Image in Indian Art', *East and West*, Vol. 30, No. 1/4, 2020, pp. 77–96.

Grimmett, Richard, Inskipp, Carol, and Inskipp, Tim, *Birds of the Indian Subcontinent*, London: Christopher Helm, 2016.

———*Pocket Guide to the Birds of the Indian Subcontinent (Helm Field Guides)*, New Delhi: Oxford University Press, 2009.

Guha, Ramachandra, 'Introduction' in Krishnan, M., *Natures's Spokesman: M. Krishnan and Indian Wildlife*, Ramachandra Guha (ed.), New Delhi: Penguin India, 2007.

Haying, Heather, 'Rhacophoridae Old World Tree Frogs', *Animaldiversityweb.org*.

Huxley, Robert, *The Great Naturalists*, London: Thames & Hudson, 2007.

Jalais, Annu, *Forest of Tigers: People, Politics & Environment in the Sundarbans*, London: Routledge, 2010.

John, Joseph, 'Bastar's Tiger Boy Passes Away', *Times of India*, 30 September 2013.

Johnsingh, A. J. T., 'Kuno is Ready to Receive Lions from Gujarat', unpublished manuscript, 2017.

Joslin, Paul, 'The Environmental Limitations and Future of the Asiatic Lion', in Divyabhanusinh, *The Lions of India*, Ranikhet: Permanent Black 2008.

Kala, Chandra Prakash, 'Traditional Ecological Knowledge, Sacred Groves and Conservation of Biodiversity in the Pachmarhi Biosphere Reserve of India,' *Journal of Environmental Protection*, Vol. 2, No. 7, 2011, pp. 967–973.

Kanchwala, Hussain, 'How Do Dolphins Sleep Without Drowning', *ScienceABC.com*, 8 July 2022.

Karanth, K. Ullas, *Among Tigers: Fighting to Bring Back Asia's Big Cats*, Chicago: Chicago Review Press, 2003.

Karve, Irawati, *Yuganta: The End of an Epoch*, Hyderabad: Black Swan, 2021. First published in Marathi in 1967 by Deshmukh Prakashan.

Kaur, Banjot, 'Gangetic Dolphins May Soon Become Extinct as River's Natural Flow Decreases: WII Report', *DowntoEarth.org.in*, 24 September 2018.

Kaur, Mandeep, Joshi, Pankaj, Sarma, Kiranmay, et al, 'Assessment of Plant Community Structure in Tal Chhapar Sanctuary, Rajasthan, India', *Species*, Vol. 21, No. 67, 2020, pp. 126–139.

Kazmi, Raza, 'The last hurrah of the 'Hurrianah' Lion *Panthera leo persica* – Part I: A chronological record of hitherto unknown references to lion hunting in present-day Haryana and related reports, *The Journal of Bombay Natural History Society*, Vol. 118, 2021, p. 177, 181.

———'The Story of the Translocated African Lions of Kuno', *Roundglasssustain.com,* 10 March 2023.

Kent, Eliza F., *Sacred Groves and Local Gods*, New York: Oxford University Press, 2013.

Khaiyam, Mohsin, 'Six Feral Horses Released in Dibru-Saikhowa National Park', *The Telegraph,* 8 March 2020.

Kosambi, D. D., *Myth and Reality*, New Delhi: Sage Publications, 2020. First edition published in 1962.

Krishen, Pradip, *Jungle Trees of Central India*, New Delhi: Penguin India, 2013.

———*The Small Plant Guide to Rao Jodha Desert Rock Park,* Jodhpur: Mehrangarh Museum Trust, 2011.

———*Trees of Delhi*, New Delhi: Dorling Kindersley, 2006.

———unpublished report about Satpura National Park.

Krishnan, M., *Nature's Spokesman: M. Krishnan & Indian Wildlife*, Ramachandra Guha (ed.), New Delhi: Penguin India, 2007.

Kurtkoti, Vinaya, 'Newly described species of scorpions from the Western Ghats highlight need for more research and conservation', *India.mongabay.com*, 18 May 2021.

Lal, Pranay, *Indica: A Deep Natural History of the Indian Subcontinent*, New Delhi: Penguin (India Allen Lane), 2016.

Lenin, Janaki, 'Evolutionary Anomalies: Killing and Eating your Kind', *Roundglasssustain.com*, 4 January 2023.

———*My Husband and Other Animals 2*, New Delhi: Westland Books, 2018.

Lyngdoh, Salvador, 'Woolly Wolf: An Ancient Lineage in the Himalaya', *Roundglasssustain.com*, 9 August 2021.

Lyngdoh, Tambor, *A Collection of Knowledge on Khasi Herbal Plants, Stories & Poems*, self-published, 2022.

Macfarlane, Robert, *The Wild Places*, London: Penguin Random House, 2008.

Marker, Laurie, Grisham, Jack, Brewer, Bruce, 'A Brief 'History of Cheetah Conversation', in Nyhus, Philip J., Marker, Laurie, Boast, Lorraine K, Schmidt-Kuntzel, Anne (eds.), *Cheetahs: Biology and Conservation*, USA: Elsevier Academic Press, 2018.

Martin, Jerry, 'I Want it All: The Checkered Keelback's Gameplan', *Roundglasssustain.com*, 12 May 2022.

———'Living Dragons: Weapons, Defences and the Water Monitor Lizard', *Roundglasssustain.com*, 27 July 2022.

———'Of Forked Tongues and Scaling For Walls: Story of the Bengal Monitor Lizard', *Roundglasssustain*, 25 May 2022.

Mehrotra, Arvind Krishna (trans.), *The Absent Traveller: Prakrit Love Poetry from the Gathasaptasti of Satavahana Halla*, New Delhi: Penguin Random House India, 2008.

Menon, Vivek, *Indian Mammals: A Field Guide*, New Delhi: Hachette, 2014.

Morell, Virginia, 'Tibetan Dogs Can Survive At High Altitudes Thanks to Ancient Breeding with Wolves', *Science.org*, 6 November, 2016.

Moxham, Roy, *The Great Hedge of India*, London: Constable, 2002.

Nair, Manoj, 'Seasons in the Sun: An Avian Rhapsody', in Singh Bindra, Prerna, Ghosh, Sonali, and Roy, Anurajan (eds.), *Wild Treasures: Reflections on Natural World Heritage Sites in Asia*, New Delhi: Aryan Books.

Naoroji, Rishad, *Birds of Prey of the Indian Subcontinent*, London: Christopher Helm, 2006.

Naveen, P., 'Madhya Pradesh: Royal family demands fort and land back in soon-to-be cheetah land, moves court, *Times of India*, 3 September 2022.

O'Flaherty, Wendy Doniger (trans.), *The Rig Veda*, London: Penguin Random House, 1981.

Pattanaik, Devdutt, 'Under the Banyan Tree', *Devdutt.com*, 26 October 2008. First published in *First City Delhi* on 25 October 2008.

Phipson, H. M., 'The Great Indian Hornbill in Captivity', *Journal of the Bombay Natural History Society*, Vol. X, 1897, pp. 307–308.

Pittie, Aasheesh, *The Living Air*, New Delhi: Juggernaut Books, 2023.

Prater, S. H., *The Book of Indian Animals*, Bombay: Bombay Natural History Society, 1965.

Rahmani, Asad, 'Tal Chhapar: The Golden Grasslands of Churu", *Roundglasssustain.com*, 6 August 2021.

Ramanujan, A. K., *The Interior Landscape*, New York: New York Review of Books, 1967.

Rangarajan, Mahesh, 'Nation's Pride', in Divyabhanusinh (ed.), *The Lions of India*, Ranikhet: Permanent Black, 2008.

———*Nature and Nation: Essays on Environmental History*, Ranikhet: Permanent Black, 2017.

Ranjitsinh, 'The Lions of India', in Divyabhanusinh (ed.), *The Lions of India*, Ranikhet: Permanent Black, 2008.

Ranjitsinh, M. K., *A Life with Wildlife: From Princely India to the Present*, New Delhi: HarperCollins Publishers, 2017.

Ray, Satyajit, *Aranyer Dinratri*, 1970, 1 hr. 55 min.

Roy, Esha, 'Cheetahs are back; economy and ecology not in conflict: PM', *Indian Express*, 17 September 2022.

———'Ladakh's plan to save its wolves: Stupas and insurance', *Indian Express*, 22 March 2022.

Sahgal, Bittu, 'Meet Billy Arjan Singh', *Sanctuary Asia*, Vol. 20, No. 9, 2000.

Sahni, K. C., *The Book of Indian Trees*, Mumbai: Bombay Natural History Society/Oxford University Press, 1998.

Schaller, George, 'Foreword' in Boparai, Shaminder, *Billy Arjan Singh: Tiger of Dudhwa*, New Delhi: HarperCollins Publishers, 2011.

Sengupta, Joydev, 'Resurrecting Tal Chhapar', *Pioneer*, 2 June 2013.

Shankar, Gauri P., Swamy, Priyanka, Williams, Rhiannon C., et al, 'King or royal family? Testing for species boundaries in the King Cobra, *Ophiophagus hannah* (Cantor, 1836), using morphology and multilocus DNA analyses', *Molecular Phylogenetics and Evolution*, Volume 165, 107300, 2021.

Sharma, Ajanta, and Zaman, Fara, '*The Great Assam Earthquake of 1950: A Historical Review*', *Senhri Journal of Multidisciplinary Studies*. Vol. 4, No. 1, 2019, pp. 1–10.

Sheldrake, Merlin, *Entangled Life: How Fungi Make our World, Change our Minds and Shape our Futures*, London: Vintage, 2020.

Singh, Arjan, *Tiger Haven*, London: Macmillan, 1973.

Singh, Shiv Sahay, 'Sunderbans Home to 96 Tigers, Bengal Forest Dept, Estimates', *The Hindu*, 30 July 2021.

Sinha, Chandrani, 'Brahmaputra's River Islands Threatened by Burning and Clearing of Grasslands', *Roundglasssustain.com*, 6 May 2022.

Sivaramurti C., *Mahabalipuram*, New Delhi: Archaeological Survey of India, 1978.

Sucksdorff, Astrid Bergman, *Chendru: The Boy and the Tiger*, tr. by William Sansom, London: Collins, 1960.

Tamar, Karin, Metallinou, Margarita, Wilms, Thomas, et al, 'Evolutionary History of Spinytailed Lizards (Agamidae: *Uromastylxi*) from the Saharo-Arabian Region', *Zoologica Scripta*, Vol. 47, No. 2, pp. 159–173.

Tandon, Prakash Narain, 'Jagdish Chandra Bose & Plant Neurobiology', *Indian Journal of Medical Research*, Vol. 149, No. 5, 2019, pp. 593–599.

Thangappa, M. L. (trans.), *Love Stands Alone: Selections from Tamil Sangam Poetry*, A. R. Venkatachalapathy (ed.), New Delhi: Penguin India, 2013.

Thapar, Romila, 'The Lion: From Pride to Metaphor', in Thapar, Valmik, Thapar, Romila, and Ansari, Yusuf (eds.), *Exotic Aliens: The Lion and the Cheetah in India*, New Delhi: Aleph Book Company, 2013.

Thapar, Valmik, Thapar, Romila, and Ansari, Yusuf (eds.), *Exotic Aliens: The Lion and the*

Tyabji, Hashim, *Bandhavgarh National Park*, Tala: Churhat Kothi, 2004.

Vats, Sharad, 'Jerdon and Tickells', *Indiabirdwatching.com*, 14 April 2020.

Verchot, Manon, and Biswas, Sanshay, 'Mangar, on the outskirts of Delhi, looks to the past to protect its future', *India.mongabay.com*, 7 September 2021.

Von Essen, Carl, *The Hunter's Trance*, Great Barrington: Lindesdesfarne Books, 2007.

Ward, Geoffrey C. and Ward, Diane Raines, *Tigerwallahs: Encounters with the Men Who Tried to Save the Greatest of the Great Cats*, New York: HarperCollins Publishers, 1993.

Whitaker, Romulus, *Common Indian Snakes: A Field Guide*, Chennai: Macmillan, 2008.

Wilson, Edward O, *Biophilia: The Human Bond with Other Species*, Cambridge: Harvard University Press, 1986.

Woodward, D. E., and Murray, James Dickson, 'On the effect of temperature-dependent sex determination on sex-ratio and survivorship in crocodilians', *Proceedings of the Royal Society Biological Sciences*, Vol. 252, No. 1334, 1993, pp. 149–155.

Wynter-Blyth, M. A., and Dharmakumarsinhji, K. S., 'The Gir Forest and Lions Part I', in Divyabhanusinh (ed.), *The Lions of India*, Ranikhet: Permanent Black, 2008.

Ylla (Camilla Koffler), *Animals in India*, London: Hamish Hamilton, 1958.

Yong, Ed, *An Immense World: How Animal Senses Reveal the Hidden Realm Around Us*, New York: Random House, 2022.

Yule, Henry and Burnell, A. C., *Hobson–Jobson: A Glossary of Colloquial Anglo-Indian Words and Phrases, and of Kindred Terms, Etymological, Historical, Geographical, and Discursive*, William Crooke (ed.), New Delhi: Munshiram Manoharlal, 2016. First published in 1886.

Zimmerman, Francis, *The Jungle and the Aroma of Meats*, New Delhi: Motilal Banarasidass Publishing House, 2011.

PICTURE CREDITS

Collett, H., *Flora Simlensis*, Calcutta: Thacker, Spink & Co., 1921 (Illustrations by Miss M. Smith): **pp. iii, 25, 151, 253, 321.**

Forsyth, J., *The Highlands of Central India*, Calcutta: Thacker, Spink & Co., 1889: **p. 9.**

Maxwell-Lefroy, H., *Indian Insect Life: A Manual of Insects of the Plains.* Calcutta: Thacker, Spink & Co., 1909: **pp. 90, 357.**

Sanderson, G. P., *Thirteen Years Amongst the Wild Beasts of India*, Edinburgh: John Grant, 1907: **p. 119.**

Stebbing, E. P., *A Manual of Elementary Forest Zoology for India*, Calcutta: Superintendent Government Printing, 1908: **pp. viii, 1, 27, 57, 185, 210, 227.**

Sterndale, Robert A., *Natural History of the Mammalia of India and Ceylon*, Calcutta: Thacker, Spink & Co., 1884: **pp. i, 74, 169, 240, 255, 274, 304.**

Whistler, Hugh, *Popular Handbook of Indian Birds*, London: Gurney and Jackson, 1935 (Illustrations by H. Gronvold): **pp. 132, 153, 289.**

Photographs by the author: **pp. 43, 105, 195, 338.**

All colour photographs in this book were taken by the author.

INDEX